ACTION

AND

CONTEMPLATION

SUNY series in
Ancient Greek Philosophy

Anthony Preus, editor

ACTION

AND

CONTEMPLATION

Studies in the
Moral and Political Thought of Aristotle

ROBERT C. BARTLETT
SUSAN D. COLLINS
Editors

STATE UNIVERSITY OF NEW YORK PRESS

Published by
State University of New York Press, Albany

© 1999 State University of New York

For information, address State University of New York Press,
State University Plaza, Albany, NY 12246

Production by Laurie Searl
Marketing by Fran Keneston

Library of Congress Cataloging-in-Publication Data

Action and contemplation : studies in the moral and political thought
    of Aristotle / Robert C. Bartlett & Susan D. Collins, editors.
        p.   cm. — (SUNY series in ancient Greek philosophy)
    Includes bibliographical references and index.
    ISBN 0-7914-4251-9 (alk. paper). — ISBN 0-7914-4252-7 (pbk. :
alk. paper)
    1. Aristotle—Contributions in political science. 2. Aristotle-
-Ethics.   I. Bartlett, Robert C., 1964-   . II. Collins, Susan D.,
1960-   . III. Series.
JC71.A7A37   1999
320'.01'1—dc21   98-31974
                                                                   CIP

10   9   8   7   6   5   4   3   2   1

CONTENTS

ACKNOWLEDGEMENTS   IX

INTRODUCTION   XI

PART ONE
ARISTOTLE TODAY
Relativism and the Possibility of Rational Moral Judgment

Chapter 1

THE REHABILITATION OF PRACTICAL PHILOSOPHY
AND NEO-ARISTOTELIANISM   3
Franco Volpi; Translated by Eric Buzzetti

Chapter 2

THE MODERN FORM OF THE CLASSICAL REPUBLIC   27
The Repression of the Judeo-Christian Heritage in
Hannah Arendt's Attempt to Renew the Aristotelian Concept of Politics
Hauke Brunkhorst; Translated by Louis Hunt

Chapter 3

DO WE NEED A PHILOSOPHICAL ETHICS?   37
Theory, Prudence, and the Primacy of *Ethos*
Ronald Beiner

Chapter 4

ARISTOTLE AND THE ETHIC OF IMPERATIVES   53
Hans-Georg Gadamer; Translated by Joseph M. Knippenberg

Chapter 5

THE NATURAL FOUNDATIONS OF RIGHT
AND ARISTOTELIAN PHILOSOPHY   69
Richard Bodéüs; Translated by Kent Enns

PART TWO
ISSUES IN THE *NICOMACHEAN ETHICS* AND *POLITICS*

Chapter 6

THE AMBITIONS OF ARISTOTLE'S AUDIENCE
AND THE ACTIVIST IDEAL OF HAPPINESS   107
David K. O'Connor

Chapter 7

THE MORAL VIRTUES IN ARISTOTLE'S *NICOMACHEAN ETHICS*   131
Susan D. Collins

Chapter 8

ARISTOTLE ON THE QUESTION OF EVIL   159
David Bolotin

Chapter 9

FRIENDSHIP AND SELF-LOVE IN ARISTOTLE'S *NICOMACHEAN ETHICS*   171
Lorraine Smith Pangle

Chapter 10

SOCRATES IN ARISTOTLE'S "PHILOSOPHY OF HUMAN AFFAIRS"   203
Aristide Tessitore

Chapter 11

ARISTOTLE ON NATURE, HUMAN NATURE, AND JUSTICE   225
A Consideration of the Natural Functions
of Men and Women in the City
Judith A. Swanson

Chapter 12

ARISTOTLE AND THRASYMACHUS ON THE COMMON GOOD   249
Wayne Ambler

Chapter 13

COMMUNITY AND CONFLICT IN ARISTOTLE'S POLITICAL PHILOSOPHY   273
Bernard Yack

Chapter 14

THE "REALISM" OF CLASSICAL POLITICAL SCIENCE   293
An Introduction to Aristotle's Best Regime
Robert C. Bartlett

LIST OF CONTRIBUTORS   315

INDEX   319

ACKNOWLEDGEMENTS

The editors wish to acknowledge the Office of Research and Development at Southern Illinois University at Carbondale, whose generous financial support made possible the able graduate assistance of Gary Mullen and Lori Phan. In addition, we are grateful for the constructive criticisms of the three anonymous reviewers at State University of New York Press.

Earlier versions of some of the chapters have appeared elsewhere. Chapter 1 appeared as "Réhabilitation de la philosophie pratique et néo-Aristotélisme" in *Aristote politique: études sur la Politique d'Aristote*, ed. Pierre Aubenque (Paris: Presses Universitaires de France, 1993); chapter 3 appeared in *Philosophical Forum* 20 (Spring 1980); chapter 4 appeared as "Aristoteles und die imperativische Ethik" in Hans-Georg Gadamer, *Werke*, vol. 2, Tubingen: J. C. B. Mohr, 1985; chapter 10 appeared as "Aristotle's Political Presentation of Socrates in the *Nicomachean Ethics*" in *Interpretation* 16 (Fall 1988); chapter 13 appeared in *Review of Politics* 47 (Winter 1985); and chapter 14 appeared as "The Realism of Classical Political Science" in *American Journal of Political Science* 32 (May 1994). Permission to reprint these articles is gratefully acknowledged.

Introduction

This collection of essays is intended to make available to a broad audience of scholars and readers some of the most interesting and important work now being done on the political philosophy of Aristotle. Our hope is to indicate the main approaches to and applications of Aristotelian political philosophy at present, and of course to contribute to them. As a contribution to existing collections on Aristotle, the volume we are presenting has several unique attributes. It confronts directly, in part one, the most fundamental and controversial question of concern to students of Aristotle today, namely the possibility of grounding moral and political action in some version of Aristotelian rationalism, and it brings together on this question the work of five leading scholars from North America and the Continent. In part two, a number of established and emerging scholars address specific questions arising from the *Nicomachean Ethics* and the *Politics* from a perspective mindful of the practical import of these questions and the overarching issue of rationalism. Many of these essays will be controversial, and we fully expect the present collection to spark debate, not only about the precise import of Aristotle's political thought, but also and more broadly about the enduring issues with which he was directly concerned.

In the last twenty years or so, there has been a sustained and systematic return to the thought of Aristotle. This return is as remarkable for the diversity of the concerns that have been brought to bear on the writings of "the Philosopher" as for the contentiousness of the debates that have ensued. And this contentiousness indicates a most welcome, but in some circles surprising, fact: the return to Aristotle today seeks above all not to learn *about* him but *from* him. To be sure, one might be tempted to trace a more or less unbroken chain of writers on Aristotle from the contemporary scholars to the German and British philologists of the eighteenth and nineteenth centuries (Immanuel Bekker, Ingram Bywater, John Burnet), to the great medieval commentators

(Thomas Aquinas, Maimonides, Avicenna, Al-Farabi), to his late Classical and Hellenistic adepts (Simplicius, Themistius, Aspasius). Like most temptations, however, this one should be resisted. For the better part of this century, such interest in Aristotle as was not linked with Roman Catholicism cannot be said to have been motivated and elevated by true philosophic passion. That is, unlike their classical and medieval forebears, the modern scholars did not typically read Aristotle to understand themselves and the world better but merely to locate Aristotle's "place" in the essentially progressive history of Western philosophy or to identify, whenever possible, the Aristotelian provenance of some of our ideas and institutions.

How then has it become permissible once again to raise the possibility, without fear of derision or attribution of delusion, that Aristotle may be right on one or more of the fundamental questions? We cannot do more than sketch some of the principal events leading to the contemporary situation. Aristotle still wielded very great influence in the Church and therefore also in the academy well into the seventeenth century, and many of the most distinguished of the modern philosophers or scientists—Galileo, Bacon, Hobbes, Descartes—sought explicitly or implicitly to undermine it. The moral and political revolutions thus set in motion brought citizens to understand human nature and hence themselves in a new way, as endowed with individual "rights," for example, at the same time as the scientific revolutions accompanying the new politics encouraged the conquest of brute nature. If the new political science with its novel understanding of nature entailed the rejection of classical philosophy, it also promised to establish a truly rational politics that would demonstrate, by its effectiveness, its superiority to all alternatives. The first great critic of the modern project, Jean-Jacques Rousseau, questioned more the goodness of the spread of the new science than its truth, fearing as he did its harmful effects on a politics he nonetheless insisted be guided by reflection on our apolitical, subrational condition in or by nature. Immanuel Kant's response to the Rousseauan criticism—an attempt both to delineate and elevate modern moral and political principles by grounding them in the idea of human freedom—was still as modern in its understanding of reason and nature as it was in its aim. It remained for Friedrich Nietzsche to question, not only the edifice built by modern political philosophy, but its very foundations.

Nietzsche discerned at the core of modern philosophy an assertion of the will or a creative imposition on an unknowable substratum and not, as its proponents themselves evidently believed, the method by which to obtain knowledge of nature. It was only a matter of time before the postwar generation of scholars in the West, under the influence of a more or less mediated

Nietzscheanism, also came to doubt the adequacy of the rational foundation of liberal democratic politics. In the social sciences, it is true, this influence first appeared merely as the necessity to separate knowable "facts" from unknowable "values," these latter being the product of the collective or individual will not subject to scientific analysis and produced or conditioned by the ineluctable but otherwise inexplicable forces of "History." But gradually scholars came to the view that one's very decision to analyze facts depended on an undemonstrated and undemonstrable value: the life devoted to reason or science cannot be known to be superior to a life devoted to its rejection or even destruction. With this questioning of the goodness of science came a pervasive doubt concerning precisely "facts" and therewith the very *possibility* of science: is not our perception of the world—more, the very "world," or "objective" reality—shaped by forces that remain hidden from us? By what right, for example, does the scientific mind claim its privileged perspective? Do not the most thoughtful of the modern scientists in fact acknowledge the necessarily hypothetical, provisional character of their alleged insights? And must not our understanding of individual rights and of the government devoted to their protection then come into serious doubt, grounded as these were originally said to be in certain insights into human nature and the world?

It is our impression that, until very recently, the majority of those in the academy who are concerned with such questions would have conceded that the rational or scientific foundation originally claimed for liberal democracy has been refuted because reason itself has been shown to be a delusion. Some have deplored this refutation as a catastrophe, others have celebrated it as a liberation; very few have questioned its truth or adequacy. And yet a growing number of people are now beginning to investigate, with a minimum of preconceptions, the fundamental claim on which so much of modern thought depends: that the self-destruction of reason is unavoidable. It is among these that the new concern with Aristotle principally comes to sight. For does not the proclamation of the death of reason presuppose that every approach to or understanding of reason has been *shown* to be defective? And can all those who concede reason's demise claim to know, and not merely to accept on hearsay or faith, the defectiveness of, say, Aristotle's philosophy? As diverse as the authors here represented surely are, the majority of them are united by their conviction that Aristotle, and hence reason, deserves a second hearing. The shaking of the foundations of philosophy has thus had the perhaps unanticipated consequence of shaking also the accepted or traditional understanding of the foundations of philosophy. Everything is once again up for grabs, and we contend that it is necessary to return to the origins of Western rationalism. This volume is our contribution to that effort.

Part one begins with Franco Volpi's searching analysis of the origins of "neo-Aristotelianism," especially in Germany. While never permitting himself to blur the many important distinctions that mark the scholars who have looked to Aristotle in the twentieth century for a means to inform practice or practical philosophy (Hannah Arendt, Eric Voegelin, Leo Strauss, Wilhelm Hennis), Volpi sketches the common ground or grounds that may be said to unite them. Seared in various ways by the experience of the collapse of reason and the corresponding praise of "resolute" or "committed" action, the neo-Aristotelian movement seeks to return to moral action both the certainty and dignity that can come only from knowledge. Although sympathetic to such attempts, Volpi concludes his essay with an important reservation or question concerning the legitimacy of all such attempts to recover Aristotle today. Hauke Brunkhorst picks up this critical thread by challenging Hannah Arendt's effort to renew the Aristotelian notion of the "political." Against Arendt's thesis that American republicanism in particular and modern republicanism in general represent a break with the Judeo-Christian heritage—that "the origin of modern revolutions lies not in Jerusalem but in Athens and Rome"—Brunkhorst contends that the project of modern republicanism, that is, its universalism, functional distinction between law, religion, and politics, positivization of the legal code, and privatization of conscience, thought, and, to some degree, speech, is "unintelligible apart from the historical background of Europe's monotheistic tradition." So far from representing a break with the Judeo-Christian tradition, then, the specifically modern transformation of classical thought is in fact this tradition's "effective-historical consequence." However the issue between Brunkhorst and Arendt is worked out, his criticisms make clear that any recovery of Aristotle and Aristotelian rationalism must confront the historical influence of our Judeo-Christian heritage, and therewith the larger question of whether modernity represents a fundamental transformation of politics and human thought. In his "Do We Need a Philosophical Ethics?", Ronald Beiner first outlines and then responds to the criticisms leveled against neo-Aristotelianism by Jürgen Habermas and those influenced by him. Suggesting that what is most needed is a heightened awareness of "the gap between a theory of practical reason and the concrete demands of practical reason itself," Beiner takes the side of Hans-Georg Gadamer in particular over that of Habermas and, offering a radical reading of the priority of praxis and ethos over theory, argues in favor of the centrality of the Aristotelian concept of prudence for practical philosophy. Against Habermas's charge that Gadamer's elevation of *ethos* and prudence devolves into a form of cultural relativism, Beiner responds that Gadamer's particular Aristotelianism presupposes "a prior fusion of Aristotelian and Kantian horizons." In the immediately following essay, "Aristotle and the Ethic of Imperatives," Gadamer himself elucidates the full meaning of this response, describing the Aristotelian and Kantian elements of this horizon as well as the character of their fusion. Finally, on the question of central importance to Aristotle's political philosophy, and to us, Richard Bodéüs offers a challenging interpretation of Aristotle's position concerning justice and natural right. Given the intimate link between the question of natural right and the possibility of rational moral judgment, Bodéüs's essay is a fitting capstone for part one. Yet his careful analysis of Aristotle's understanding of justice also prepares the ground for part two, in which our contributors address specific questions in Aristotle's *Nicomachean Ethics* and *Politics*.

Seeking to challenge dominant or traditional readings of Aristotle and to cast new light on his work, these essays tackle key elements of Aristotle's moral and political thought: his careful but far-reaching presentation of the relation between politics and philosophy, and of the relative status of the political and philosophic lives; his discussions of moral virtue, justice, and friendship; his complex view of nature and human nature, especially in its male-female duality; and his challenging treatments of the problem of the common good, the foundation of the political community, and the nature of the best regime. These essays, which will contribute to discussions of textual interpretation and debates about specific elements of Aristotle's thought, largely speak for themselves. But in general they are unified and find their most serious purpose in drawing attention to the remarkable depth of the realm of practice or action, and to the moral and political guidance we may draw from it. Of course, the realm of action or practical life in Aristotle's political philosophy is not simply self-contained but in a complex way leads to and may well depend upon the activity that distinguishes the contemplative or philosophic life. This is not a contention with which all our authors might agree, at least not without qualifications, yet it is clear that this aspect of Aristotle's thought—the subtle, graceful way in which he investigates the possibilities of action and contemplation—is responsible for the current revival of his political philosophy, a welcome renaissance this book hopes to encourage.

Part One

ARISTOTLE TODAY

RELATIVISM AND THE POSSIBILITY OF RATIONAL MORAL JUDGMENT

CHAPTER 1

THE REHABILITATION OF PRACTICAL PHILOSOPHY AND NEO-ARISTOTELIANISM

FRANCO VOLPI

Translated by Eric Buzzetti

THE GERMAN DEBATE ON "PRACTICAL PHILOSOPHY"

From the beginning of the sixties until the end of the seventies, an intense debate took place in Germany that has become famous under the title "The Rehabilitation of Practical Philosophy."[1] From a general perspective, one can distinguish two main moments in the genesis and unfolding of that debate. The *first moment*, prepared by the writings of some political philosophers of German origin who emigrated to the United States, like Leo Strauss, Eric Voegelin, and Hannah Arendt, came to maturity in the sixties and was mainly characterized by the rediscovery of the relevance of Aristotle's model of practical philosophy, and then of Kant's, and by the attempt to use these models to offer a new philosophical examination of the realm of action. The *second moment* had above all a theoretico-systematic character, where the problems raised by the rediscovery of the Aristotelian and Kantian models were approached and treated in the context of a more general discussion involving the main contemporary German philosophical schools, like the old Frankfurt school of

3

Hegelian-Marxist inspiration (Theodor Wiesengrund Adorno and the young
Jürgen Habermas), critical rationalism (Hans Albert, Hans Lenk and, in a certain respect, Ernst Topitsch), the philosophical hermeneutics of Hans-Georg
Gadamer and his student Rüdiger Bubner, but also Joachim Ritter and his
school (Hermann Lübbe, Odo Marquard, Willi Oelmüller, Günther Bien,
Reinhart Maurer), the constructivism of the school of Erlangen and Constance
(which was founded by Paul Lorenzen, developed by Friedrich Kambartel and
Oswald Schwemmer, but then disbanded) and, finally, the new Frankfurt
school of Karl-Otto Apel and the later Habermas, with his project of an ethics
of discourse based on a transcendental or universal pragmatics. To a greater or
lesser extent, the most prestigious and most renowned representatives of contemporary German philosophical thought participated in the complex discussion that developed. This discussion likewise involved and motivated thinkers
active in disciplines that were not, strictly speaking, philosophical, to take a
stance: for example, the sociologist Niklas Luhmann (and his critique of the
obsolescence of the category "end"),[2] the ethnologist Konrad Lorenz (especially
in his discussion of the biological genesis of moral conduct as a residue of
instinctive rules),[3] or again the anthropologist Arnold Gehlen (through his
anthropo-biological grounding of institutions).[4] One can date this theoretico-
systematic phase of the debate back to 1969, that is, to the date of the ninth
German Convention of Philosophy where, in the presentations of Paul Lorenzen
(*Das Problem des Szientismus* [The Problem of Scientism]), Jürgen Habermas
(*Bemerkungen zum Problem des Begründung von Werturteilen* [Remarks on the
Problem of the Foundation of Value Judgements]), and Richard M. Hare
(*Wissenschaft und praktische Philosophie* [Science and Practical Philosophy]),
the discussion of the problems involved in the rediscovery of practical philoso-
phy was freed of its reference to the models of the past and was conducted on
the basis of more contemporary points of view, perspectives, and philosophical
positions.

THE MOTIVATIONS AND THE ROOTS
OF NEO-ARISTOTELIANISM

However this debate may be understood as a whole, one can say that its
origin is essentially found in philosophical positions which, while fairly different from one another, were later brought together under the single designation
"neo-Aristotelianism."[5] The two most important texts in this respect, which
can be regarded as having started this debate, are Hannah Arendt's well-known

book, *Vita activa*, published first in the United States in 1958 under the title *The Human Condition*, and then translated into German in 1960,[6] and Hans-Georg Gadamer's equally famous book, *Wahrheit und Methode* [*Truth and Method*],[7] published in the same year. In *Vita activa*, H. Arendt drew the attention of contemporary thought to the Aristotelian account of *praxis* and to its fundamental character for understanding the phenomenon of *the political* (as distinguished from *politics*) in light of the tyrannies of production and labor characteristic of the modern world. Gadamer too, in a chapter of *Wahrheit und Methode*[8] which later became famous, emphasized that Aristotle's ethics remains relevant precisely on the grounds that the Aristotelian account of the knowledge guiding human action and life, namely *phronēsis*, prudence, remains of interest.

These texts represent only the two most famous examples of a fairly widespread recovery of the Aristotelian understanding of *praxis* and of the ethical and political knowledge with which it is concerned. This recovery, essentially a German phenomenon, occurred at a moment of particularly profound crisis within the disciplines that had traditionally dealt with human action—ethics and politics notably—as well as the human and social sciences which, in our century, had progressively asserted themselves as the only knowledge pertaining to human action that could rightly call itself scientific.

The case of political science can be regarded as paradigmatic in this regard. Indeed, even after having achieved epistemological dignity in its own right, it nevertheless finds itself, in the contemporary age, in the midst of a crisis concerning its conceptual foundations and in a state in which its identity as a discipline is fairly weak, not only because it has progressively become a purely empirical and descriptive science, but also because it is torn by a conflicting plurality of methods which offer themselves at once as the most effective and as the only ones capable of describing adequately the phenomena of politics.[9] The work of Hannah Arendt, as well as that of Leo Strauss and Eric Voegelin, represents in this respect a bold denouncement of the impasses and naivetés of modern political *science*, against which these authors hold up the relevance of classical political *philosophy*. The same could be said of the human and social sciences: even though their birth and organization into a field of scientific knowledge is a fairly recent event, they too have been shaped from their beginning by problems of method and epistemological self-representation. On this subject, it would suffice to recall the quarrel over the sociological method (*Methodenstreit*) that developed in the last twenty years of the past century and with which the names of Carl Menger and Gustav Schmoller are associated; the debate over value judgements (*Werturteilstreit*) that took place, starting from

1909, at the Conventions of the Verein für Sozialpolitik [Association for Social Policy] and the Deutsche Gesellschaft für Soziologie [German Society for Sociology] and which remains associated with the work of Max Weber and Werner Sombart; the controversy over the sociology of knowledge; or again and finally, the debate over the positivistic or dialectical method in sociology, known as *Positivismusstreit*, that involved Adorno, Popper, and their schools.[10]

In light of all these problems, the recovery of the practical philosophy of the Aristotelian tradition offered itself as an alternative solution insofar as it was recovered as an alternative paradigm of knowledge for modernity and for the unitary notion of science that characterizes modernity. Indeed, the tradition of the *philosophia practica*, which one can date back to Aristotle and, more precisely, to the Aristotelian structuring of the *epistēmai*, refers to a field of knowledge whose object is human action, a field that is distinct from both the *philosophia theoretica* as well as the *philosophia mechanica* and the *artes*. According to the tradition that took root especially in the medieval encyclopedias, that field was tripartite: it included *ethics*, the knowledge concerning individual action, *economics*, the knowledge concerning the *oikos*—hence the household as a whole—and *politics*, the knowledge concerning action in the political community (*koinōnia politikē, communitas civilis*).[11]

In fact, independently of a precise and rigorous reference to the Aristotelian classification of knowledge, the tradition of a discipline of practical philosophy, with its tripartition, was formed and remained alive from the Middle Ages onwards essentially in the scholastic culture of encyclopedias[12] and in the academic structuring of knowledge by discipline produced by the German universities.[13] Indeed, from the second half of the thirteenth century onwards, with the rediscovery of Aristotle's *Ethics* and *Politics*, the tendency previously dominant in university education to treat morality and politics as dependent on metaphysics and theology was inverted. The preliminary conditions essential to the creation of an autonomous *philosophia practica*—autonomous as a discipline at least—could at that point be met.[14] Indeed, in the universities, in addition to the classes of the *organicus*, where one studied the books of the *Organon*, and those of the *philosophus naturalis* and the *metaphysicus*, the study of philosophy also included the classes of the *ethicus*, that is, the study of the *Ethics* and the *Politics*; later, the study of economics and money-making was also added. The *philosophia practica* thus became an official subject of education and, at least in Germany, remained so until almost the end of the eighteenth century.[15]

In this tradition of scholastic and university teaching of the *philosophia practica*, which drew its inspiration from Aristotle but was increasingly removed from Aristotelianism, Christian Wolff's treatise *Philosophia practica universalis* (1738–1739) occupies a particular place and can be regarded as the last great testimony to that tradition. Here the philosophia practica is called *universalis*,[16] since it provides the foundation of the formal tripartition of the practical disciplines by being at the basis of the *Philosophia moralis sive Ethica*, the *Oeconomica*, and the *Philosophia civilis sive Politica*. Indeed, Wolff's treatise represents the last systematic effort to structure and organize the practical disciplines according to the Aristotelian model of knowledge, even though, strictly speaking, there remains from Aristotle only the formal external scaffolding and the arrangement of the subject matter, and despite the fact that the method taught by Wolff was the mathematical method.[17]

THE MODERN ALTERNATIVE TO PRACTICAL PHILOSOPHY

This "tradition," moreover, will lose out to the predominant position of modernity. Indeed, from a very general perspective—and leaving aside a more precise examination of the complex transformations characterizing modernity —one can say that in the configuration of the modern system of knowledge according to the ideal of *scientia*, either the self-understanding of the disciplines concerned with human action or their relative value in the general classification of knowledge change radically. They change in comparison to the place these disciplines had either in the ancient system of the *epistēmai* or in the medieval one of the *disciplinae* and the *artes*. Among the various factors characterizing this change, a paradigmatic value must be attributed to the identification of *scientia* with *theōria* and to the spreading of the notion that method is a guarantor of universality and scientific rigor. One can say that the application of method to science understood as theory, that is, the elevation of method, in the context of a theoretical understanding of knowledge itself, [to the status of] ideal parameter of knowledge, had a destructive impact on the structuring of the realm of knowledge traditionally referred to as *philosophia practica* and distinguished, as such, from the *philosophia theoretica* and the *philosophia mechanica* or the *artes*.

Now, if one presupposes that the mathematical method represents the paradigm of knowledge in general, two consequences are possible. On the one hand, the realization that this method is inapplicable to the realm of the *philosophia practica*—in other words, to the field of knowledge that guides action— leads one to conceive of it as a kind of *philosophia minor*, as a knowledge that has only a provisional and approximate character; on the other hand—and such is the predominant opinion in modernity—human action is accepted as an object of knowledge, not in the sense that it is concretely guided by that knowledge, but in the sense that it is accepted as the field of a possible exercise of knowing—as a world, in other words, which, like that of nature, can be grasped and described rigorously in its mechanisms and operation. At that point, the idea arises of applying a knowledge as rigorous as mathematical knowledge to ethics (Spinoza), politics (Hobbes), law (Pufendorf), and economics (Petty).

The thought of Kant, a crucial point in the development of modern philosophy, represents the most consistent attempt to correct that tendency within [the confines of] an acceptance of the modern notion of reason. Since it is impossible in the context of this article to examine how Kant offers an understanding of practical knowledge which differs from both the objectivistic paleomodern tradition and that of the *philosophia practica* of Aristotelian origin, let it suffice to recall the radicalness and the decisiveness with which Kant separates the examination of man as a being belonging to the order of nature—and hence subject to physical causality—from the examination of man as belonging to the order of freedom. This [separation] gives rise to the Kantian distinction between the theoretical and the practical use of reason, between the metaphysics of nature and the metaphysics of morals, between the physiological and the pragmatic examination of man: the one aims at determining "how nature shapes man," the other at "how man as a free being does, or can and should, shape himself."[18] What must be emphasized here is that, through his practico-moral examination of action, Kant seeks to restore to this knowledge a guiding character. He thereby introduces a remarkable change away from the predominant tendency in the modern age, according to which one regards human action as a possible object of rigorous scientific knowledge and thus extends also to that object the ideal of objective knowing, solely reportorial and descriptive.

In light of that development, the attribution of a scientific character to the *Geisteswissenschaften* (Sciences of the Mind)[19]—a term that was coined to translate the English *moral sciences*[20]—does not represent a break, but rather a continuation and a radicalization. Indeed, to be effective, the extension of the ideal of rigorous and universal knowledge to any reality requires the recognition of the diversity and specificity of the scientific realms and, consequently, the abandonment of the unity of the method. It is this very thematizing of the specific characteristics of the knowledge of the sciences of the mind that Dilthey defines as the task of a "critique of historical reason"; it would make scientific knowledge possible in the realm of the *res gestae*—that is, objective and rigorous knowledge—since an application of the scientific method appears impracticable or reductive in that case. But what does not change and is, on the contrary, radicalized in the very process, is the typically modern manner of examining human action and the relation between action and the knowledge that examines it. Indeed, action remains the *object of a descriptive examination*; in other words, it is *objectified* and *reified* as the field of a reportorial and factual analysis. The corresponding knowledge, in turn, is no longer a practico-moral knowledge capable of guiding action, but simply becomes a theoretical and neutral observation and description of the dynamics and regularities characterizing action. It does not guide action by indicating ends for it, but it sees and foresees actions, just as the physicist sees and foresees the movements of nature.

In other words, it is precisely in order to guarantee the effectiveness of the link between truth and method that the methodology of scientific analysis must be diversified with a view to the specific objects being examined. And yet, in this differentiation, the ideal of knowledge presupposed by the sciences of nature as well as the sciences of the mind (of culture, of man), by the nomothetic as well as the idiographic disciplines, remains the same. It is the ideal of a rigorous, objective, universal, and neutral knowledge, guided and controlled by method. It follows, as Gadamer has emphasized, that even the extramethodical experiences of the truth like art, history, morality, and politics, are reduced (brought back) to the horizon of a methodical and scientific knowledge. The knowledge that guides morality, ethics—the *moral sciences*[21]—becomes at that point the neutral knowledge of the sciences of the mind, of culture, or of man. Their examination of action conforms to the ideal of objectivity and descriptive universality of scientific knowledge; the practico-moral examination of old becomes a theoretico-reportorial examination and loses in this way the content of truth that had belonged to it in the former tradition.

This transformation is sanctioned for good by the famous thesis of axiological neutrality (*Wertfreiheit*). Once the knowledge of the human and social sciences is defined as descriptively neutral—a definition which is closely linked to the acknowledgement of the scientific character of these sciences—that knowledge is released from any practico-guiding function; it is released, in other words, from the connection with values that—according to a notion that is also typically modern[22]—should guide action, choices, and human life as a whole. Descriptive neutrality becomes at a certain moment a feature immanent to reason as such, which is thereby gradually stripped of its substantive content and progressively develops in the direction of mere instrumentality and mere functionalism. By becoming incapable of guiding life, it loses its importance for it, its *Lebensbedeutsamkeit* (life-significance).

THE OPPOSITION OF
NEO-ARISTOTELIANISM TO MODERNITY

It was against that development and that modern understanding of action that the German neo-Aristotelians declared the necessity to rehabilitate the practical philosophy of the "Aristotelian tradition," despite the serious difficulty of recognizing an essential and continuous core characterizing that tradition in a way that is Aristotelian in actual fact. In truth the neo-Aristotelians, without exhibiting an explicit and rigorous awareness of the Aristotelian account of practical knowledge, have instead drawn freely from it by following rather different demands and perspectives. [They did so] in order to derive from that account elements suited to the depiction of an understanding of practical rationality capable of opposing and, in a word, of correcting the modern notion that knowledge must be unitary and methodical, objective and descriptive, and applicable to Being as a whole. This is why the recovery of the Aristotelian conception of practical rationality has been determined by the point of view motivating it and by the general expectations it raised, that is, by the thought of using that conception as a response to the crisis of the modern understanding of knowledge. In addition, the attention paid to Aristotelian practical philosophy is differently inflected depending on the different disciplines in which it is seen. Therefore, it ought to be said that the overall designation "neo-Aristotelianism" must be understood in fairly general terms, and all the more so since the neo-Aristotelians limit themselves to the recovery of certain aspects or certain specific accounts, which they isolate from the context of the Aristotelian understanding of knowledge and which they use in accordance with the questions that concern them.

An overview of the positions that have contributed to the reawakening of interest in Aristotle's practical philosophy and are accepted on that account, especially in Germany, as in a certain way neo-Aristotelian, indicates better than any analysis could the relative character of this collective denotation. The relevance of Aristotelian practical philosophy has been rediscovered in the realm of political science (Leo Strauss, Eric Voegelin, Hannah Arendt, Wilhelm Hennis, Hans Maier); likewise, in the realm of historical science, reference to the old social orders in which practical philosophy had taken shape has provided the motivation for research in social history which—opposing the progressive view of history—have made a theme of the transition from the vetero-European medieval world to the modern world of industrial bourgeois society (Otto Brunner, Werner Conze). In the science of law, the attention paid to Aristotle has focused on the recovery of the topico-dialectical method (Theodor Viehweg,

Chaïm Perelman). In pedagogical science, it has provided the motivation for a rehabilitation of the humanistic, rhetorical and literary tradition (a tradition for which was important the debate between Joachim Ritter and Helmut Schelsky on the function of the *Geisteswissenschaften* (Sciences of the Mind) in the University, [a debate] that took place at the beginning of the sixties). More recently still, the studies of Jürgen-Eckhart Pleines, a student of Gadamer, deserve to be singled out. Finally, very remarkable attention has been paid to the practical philosophy of Aristotle in philosophy itself (Hans-Georg Gadamer, Joachim Ritter, Günther Bien, Klaus Held, Rüdiger Bubner).

THE FUNDAMENTAL PROGRAMMATIC
THESES OF NEO-ARISTOTELIANISM

Faced with this situation of widespread interest, and instead of lingering over an examination of manifold and various positions, it is fitting to try to recognize the elements that characterize and unite these positions and thereby allow for the denotation "neo-Aristotelianism." It seems to me that these characterizing elements can be reduced to three epistemic intuitions or three fundamental theses which the neo-Aristotelians recover from the Aristotelian understanding of *praxis*. These theses are: (1) the affirmation of the autonomy of *praxis* from *theōria*; (2) the delimitation of *praxis* from *poiēis*; and (3) the determination of the specific characteristics of the knowledge of *praxis*, of practical rationality.

1) *Theōria* and *Praxis*

It is known that Aristotle, unlike Plato, distinguishes for the first time in a systematic manner between the attitude of *theōrein* and that of *prattein* and, consequently, between the scientific dispositions corresponding to practical and theoretical knowledge. This differentiation is done by means of criteria that are, without any doubt, closely linked historically to the Aristotelian classification and understanding of knowledge, and yet they possess in themselves their own specific plausibility, which the neo-Aristotelians invoke. They are as follows:

a) The diversity of the end pursued in each case: in *theōria* that end is the truth (*alētheia*); in *praxis*, it is the success of *praxis* itself,[23] that is, acting well and living well, the *eu prattein* and the *eu zēn*. This implies a difference in the epistemological status of the scientific disciplines that correspond to these two attitudes: the theoretical sciences carry out a contemplative and reportorial examination of the truth of the natural and celestial realities which do not depend on human beings, whereas practical knowledge—which also has the character of scientific knowledge—is oriented toward the understanding of *praxis* whose success it pursues.[24]

b) The different modes of Being of the being respectively examined: in the case of the theoretical sciences, the being examined possesses a stability of Being superior to that of human action, which is the object of practical philosophy. Indeed, human actions do not have the character of necessities, they are not *anankaia*, things that cannot be other than they are (*ta mē, endechomena allōs echein*).[25] Human actions, however, do not happen in a completely unpredictable manner, by chance (*apo tuchēs*), since in that case, according to the Aristotelian principle that there is no science of the accidental event, it would not be possible to subject them to an epistemic examination. The character of Being of human actions, which are the object of practical science, lies therefore between the necessary and the accidental, in the realm that possesses the relative regularity of that which, as Aristotle says, happens *hōs epi to polu* [for the most part].

c) The different degrees of precision (*akribeia*) that one can achieve[26]: given the changeable and variable make-up of their object, the practical sciences cannot attain the same degree of precision as that possible, for example, in mathematics. But, since this lesser precision does not stem from a lack of knowledge, but rather from the very nature of the being that is the object of the knowledge, Aristotle does not deny the scientific character of practical knowledge. Nor does he regard it—as it was done later in the scholastic tradition—as a sort of lesser science, as if the *philosophia practica* was a kind of *philosophia minor*: practical knowledge is, admittedly, only a likely knowledge, not in the sense that it would be an approximation of what is true (*verisimilitudo*) without ever attaining the truth, but rather in the sense that it is exactly the truth of what is probable (*probabilitas*).

d) The difference in the modes of argumentation respectively employed: because of the specific characteristics determining it, practical knowledge is not structured in an apodictic but rather in a topico-dialectical manner. For example, taking the practical syllogism, one can say that it has the same rigor and the same necessary character as the *apodeixis* [proof], although it is not based on necessary and true premises, but only on probable premises, on noteworthy or generally accepted opinions (*endoxa*), so that the conclusions it reaches can have themselves only a probable, topico-dialectical character. Even though this point apppears plausible from a general perspective, I know well that it is fairly controversial, and I do not forget that in order to give a satisfactory answer on this point, it would be necessary to distinguish between the rationality of the prudence that guides action and the rationality of the scientific knowledge of action.[27]

2) *Praxis* and *Poiēsis*

In Aristotle's work, and once again unlike in Plato's,[28] one finds the first systematic delimitation of *praxis*, and of practical knowledge (*phronēsis*), from *poiēsis*, and from the knowledge pertaining to it, the *technē*.[29] The difficulty as well as the importance of this delimitation stems from the fact that both *praxis* and *poiēsis* present themselves as action aiming at a goal; likewise, the two corresponding types of knowledge, *phronēsis* and *technē*, offer themselves as knowledge capable of guiding action toward success. The difference can be perceived in the way the success of the action itself is established: in the case of *poiēsis*, the success can be recognized in the product, in the *ergon*, which remains after the poietic action has been executed; by contrast, the success of the *praxis*, which leaves behind no concrete observable product, can only be measured by the quality, by the perfection (*aretē*) of the execution of the *praxis* itself (which is a *kinēsis* and, in its perfectly successful form, an *energeia*). This is the meaning of the Aristotelian distinction between *poiēsis*, understood as a doing that does not have its goal in itself, but outside of itself, in the *ergon*, and *praxis*, understood as an action that has its goal in itself, that is, in the perfection of its execution. Consequently, there is a close link between the moral being of the subject who carries out a *praxis* and the perfection of the *praxis* itself, whereas the perfection of the *ergon* is relatively independent of the [moral] being of the *technitēs* [craftsman].

3) The Specificity of the Knowledge of *Praxis*

The specificity of practical knowledge demands that it be distinguished from both theoretical as well as technical knowledge. The first demarcation, as we have just seen, is very clearly drawn on the basis of the difference between the kind of being *praxis* and *theōria* respectively know. The second demarcation cannot be based on the difference in the ontological nature of the being examined, since both *technē* and *phronēsis* deal with a kind of being that is *endechomenon allōs echein* [capable of being otherwise]. As a result, Aristotle here abandons the objective criterion used for the determination of *epistēmē* and considers the diversity of the subjective disposition on which *technē* and *phronēsis* are respectively based. Thus, in the text that is of capital importance on this point, the sixth book of the *Nicomachean Ethics*, Aristotle separates terminologically and conceptually in a very rigorous manner the knowledge dealing with human actions, with *praxeis*, from technical knowledge; he distinguishes between *phronēsis* and *technē*. There remains a problem nonetheless since, even in that text, Aristotle appears to ground this division not directly but only by referring to the fact that these two sorts of knowledge deal with two different sorts of doings, already distinguished from one another. Yet he gives indications for a distinction —if not systematic, at least, say, phenomenological—between the knowledge of *phronēsis* and that of *technē*:

a) *Phronēsis* is not concerned with particular actions as such, as *technē* is, but only insofar as they contribute to the success of the blessed life as a whole. It is *pros to eu zēn holōs*.[30]

b) *Technē* and *phronēsis* are two different types of knowledge, insofar as they are concerned with two different genera, *technē* and *praxis*,[31] and that difference lies in the fact that *technē* has an end outside of itself whereas *praxis* has its own success as its end (*eupraxia*).[30]

c) *Technē* and *phronēsis* are both defined as *hexis meta logou* [a condition with *logos*], but *technē* is said to be *hexis meta logou alēthous* [a condition with true *logos*],[33] a definition where truth is a constituent element of the *logos* that accompanies the *hexis*, whereas *phronēsis* is defined as *hexis alēthēs meta logou* [a truthful condition with *logos*], a formula whereby truth determines the *hexis* itself.[34] By this, Aristotle probably wants to emphasize the importance of the correctness of the *hexis* for practico-moral knowledge—without which there would not be *phronēsis*, but only *deinotēs* [cleverness][35]—whereas in the case of practico-technical knowledge, he emphasizes the importance of the truth of the *logos*, bringing to light thereby a difference in the analogy of the definitions of the two types of knowledge. Moreover, and closely connected with the foregoing, it would be necessary to take into consideration that *technē* can be effected in opposites (for example: the physician knows how to cure an illness as well as how to bring about death) whereas *phronēsis* can only exist in the virtuous accomplishment of the action, as well the fact that in *technē*, as Aristotle emphasizes, the one who errs voluntarily is to be preferred, while in *phronēsis*, it is the one who errs involuntarily.[36]

d) There is a virtue of *technē*, a perfection (*aretē*), but there is no [virtue] of *phronēsis*.[37] This assertion can be added to the thesis explained in *EN*, II.5 according to which practical virtue, being *stochastikē tou mesou* [skillful in aiming at the mean], can attain the goal (*kathorthoun*) in only one manner (*monachōs*), whereas one can be mistaken in several ways (*pollachōs*).[38] Likewise, there cannot be different degrees of *phronēsis*, but it can exist only insofar as it is realized, insofar as it is perfect. This also implies that in *technē*, one attains perfection by exercising, and even through errors, whereas in *phronēsis*, one does not learn through errors. In other words, one does not become virtuous by practicing vice.

e) An additional difference is that *phronēsis*, as Aristotle says toward the end of *EN*, VI.5, is not only a *hexis meta logou*, but something more. Curiously, he does not say what this "more" is but limits himself to giving one application of it, saying that, whereas every *hexis* can be forgotten, *phronēsis* cannot.[39]

On the basis of these indications, it is certain that, even though Aristotle very often uses examples borrowed from the technical arts in the ethical treatises, and especially from medicine, he does not for all that equate the knowledge of *phronēsis* with rules of good conduct, with technical knowledge, as if moral knowledge consisted in the application of a model, of an *eidos* of the perfect man to the particular situations of human life.[40] Likewise politics, as practical knowledge, cannot be reduced to a technique for the preservation of life (or power) but, once the management of the needs of life (*oikonomia*) has been satisfied and accomplished, it reveals itself as the stage open to the problem of choosing the best possible way of life, to the problem of living well (*eu zēn*). The problem remaining open in my view is that of the distinction between *phronēsis* and practical science, a distinction which Aristotle himself emphasizes[41] but which generally tends to be abolished among the German neo-Aristotelians. One can only understand this distinction in a satisfactory way if one states with sufficient precision the distinctiveness of the Aristotelian account of *epistēmē* within a more general historical context, that is, if one compares it either to the Platonic understanding of *epistēmē*, or else to the modern understanding of *scientia* insofar as it is identified with *theōria*.

Thanks to his effort to delimit the epistemological field of *praxis*, Aristotle arrives at a differentiation of the types of scientific knowledge which not only saves the phenomena, but also allows him to defuse the disturbing tension between *epistēmē* and *doxa* that had taken form among the Presocratics (in Heraclitus and Parmenides) and had deepened even more profoundly among the sophists and in Plato, threatening the subsistence of the *philosophia* and the *epistēmē* which had just been established. Indeed, to establish the possibility of an epistemological examination of the realm of *praxis* is not only to save the autonomy of that realm; it is also to define and delimit the realm of *theōria*[42] and to save its possibility from the threat of an open conflict with *doxa*. On the other hand, the particular character of practical science allows Aristotle to bring about a kind of rehabilitation of *doxa* to the extent that, given the differentiation of the epistemological degrees of universality and precision, there is no longer any reason to set up a total and radical opposition between *doxa* and *epistēmē*.

When *scientia* comes to be identified with *theōria* in the Middle Ages, and even more so in the modern age—an identification in which modernity's ideal of a unitary and methodical knowledge finds its origin and under the aegis of which it develops—the precious work of differentiation done by Aristotle is lost for good, even though the scholastic and encyclopedic classifications of knowledge retain the formal structure of the Aristotelian classification. Thus, the "scientific" understanding of practical knowledge set before us by the moderns, for example by Spinoza in ethics, Hobbes in politics, Pufendorf in law, and Petty in economics, represents, paradoxically, a regression toward a pre-Aristotelian understanding of practical knowledge (and of the relation between theory and *praxis*). The fundamental problems of the modern determination of the sciences of action are also born of this [regression].

CONCLUDING CONSIDERATIONS

It is precisely with regard to these unresolved problems that the German neo-Aristotelians, through the "rehabilitation of practical philosophy," have drawn once again on Aristotle. To speak the truth, they did so somewhat freely and were, in my view, more driven by the difficulties of modernity and by an anxious desire to solve them than by the need to understand in actual fact the historical and conceptual transformations that have led modernity to regress below the level of the Aristotelian account of practical knowledge. Indeed, all the intuitions and all the programmatic theses vigorously maintained by the German neo-Aristotelians correspond without a doubt to problems and demands felt in the contemporary self-understanding of the practical disciplines and, in particular, to the demand that a capacity to guide be restored to the knowledge that concerns action. In the critical opposition to description, to the solely reportorial and neutral character of the examination of action developed in the social and human sciences, the paradigm *par excellence* of the knowledge adequate for *praxis* is rediscovered in Aristotelian *phronēsis*. Indeed, in the Aristotelian conception, phronetic knowledge— even though its dignity is inferior to that of the theoretical knowledge of sapience (*sophia*) because of the lesser degree of perfection of Being of its object, namely, human actions rather than divine and celestial realities—possesses nevertheless a feature that theoretical knowledge lacks, namely, the capacity to command, to guide action.[43]

By emphasizing the guiding character of practical knowledge, the neo-Aristotelians mean to oppose the new intellectualisms propounded in ethics and politics; they seek in that feature of practical knowledge a basis of support to bring together, in the realm of action, the moment of knowing and that of action, to bring closer together "knowledge of what is good" and "doing well." To do so, they also rehabilitate the element of decision, of deliberate choice, of *proairesis*, an element which, especially within the modern horizon of the theoretical misunderstanding of practical knowledge, has often been regarded as an imponderable and irrational element. Some take issue with it and purge it from their theories, others extol it as the root from which action originates—political action in particular. Against these two extremes—theoricism and intellectualism on the one hand, voluntarism and decisionism on the other—the neo-Aristotelians intend to open the way to a reconciliation between *reason* and *decision*.[44]

Moreover, among some neo-Aristotelians, this critique of ethical intellectualism is connected with a critique of the dissociation between morality and ethics, with a critique, in other words, of the typically modern separation of the rationality and universality of the principles of action, on the one side, and, on the other, the context-based, opaque, particular and historically conditioned character of the institutions and concrete mores in which concrete action takes place and shape. Against this dissociation and this separation, the neo-Aristotelians assert the necessity of an interpenetration of morality and ethics, of universality and concrete determinations, since it is only in the concrete character of *ēthos* [custom], mores and institutions that practical rationality can be fulfilled by attaining the genuine universal, that is, the concrete universal. Besides, all of this amounts to a critique of utopia; in other words, [it amounts] to a critique of this abstract morality and rationality which believes it can anticipate in a theoretical description the content of the happy life, and which seeks to revolutionize the existing *ēthos* and *nomos* [law] on the basis of its image of the blessed life.

However this may be, if the neo-Aristotelians had any merit, it was indeed that they reawakened a critical consciousness toward the modern understanding of action and the knowledge that must correspond to it. While the neo-Aristotelian recovery of practical philosophy has been stained by the dubious attempt to recycle pieces of Aristotelianism, by their use in heterogeneous contexts and by the rehabilitation of models of practical rationality like prudence, it has [nevertheless] resubmitted to our attention an understanding of action and of the knowledge that pertains to it which, while ancient, retains all of its validity. In the cultural self-representation of the contemporary age, which is in disarray after the crisis of dialectical thought and tormented by the furious winds of antidialectical thought, the rehabilitation of practical philosophy has opened a perspective from which it is once again possible to examine in a critical manner the identification of science with theory posited in modernity, as well as the paleomodern and modern notion of reason and its development in the direction of mere instrumentality and functionalism.

Undoubtedly, many problems remain open. I would like to limit myself to indicating briefly the one that appears to me most disturbing. Phronetic knowledge, as we have seen, is rehabilitated by the neo-Aristotelians in the general context of an attempt to respond to the crisis of the modern notion of reason, deprived of any substantiality and incapable of indicating in a compelling manner ultimate ends for human action. Hence [that knowledge] is invoked to help us in the context of a new, foundational project. But it is appropriate to wonder whether *phronēsis* is not, in Aristotle, a knowledge concerned with the means suited to attain an end and not the end itself. And since what the modern world lacks, in all of its "im-prudence," are undoubtedly not the means, which science places ever more at its disposal, but precisely the ends themselves, how can one hope to obtain indications regarding the ends through a rehabilitation of *phronēsis*? In Aristotle, *phronēsis* could guarantee the balance between the effectiveness of the means and the moral quality of the ends and hence, ultimately, the success of the action, because it was conceived of in the specific context mapped out by practical science and in the more general one of its anthropology, its cosmology, and its metaphysics. For that reason, it was capable of using operative concepts derived from these contexts. Among the neo-Aristotelians, by contrast, the recovery of *phronēsis* runs the risk of missing its goal since phronetic knowledge is here understood within a postmetaphysical horizon, within a horizon which is fairly flat and weaker than Aristotle's; in other words, [it is understood] within a minimal horizon, or even in the absence of any context, of any signpost from which phronetic knowledge could derive any guidance. Given such absence, *phronēsis* loses its moral qualification and runs the risk of being reduced to a mere skill, to a *deinotēs* or a *panourgia*, or else, as it has been objected to Gadamer, the German defender *par excellence* of a philosophy of *phronēsis*, it lays itself open to the risk of becoming an ideology, and in particular, as it has been maintained, the ideology of a pleasant moderate cultural relativism of conservative leaning.

It is because of this very predicament of disorientation of the contemporary world, and in the wake of this forced abstinence that has given rise to what I would call a situation of postmetaphysical bewilderment, that a compelling question demands an answer from us. This question, to paraphrase a famous Kantian title, could be formulated as follows: what does it mean to guide oneself in action? Nobody, neither the neo-Aristotelians nor their adversaries nor anybody else, can say today that he has an answer to this question. Do they have a strategy to contain the situation? Maybe. An aid to remedy the crisis?

They probably do as well. But the more one contains, the more one remedies, and the more acute becomes the feeling of bewilderment. It is for this reason that, despite quite a few unilateral decisions and exercises of force, the considerations and problems brought to our attention by the rehabilitation of practical philosophy and the neo-Aristotelians retain a disturbing relevance.

NOTES

The translator wishes to thank Judith Adam, Robert C. Bartlett, Jeffrey J. S. Black, Susan D. Collins, Matthew K. Davis, Ron C. Lee and Devin Stauffer for their comments on earlier drafts of this translation. All bracketed passages have been added by the translator.

1. The first general collection of essays on this debate was put together by M. Riedel, ed., *Rehabilitierung der praktischen Philosophie*, 2. vol. (Freiburg im Breisgau, 1972–1974). For an overall reconstruction of the debate, I take the liberty of referring to my article: "La rinascita della filosofia pratica in Germania", in *Filosofia pratica e scienza politica*, ed. C. Pacchiani (Abano and Padua, 1980), 11–97. For an analysis of certain particular aspects [of the debate], cf. A. Da Re, *L'etica tra felicità e dovere. L'attuale dibattito sulla filosofia pratica* (Bologna, 1986); L. Cortella, *Aristotele e la razionalità della prassi. Una analisi del dibattito sulla filosofia pratica aristotelica in Germania* (Rome, 1987).

2. Cf. N. Luhmann, *Zweckbegriff und Systemrationalität* (Frankfurt, 1968); cf. also the controversy with Jürgen Habermas in idem, *Theorie der Gesellschaft oder Sozialtechnologie. Was leistet die Systemforschung?* (Frankfurt, 1971).

3. Cf. especially K. Lorenz, *Das sogenannte Böse. Zur Naturgeschichte der Agression* (Vienna, 1963).

4. Cf. A. Gehlen, *Urmensch und Spätkultur* (Bonn, 1956), and idem, *Moral und Hypermoral* (Frankfurt and Bonn, 1969).

5. I have examined and tried to elucidate the particular meaning and problematic character of this designation in a paper, "Che cosa significa neoaristotelismo?," which I delivered at an Italo-German seminar organized in October 1984 by the University of Padua, in Brixen (Südtyrol). It was first published under the title: "La riabilitazione della filosofia pratica e il suo senso nella crisi della modernità," in a volume of the journal *Il Mulino* devoted to the problems of contemporary ethics (*Il Mulino* 35 (1986), 928–49), and then, under its original title, in E. Berti, ed., *Tradizione e attualità della filosofia pratica* (Genoa, 1988), 111–35. Cf. also the critical contextualization suggested by E. Berti, "La philosophie pratique d'Aristote et sa 'réhabilitation' récente," *Revue de Métaphysique et de Morale*, 45: 249–66. For an analysis of the typically German association of neo-Aristotelianism and conservatism, cf. Schnädelbach, "Was ist Neoaristotelismus?," in the collection of essays by W. Kullmann, ed., *Moralität und Sittlichkeit. Das Problem Hegels und die Diskursethik* (Frankfurt, 1986), 38–63. Schnädelbach does not question this association, however.

6. H. Arendt, *The Human Condition* (Chicago, 1958); German edition: *Vita activa oder vom tätigen Leben*, Stuttgart, 1960.

7. H.-G. Gadamer, *Wahrheit und Methode. Grundzüge einer philosophischen Hermeneutik* (Tübingen, 1960).

8. It is the chapter entitled: "Die hermeneutische Aktualität des Aristoteles" (H.-G. Gadamer, *Wahrheit und Methode*, 295–307).

9. Cf. R. H. Schmidt, ed., *Methoden der Politologie* (Darmstadt, 1967); H. Schneider, ed., *Aufgabe und Selbstverständnis der politischen Wissenschaften* (Darmstadt, 1967).

10. Cf. H. Albert and E. Topitsch, eds., *Werturteilstreit* (Darmstadt, 1979); V. Meja and N. Stehr, eds., *Der Streit um die Wissenssoziologie*, 2 vol. (Frankfurt, 1982); *Der Positivismusstreit in der deutschen Soziologie* (Neuwied and Berlin, 1969).

11. This tripartition of practical knowledge was not established by Aristotle. Admittedly, Aristotle distinguishes between different forms of *phronēsis*, with regard to action in the *polis*, action in the *oikos* and individual action (for example *EN*, VI.8) but, in general, if we want to maintain the notion of an articulation of practical knowledge in Aristotle, we ought to think rather of a bipartition of that knowledge into ethics and politics. The tripartition was probably born in the wake of the great influence of the pseudo-Aristotelian *Oikonomikos*. As for the general classification of knowledge into theoretical, practical and poietic disciplines, cf. *Top.*, VII.1, and *Metaph.*, A.I (where Aristotle distinguishes between the theoretical and practical disciplines). The complete tripartition is found at *Top.*, VI.6; VIII.I; *Metaph.*, E.I; K.7; *EN*, VI.2; the distinction between practical and poietic sciences, at *De Caelo*, III.7; *Metaph.*, L.9.

12. The tripartition of practical knowledge into ethics, economics. and politics—which is linked to the Aristotelian classification of the sciences (theoretical, practical, poietic) and is an alternative to the Hellenistic articulation of knowledge into logic, ethics, and physics (an articulation which Cicero attributes to Plato, but which Sextus Empiricus traces back to Xenocrates)—is introduced in the Latin culture by Boethius (in his commentary on the *Eisagōgē* of Porphyry) and is found in almost all the most important encyclopedias of the Middle Ages such as, to name only the best known, the *De artibus ac disciplinis* of Cassiodorus, the *Etymologiae* of Isidore of Seville, the *Speculum quadruplex* of Vincent of Beauvais, the *Didascalicon* of Hugh of St. Victor, the *De divisione philosophiae* of Dominicus Gundissalinus, the *De ortu scientiarum* of Robert Kilwardby. Cf. J. Mariétan, *Problème de la classification des sciences d'Aristote à saint Thomas* (Paris, 1901); J. Koch, ed., *Artes liberales. Von der antiken Bildung zur Wissenschaft des Mittelalters* (Leiden, 1959, 1976); J. A. Weisheipl, "Classification of the Sciences in Medieval Thought," *Medieval Studies* 27 (1965), 54–90; M. de Gandillac, ed., *La pensée encyclopédique au Moyen Age* (Neuchâtel, 1966); *Arts libéraux et philosophie au Moyen Age*, Actes du IVe Congrès international de philosophie médiévale, 27 août–2 septembre 1967 (Montreal and Paris, 1969); I. Hadot, *Arts libéraux et philosophie dans la pensée antique* (Paris, 1984). The tripartition of practical knowledge according to the Aristotelian classification of the sciences is also recovered by the modern encyclopedic tradition beginning with Francis Bacon. But in that case, it is increasingly combined with the tripartition of knowledge, of Hellenistic origin, into logic, physics, and ethics (cf. U. Dierse, *Enzyklopädie. Zur Geschichte eines philosophischen und wissenschaftstheoretischen Begriffs* [Bonn, 1977]; W. Schmidt-Biggemann, *Topica universalis. Eine Modellgeschichte humanistischer und barocker Wissenschaft* [Hamburg, 1983]).

13. Cf. the works of H. Maier, "Die Lehre der Politik an den älteren deutschen Universitäten" (1962), in H. Maier, *Politische Wissenschaft in Deutschland. Lehre und Wirkung*, erweiterte Neuausgabe (Munich, 1985), 31–67, 247–62; H. Maier, *Die ältere deutsche Staats- und Verwaltungslehre (Polizeiwissenschaft)* (Neuwied and Berlin, 1966, 1986). More generally, see the classic study of H. Denifle, *Die Entstehung der Universitäten*

des Mittelalters bis 1400 (Berlin, 1885 [repr. Graz, 1956]), and the rich bibliography contained in R. Graf von Westphalen, *Akademisches Privileg und demokratischer Staat. Ein Beitrag zur Geschichte und bildungspolitischen Problematik des Laufbahnwesens in Deutschland* (Stuttgart, 1979).

14. Ethics had been taught as an autonomous discipline in the faculty of arts in Paris since 1215. First, the teaching was based on the translation of Book II and Book III.1 of the *Nicomachean Ethics*, that is, on the *ethica vetus*, which included especially the theory of the virtues; then, Book I was also used, the *ethica nova*, which included the doctrine of happiness; finally, one had at one's disposal the complete translation of Robert Grosseteste (1246–1247). After the translation of the *ethica nova*, the effort to reconcile Aristotelian ethics with theology was a particularly arduous task, which led to a narrowing of the scope of the Aristotelian doctrine of *eudaimonia* and to its subordination to the theological doctrine of heavenly *beatitudo*. This [effort] also implied a theoretical understanding of ethics leaning toward *ethica docens* rather than *ethica utens*. On these problems, in addition to the studies of such pioneers as M. Grabmann, Ph. Delhaye and O. Lottin, we now have at our disposal the excellent monograph of G. Wieland, *Ethica- scientia practica. Die Anfänge der philosophischen Ethik im 13. Jahrhundert* (Münster, 1981). The studies of Ph. Delhaye have been recently collected under the title: *Enseignement et morale au XIIe siècle* (Freiburg, 1988).

15. The reasons for this persistence are numerous and fairly complex: the influence of the process of Aristotelizing the thought reformed by the *praeceptor Germaniae* Ph. Melanchthon; the resistance with which the German political culture opposed to the penetration of the modern notion of the State in the Machiavellian or Hobbesian sense, which represented the most powerful antithesis of the Aristotelian conception of politics as a practical science; finally, the progressive assimilation of novel elements like the jus-naturalistic or cameralistic traditions and the new [science of] economics, which were recovered in Germany within the tradition of *philosophia practica*. On the spreading of political Aristotelianism in Germany, in addition to the studies by H. Maier cited above, see M. Riedel, *Metaphysik und Metapolitik. Studien zu Aristoteles und zur politischen Sprache der neuzeitlichen Philosophie* (Frankfurt, 1975); V. Sellin, *Politik*, in O. Brunner, W. Conze, and R. Koselleck (eds.), *Geschichtliche Grundbegriffe. Historisches Lexikon zur politischsozialen Sprache in Deutschland*, vol. IV (Stuttgart, 1978), p. 789–874; finally, in general, P. Petersen, *Geschichte der aristotelischen Philosophie im protestantischen Deutschland* (Leipzig, 1921).

16. In the *Ratio praelectionum Wolffianarum in mathesin et Philosophiam universam* (1718), Wolff notes in that connection: "Philosophiae practicae universalis nomen hactenus inauditum inter Philosophos, nec minus res ipsa ignorata: mihi tamen haec disciplina utilis ac necessaria videtur ad Philosophiam practicam rite constituendam" (The name universal practical philosophy has been hitherto unheard among philosophers no less than the thing itself has been unknown; nevertheless, this discipline seems to me useful and necessary with a view to instituting practical philosophy in the proper way) (VI.2).

17. Outside of the scholastic and university tradition, of which Wolff can be regarded as the last great representative, it would be necessary to examine the presence of Aristotelianism in other areas where knowledge is transmitted: for example, in literary genres like the literature of the "mirrors of the prince," the *Hausväterliteratur*, and in the literature of

good behavior and of "civil conversation." On that point, the researches of E. R. Curtius, *Europäische Literatur und lateinisches Mittelalter* (Berne and Munich, 1948), regarding literature, and those of O. Brunner, *Neue Wege der Verfassungs—und Sozialgeschichte* (Göttigen, 1968), and idem, *Adeliges Landleben und euröpaischer Geist* (Salzburg, 1949), regarding history, remain fundamental.

18. "Die physiologische Menschenkenntnis geht auf die Erforschung dessen, was die *Natur* aus dem Menschen macht, die pragmatische auf das, was *er* als freihandelndes Wesen aus sich selber macht, oder machen kann und soll" (The physiological knowledge of man arises out of the investigation into how *Nature* shapes man; the pragmatic [knowledge of man], into how *he* as a free being does, or can and should, shape himself) (I. Kant, Anthropologie in pragmatischer Hinsicht, Akademie-Ausgabe, vol. 7, 117).

19. Cf. K. Chr. Köhnke, *Entstehung und Aufstieg des Neukantianismus. Die deutsche Universitätphilosophie zwischen Idealismus und Positivismus* (Frankfurt, 1986), p. 468, note 64.

20. English in the original.

21. English in the original.

22. As Heidegger, especially, has shown: cf. *Einführung in die Metaphysik* (1935), Gesamtausgabe, vol. 40, s. 57, 205–8; *Nietzsches Wort "Gott ist tod"* (1943), Gesamtausgabe, vol. 5 (= *Holzwege*), 209–67, 227ff.; cf. also *Brief über den Humanismus*, Gesamtausgabe, vol. 9 (= *Wegmarken*), 313–64, p. 349ff.; finally see also C. Schmitt, *Die Tyrannie der Werte*, in *Sekularisation und Utopie*, Ebracher Studien, E. Forsthoff zum 65. Geburtstag (Stuttgart, 1967), 37–62.

23. Cf. *EN*, II.2, 1103b26–29.

24. *EN*, VI.2, 1139a26–27.

25. Cf., for example, *EN*, VI.3, 1140a1–2.

26. Cf. especially *EN*, I.1 and II.2; IX.2, 1165a12–14; see also H. Bonitz, *Index aristotelicus*, 27b–28a (*sub voce akribeia, akribēs*).

27. On this question and, in general, for a study of the Aristotelian understanding of *phronēsis*, see P. Aubenque's monograph, *La prudence chez Aristote* (Paris, 1963, 1986).

28. Plato classifies scientific knowledge according to a dichotomy—theoretical and practical sciences—but his characterization of "practical" is radically different from that of Aristotle for the reason that he does not distinguish between *praxis* and *poiēsis*. As one sees very clearly in the *Statesman*, Plato regards the manual character [of practical knowledge] as a criterion to distinguish [it] from theoretical knowledge. Practical knowledge is therefore essentially the knowledge provided by the arts. The theoretical sciences, on the other hand, are of two kinds: either they give rise to judgments, or else they produce new realities that did not previously exist. Politics is regarded as a theoretical science of this kind, and it is theoretical because it does not involve the use of the hands (*Statesman*, 259e8–11).

29. Cf. *EN*, VI.4–5.

30. *EN*, VI, 5, 1140 a 28.

31. *EN*, VI.5, 1140b3–4.

32. *EN*, VI.5, 1140b6–7.

33. *EN*, VI.4, 1140a20–21.

34. *EN*, VI.5, 1140b5, repeated exactly in line 1140b20 with the same attribution of *alēthē* to the *hexis*. There is no reason, in my view, not to preserve this different attribution; it obviously indicates a difference between *technē* and *phronēsis*. This difference is completely obliterated if one accepts the suggestion of Susemihl and Stewart (followed by Apel and Tricot but rejected by Gauthier-Jolif), who correct *alēthē* twice, which agreed with *hexis*, by replacing it with *alēthous*, made to agree with *logou*. This correction establishes too close an analogy with the definition of *technē*, an analogy which runs the risk of obliterating the difference which Aristotle expresses here through the terminological subtlety of his definition.

35. Cf. *EN*, VI.13, 1144a23–29.

36. *EN*, VI.5, 1140b22–24.

37. *EN*, VI.5, 1140b24–25.

38. *EN*, II.5, 1106b26–31.

39. *EN*, VI.5, 1140b28–30.

40. On this point, Gadamer has given fundamental indications in the chapter of *Wahrheit und Methode* quoted above, which he obviously borrowed from the interpretation of Book VI of the *Nicomachean Ethics* given by the young Heidegger in his lectures (particularly in the introductory part of the course he taught at Marburg in the summer semester of 1924), [an interpretation] which was known to Gadamer.

41. Cf., for example, *EN*, VI.9, 1142a23–24. Broadly speaking, one can distinguish four strands in the history of the interpretation of this distinction: (1) one strand emphasizes the practical character of *phronēsis* and, by contrast, the descriptiveness of practical science (J. Walter, E. Frank); (2) the opposite strand emphasizes the singleness of practical knowledge, which can be at once a guidance of action (*phronēsis*) and a scientific examination of actions (G. Teichmüller, R.-A. Gauthier and J.-Y. Jolif, W. F. R. Hardie); (3) a third strand attributes to practical knowledge as a whole a topico-dialectical character (A. Grant, J. Burnet, W. Hennis, G. Bien); (4) there is, finally, a last strand opposed to this attribution, arguing that, since Aristotle denies that dialectics is a science, to attribute to practical philosophy a topico-dialectical character would amount to denying that practical philosophy is scientific knowledge (F. Susemihl, H. Kuhn, J. A. Stewart, O. Gigon, H. H. Joachim).

42. Pierre Aubenque brought to light a fundamental point when he noted rightly that "L'originalité d'Aristote ne consiste donc pas, comme on le croit parfois, dans l'affirmation du caractère pratique de la prudence, ni d'ailleurs dans celle de son caractère intellectuel. Car Platon n'avait jamais dit autre chose de sa sagesse, qui, indifféremment appelée *sophia* ou *phronesis*, était déjà indissolublement théorique et pratique. Et tel était déjà le sens de la doctrine socratique de la vertu-science. L'originalité d'Aristote consiste, en réalité, *dans une nouvelle conception des rapports de la théorie et de la pratique*, conséquence elle-même d'une rupture pour la première fois consommée dans l'univers de la théorie" (Hence Aristotle's originality does not consist, as it is sometimes believed, in the establishment of the practical character of prudence, nor again in that of its intellectual character. Plato had never said anything different of his wisdom which, indiscriminately called *sophia* or *phronesis*, was already indissolubly theoretical and practical. And this was already the meaning of the Socratic doctrine of virtue-science. Aristotle's originality, in truth, consists *in a new way of conceiving of the connections between theory and practice*, itself the consequence of a break

consummated for the first time in the universe of theory) (P. Aubenque, *La prudence chez Aristotle*, 144; our emphasis).

43. *Phronēsis* is *epitaktikē* (*EN*, VI.11, 1143a8).

44. It is significant that those who have clung to the Kantian paradigm of practical knowledge have endeavored to wring out of the faculty of judgement (*Urteilskraft*) an analogous function of guidance. By developing an hypothesis originally offered by Hannah Arendt, they have used in that function the Kantian determination of the reflective judgement (*reflektierende Urteilskraft*), insofar as it is set apart from the determining judgement in the *Kritik der Urteilskraft*. By abstracting completely from the Kantian understanding of ethics and politics, they have tried to regard the reflective judgement as the paradigm of the knowledge adequate for *praxis*. Differing from both reason (*Vernuft*), as a faculty of coherent thinking, and intellect (*Verstand*), as a faculty of autonomous thinking, the faculty of judgement, as an "enlarged mode of thinking" (*erweiterte Denkungsart*) is based on this principle: "an der Stelle jedes andern denken" (in place of every other thinking). As such, it can be suitably applied to the realm of ethics and politics as the medium of a universality closely connected with the concrete character of particular situations.

CHAPTER 2

THE MODERN FORM OF THE
CLASSICAL REPUBLIC

*The Repression of the Judeo-Christian Heritage
in Hannah Arendt's Attempt to Renew the
Aristotelian Concept of Politics*

HAUKE BRUNKHORST

Translated by Louis Hunt

The world of the political is a pagan world. The concept of the citizen is
as foreign to biblical thought as that of the republic. "Nothing is more foreign
to us Christians than public affairs" writes the Roman jurist and later founding
father of the Catholic Church, Tertullian, at the beginning of the third
century.[1] Hannah Arendt quotes him as proof of her thesis that the teaching of
the Bible is political only in the negative sense of a freedom from politics.[2] In
the constitutional revolutions of the eighteenth century, however, modern
European society returned to its origins in the Greek *polis* and the Roman *res
publica*. The politics of the modern age—exemplified in the rapid success of the
American Revolution—has daringly carried out a radical break with the Judeo-
Christian tradition. With this break it corrected the deceptive path, grounded
in Platonic idealism and biblical monotheism, which led to forgetfulness of
plurality, and overcame the old European onto-theology. At the end of the
1950s Arendt maintained that the understanding of freedom in the Western

democracies was far removed from that of the Roman citizen, Paul—an under-standing of freedom that, as Paul knew, was foolishness in the eyes of the Greeks. The foolishness of the Pauline doctrine of freedom is now a matter of the past: "The free world understands by freedom not: 'Give to Caesar what is Caesar's and to God what is God's,' but the right of everyone to take a hand in those affairs which were once the prerogative of Caesar. Precisely the fact that in our public life we are more concerned about freedom than anything else proves that we no longer live publicly in a religious world."[3]

The central thesis of the book *On Revolution* is that the origin of modern revolutions lies not in Jerusalem but in Athens and Rome. Neither "Christian equality nor Christian freedom could ever have led of their own accord to the idea of 'government of the people, by the people, for the people' nor to any other modern definition of political freedom."[4]

For Hannah Arendt, the decisive achievement of the revolutions of the eighteenth century lay for this reason not in liberation from burdensome servi-tude and self-imposed immaturity but in the common founding of a free repub-lic. The liberation of those who labor and are heavy-burdened, the humiliated and insulted, out of poverty and servitude is the goal of social *rebellion*, while genuine political *revolution*, since it is concerned with the "foundation of free-dom," can only be the work of free men who are not driven by "prepolitical need."[5] The republican act of founding separates the truly political "will to free-dom" from the merely negative, biologically compulsive "longing for libera-tion."[6] Not negative, but positive freedom stands as the foundational event of modern democracy.[7]

Hannah Arendt's work, composed in exile, can be read as an extraordi-nary attempt to rescue the knowledge of the original power of the republican founding event from oblivion and repression. For this reason she greeted effu-sively attempts to renew the spirit of the republic, whether it was in the bloodily suppressed Hungarian uprising of 1956 or in the student revolts at the end of the sixties in America.[8] Conversely, she defined the essence of totalitarianism as the destruction of the political and the extinguishing of all republican free-dom.[9] And she saw the real threat to the Western democracies in the consumer-istic identification of freedom and security, in the loss of civic virtue, in the destruction of positive by negative freedom.[10] The will to freedom is fundamen-tal to all public affairs; the longing for liberation, however justified it may be, remains always a merely private interest.

Where the public will to freedom fails to set limits to this private interest, the "conspiracy of poverty and necessity" will in the end destroy the republic.[11] In its technological-scientific self-understanding, in the economic and technological structure of the social basis, and in the new "social question," modern society as defined by private interests has unleashed antipolitical forces which in a crisis situation unite to form a potentially totalitarian power. The political authority charged with protecting the public space of freedom has not always proved equal to this power. This is a danger, whose first great negative example was the Jacobin terror, and which found in totalitarianism the historically perfect form of a hell on earth. But it is also a danger that lies dormant in the prosperous institutions of the modern social and welfare state, institutions that have made the consumer king and in which the political apathy of the lonely masses has long been apparent. In the West the republican utopia of an order of equality without a ruler threatens to degenerate into the "rule of nobody."[12] The important figures of the republic, mayor and council, become the easy prey of hungry wandering rats, and Heinrich Heine in his late poem on the "social question" did not shrink from pointing out the consequences and mocking classical republicanism:

> There are two kinds of rat:
> One hungry and one fat.
> The fat ones stay content at home,
> But hungry ones go out and roam.
>
> These wild and savage rats
> Fear neither hell nor cats;
> They have no property or money too,
> So they want to divide the world anew.
>
> These roving rats, alas!
> Are near us now en masse
> I hear their squeaks—straight on they press—
> Their multitude is numberless.[13]

They come out of the *oikos* and stream into the *polis* in order to fatten themselves in the light of the public realm. Their motif is hunger and their melody an abstract-universal "slave morality," which is enraptured by simple equality and by a justice, knowledge of which requires no particular insight and ability, no rhetorically versed common sense, no virtue rooted in experience of life and no political prudence. The beautiful, republican virtuoso freedom is swallowed up by the terrifying rebellion of the belly.

> We're lost—O woeful fate!
> They're already at the gate!
> The mayor and the council shake and pray,
> They don't know what to do or say

No finespun talk can help, no trick
Of old outdated rhetoric.
Rats are not caught with fancy isms—
They leap right over syllogisms.
When bellies are hungry, they only make sense
Of soup-bowl logic, breaded arguments,
Of reasoning based on roast beef or fish,
With sausage citations to garnish the dish.
A codfish, silently sautéed in butter,
Delights that radical gang of the gutter
Much more than the speeches of Mirabeau
And all orations since Cicero.[14]

Heine's ridicule is directed against a restorationist republicanism that has long since degenerated into a facade for a possessively individualistic class society: "They preach publicly water and drink secretly wine." Hannah Arendt on the other hand wants to renew the original force of the republican spirit. But the classical form of the republic fails in the face of the self-generated problems of a complex, functionally differentiated society. In this respect Heine's polemical poetry exposes the sociological weakness of Hannah Arendt's political theory. Modern civil society, which forms a legally institutionalized system of private autonomy between the genuinely private sphere of the family, where socialization primarily takes place, and the apparatus of state authority, eludes an analysis in terms of the dichotomies of *polis* and *oikos*, of public and private affairs, of action and production, which Hannah Arendt borrows from the classical conceptions of the republic and the political.

The exclusion of economic and social themes from the sphere of political discourse leads to a technically reduced understanding of the social and welfare state. The social question is in its core—as the question of slavery already was for Aristotle—a technical problem for which there are scientific solutions established essentially outside the genuine political sphere. To fill hungry mouths requires no republican rhetorical arts, "a codfish, silently sautéed in butter" is here exactly the right answer.

Hannah Arendt's vehement rejection of feminism can also be explained on the basis of her retention of a strict separation of political and private issues. The relation of the sexes—no less than that between master and slave—is essentially a deeply private affair and must be solved in the "darkness of the household." It can only be politicized at the expense of the republican spirit. The dam breaks. One does not speak of the private in the public. Knowledge of these limits belongs to the silent background consensus, the tacit consent, which constitutes the space of the political, and for this reason it should not be made into a political issue. For Hannah Arendt, "ruling" and "paternalism" are both fundamentally unpolitical phenomena. Her republican ideal is that of *isonomy*, the rulerless, politically active self-organization of citizens with equal rights. This is the deeper reason why she is just as persistent in denying the political dimension of the "social question" and the class struggle as she is in denying the political character of feminism.

The anthropologically based primacy of public over private freedom has a restorationist tendency as well. Only that person should belong to the community of equal citizens who proves to be of equal rank in politically active engagement. For this reason, the equality of human beings was originally the equality of a limited number of active citizens who lived and acted together in a limited space. This position obviously has elitist, antidemocratic consequences: "Precisely where the gap between rulers and ruled has closed there develops the danger that public and private interests will blend together in a highly unappetizing and destructive fashion."[15] In order to protect both the private autonomy of the passive citizen and the public autonomy of the active citizen, Hannah Arendt proposes a hierarchical, social differentiation between a right of political participation limited to active citizens and a share in private freedoms and social rights for all citizens.[16] This is by no means surprising but merely the logical consequence of the primacy of public over private autonomy.

Hannah Arendt's republicanism is restorationist finally in its fixation on a past but forgotten founding event. The new beginning made by the revolution is transfigured in civil-religious commemoration into a quasi-sacred core of republican identity. The emphasis lies not on the future-oriented legislative competence of the people but rather on the past-oriented evocation and renewal of the extraordinary spirit of the laws.[17] Arendt interprets civil disobedience for this reason defensively as protection of the constitution and not offensively as a new interpretation and extension of the existing constitution. Civil disobedience is an act in which citizens spontaneously unite in order to restore the original power of the founding event. It is supposed to check the progressive erosion of the political that occurs with the routinization of the charisma of the founding and the consumeristic privatization of the public good. The emphatically political dimension of civil disobedience consists not in the voluntary opening up of the democratic process of legislation to marginalized issues and to excluded persons and minorities, but in the reestablishment of the community of virtue—lost in the passage of time—out of which the republic first emerged. Arendt thus sees the genuine sense of civil disobedience in the public recollection of the moral content of the reciprocal agreement with which the founders of the republic pledged "active support and enduring participation in all affairs of public moment."[18]

Despite these restorationist tendencies, Hannah Arendt's recollection of the repressed republican idea of founding touches on the decisive weakness of the liberal self-understanding of modern politics. The revolution that led to the victory of the liberalism of freedom from politics was a republican one. In its identification of freedom with freedom from politics, liberalism is the secular heir of the Christian tradition. With the idea of republican freedom, however, a constitutive element of old Europe has wandered into modern democracy, an element that has pagan roots and cannot be reduced to liberal freedom from politics.

When Lincoln in his funeral oration after the terrible battle at Gettysburg defined democracy as "government of the people, by the people, for the people," he in fact fell back on the pagan idea of the republic, i.e., on the idea of the public self-organization of free and equal citizens. What Lincoln understood by such freedom differed fundamentally, however, from the famous classical document of republican freedom, the funeral oration of Pericles.[19] Lincoln—no differently than Jefferson, Locke, Rousseau, or Kant before him—gives a radical, new interpretation to the classical idea of the republic in the light of the Judeo-Christian inheritance of negative freedom. I consider the secularization thesis suggested by Hannah Arendt, according to which Western democracy is attributable to a "sharp break between Christian traditions and political modernity," to be false. In my view, this claim misses precisely the point of the modern transformation of classical thought. I will show this in what follows.

The primary distinction between modern and classical republicanism is that the former has overcome the abstract opposition between the virtuous *citoyen* and the self-interested bourgeois in favor of a mediation of both positions in the process of legislative will-formation.[20] Public self-organization is now understood as the lawful influence on social relations of power and no longer as the exclusion of private interests. The general laws that the people decide for themselves in a fair procedure are supposed to filter the general interests out of the multiplicity of particular interests. Moreover, the laws regulate only the external relations of the citizen. Whatever is not forbidden is permitted. The sovereign legislature has no access to the "law of the heart." The *Contrat Social* begins with the statement that the democratic sovereign can only change the laws, not human beings. This is the very opposite of Aristotle's position. An externally effective, institutionalized, positive-legal process takes the place of virtue, which is no longer necessary in order to arrive at rational regulations. Through the formality of law and the limitation of the "will to freedom" to legislation, a solidarity among friends is converted into a solidarity among strangers who may have no desire for greater intimacy. The liberation of the citizen from the obligation to be virtuous puts the censor out of work and renders superfluous the ontological distinction between *citoyen* and bourgeois. Ingeborg Maus has developed this decisive point with particular sharpness: "The sphere of the political as the place of the *citoyen* is not distinguished from that of the *bourgeois* by a specific 'field.' In the legal theories of Kant and Rousseau the political does not constitute an arena 'beyond the social.' For this reason, the political has no issues of its own, but only social issues." "Even the choice of these issues," according to Ingeborg Maus, "is decided not from a political perspective but from a social one."[21]

This is the reason why slavery, the class society, and the subordination of women in their careers *and* in the family could become issues for the political self-organization of a citizen body. The question of where the boundary currently lies between public and private autonomy is an eminently political question. The dispute about these limits constitutes public will-formation. And in this dispute, as the women's movement has shown, the door to the home no more sets an a priori limit to debate than the door to the factory did in its day. As the private-autonomous consumption of the products of labor becomes the subject of political and legal dispute about "exploitation" and "social justice," we learn that something we previously considered to be private is in truth a public affair. The public condemnation of the private consumption of female sexuality as "marital rape" lets us know that the earlier distinction between a private and a public sphere cannot have been in the common interest.

Insofar as modern republicanism uses public autonomy for the legal development of private-autonomous spaces for freedom, it gives free play to the motif of a radical critique of ruling that does not stop at any social issue. And this motif is not the inheritance of Roman republicanism but returns to the biblical idea of a free association. In the *Book of Judges* (8:22), which in no sense corresponds to the conception of theocracy assumed by Hannah Arendt, but is rather an example of "regulated anarchy" (Christian Sigrist), Gideon rejects the offer of the royal crown with the words: "I will not rule over you, and my son will not rule over you; the Lord will rule over you." This passage formulates a principled reservation against every form of the rule of some human beings over others. While for the Greeks and Romans isonomy or republican government implied a principled reservation against all ruling of some citizens over others, the thought that every form of the rule of some human beings over others stands under a principled reservation about legitimacy, breaks open the horizon of their political thought. It is this thought that appeared foolish in the eyes of the Greeks. The modern form of classical republicanism is due to the integration of this reservation about legitimacy. In this model of democratic self-legislation, though ruling is not excluded, the critique of ruling is internalized as the most important republican institution. Modern fundamental rights are institutions that, in interplay with a universalistic morality and the functional differentiation of society, make possible a radical critique of ruling, including a critique of the latent ruling that has been channeled into social institutions.

Moreover, Hannah Arendt is wrong to assume that the abstract universalism with which the Jews and Christians provoked the Greeks and Romans is political merely in a negative sense. As Harold Berman has shown, the legal revolution of the eleventh and twelfth centuries demonstrates the power of this universalism to found states.[22] The application of absolute notions of justice developed in the Bible to traditional Roman law in no sense led to the destruction of existing institutions, but rather put the law itself under the pressure of rationalization and contributed to the institutional differentiation of law and morality, church and state. Because this universalistic morality was too abstract for the ancient republic of virtue, it provoked, to a previously unheard of degree, the complementary development of positive law as an instrument of social self-regulation. The differentiation of positive law and the final secularization of modern politics remain unintelligible apart from the historical background of Europe's monotheistic tradition. To put this point sharply: That our rights are trump cards to be played where the cross hangs represents not a break with the Judeo-Christian tradition but its effective-historical consequence. The functional distinction between law, religion and politics, the positivization of the legal code and the existence of a minimal state governed by the rule of law in which conscience, thought and, in part, speech is free from the oppression of the community are already there prior to the founding of new republics in the constitutional revolutions of the eighteenth century. In these revolutions, not only is the republic established as a communicative power, which is Arendt's central point, but at the same time the republic is established as a project for the democratic development of all rights. This is a project which Lincoln called an "unfinished work"; a work that is unconcluded and unfinishable because it is guided by the normative premise of not excluding any issue or voice. This is a normative principle that is unintelligible to the political thought of the Greeks and Romans. For this reason democracy is also, as Lincoln again puts it in his Gettysburg Address, a global affair that cannot be limited to particular cities or territories. By defining the people of a state, and not, for example, an ethnic community of descent,[23] as a "permanently constituting" sovereign, Kant connected the Roman idea of the institutional founding of a legal collectivity with the Biblical promise of an uncertain, but auspicious future, without needing for this purpose to fall back on religion or transcendence as supports. It is this hope for something that, if we are fortunate, could be unimaginably better than the present that distinguishes modern republicanism from Hannah Arendt and the pagan polis.

NOTES

1. "Nobis nulla magis res aliena quam publica," Tertullian, *Apologeticum*, 38, cited in H. Arendt, "Religion und Politik," in *Zwischen Vergangenheit und Zukunft* (München, 1994).

2. Arendt, Ibid., 310.

3. Ibid., 311.

4. Ibid., 310.

5. H. Arendt, *Über die Revolution* (München, 1974), 116, 184.

6. Ibid., 39.

7. H. Arendt, Ibid., 39.

8. H. Arendt, *Macht und Gestalt* (München 1970).

9. H. Arendt, *Elemente und Ursprünge totalitärer Herrschaft* (München, 1986), 102ff., 240ff.

10. Cf. H. Arendt, "Freiheit und Politik," in *Neue Rundschau* 69 (1958): 671.

11. *Über die Revolution*, 75.

12. H. Arendt, *Vita activa* (München, 1981), 45.

13. Heinrich Heine, "The Roving Rats" ("Die Wanderratten") trans. Hal Draper, in *The Complete Poems of Heinrich Heine* (Oxford: Oxford University Press, 1982), 783–85.

14. Ibid.

15. *Über die Revolution*, 323.

16. Ibid., 355, 359ff.

17. Cf. I. Maus, "'Volk' und 'Nation,'" *Blätter für deutsche und internationale Politik* 5 (1994): 603ff.

18. H. Arendt, "Ziviler Ungehorsam," in *Zur Zeit* (München, 1989), 144.

19. Cf. H. Brunkhorst, *Demokratie und Differenz: Vom klassischen zum modernen Begriff des Politischen* (Frankfurt, 1994), 143ff.

20. The word *Willensbildung* commonly refers to the process of political debate. I have translated the term literally in order to bring out the connection with the problem of the "general will." Tr.

21. I. Maus, "'Volk und 'Nation,'" 611; cf. H. Brunkhorst, *Demokratie und Differenz*, 186ff.

22. H. Berman, *Recht und Revolution* (Frankfurt, 1991).

23. Hannah Arendt does not sufficiently distinguish between the French model of a people or nation politically united by a state (*Staatsvolk*) and the understanding of the state as rooted in an ethnic nation (*Volksstaat*) which was effective in Germany.

CHAPTER 3

DO WE NEED A
PHILOSOPHICAL ETHICS?

Theory, Prudence, and the Primacy of Ethos

RONALD BEINER

One of the more interesting developments in moral theory in recent decades has been a very notable resurgence of modes of thought inspired by Aristotle's *Nicomachean Ethics*. Needless to say, this turn back to Aristotle within contemporary moral and political theory did not please everyone. In particular, Habermas and his followers charged that neo-Aristotelianism, with its appeal to notions like *ethos* and *phronēsis*, rendered morality entirely dependent on the contingencies of given constellations of social life, and therefore abdicated the proper task of a moral theory, which is to supply universalist moral principles, as Kant, for instance, aspires to do in his practical philosophy. This essay tries to offer a response to the Habermasian challenge to neo-Aristotelian ethics. The object of my argument will be a heightened awareness of the gap between a *theory* of practical reason and the concrete demands of practical reason itself; this will, I think, allow me to defend Gadamer and other neo-Aristotelians against Habermas's charge that they hark back to an outdated philosophy that rests solely upon, as he disparagingly terms it, substantive "worldviews."[1] If Gadamer is correct in arguing for the centrality of notions like prudence and *ethos* to the constitutive reality of moral life, then Habermas's demand that ethics be grounded in "theoretical knowledge" can be seen as basically hollow. Gadamer's emphasis on the ineradicable concreteness of practical knowledge suggests that even the full realization of Habermas's program (or any comparable one) leaves the tasks of practical reason in their actual content essentially untouched. Gadamer states in one place that it was "on the basis of reasons and not out of neglect" that Heidegger in the *Letter on Humanism* balked at Jean Beaufret's plea for a new Heideggerian ethics. What were those reasons? An elucidation of these grounds will, I hope, help to clarify the limits of what one can accomplish with a new philosophical ethics.

Let us, then, start with an account of Habermas's challenge to the neo-Aristotelians. Habermas writes:

> Classical natural right is a theory dependent on world views. It was still quite clear to Christian Wolff at the end of the eighteenth century that practical philosophy "presupposes in all its doctrines ontology, natural psychology, cosmology, theology, and thus the whole of metaphysics." The ethics and politics of Aristotle are unthinkable without the connection to physics and metaphysics, in which the basic concepts of form, substance, act, potency, final cause, and so forth are developed. . . . Today it is no longer easy to render the approach of this metaphysical mode of thought plausible.[2]

The nub of the argument so far is, clearly, that classical ethics is inseparable from classical metaphysics, and that the awareness of this inseparability has prompted contemporary advocates of Aristotelianism to shy away from a forthright systematic account of their principles (for obviously they lack the means to resuscitate an obsolete metaphysics).[3] This critique is, in my opinion, quite effectively negated by Alasdair MacIntyre. In the following passage, MacIntyre addresses the widespread assumption that "ancient and medieval beliefs, including Aristotelian beliefs, in the objectivity of the moral order required as a foundation . . . or were 'based upon' theories about human nature and the nature of the universe":

> This is an important, although a common misreading of the structures of ancient and medieval thought which projects back on to that thought an essentially modern view of the ordering of philosophical and scientific enquiries. On this modern view, ethics and politics are peripheral modes of enquiry, dependent in key part on what is independently established by epistemology and by the natural sciences (semantics has now to some degree usurped the place of epistemology). But in ancient and medieval thought, ethics and politics afford light to the other disciplines as much as *vice versa.*

Hence from that standpoint, which I share, it is not the case that *first* I must decide whether some theory of human nature or cosmology is true and only *secondly* pass a verdict upon an account of the virtues which is "based" upon it. Rather, if we find compelling reasons for accepting a particular view of the virtues and the human telos, that in itself will place constraints on what kind of theory of human nature and what kind of cosmology are rationally acceptable.[4]

Precisely the same point is made by Gadamer in the context of a challenge to recent efforts to derive a new ethics from the thought of Heidegger: "The Aristotelian-Kantian inheritance still carries weight precisely because it is not grounded upon a metaphysics. Here I fail to see in what way Heidegger's [challenge to traditional metaphysics] lends itself to a direct application for the problem of a philosophical ethics. I think that Heidegger has warded off the question of an ethics on the basis of reasons and not out of neglect."[5] In other words, it is not incumbent on Heidegger to produce a "new" ethics, for the older ethical traditions have retained their abiding validity (or such validity as is proper to them). The debunking of traditional *metaphysics* does not at the same time suffice for the debunking of corresponding ethical traditions; so, at least in principle, traditional ethics can survive the demise of traditional metaphysical worldviews. What is decisive, of course, is whether these ethical traditions continue to be reflected in the actual life and practices of historical societies; and this is something that is entirely independent of the efforts of philosophers and theorists. It is, as Gadamer—following Heidegger as much as Aristotle—terms it, a matter of *ethos*.

As the next stage of Habermas's polemic makes clear, however, Habermas is fully aware that certain qualified "Aristotelians" like Gadamer "withdraw" the *theoretical* claim of practical philosophy. As Habermas puts it, "they *reduce* it to a hermeneutics of everyday conceptions of the good, the virtuous, and the just"[6] (hence his reference to this as "reductive," that is, reduced or contracted, Aristotelianism). However, in Habermas's view this tactical retreat does not rescue Aristotelianism from its contemporary predicament, but merely proves that such an emasculated Aristotelianism is incapable of meeting the demand that it *validate* itself at the level of theoretical knowledge:

> If philosophical ethics and political theory can know nothing more than what is anyhow contained in the everyday norm consciousness of different populations, and it cannot even know this in a different way, it cannot then rationally distinguish legitimate from illegitimate domination. . . . If, on the other hand, philosophical

ethics and political theory are supposed to disclose the moral core
of the general consciousness and to *reconstruct* it as a normative
concept of the moral, then they must specify criteria and provide
reasons; they must, that is, produce theoretical knowledge.[7]

Implicit in this critique is a concern about the inherent *particularism* of
any appeal to the prereflective *ethos* of given communities (hence the demand
that these moralities be theoretically "reconstructed"). The answer to such a
challenge can be located, I think, in Gadamer's reference to "the Aristotelian-
Kantian inheritance"; for I think there can be little doubt that Gadamer, no less
than Habermas, wishes to draw upon the Kantian universalism that is (today)
also a part of the given ethical consciousness. Gadamer is *not* an Aristotelian in
the sense that he wishes to revert ultimately to the self-assured political convictions of a particular privileged community (say, the Athenian polis). The ethical insight underlying Habermas's appeal to universal postulates of linguistic
reason—an appeal that he sees as necessary to guard against the invidious
implications of any such particularism—has already been "fused" into the more
comprehensive ethical tradition that Gadamer invokes. Consider the following
sentence from *Truth and Method*, referring to *sensus communis* as "the sense that
founds community": "What gives the human will its direction is not the
abstract generality of reason, but the concrete generality that represents the
community of a group, a people, a nation, *or the whole human race*."[8] This is
not, I think, a sentence that could have been written by Aristotle. In short,
Habermas's fears that the renunciation of a steadfast "theoretical" grounding
for ethics will endanger the best universalistic impulses of modernity overlooks
the fact that Gadamer's "Aristotelianism" (denoting a participation in commu-
nally accepted basic norms) presupposes a prior fusion of Aristotelian *and*
Kantian horizons.[9]

  At this point, it starts to become rather unclear whether an Aristotelian
like Gadamer has any more trouble distinguishing between legitimate and illegitimate consent than does Habermas; and if so, unclear also what exactly is
gained by the heroic theoretical labors that Habermas's project of a philosophical ethics requires. Gadamer, as we have seen, holds that Heidegger had good
reasons for turning aside the demand for a philosophical ethics. To the question
that stands at the head of our essay, then, Gadamer answers: No, we do not
need a "new" philosophical ethics, for the ethics already to hand within the tradition are perfectly sufficient, and in any case, no "new" ethics can serve to
restore the *ethos* that animates ethical practice if indeed that *ethos* has dissipated
within the life-practices of our society. This explains, more lucidly than

Heidegger's account in the *Letter on Humanism*, why Heidegger was compelled to refuse Jean Beaufret's famous demand for a Heideggerian ethics.

When Heidegger asserts, in the *Letter on Humanism*, that the tragedies of Sophocles "preserve the ethos in their sagas more primordially than Aristotle's lectures on 'ethics,'"[10] what is perhaps most interesting about this claim is the possibility that Aristotle himself might not have dissented from it in any decisive respect. That is, the conceptual articulation of the Greek *ethos* offered in the *Ethics* may have been composed from within an awareness that the essential force of this *ethos* had already exhausted itself. If so, Heidegger's seeming critique of Aristotle would actually agree with Aristotle's own awareness that he was describing an ethical culture that had been, since the emergence of the Sophists, in the process of losing its sway. In the same vein, Gadamer remarks that even so gifted a theorist as Aristotle could do nothing to restore *ethos* to the polis.[11]

Habermas, it seems, tends to trace Gadamer's aversion to a systematic ethics to the latter's reverence for cultural tradition, which involves a kind of idealistic historicism, which in turn leads easily into cultural relativism.[12] In my judgment, this is not at all the source of their theoretical disagreement. Rather, Gadamer's position derives from his emphatic understanding of the tense relationship between theory and prudence. As early as *Truth and Method*, Gadamer refers to how the Roman concept of the *sensus communis* contains "a critical note, directed against the theoretical speculations of the philosophers; and that note Vico sounds again from his different position of opposition to modern science."[13] More significantly, Gadamer's constant emphasis on Aristotelian *phronēsis* is meant to bring to mind a polemical opposition between abstract theory and concrete prudence. According to Gadamer, Aristotle's distinction between the ideas of *sophia* and *phronēsis* was "developed by the peripatetics as a critique of the theoretical ideal of life."[14] *Phronēsis* is practical knowledge "directed towards the concrete situation"; "it must grasp the 'circumstances' in their infinite variety."[15] It is just this infinity of circumstance that theory as such is incapable of anticipating; and if ethical theory is in principle unequipped to deal with the concrete situation, this means that it stops short of precisely that concreteness that is at the heart of all moral knowledge.

The fact that Aristotle's ethics offers the merest sketch of what it is to achieve the mean in one's ethical conduct is an acknowledgment of this necessary limitation of theory.[16] What Gadamer ultimately draws from Aristotle's practical philosophy is the notion that one is always already participating in shared norms by which one is antecedently shaped, and that "the ideal of the nonparticipating observer" who stands above it all is therefore a bogus one.

While the given normative consciousness should never be conceived as immutably fixed and beyond criticism, "it would surely be an illusion to want to deduce normative notions *in abstracto* and to posit them as valid with the claim of scientific rectitude," for this would be to preempt the rightful task of *phronēsis*.[17]

Here we confront what Gadamer, in his 1961 lecture "On the Possibility of a Philosophical Ethics," refers to as the vexing "dilemma" of all philosophical reflection on ethics[18]: namely, that in order to philosophize about ethical norms, one must distanciate oneself from them, whereas in order to have experience of these norms at all, so as to be acquainted with that about which one philosophizes, one must first of all participate in them—and this participation never completely ceases, even in the furthest flights of theoretical distanciation. (This dilemma is not so pressing in the case of, say, a philosophy of natural science, where the content of the norms one seeks to validate does not enter into the very being of the philosophical observer who reflects on them, as *is* true—and necessarily true—for the moral philosopher.) This unavoidable tension between distance and involvement is at the heart of Gadamer's hermeneutics. The intractability of this dilemma carries important implications for any attempt to define a philosophical ethics. For Gadamer, it implies an essential finitude that characterizes any endeavor to bring philosophical reflection to bear upon ethical life. This finitude or conditionality of moral reflection is visible not only in the ethics of Aristotle, but even, as Gadamer shows, in the seemingly more ambitious attempt by Kant to ground moral principles. Kant, like Aristotle, insists that his moral philosophy makes available no new moral content, but merely clarifies and articulates the moral experience already shared in by ordinary people throughout the ages. Kant notes that a fault-finding reviewer of the *Foundations of the Metaphysics of Morals* "really did better than he intended when he said that there was no new principle of morality in it but only a new formula. Who would want to introduce a new principle of morality and, as it were, be its inventor, as if the world had hitherto been ignorant of what duty is or had been thoroughly wrong about it."[19]

The import of Kantian formalism, as understood by Gadamer, is less to inform us of the content of our duty than to confirm what duty *is*, in its very nature (to remind us of its unconditionality, when reason itself tempts us to treat duty as something that can be finessed). The purpose of Kant's ethics, on this reading, consists not in telling us what we ought to do, but rather, in telling us what it *means* to be subject to an "ought," what it *is* to be morally bound. According to Gadamer, Kant's attempts to derive content from the formula of the categorical imperative are entirely unpersuasive and contrived, and so what remains is the mere *form* of moral experience as the steadfast search for what is unconditionally valid and binding. Therefore *phronēsis*, far from being displaced, retains its indispensable function within the drama of trying to *apply* the demand for moral unconditionality. Once again, the heart of moral experience lies in finding oneself cast into the concreteness of an ethical situation where no predetermined rule dictates an answer.[20]

As Gadamer puts it, practical philosophy, with its insistence on *phronēsis*, "does not propose any new ethics, but rather clarifies and concretizes *given* normative contents,"[21] and this, as we have seen, applies as much to Kant as to Aristotle. These given normative contents can only be supplied by *ethos*, which in turn is a function not of reflective consciousness but of our very being as shaped by life in society. So we see that what is most relevant to the understanding of contemporary practical reason is not the theoretical or meta-theoretical grounding of principles, but the historical question of why the *ethos* of a coherent ethical life has decomposed. And for this purpose a historical reckoning such as that offered by Alasdair MacIntyre in *After Virtue* is a great deal more helpful than Habermas's attempt to supply grounding principles.[22]

Part of the explanation for the primacy of *ethos* is that in order for moral convictions to have force within the life of concrete societies, ethical intuitions must possess a great deal more self-certainty than they could possibly gather from merely theoretical demonstrations. (An insight of this kind is present in Hegel's and Nietzsche's analyses of Socrates, whose very appearance is seen as a symptom of moral decline within the polis.) As even Habermas concedes, "the difference between what we always claim for our rationality and what we are actually able to explicate as rational can in principle never be eliminated."[23] But for the demands of situated praxis, this is simply not enough: one must act *as if* unreflectively embodying a sure sense of what is good and right; one must command a kind of practical assurance that even the strictest, most rigorous set of arguments fails to supply.[24] This is something made possible only by character and habituation, never by rational argument as such. As an Aristotelian would say, in order to live virtuously and to make the right choices, one's soul must be shaped by certain habits of virtuous conduct, in a way that renders superfluous, recourse to strict arguments. Judged by these purposes, the achievements of theory always fall short. This does not mean, of course, that the adequacy of one's judgments is measured by pure inner conviction; it means only that one's capacity to discriminate between good and bad judgments cannot be reduced to an abstract science.

Here we perceive the grounds of the tremendous modesty that characterizes Aristotelian ethics. Gadamer writes entirely in the spirit of Aristotle when he speaks of his "profound scepticism regarding the role of 'intellectuals' and especially of philosophy in humanity's household of life": "The great equilibrium of what is living, which sustains and permeates the individual in his privacy as well as in his social constitution and in his view of life, also encompasses those who think. . . . [Even the Greeks, with their exaltation of *theoria*,] knew that such theory is embedded within the practice of conditioned and lived life and is borne along by it."[25]

Habermas also, to be sure, often gives expression (especially in some of his more recent statements) to a similar sense of modesty in relation to the self-defined understandings of given societies.[26] The fundamental difference between them can, I think, be put as follows: For Habermas, any practical judgment insofar as it has not been theoretically validated is to that extent somehow suspect, or clouded by suspicion, as to its possible groundlessness. For Gadamer, on the other hand, any theoretical judgment as such carries a certain measure of stigma insofar as it stands unmediated by the concreteness of a particular social experience. It seems to me possible and desirable to embrace both of these points of view in a way that does justice to the imperishable tension between theory and practice.

The issue is not one of truth versus relativity, as Habermas tends to present it, nor of validated knowledge versus unvalidated opinion; the issue, rather, is one of the truth of generality versus the truth of specificity—that is, truth at the level of abstract principles versus truth embedded in immediate circumstances. Aristotle certainly does not repudiate the idea of moral truth when he insists that *phronēsis* can only embody itself in the local encounter with "ultimate particulars." Nor does Gadamer. So it is not any kind of moral scepticism that prompts doubts about the project of a philosophical ethics, but instead the worry that it will have very little to teach us at the real locus of our ethical experience. What is intended is not an attenuation of moral reason, but its confrontation with an alternative account of moral reason—its "localization," one might say.[27] To use Gadamer's terms, the choice is between judging "from a distance" and judging from within "the demands of the situation"; so it is not a question of whether moral truths exist but of whether one gains access to these truths "from the inside," or whether they are imposed from "outside" shared moral experience.

Gadamer's Aristotelian insight into the primacy of *ethos* may be expressed as follows: Good theory is no substitute for good socialization, and even the best theory is utterly helpless in the face of bad socialization.[28] Habermas, it would appear, agrees entirely with this formulation:

> Moral theory proceeds reconstructively, in other words after the
> event. Aristotle was right in his opinion that the moral intuitions
> which theory clarifies must have been acquired elsewhere, in more
> or less successful socialization processes.[29]

> How could anyone focus on moral intuitions and reconstruct
> them, before having them—and how do we get them? Not from
> philosophy, and not by reading books. We acquire them just by
> growing up in a family. This is the experience of everyone. . . .
> There can't be anyone who ever grew up in any kind of family who
> did not acquire certain moral intuitions.[30]

These statements certainly appear to draw Habermas as close to
Gadamer's Aristotelianism as it is possible to get. And yet there remains a crucial gulf between them that may be discerned from the wide divergence in their
respective stances toward modernity. For Habermas, modernity in itself is a
gain, for it opens more and more aspects of human life to free, uncoerced
examination and discursive argument, which renders these practices more
"rational," and therefore more free. For Gadamer, in contrast, the effect of such
"rationalization" may be to loosen the hold of these practices (whether they are
legitimate or illegitimate) insofar as they depend on *ethos*. Thus Habermas,
while he seems to concede a great deal on the question of habituation, still does
not follow through the full implications of his own admission of the primary
role of moral socialization, as can be seen, above all, in his equation of modernity as such and emancipation. (How can the content of ethical life rest upon
both habit *and* rational consensus? Surely this is an either/or.) For Gadamer, on
the other hand, the legacy of modernity is far more ambiguous, for the rational
and discursive examination of ethical practices may, in itself, contribute to the
dissolution of those practices, to the extent that these practices express not our
"consciousness" but our "being" as shaped by prereflective habituation.[31]
(Consider the decline of the work ethic, the atrophying of shared culture, the
decomposition of the family itself, and so on.) What may be inferred from this
observation is not necessarily that these practices were in essence illegitimate,
but rather, that there is a tension between *ethos* and "rationalization" (that is,
reason in the *Enlightenment* sense of bringing-into-explicit-consciousness)—a
tension that Habermas persistently fails to acknowledge.

In a curious way, the contrast between these two positions vis-à-vis
modernity shows Gadamer to be *less* of a relativist, more of a universalist, than
Habermas; for whereas Habermas seeks to vindicate the universalistic truth contained within *our own* modern, Western rationality, Gadamer seeks to recover

the truths of other times and other cultures that have been eclipsed by Western modernity. The irony is that Habermas, for all of his antihistoricism, embraces the supposedly higher claims of our own epoch, while Gadamer, criticized for his "historicism," is much more sceptical of the putative gains of modernity, and therefore further removed from the presumptions of the present.[32]

To reinforce our case, let us consider another Habermasian critique of Gadamer. Albrecht Wellmer, writing in defence of Habermas's project, offers the following characterization—mistaken in my view—of what he calls the "left-Aristotelian" position.[33] The heart of this position, as he describes it, is the idea that while rational argument and agreement is certainly possible with respect to specific issues and problems, there are nonetheless basic norms, constitutive of political legitimacy, that are not in principle subject to rational dialogue. The crucial question here, as Wellmer construes it, is whether limits can be drawn, beyond which *in principle* rational argument and rational agreement are out of reach. If, in engaging in any rational discussion, we pursue a discursive continuum that leads to progressively more and more basic assumptions, then it is hard to see how any such "boundary line" can ever be justifiably drawn. And if this boundary line can never be located in a fixed or determinate way, it follows, for Wellmer, that "no norms, institutions or interpretations are in principle exempt from the possibility of critical examination."[34] If this is intended as a refutation of Gadamer (Hannah Arendt is the only thinker explicitly mentioned by Wellmer), I think it fails to hit the mark. The basic premise of Wellmer's argument (the interminable continuity of rational discourse) is, in my opinion, sound, but it does not yield the conclusion that he seeks to draw from it (that is, the refutation of "left Aristotelianism"). What the argument obscures is a fundamental ambiguity surrounding the term "in principle." I think that Gadamer (and Arendt, for that matter) would happily admit that there are no principled limits to rational discussion of social norms. (This is, after all, what defines the tradition of political philosophy.) What *is* at issue, though, is whether it is realistic to demand or expect that such rationally-arrived-at consensus could actually uphold the life of an entire society (or whether it is even coherent to posit such a consensus as an ideal norm at which to aim). Here indeed Gadamer would fault Habermas's theory for rationalistic utopianism. If, as any "left Aristotelian" must believe, *ethos*, not rational agreement, is the condition of virtue, it would be completely implausible to posit the possibility of a good or reasonable society, any more than any other society, founded upon rational consensus. To say this, however, is not to banish notions of reason and unreason in the evaluation of different societies. The idea that social norms should not be submitted to critical reason is hardly a view one would expect from a devoted student of Plato and Aristotle like Gadamer. (To put the point rather provocatively, one might say that where Gadamer opposes critical theory is not in its commitment to reason but in its sociological naiveté—a naiveté that is, of course, as critics from Rousseau and Hegel onwards have insisted, a crucial aspect of the legacy of Enlightenment rationalism.)

Habermas himself, of course, denies that the idea of rational consensus is any kind of utopian ideal; rather, he insists that it furnishes merely a critical standard for distinguishing the legitimacy or illegitimacy of given forms of social organization. But even as a standard for judging actual societies, such a regulative idea presupposes that it is meaningful to conceive of societies whose members are not just socialized *to* reason but socialized *by* reason,[35] and it is the coherence of precisely this conception that is here in question. Furthermore, if Habermas agrees with Gadamer that philosophical ethics is necessarily situated posterior to ordinary moral consciousness, and that to this extent no such ethics, however well-grounded, can actually "preempt" practical judgment, and if he agrees that even the most impeccably grounded theory leaves open the task of application with respect to particulars,[36] what in substance remains of Habermas's demand that everyday communication receive a "justification or grounding" whose validity is elevated above "the mere de facto acceptance of habitual practices?"[37] Is it not the case that the challenge to supply reasons or grounds for a particular judgment will arise *within* the immediate situation of praxis, as Gadamer thinks, and that a formal inquiry into conditions of validity such as Habermas pursues will have little or nothing to contribute toward satisfying the internal demands of practical reason in all its immediacy and concreteness? We are left, it seems, more unsure than ever about what one may hope to accomplish with a systematic *"Diskursethik"*—apart from seeking merely to repel the most virulent forms of relativism. But even supposing that this last intention defines the sole object of the enterprise,[38] one might still ask: Does one need a systematic ethics in order to fend off relativism, as Habermas implies in relation to Gadamer?[39]

The disputation between Gadamer and Habermas ultimately comes down to a question of the relative priority of theory and prudence. Habermas's position, as we saw in the passage I quoted from "Legitimation Problems in the Modern State," is that a reliance upon prudence alone, without resort to theoretical criteria, risks sliding into a denial of universal principles of justice and equality. Therefore *phronēsis* is not enough: one requires theoretical knowledge of correct norms. Gadamer's clearest and most forceful answer to this challenge is contained in his letter to Richard Bernstein, appended to *Beyond Objectivism and Relativism*:

Aristotle's *Politics* . . . comes into its own and makes the transition from ethics to politics only because it presupposes the results of the *Ethics*: first and foremost, a common, shared normative consciousness. The *Politics* proposes, so to speak, the doctrine of a political constitution for a society that still knows what *ethos* and *phronesis* are. Both your own [Bernstein's] and Habermas' argument assert that this is precisely the knowledge we no longer possess today. This fact fundamentally alters the task of the transition from ethics to politics; if I understand correctly, it now becomes the transition from practical philosophy to social science. But practical philosophy insists on the guiding function of *phronesis*, which does not propose any new ethics, but rather clarifies and concretizes given normative contents. To this extent, I share Rorty's criticism of Habermas' claim to scientific status. As I have put it elsewhere, I cannot really make sense of a *phronesis* that is supposed to be scientifically disciplined, although I can imagine a scientific approach that is disciplined by *phronesis*.[40]

The priority of *phronēsis* over science that Gadamer here asserts follows from the dependence of any ethical understanding upon *ethos* or habituation (as Gadamer puts it: one cannot be convinced by argument to be virtuous). If in fact the technicization of modern life, or the "disenchantment of the world," or whatever, has caused us to lose this *ethos*, then no theoretical grounding of a philosophical ethics could possibly allow us to recover it. In that case, our situation would be truly desperate; it would be as forlorn as Heidegger describes it when he says that "only a god can save us"—namely, the descent of a new *ethos* as a dispensation of being. But here Gadamer is just as critical of Heidegger as he is of Habermas: just as no philosopher can legislate a new *ethos*,[41] so no philosopher can rule out new constellations of ethical life arising out of existing communal solidarities. (It is in reference to *Heidegger* that Gadamer speaks of the "terrible intellectual hubris" involved in dismissing "life as it is actually lived with its own forms of solidarity."[42]) The *ethos* may indeed be tenuous in the technological age we now inhabit, but if it were genuinely as bleak as Heidegger expresses in his cry for new gods, then certainly no provision of a philosophical ethics would yield consolation enough.

Notes

1. Jürgen Habermas, "Legitimation Problems in the Modern State," in *Communication and the Evolution of Society*, trans. T. McCarthy (Boston: Beacon Press, 1979), 201.

2. Ibid. Cf. Habermas's combative references to neo-Aristotelianism in "Discourse Ethics: Notes on a Program of Philosophical Justification," in Habermas, *Moral Consciousness and Communicative Action*, trans. Christian Lenhardt and Shierry Weber Nicholsen (Cambridge: MIT Press, 1990), 44, 98–99.

3. Leo Strauss, one of the targets of Habermas's critique, admits as much in *Natural Right and History* (Chicago: University of Chicago Press, 1974), 7–8.

4. Alasdair MacIntyre, "Bernstein's Distorting Mirrors," *Soundings* 67, no. 1 (1984): 38–39.

5. Hans-Georg Gadamer, "Gibt es auf Erden ein Maß?" *Philosophische Rundschau* 32, no. 1/2 (1985): 18. Cf. Gadamer, *Truth and Method* (New York: Seabury Press, 1975), 278: "By placing limits on the intellectualism of Socrates and Plato in his enquiry into the good, Aristotle became the founder of ethics as a discipline independent of metaphysics." See also Gadamer, *Reason in the Age of Science*, trans. F. G. Lawrence (Cambridge: MIT Press, 1981), 117: "The expression *practical philosophy* intends precisely to say that it makes no determinate use of arguments of a cosmological, ontological, or metaphysical sort for practical problems."

6. Habermas, "Legitimation Problems in the Modern State," 202, my italics.

7. Ibid., 202–3. Habermas alludes in this context to the experience of National Socialism, where the participation in a shared ethical consciousness provided absolutely no bulwark against political evil.

8. Gadamer, *Truth and Method*, 21, my italics.

9. For a discussion of similar themes, cf. MacIntyre, "Bernstein's Distorting Mirrors," 39–40. For a more direct statement by Gadamer, see also his letter to Richard J. Bernstein, published as an appendix to Bernstein's book *Beyond Objectivism and Relativism* (Philadelphia: University of Pennsylvania Press, 1983), 264, where he states that the aspiration to universal freedom "has been self-evident to any European since the French Revolution, since Hegel and Kant."

10. Martin Heidegger, *Basic Writings*, ed. D. F. Krell (New York: Harper and Row, 1977), 232–33.

11. Gadamer describes the cultural drama of this ebbing of the *ethos* in the context of his commentary on Book X of *The Republic* in "Plato and the Poets" in *Dialogue and Dialectic*, trans. P. C. Smith (New Haven: Yale University Press, 1980), 39–72.

12. That the fear of relativism remains Habermas's chief objection to hermeneutic philosophy can be seen from his more recent essay, "Philosophy as Stand-In and Interpreter," in *After Philosophy: End or Transformation?* ed. K. Baynes, J. Bohman, and T. McCarthy (Cambridge: MIT Press, 1987), 304, 307–9, 314. See also Habermas,

"Interpretive Social Science vs. Hermeneuticism" in *Social Science as Moral Inquiry*, ed. N. Haan, R. Bellah, P. Rabinow, and W. Sullivan (Berkeley: University of California Press, 1983), 258.

13. Gadamer, *Truth and Method*, 22.

14. Ibid., 20.

15. Ibid., 21.

16. Cf. Gadamer, *Reason in the Age of Science*, 112, 133–34; also, Gadamer, *Truth and Method*, 286; Gadamer, "On the Possibility of a Philosophical Ethics: in *Kant and Political Philosophy: The Contemporary Legacy*, ed. Ronald Beiner and William James Booth (New Haven: Yale University Press, 1993), 369.

17. Gadamer, *Reason in the Age of Science*, 135.

18. Gadamer, "On the Possibility of a Philosophical Ethics," 363.

19. Immanuel Kant, *Critique of Practical Reason*, trans. L. W. Beck, 3d ed. (New York: Macmillan, 1993), 8n.

20. Gadamer, "On the Possibility of a Philosophical Ethics," 371: "The recipient of Aristotle's lectures on ethics must be immune to the peril of wanting to theorize simply in order to extricate himself from the demands of the situation. It seems to me that the abiding validity of Aristotle consists in his holding this peril constantly in view. As Kant did with his formalism, Aristotle too expelled all false claims from the notion of a philosophical ethics."

21. Bernstein, *Beyond Objectivism and Relativism*, appendix, 263, my italics.

22. In "Discourse Ethics" (43–45, 98–102), Habermas conceives only deontological ethics as cognitivist, and therefore totally misreads MacIntyre as a noncognitivist "sceptic." The acknowledgment that Aristotelians like Gadamer and MacIntyre *are* moral cognitivists would force Habermas to rethink his strange assumption that one must be a Kantian in order to avoid moral scepticism. The same misapprehension arises in Habermas's debate with Charles Taylor in *Kommunikatives Handeln*, ed. Axel Honneth and Hans Joas (Frankfurt: Suhrkamp, 1986), 35–52, 328–37. Seeking to repulse Taylor's critique, Habermas replies on behalf of "a formal *and cognitivist* ethics" (333, my italics)—as if to suggest that these terms are synonymous, or as if Taylor's Aristotelian perspective were any the less cognitivist.

23. Habermas, "Questions and Counterquestions," in *Habermas and Modernity*, ed. R. J. Bernstein (Cambridge: MIT Press, 1985), 195 (quoting Herbert Schnädelbach).

24. Cf. Gadamer, "On the Possibility of a Philosophical Ethics," 369: "What is meant by *hexis* [habit] is not a possibility of this or that, as with capability and knowledge, but rather a naturelike state of being, a 'thus and not otherwise.'"

25. Gadamer, "The Heritage of Hegel," in *Reason in the Age of Science*, 58–59.

26. Habermas, *Autonomy and Solidarity*, ed. P. Dews (London: Verso, 1986), 160–61, 170–71, 204ff.

27. In this respect, Gadamer and Habermas stand together in opposition to French postmodernists, such as Derrida and Lyotard, and their American followers, such as Rorty. For a critical response by Gadamer to French "deconstructionism," see Gadamer, "Reply to Jacques Derrida" in *Dialogue and Deconstruction: The Gadamer–Derrida Encounter*, ed.

Diane P. Michelfelder and Richard E. Palmer (Albany: State University of New York Press, 1989), 55–57. It bears observation that Gadamer, in his letter to Bernstein (see note 9 above), at least implicitly sides with Habermas in criticism of Rorty, just as he sides with Rorty in criticism of Habermas. Habermas typically conflates Gadamer's hermeneutics and Rorty's pragmatism (see "Philosophy as Stand-In and Interpreter," 299, 304–5, 309, 314). In my view, the critique of Rorty as a relativist is somewhat easier to sustain, at least insofar as Rorty plays up relativist themes in order to give added bite to his antifoundationalist rhetoric.

28. Cf. "Gadamer on Strauss: An Interview," *Interpretation* 12, no. 1 (January 1984): 10: "As you know, we are formed between the ages of fourteen and eighteen. Academic teachers always come too late. In the best instance, they can train young scholars, but their function is not to build up character. After the war, I was invited to give a lecture in Frankfurt on what the German professor thinks of his role as an educator. The point that I made was that professors have no role to play in that regard. Implied in the question at hand is a certain overestimation of the possible impact of the theoretical man. That is the thought behind my attitude."

29. Habermas, *Autonomy and Solidarity*, 171.

30. Ibid., 207–8.

31. Cf. Gadamer, "On the Possibility of a Philosophical Ethics," 370: "Ethical practice . . . depends so much more on our being than on our explicit consciousness." Hence Gadamer's attempt to redeem the pre-Enlightenment sense of "prejudice": *Truth and Method*, 235ff.

32. For a more radical challenge to Habermas's "universalism," cf. Richard Rorty, "Habermas and Lyotard on Postmodernity" in *Habermas and Modernity*, 165–66. As if to underline the irony, Rorty seeks to enlist Habermas's affirmations of modernity in Rorty's own frankly historicist cause.

33. Albrecht Wellmer, "Reason, Utopia, and the *Dialectic of Enlightenment*," in *Habermas and Modernity*, 59.

34. Ibid., 60–61.

35. That the latter possibility is still entertained by Habermas is evident in "Questions and Counterquestions," 197, when he asks, "Does it not remain an open question whether or not the social integrative powers of the religious tradition shaken by enlightenment can find an equivalent in the unifying, consensus-creating power of reason?" (Cf. *Habermas and Modernity*, 92.) I believe that Gadamer would view this unwavering commitment to the Enlightenment idea of reason as a symptom of the "intellectualism" to which Gadamer's Aristotelianism is opposed. (See *Truth and Method*, 278, and "On the Possibility of a Philosophical Ethics," 367).

36. Habermas, *Autonomy and Solidarity*, 171, 204–5, 207. Habermas wrestles with these questions in "Discourse Ethics," 98–109.

37. Habermas, "Philosophy as Stand-In and Interpreter," 314.

38. Habermas, *Autonomy and Solidarity*, 160–61; "Discourse Ethics," 98.

39. Gadamer's antifoundationalism is clearly expressed in the foreword to the second edition of *Truth and Method*, where he concedes that his hermeneutical philosophy

"does not satisfy the demand for reflective self-grounding." "But is the dialogue with the whole of our philosophical tradition, in which we stand and which, as philosophers, we are, groundless? Does what already supports us require any grounding?" *After Philosophy: End or Transformation?* ed. Baynes, Bohman, and McCarthy, 349. Also, see the exchange between Gadamer and Karl-Otto Apel in *Rationality To-day*, ed. Theodore F. Geraets (Ottawa: University of Ottawa Press, 1979), 348–49. For Habermas's own disavowal of foundationalism, see "Discourse Ethics," 94–98, "Interpretive Social Science vs. Hermeneuticism," 260–61.

40. Bernstein, *Beyond Objectivism and Relativism*, appendix, 262–63.

41. This was Rousseau's grim insight: that intellectuals or theorists can do much to *undo* the *ethos* of a sound political community, but they can do little to restore it once it is lost. For a similar line of thought, cf. Heidegger, "Why Do I Stay in the Provinces?" in *Heidegger: The Man and the Thinker*, ed. T. Sheehan (Chicago: Precedent, 1981), 29.

42. Bernstein, *Beyond Objectivism and Relativism*, appendix, 264. Cf. "Gadamer on Strauss," 9–11; Strauss and Gadamer, "Correspondence Concerning *Wahrheit und Methode*," *Independent Journal of Philosophy* 2 (1978): 8, 10; *Truth and Method*, xxv.

CHAPTER 4

ARISTOTLE AND THE
ETHIC OF IMPERATIVES

HANS-GEORG GADAMER

Translated by Joseph M. Knippenberg

The imperativistic character of human moral experience is certainly an essential point of view for every reflection. By contrast, "sagezza" could be rendered as the practical virtue of *phronēsis* and as reasonableness, discretion, or prudence (*prudentia*). As these correspondences clearly show, "*phronēsis*" can appear as a merely pragmatic modification, in which the strict obligatoriness of the moral law mitigates itself into the easy expediency of a rule of prudence. Thus Kant in his famous grounding of the moral law and its obligation contrasted the "categorical" imperative as higher than the imperatives of prudence or skill.

But one can also emphasize these connections differently. Whoever learned to think in the tradition of neo-Kantianism, as I did, and as a result learned to look at the controversial figure of Kantian formalism with a critical eye, has to miss the richness and the breadth of moral truth and reality that one finds in Aristotle. The Aristotelian working out of the rational element in moral behavior helps present ethics in all its differentiated multiplicity. That which is called by the Greek name *phronēsis* is an essential moment of moral being that belongs to everything we call "virtue." Since Socrates showed that the good and virtue are not self-evident and do not consist in the mere choices

53

of heroic exemplars and their successors, the question of the good has been placed in a new consciousness; the demand has been made to justify one's own being and conduct and to be ready to give an account of oneself. But then one must concede that every attempt to give an answer to the Socratic question about the good always contains the inner connection between *ethos* and *logos* and therewith also the balance between the developed habituation through cultivation and moralization and a self-consciously rational giving of accounts. The name "ethics," that Aristotle, the founder of this philosophical discipline, introduced, should not permit us to forget that he, like Plato, is a successor to the Socratic question. He interpreted the Socratic equation of virtue and knowledge in such a way as to include the giving of accounts as part of the moral essence of ethics, thereby founding a tradition that survives into modernity under the title of "ethics" or "practical philosophy." It includes not only the deliberation and the ordering of the individual's life in society, but even also the ordering of the social arrangements themselves that govern the common life of people in social bonds. Thus practical philosophy also encompasses so-called political science along with ethics and implies both when it is called "practical philosophy."

Thus it is significant that in the course of the nineteenth century the title "politics," which indicates the second part of Aristotle's practical philosophy, changed its meaning. The Aristotelian lecture on politics can and must serve as a part of the more general inquiry of practical philosophy into the right way of life. Until the middle of the nineteenth century, German authors (and presumably also others) still understood "politics" as this portion of a philosophical science. This reflects philosophy's claim, as intimate as it is irrefutable, to help determine practice, even political practice.

The change in the meaning of the concept of "politics" that I have sketched permits us to acknowledge another sort of background. Like ethics, politics bases itself on a presupposition. Ethics—that is, the *ethikē* or, in the Aristotelian usage, *ta ethika*—presupposes ethos or customary mores [*Sitten*]. Politics presupposes the *polis* and everything implied by its existence. Above all, that means that the *polis* has its gods. Later this is fundamentally advanced as the Roman empire continues to serve the fundamental sacral orders of Greco-Roman life. Thus even the "*civitas Dei*" itself follows this tradition. Hence also according to the Christian understanding *prudentia* is not only the knowledge of the means of political action, but also one of the great "virtues" that even in the doctrine of the church is not denied its connection to the salvation of man and to the divine. Only with incipient modernity did this background disappear, so that *prudentia* came to be understood technically as mere knowledge of the proper means. Therewith it came in the end to be indistinguishable from that which according to Aristotle is not *aretē*, but rather a dubious capacity (*deinotēs*) (*EN* 1144a23ff).

This implies for Kant the distinction between technical imperatives of cleverness and the laws of morality [*Sittlichkeit*]. Behind this lies once again the distinction between the meaning of causality and its categorial significance [*Seinsgeltung*] and the "causality of freedom." As is well known, however, freedom is not for Kant simply a fact, but rather a fact of reason, that is, not an object of experience for science. The new opposition between is and ought, which governs post-Kantian philosophy of science, relies upon this distinction in Kant's moral philosophy. Only if something is a pure fact and itself has absolutely no relation to the good is it readily available through knowledge. The realm of oughts, which is restricted to relations to the good, does not deal with facts but rather with "values."[1]

So in the aftermath of Kant, the realm of the ought and values was not considered knowable by modern science. This finally led to the strict juridical distinction between so-called judgments of fact and "judgments of value," which decayed absolutely in the semantic change.

At the same time the designation "political science" or "politology" took the place of this philosophy of "politics." In this is expressed the radical scientific change that in the era of modern science led to the collapse of the Aristotelian metaphysical tradition. A new concept of knowledge [*Wissenschaft*] asserted itself. Thus John Stuart Mill in the concluding chapter of his *Inductive Logic* treated of traditional practical philosophy, which he called "moral sciences," as an admittedly very imprecise sort of experiential science. The translation of this title into the German "*Geisteswissenschaften*" has struck deep roots in Germany. Therein began yet another moment than that of methodological science, and that is the heritage that lies in the Hegelian concept of the objective spirit. Through it the modern concept of science has truly modified and enriched itself. Dogmatists would say that it has "watered itself down." The *Geisteswissenschaften* are truly not merely a section of the sciences, but are, despite all their imprecision, the actual carriers of the great burden of the tradition that has been expressed in the Hegelian concept of spirit and its cultivation and lives on in other languages as "humanities" or "lettres."

Seen from this point of view, the imperativistic truly seems too narrow as a point of departure. The question arises as to whether the role of the doctrine of duties can be so determinative for ethics and if the ethic of imperatives can even constitute the whole. In truth, it is merely the remaining inheritance of the Stoic tradition from classical antiquity. The Stoa taught the withdrawal

from everything that was not particularly our own. Otherwise we are help-
lessly subject to the alternation of fortune and misfortune. The ideal of Stoic
equanimity includes in the end also the withdrawal from all public things,
however those happened to be understood by the Greeks of the Hellenistic
age and in the age of the Roman emperors. This should lead especially well into
the modern scientific disposition that admittedly as a consequence leads into
the narrow pass of modern subjectivism.

The opposition between is and ought has certainly always been an aspect
of morality. But it found its formulation only in modern times, for only now is
"being" (or, currently, "fact") without any connection to the good. With respect
to the narrowness of every ethic of imperatives, we must always again turn our
gaze to the whole of the moral-political world and thus return to Aristotle, the
founder of practical philosophy, who at the same time created a "teleological"
physics that for a millennium and a half was physics. In Aristotle there is neither concept of duty nor an intelligible word for it, just as there is no word for
the concept of obligation [Sollen]. Of course, one occasionally made use of a
somewhat surprising Greek expression, which one liked to translate as "ought":
hōs dei, "as it is necessary." One encounters the word deon in the company of
agathon, the good, in the connection agathon kai deon, ("good and binding").
To deon means the binding, the obligatory [das Bindende, das Verbindliche]. It
points less to a demand that is placed on the individual as obligatory than to
the common basis of binding, on which all morals and the formation of social
life are grounded.

The later Stoic concept, the kathēkon, that which one deserves and which
is appropriate, sounds less like an obligation [Sollen] than like a possession
[Haben]. The transformation of kathēkon and kalon into the Latin "officium"
represents, it seems to me, the decline of the free polis and the transition to an
increasing dependency and bureaucracy. Thus this brought with it the new integration of Stoic thought into the sacrally and politically living Roman world of
the republic and ascribed to the concept of duty its central role in ethics. Only
since Cicero has the word "officium," obligation [Obliegenheit], become common. The German word Pflicht [duty] is a Germanization that originated in the
eighteenth century. And Garve's translation of officium in Cicero led to the coin-
ing of the concept of duty, in which one could still hear echoes of its Roman
ancestry and the presence of the political. Kant's adoption of this concept and
his analysis led in a further step the concept of the imperative from grammar
into ethics.

We are here far removed from the actual realm of theoretical knowledge,
as it has been developed as a model in the ideal proofs of mathematics and its

methodical creation by the Greeks. Even the so-called "deontic" logic, about which there is so much talk nowadays, can truly only make it possible to describe with logical means the structure valid for all *technical* thinking. It still owes what is decisive to *practical* knowledge. Thus the use that Aristotle in the *Ethics* makes of the so-called practical syllogism and of his logical doctrine of conclusions shows that it in truth is always a technical syllogism. This is entirely true of the decisive founding of modern mathematics. Since mathematics permitted the development of modern mathematical natural science for the modern assimilation of the human experience of the world, syllogisms have also absolutely lost their scientific meaning (one thinks of Liebig's critique of Bacon). The concept of science that begins with mathematics and that governed Greek thinking developed the logic of proofs, that is, the derivation from a first beginning, the principle. Under the rule of the universal, the particular becomes an example and, in modern natural science, an example of the law of nature. Therewith neither in the natural sciences nor in the realm of culture can the logic of research do justice, if it is supposed sufficiently to justify practical philosophy as a science in the research and knowledge realms of the so-called *Geisteswissenschaften.*

For this reason the return to Aristotle has a new meaning. Aristotle certainly came to be the founder of practical philosophy, as he established it on its own over against the ideal of science, the "*mathēmata*," and his comprehensively developed "physics" and did not treat it as a specification of theoretical philosophy. In an explicit polemic, Aristotle distinguished the human good, after which he inquired, from the universal idea of the good, about which Socrates asked in so many ways in the Platonic corpus. If Plato unifies the good of the soul, the good of the *polis*, and the good of the universe, this magnificent Pythagorean vision of the world is established on a numerical-theoretical basis. This could not promise any proper satisfaction in the search for happiness to the human life struggling in its tasks and for its goals. The famous anecdote about the Platonic lecture "On the Good" and its reception by the Attic public testifies to this fact. In his polemic counterconstruction, Aristotle does not build practical philosophy on the general idea of the good; rather, his point of departure (principle, *archē*, the first beginning) is the "that" [*das Dass*] (*to hoti*).

Of course, in this we are not to understand an ascertainable fact, a "*factum brutum.*" That upon which moral reflection and especially the reflection of philosophy is to be grounded, if we are to concern ourselves with exposing to view the moral dimension, is much more the human understanding, which they always already possess in their lives and social lives. This has worked itself out in Greek society in a series of life-projects on which Aristotle seizes (*EN* Bk. III).

There hedonism is presented as the projection of a life goal onto the gratification of desires. There he projects the pragmatically successful as the goal of political life, which finds its fulfillment in the honor one receives. Finally, there is yet another projective trajectory [*Entwurfsrichtung*] that completely exceeds everything teleological. That is the projection of the *kalon*, the beautiful, that is free of any calculation and therefore is good "in itself." Hence "*aretē*" is good in itself, whether one sees its highest goal in acting or in observing. This is what is meant by the "that" as a point of departure. It rests on the self-projection [*Selbstentwürfen*] of human existence [*Dasein*]. This has nothing in common with the ideal of a demonstrable knowledge or a derivative of the more specific from the general. The founding thought and ideal of certainty of the moderns in this connection see themselves placed before a completely different forum. Yet the pressure of the proof-ideal that here comes up against its limits shows itself everywhere in contemporary philosophy. It shows itself in the expression "final founding" [*Letztbegründung*], which Husserl himself took up again in order to fit his phenomenological research project [*Forschungsgesinnung*] into the system of German idealism and its neo-Kantian successors and to bow before it. But can ethics or practical philosophy even support such a scientific founding and justification? In the face of the situation's demands, wouldn't a mere application of a general [principle] to a particular instance promise a false relief, rather than requiring the person to make a responsible decision? As if it were sufficient to follow rules in this realm!

But must one not state the question in yet a more general way? What task can philosophy even have in the realm of moral and political practice? This is the actual question at the heart of practical philosophy. Philosophical reflection is a theoretical movement of thought. The reflection that would constitute practical philosophy would nevertheless with inner necessity have to make the claim not only to know what the good is, but also to contribute to it. Thus it is in any event for the decision that faces a person in acting or abstaining: he wants to know what is best. From this point of view must one understand the fundamental question of practical philosophy, a question that is posed just as much in an era of a comprehensive philosophical knowledge—what the Aristotelian interpretation of the world aspired to—as in the era of modern science. Thus our task is a double one. We must not just make the horizon of the Aristotelian project conscious of its orientation to the world and therewith bring our own concepts necessarily into play. On the other side, we must also take up again Kantian moral philosophy and see it for what it is [*in ihrem Rechte zu sehen*]. For in an era of modern science and its lustrous ignition through the ideals of the modern Enlightenment, Kant was the first to rediscover the fundamental question of practical philosophy.

Kant himself admitted that Rousseau set him straight. In fact, his founding of the "categorical imperative" did not serve the purpose of opening a new realm of sovereign self-legislation for the autonomy of the subject. On the contrary, it served to ground moral obligation on moral freedom over against the presumptuousness of a universal enlightened cleverness. What we here call grounding and founding [*gründen und begründen*] certainly cannot mean the same as what passes for ground and founding in theoretical explanations. As Kant showed, freedom is not a fact of theoretical reason that one can demonstrate, but rather a fact of reason, which one must assume if one wishes to understand oneself as a person. To wish to demonstrate freedom is in Kant's eyes as mistaken as to derive ethics from the highest principle of the good is in Aristotle's eyes. Kant's *Groundwork of the Metaphysic of Morals*, his deepest work of moral philosophy, explicitly poses the question of what business philosophical reflection has where the human heart and the subtlety of human conscience bring about a precision of self-examination and deliberation that cannot be exceeded by anything. Thus with Kant, as with Aristotle, the point is not to ground moral obligation conceptually by means of theoretical reflection. Morality and ethical behavior [*Moralität und Sittlichkeit*] do not demand especially great gifts for understanding or an educated capacity for thinking. On what ground, then, does philosophical reflection have the right to claim practical influence on human moral existence, as of course philosophy openly claims? The answer lies in this: human beings always, even if usually in an unclear way, subordinate their concrete decisions to a general setting of goals; that is, they have a practical philosophy. This explains why in one sense one must have a more proper thinking. We see that Kant's *Groundwork of the Metaphysic of Morals* answers this question.

Aristotle was well aware that practical philosophy could do nothing other than contribute to this striving for knowledge and self-understanding that is always already active in human action and decision and to bring greater clarity to what hovers vaguely, as in his pointing to the goal that helps the archer hit his target (*EN* 1093a23ff) or in a more precise articulation of a goal that is already known (*EE* 1214b11).

The German situation at the end of the First World War was especially prepared for this question. The phenomenological school had under the leadership of Husserl and thanks to his descriptive patience and mastery recaptured the question-horizon of the lifeworld and shown that one had to go back behind the scientific horizon and its epistemological illumination that totally encompassed the nineteenth century. Knowledge of the lifeworld is always a kind of advancement and working out of a deliberation that is rooted in life itself and unfolds itself in life's practice. It must thus be practical knowledge that can alone be here in question, whether one wishes to call the "virtue" of this knowledge deliberation [Besinnung], circumspection [Besonnenheit], cleverness, or prudentia. The critique that before this Kierkegaard had already made of Hegel's totalizing dialectical synthesis now gained influence on the phenomenological readiness to shed light on the lifeworld in itself. It will be shown that, despite the differences, it was just this motive that Aristotle, like Kant, had sought to give conceptual expression.

The critique of the scientific belief of the liberal age made use of the Kierkegaardian concept of "existence" [Existenz], which he had advanced against Hegel's all-encompassing synthesis. Now, in our century, the issue is of course not another critique of Hegel's speculative idealism. The issue is now rather the epistemological methodology of the reigning neo-Kantianism. Against that, one began to ask oneself what the rationality actually is that is transparent to practical, living people and that apparently differentiates itself fundamentally from the theoretical rationality of science. For this, Aristotle can be even more helpful than Kierkegaard. After all, Aristotle's entire ethics is ruled by the question of the allo eidos gnōseos[2], of the "other form of knowledge," which concerns life.

Here we must begin a hermeneutical reflection. One would be subject to a naive dogmatism if one raised all the texts that have come to us through the accidents of ancient tradition up to the reflective level of modern scientific literature. Neither the Platonic dialogues nor the Aristotelian treatises lend themselves to this classification. Even if we possess the critical reports about Platonic thinking and teachings from Aristotle and other later witnesses, the Platonic dialogues present to us wide-ranging knowledge about Plato's thinking. That the dialogues in their mimetic style present Socrates and always leave open only a limited area for the expression of concepts does not change anything. By contrast, Aristotle is concerned with the construction of concepts. But Aristotelian ethics still sets itself the task of translating living language into the language of concepts. Thus Aristotle, especially in his doctrine of the intellectual virtues, the "dianoetic virtues," establishes a test with five expressions, all of which have synonyms in Plato; that is, they are used in entirely the same way. They are technē, epistēmē, phronēsis, nous, and sophia. Aristotle characterizes these five concepts as hexeis tou alētheuein, as means of being that which is known [Seinsweisen des Wissendseins] or of preserving the truth. All forms of knowledge that are mere assumptions or views or opinions cannot really be called knowledge because they leave opening for error. These five ways of knowing are five forms of steadfastness over against all mistakes and concealments. It will be proven that among them only *sophia*, wisdom, and *phronēsis*, practical reason, are true "excellences" or virtues for Aristotle.

I am indebted to Heidegger's seminar in Freiburg in the summer semester of 1923 for this insight into the central meaning of this analysis of the dianoetic virtues.[3] Obviously, the penetrating analysis of these concepts finally serves the purpose of distinguishing *phronēsis*, the special kind of practical knowledge, from other forms of knowledge that find their fulfillment in theoretical or technical uses.

Let us begin with the Greek expression *logon echein*. This is an expression that was common and useful in both theoretical and practical senses. *Logon echein* can mean "possessing a proof." In this way the scientific ideal of mathematics would best be indicated. Of course, for the Greeks mathematics became, because of its ideal and logic of proofs, absolutely the primary science. Precisely through its logic of proofs the Greeks for the first time made the mathematical knowledge of the Egyptians and the Babylonians into a science. This is fully confirmed by the third chapter of the sixth book of the *Nicomachean Ethics* that describes the concept of "*epistēmē*" with respect to mathematics, particularly later Euclidean geometry. *Epistēmē* is a kind of knowledge that rests on the possession of proofs.

Now, there is another meaning of *logon echein*, a moral meaning on which Aristotle consciously plays, both in the thirteenth chapter of the first book and the first and second chapters of the sixth book of the *Nicomachean Ethics*. *Logon echein* is "to give an account" and is also spoken of the way in which one listens to the father. That is: with respect. Respect is not blind submission to the will of another. It is much more participation in the superiority of a knowledge that one recognizes as an authority. To have respect does not mean to trust another against my own conviction, but rather to permit another to participate in determining my own conviction. In Aristotle this is perfectly clear in the precise interpretation that he devotes to the cultivation [*Bildung*] of the correct conviction and therewith the discovery of the correct decision; this he designates "*prohairesis*." This defines precisely the free demeanor of the practical-moral person who is a citizen of his city. (Slaves do not have *prohairesis*).

One must guard oneself against the dogmatism of doxographical pedantry. Hermeneutics teaches us to attend to the distinction between a philosophical treatise, on the one hand, and a literary work of art like the Platonic dialogues, on the other. This is shown in the treatment of the parts of the soul that one encounters in both forms of literary tradition, in Aristotle as in Plato (*De. An.* A 5, *Rep.* IV). The doctrine of the parts of the soul is developed extensively in the Platonic *Republic.* There, in the end, it serves the purpose of demonstrating the unity of the soul in its articulated multiplicity, and also the unity of the *polis*, on whose harmonious agreement the happiness of both the soul and the city rests. Nothing is as unredeemed as a civil war or an irredeemably torn person. Not seldom do we encounter in Plato in mythic analogy how the inner part of the soul is threatened by division and how it returns to unity and agreement. The labyrinth of the human heart was from the oldest times as present to the Greeks as the horrors of civil war. It is in no way a criticism if Aristotle in the *Nicomachean Ethics* makes use of the concepts of *logon echein, alogon*, and so on and attenuates the meaning of their distinction. There he finds the elegant image of the distinction between concave and convex. It appears that here the same thing is described in different aspects and that the entire difference consists in the manner of description. The soul is as much one as is a curve that is seen from one side as hollowed out and from the other as bent. Thus Aristotle in *De Anima* (B 4) expressly insisted that there are not parts of the soul in the same sense that there are parts of the body, its limbs and organs. Much more so is the soul always one and, as the one that it is, applies itself to the various directions of its possibilities.

In Aristotle's understanding, this is heartening. If one then encounters the differentiation of the moral virtues from the dianoetic virtues, it makes methodological sense. Aristotle wishes to show unambiguously that there can be no *ethos* without *phronēsis* and no *phronēsis* without *ethos*. They are two aspects of the same fundamental human inheritance. Man has *prohairesis*; he must choose. He has a free choice, but he is not free to choose. Thus he can say of *prohairesis* that it is a yearning in which there is thought or also that it is thinking in which there is a yearning (*orexis dianoētikē* or *dianoia oretikē*, *EN* 1139b5). It is mistaken from the beginning to separate this kind of thinking (and therewith knowing) from morality. The entire theme of *phronēsis* is included in the question: what actually does it mean when *ethos* is described as something that contains *logos*?

What is *logos*? Aristotle in full consciousness takes up the Socratic inheritance. He observes precisely that virtue is conduct *with logos* and that this does not merely mean that our conduct implies a *logos*, a law (*kata ton logon*). Rather it means that this conduct is *meta tou logou*, that it does not merely imply thinking, but thinking is in the middle of it.

Aristotle poses for himself the formidable task of distinguishing this thinking, this form of knowledge, this knowledge of the *phronēsis* that guides practices, from other forms of knowledge that operate as theoretical knowledge or as knowledge mastery of production and manual knowledgeability. In such conceptual coinages Aristotle seeks to follow the signs of speech usages. So we encounter the word "*phronēsis*" and also the particular word "*phronimos*" principally in practical contexts, where they mean rationality and capacity for understanding. Through this, *phronēsis* is distinguished from *sophia* (occasionally *sophos*) and properly from *epistēmē*, which I call "knowledge" [*Wissendsein*]. Naturally, such conceptual determinations are not binding rules for speech usage. In the use of speech in the lifeworld, these expressions often fade into one another, as they do in Plato. It was for precisely this reason that Aristotle undertook his conceptual analysis. It is completely unambiguous how he tried to learn something from language for which the proper conceptual materials were not yet available.

We can illustrate this especially nicely with the concept of "*sunesis*" which is closely related to *phronēsis*. In German, we can use the word "understanding" [*Verständnis*]. We can also see a virtue in it, if someone is full of understanding [*Verständnisvoll*]. When we say this in German—and there are probably good equivalents in other languages—we do not mean that he understands and comprehends well, but rather that he wishes to understand another, that is really to understand "him." But *sunesis* passes in Greek usage only for the capacity to learn, that is, as the talent for comprehension in the theoretical realm. On the other hand, in the *Nicomachean Ethics* Aristotle is looking for the other form of knowledge that determines a person's practical conduct and being. So here he places *sunesis* in the context of a series that culminates in *phronēsis*, which signifies political and human concern with the good and with "*aretē*." Things like *gnōmē* (insight) and *suggnōmē* (forbearance) appear in the same series. Thus Aristotle determines the entire series *phronēsis, sunesis, gnōmē, suggnōmē* unambiguously in accordance with the orientation of that *allo eidos gnōseos*, that other way of knowing, that is apparently not mere knowledge, but rather a knowledge that rises from the being of a person, his human existence [*Wesen*], his character, the formulation of his entire human demeanor. That is the knowledge that Aristotle seeks and that is decisive for human life, prospering, and happiness. Here we are absolutely not concerned with imperatives in the usual sense.

It remains properly to determine Kant's contribution and relate it to our question. There can be no doubt that Kant was not the discoverer of a doctrine of duties. On the contrary, he moved in an already fully developed tradition of a doctrine of duties that in the final analysis must be viewed as Stoic, not primarily Mosaic. The concept of duty describes fundamentally only the simple self-evidence with which a well-grounded character holds fast to the maxims of his action. Thus, as his presentation in the first section of the *Groundwork* shows, Kant does not play a founding role. His aim was to determine the essence of moral reason on which all obligation is founded. We already saw that he did not undertake to ground the whole of moral self-determination on the omnipotence of subjectivity, although this is how, above all, Fichte, Schiller, already also Reinhold, and in any event the entire post-Kantian tradition understood him.

As is well-known, Kant used the expression "autonomy." In a book that unfortunately, however, is not sufficiently read and considered any more,[4] Gerhard Krüger has shown that "autonomy" does not ground the origin and validity of the moral law, but rather should guide me in the judgment of what should for me be the case. It belongs to the typic of judgment, as Kant himself mentioned in this context in the *Critique of Practical Reason*. It is merely a kind of demonstration that serves our judgment if we wish to hold fast onto what in this case the moral law demands. "Autonomy" explains the capacity of our maxims to be universalized and the exceptionlessness that resides in the concept of law. This is demonstrated through a comparison with the law of nature, the legal order of a society, or with a metaphysical kingdom of ends. The "typic" of autonomy must thus be understood as arraying itself against that tendency of human nature that Kant, at the end of the first part of the *Groundwork*, characterizes as the sophistry of passion or as the inclination to quibbling. Kant thereby assumes that in themselves virtue and uprightness could not be anything that could be attained first through higher talents for understanding or even conceptual clarity and precision. It is a presumptuous undertaking of the Enlightenment to believe in the perfectibility of a human being with the assistance of his understanding and science. Insofar as we can even talk about it, the moral progress of humanity must be seen in other ways than through elevated human knowledge and capacity.

Now, it is the case that there is in every person so much effective reason, precisely also in his moral deliberations, that he is always also tempted to bring it to bear against the obligatoriness of what is recognized as right. That is what Kant meant by "quibbling." It is surely the case that one acknowledges the obligatoriness of the moral law, but in special cases one undertakes to ground an exception. The task thus is to refute the "dialectic of exceptions" that acknowledges something as valid and still excepts oneself from it. This is precisely the same as what is graspable in the other models of which Kant's formulations of the categorical imperative make use, the laws of nature and of right. This must also be compulsory for perhaps the least dispensable requirement of morality that Kant found when he says that one could never use another person merely as a means, but must always at the same time acknowledge him as an end in himself. This fundamental law of humanity—certainly the most beautiful inheritance of Christian culture for humanity—is today just as strongly evident as the laws of nature and justice are through their own definitions.

Therefore it is completely mistaken to apply Kant's famous critique of eudaimonism to the great tradition of practical philosophy, which begins with the Aristotelian founding of this discipline. It is also according to Kant a natural tendency of a human being to care for his welfare and happiness. Now, in Aristotle there is nothing about virtue as the demand of morality to be followed as a means for the sake of such happiness. What Aristotle recommends when he designates the virtue as the mean between the evils is not a well-considered cleverness about life. A concern with one's own welfare certainly belongs to the nature of man and his striving, so long as he is not necessitated by a higher moral duty to denigrate his own inclinations out of respect for others and for the "moral law." By contrast, the eudaimonism that Kant criticizes suggests that one should with cleverness about life so arrange everything that one attains one's greatest flourishing and therewith so-called happiness. Against this assertion and in the face of the apparent multiplicity of human dreams and calculations about happiness, Kant critically offered the universality of the *categorical* imperative.

One does not do justice to his position if one does not see it in polemical conflict with the enlightened thought of the epoch. He does not offer a foundation of morality, but rather a defense of the doubts that follow from the Enlightenment's epistemological arrogance in the sense that Rousseau criticized it. Thus Kant is not subject to the vanity and the glitter of his successors. They extended the primacy of practical reason to the realm of theoretical knowledge and therewith to the entire scientific culture of the modern, after Galileo and his successors. They have once again made it bow to the primacy of the concept of purposiveness and hence have also made the primacy of practical reason valid for the theoretical use of reason. We are thankful to them for an endless wealth of anthropological and moral insights. But we cannot fail to appreciate that with these the particular task of reason is not satisfied: to arrive at a consistent relationship between these so different intellectual tasks related to science and action. If one derives and attempts to confirm a priori the results of natural scientific research from a teleological point of view, one conceals from oneself precisely the moral tasks that human knowledge and ability require of the researchers and that for the sake of the good and therewith human coexistence on this earth are required of us all. Despite all the critiques of the narrowness of

his distinctions, Kant is right on the main point: to validate the moral task over
against a growing scientific-technical extension of power. In this it seems to me
also that by comparison with German idealism and its riches Kant is best at
protecting our particular heritage. The world of science in its business of
research cannot on its own wish to conform to human purposes. Science as
such cannot afford this without thereby betraying itself and putting itself into
political dependency. It is much more the task of all human beings and their
practical reason. Humanity will survive in the event that it succeeds, through a
considerate rationality, a "*phronēsis*" in the old Aristotelian sense, in bringing
under control the frightful destructive power that thanks to science has reached
human hands. Coercive political power cannot accomplish this because it is
always inclined to misuse that power.

In recent times one has spoken of the two worlds in which humanity
finds itself: the world of natural science and that other, that is presented
through human culture and its riches. The English writer Snow, who first
established this critical formulation, still seriously believed that he had to complain about the dearth of natural scientific knowledge in human educational
life. He was deeply mistaken, even if he perhaps also recognized a weakness in
the then-current education in the elite English universities. The question is not
if human accomplishments and therewith the attainments of science for our
knowledge of the world have enough access to people's spirits. The reverse is the
particular life-question for humanity: will it succeed in tying the frightful esca-
lation of human ability to rational purposes and in working it into a rational
order of life? This will never be accomplished through the mere increase in
human ability, but rather only through insight and growing solidarity among
human beings. This has been conceptualized as the heritage of Aristotle's practical philosophy for the West and has had a corresponding socially cultivating
effect also on the other culture through the great messages of the religions.
Among the extraordinary accomplishments of Kant is that he understood how
to think about religion "within the limits of reason alone" and thereby showed,
even in a pluralistically divided world, ways to take a step on the path toward
the dream of perpetual peace.

NOTES

The translator is grateful to Jason Wirth, for generously sharing his knowledge of Heidegger and Gadamer, and to Colleen Grogan, for working cheerfully at the word processor.

1. Compare my work on the history and limits of the concept of value in *Ges. Werke*, Vol. 4: "Das ontologische Problem des Wertes," 189–202, and "Wertethik und praktische Philosophie," 203–215 ["The Ontological Problem of Value" and "The Ethic of Values and Practical Philosophy"].

2. Cf. *EN* 1142b33, 1142a30; *EE* 1246b36.

3. Some of my later works in volumes 5 and 6 of the Collected Works clearly show this. In the meantime, I have brought forward new observations about Aristotle's construction of concepts here (given the opportunity by an Italian lecture in Gallarate) and shed new light from another point of view in the previous essay, "The Socratic Question and Aristotle," dedicated to K.-H. Ilting. These essays are connected with "On the Possibility of Philosophical Ethics," (Vol. 4, 175–188), which lays the foundations for this inquiry.

4. G. Krüger, *Philosophie und Moral in der Kantischen Kritik* [Philosophy and Morality in the Kantian Critique] (Tübingen, 1931).

CHAPTER 5

THE NATURAL FOUNDATIONS OF
RIGHT AND ARISTOTELIAN
PHILOSOPHY

RICHARD BODÉÜS

Translated by Kent Enns

The very complex relations that contemporary philosophy maintains
with ancient philosophy, that of Aristotle in particular, are not exempt from
prejudice. I believe it is up to the historian to observe these prejudices.

A favorable prejudice, induced by the antimodernism of a segment of
contemporary philosophic movements, gladly recommends a positive return to
Aristotelian thought on the question of natural right.[1] An inverse, unfavorable
prejudice, induced by modernist movements, demands, to the contrary, a defiance with regard to this same thought which it negatively criticizes.[2] These prejudices, however, do not hinder philosophers, whether partisans or adversaries
of a return to Aristotle, from sharing the common concern of remedying the
weaknesses of the narrow positivism of the majority of jurists for whom right
would not have a source other than positive law itself. It is not therefore in their
shared resistance to narrow logical positivism that the partisans and adversaries
of a return to Aristotle find the ground of their difference. Their difference
arises from an opposition in the manner believed to be most appropriate for
remedying the weaknesses of logical positivism. And it is this very opposition

which guides the one group to look favorably on Aristotelian theses on natural right, and the other to regard these same theses with a certain suspicion.

For, faced with the practice of contemporary jurisprudence that is governed by constitutional right and fundamental laws (Charter or Declaration of Rights, Bill of Rights, etc.), the philosopher confronts the following dilemma: either the philosophy of right, like the science of the jurist, should always avoid a normative jurisprudence, and thereby not escape the reproach, made by Hume, of confusing "what is" (fact) with "what ought to be" (right); or it is inevitable, even for the jurist, to have recourse to a normative jurisprudence, as R. Dworkin thinks, if only to justify fundamental laws; in which cases, it is advisable to search for these foundations outside of positive right.[3] Not satisfied with the pretension of a strictly interpretive jurisprudence to ground right, contemporary philosophy tends to seek norms suitable for justifying the law in terms other than the law itself.[4]

But this search tends to follow contrary paths. The inheritors of classical rationalism attempt to deduce a priori the norms in question from universal principles of natural reason (pure reason in the Kantian or neo-Kantian traditions); thus, they defend the assumptions of modernity—liberty and equality—and, to this extent, prudently maintain their distance with regard to Aristotelian thought.[5] Self-styled antimoderns, on the other hand, rely on natural reason to set out a posteriori the norms of positive right that they judge to conform with nature and, to this extent, they are inclined to reread Aristotle with a favorable prejudice.[6]

Though often supported by the notion that a certain abstract universalism would be incompatible with juridical realism, this favorable prejudice nonetheless exposes these partisans of a return to Aristotle to several misunderstandings. The most evident of these misunderstandings arises from an unfortunate approximation that consists in assimilating Aristotelian thought to ancient thought in general and, particularly, in not respecting the distance that separates Aristotle from the Stoics. But this approximation exposes the adversaries of a return to Aristotle to the same misunderstanding in their unfavorable prejudice.[7] Simply, what would turn the one group away from Aristotle is what would lead the other group to follow him, that is, an approximate vision of his thought on natural right.

Indeed, there is not in Aristotle, as there is in the Stoic materialists, this idea of natural reason present to each man and homogeneous with the universal reason that rigidly governs nature.[8] In the absence of this idea Aristotle could not therefore count on a norm of right inscribed, as in the universe, on the intelligence of every legislator and from which the philosopher could draw principles as absolute imperatives. Nor in Aristotle could a norm of universal right (followed only by legislators who legislate correctly) be a transcendent norm in the manner of Platonic justice;[9] rather, if such a universal norm exists, it therefore should be immanent in nature. But the principle that explains the strictly natural evolution is certainly not without analogy to that which should regulate and justify the strictly human evolution, as long as a final principle is invoked by Aristotle to justify the former as explaining the latter ("nature is the end" *Politics* I.2 1252b32). But as everyone knows, outside of human things, the natural end is attained and is therefore observable in what happens most often; and the exception immediately shows itself as a monstrosity against nature—while in the order of human things, things do not work the same way.[10] If in this order a normative criterion could be observed in what happens most often, this would mean that for Aristotle, in a certain way, the most frequent fact coincides with right. It is very doubtful that Aristotle thought such a thing.

If "nature" understood in terms of an end had been for Aristotle a norm of right, it is certainly not in the most frequent provisions of positive right that he would invite legislators to identify such a norm, but rather in the natural end of right itself or of the law, by an appropriate reflection that is not guided by any observation of the diverse contents of positive laws. However, I know of no one, either among the partisans or among the adversaries of a return to Aristotle, who is seriously occupied with judging ancient philosophical theories according to this hypothesis. The former maintain a questionable interpretation of the *Nicomachean Ethics* which opposes natural justice to legal justice. In response to this opposition the latter maintain an equally questionable interpretation of the *Politics*, which distinguishes a natural slave from a legal one, hoping thus to show the weakness of the norm of right that Aristotle, according to the former, had sought in nature.

The interpretation of the *Nicomachean Ethics* V.10 (1134b18ff.) invoked by the partisans of a return to the natural right advocated by Aristotle, is a questionable interpretation to the extent that it tends to accept as given that, in this passage, philosophy distinguishes natural right and positive law under the names of "natural justice" and "legal justice."[11] In reality, and I shall return to this, the distinction Aristotle makes is, by all appearances, a distinction *within* positive right between what is natural and what is legal—that is, purely conventional. Thus there is perhaps no reason to see in this the manner in which the philosopher conceived of the relations between positive right and some natural norm of right, nor for that matter to suppose, as does the common interpretation of Thomistic origin,[12] that Aristotle held positive right or positive laws to be a necessary particularization of natural right or natural law. This supposition could hardly be drawn from what Aristotle affirms elsewhere as an unwritten natural law shared by all men,[13] and it seems inevitably to lead to an impasse. If indeed, as one imagines, Aristotle here assimilates natural right or justice to the least significant of unwritten laws that positive right particularizes, how could he maintain that this law changes as does positive right (1134b32–33)? This impasse is overcome only by a kind of hypothesis that situates Aristotle and his changing natural law on the side of Hegel and his historical development of reason.[14]

On the other hand, the interpretation of *Politics* I (chs. 2–6) cited by the adversaries of an Aristotelian natural right,[15] is, as well, a questionable interpretation to the extent that it supposes that the distinction made by Aristotle between natural slavery and legal slavery is destined to justify the latter by nature (I will return to this). The interpretation of these sections of the *Politics* is equally questionable to the extent that it avoids clarifying the precise reason why Aristotle holds that certain beings are servile "by nature." One suspects that Aristotle is here the victim, if not of a deceptive ideology,[16] at any rate of a contingent historical situation. For he takes as natural what was in his time a given fact—as if the most common beliefs in the human world were "natural" for Aristotle, and according to this hypothesis he is reproached for confusing fact with right.[17]

It is not easy, we admit, always to know with certainty the meaning of Aristotelian claims. But this difficulty is a serious motive for resisting overhasty readings, whether sympathetic or adversarial, which lead some present-day theorists of right to retrieve Aristotle's thought for their own benefit and others to keep their distance.

The historian's vocation is to inquire into the documents of this thought as clearly as possible before judging it. I propose, to this end, to try to see first how Aristotle seems to avoid the kind of dilemma that the practice of jurisprudence today poses to those who investigate the principles of right.

THE PRINCIPLES OF RIGHT
ACCORDING TO ARISTOTLE

First, one must know if and to what extent law can be rendered for Aristotle without norms that are exterior to positive law. The well known texts on "equity" respond in part to this question.[18] Aristotle recognizes as equitable "the just that is not regulated by the law, but constitutes a correction of the just defined by law" (*Nicomachean Ethics* V.14 1137b12–13). And he explains:

> Each time that the law makes a universal statement and confronts,
> on this point, an exception to the universal, then it is proper, to the
> extent that the lawmaker leaves something out or oversimplifies a
> particular matter, to correct the omission according to what the
> lawmaker himself would have pronounced had he been present, or
> to legislate as he would have, had he known. (1137b19–24)

The cases envisaged by Aristotle are ones where the law, already interpreted in a
certain way, does not apply and where, consequently, it seems an exterior rule
should be invoked by the law. But Aristotle does not thereby insist any the less,
even in such cases, on the fact that the defect of the law should be redressed by
an exact judgment conforming to what the lawmaker would have pronounced
if he had had knowledge of the exception that he had not foreseen. It would be
difficult to account for this insistence if Aristotle thought that the rule of equity
was independent of the law understood as defective, and its principle differed
from the principle (inadequately) expressed by the author of this law. In these
conditions, equitable jurisprudence, which is in question here, seems of an
interpretive nature. I understand by this that for Aristotle the equitable judgment is still interpretation of the positive law itself, not of some independent
and superior norm that would have to be called moral, for instance. Equitable
jurisprudence certainly is not a strict interpretation of the law, such as that
which operates in the application of it to particular cases foreseen by the lawmaker. But it is nevertheless a reinterpretation of the law according to its own
principles; it rigorously avoids what is not already the rule posed by it, and it
limits itself on the whole to saying better what is already said imperfectly by
positive law, without reference to some principle of another nature.

Another Aristotelian thesis tends in the same direction and shows the
considerable importance that he accords to interpretive jurisprudence. It is the
thesis of the "constitutionality of law," a thesis that eminently conforms with
contemporary juridical usage and also with its usage in antiquity where the trials
of illegalities had the function of our constitutional courts. Aristotle writes, "It
is with a view to the function of political regimes that the laws ought to be
established and that they are established" (*Politics* IV.1 1289a13–14; cf. III.11
1282b10–11).[19] The resemblance between this principle and the one that regulates equitable jurisprudence is very evident. Just as equity cannot be established in indifference to or ignorance of positive law, but rather the immanent
rule should imperatively inspire the correction of law, in the same way positive
laws themselves cannot be established in ignorance of the very constitutional
regime under which they are promulgated, but rather they must of necessity
conform to the principles which determine the form of that regime. Like the

jurist who must keep the lawmaker's principle in sight while seeking to perfect that work, the lawmaker himself must keep in sight the principle of the founder: he must "harmonize" his law with the intention of the founder (see *Politics* VII.13 1331b30). In this light the task of lawmaking, like that of equitable jurisprudence, is of a truly interpretive nature. Basically, the constitution (written law or custom—see III.16 1287b5–6) is to the particular law what the particular law is to the equitable: a general principle informing the application of law in each case. Jurisprudence, in its strictly interpretive capacity (in the application of a law to foreseen cases) or in its reinterpretive capacity (in the search for equity in unforeseen cases), is therefore the work of lawmaking itself, whether it pronounces, on one question of right, what is in conformity with actual constitutional rules, or whether it corrects, on another point, a regime's defects in relation to its fundamental rules.

A standing regime could well contain defects that denature it because these defects prove to have consequences contrary to the regime's foundation (contrary to its "hypothesis" as Aristotle says, *Politics* II.9 1269a32). The regime so affected should therefore be corrected by the lawmaker whose jurisprudence is then of exactly the same reinterpretive kind that establishes equity. A perfect example of such a defect that jeopardizes the regime is the Spartan law's neglect of women: "leaving be what pertains to women is a threat that goes against the intention of the constitution because the lawmaker who had wanted to make the whole city hardy . . . neglected women" (*Politics* II.9 1269b12–14 and 19–22). This situation that demands repair is comparable to the one that demands an equitable judgment when confronted with a defective law, because the law intended to repair it should correct the constitutional regime as the equitable should correct the justice of the law. It therefore presupposes an appeal to the norm immanent in the defective regime, as equitable jurisprudence presupposes an appeal to the norm immanent in the defective law.

The importance Aristotle accords to interpretive jurisprudence is measured precisely by the fact that such a jurisprudence is at work not only in the application of laws to foreseen cases, and in the search for equity in unforeseen cases, but also and above all in lawmaking itself, which is always called upon to refine existing constitutional rules or to correct what upon closer examination does not strictly conform to right.

Now, in all these cases, interpretive jurisprudence makes of positive right the universal rule of right. This is so in the form of the positive laws that regulate justice or whose immanent norm regulates equity, and it is also so in the form of the fundamental rules of the actual constitution that determine the orientation of the particular laws or whose immanent principle requires certain corrective laws. Under these conditions one wonders how Aristotle escapes Hume's reproach of confusing what is with what ought to be, since according to Aristotle right always seems to conform to what is—that is, particular laws or positive constitutional laws.

And, to begin with, does he escape this reproach? Yes, if in a clear and unambiguous manner Aristotle defends the idea of "unjust laws." Now, this is not only the case, but it is so in a precise context that permits one in addition to understand easily how to reconcile this idea perfectly with the theses that we just discussed. After stating the principle of the constitutionality of the laws, Aristotle adds, "It is thus evident that the laws conforming to the correct constitutions are necessarily just, while those conforming to deviant constitutions are not just" (*Politics* III.11 1282b11–12).

We know that Aristotle distinguishes several forms (or species) of constitutional regimes and that he separates them according to two criteria. Now, if the first of these criteria, which separates aristocracy from the republic for example, is one in which a greater or lesser number of citizens hold power (a minority or a majority, for example), the second, on the contrary, is the criterion of their correctness. Aristotle states, "it is clear that all constitutions that seek the common interest are correct constitutions and conform to what is simply just, while those that seek only the exclusive interest of those in power are completely faulty and are deviations from the correct constitutions" (*Politics* III.6 1279a17–20). There is surely in Aristotle a principle that allows him to escape Hume's reproach and is at bottom a superior principle of justice. It is one that allows him to distinguish between just laws and those that are not; he therefore returns to subordinating positive right to a requirement that its positivity does not necessarily fulfill. According to this rule, only the actual positive right in correct constitutions can respond to the requirement of justice pure and simple, that is, without qualification.

It is important to know if with such a rule Aristotle in the end leaves room for a noninterpretive jurisprudence. At first it appears that he does because justice seems to be an ethical norm—one that is called upon to measure right in a sovereign manner. But we must guard here against a grave error. The notion of submitting the law to an ethically superior requirement, of founding right on morality and of thus recognizing the necessity of a normative jurisprudence, is a typically modern idea that defends the priority of the good of the individual over the good of the state and that of the person over the citizen. Moreover, this idea is at the center of "liberal" thought and the target of "communitarians" who consequently here find a reason to reclaim Aristotle.

What is at stake in interpreting Aristotelian ideas on this point is therefore a serious matter.

These ideas rest on a few words: "there is a political good and it is justice, that is, the common interest" (*Politics* III.12 1282b16–18). In the context we have just seen, such formulations make of justice or the political good a principle destined to measure right, which is to say, positive laws (products of the political if ever there were any: "laws are like works of the political" [*Nicomachean Ethics* X.10 1181a23]). But they do not make of justice or of the good an ethical norm independent of and superior to the political: Aristotle states very precisely that justice is the political good itself. There is therefore no reason to believe that Aristotle here invokes under the name of justice the good of the individual or of the moral subject and opposes it to the products of the political reputed to be good—the laws. Aristotle is not "liberal" on this issue. On the other hand, these same formulations effectively identify the common interest with the political good. But they do not oppose this common interest to individual interest; rather they oppose it to the exclusive interest of one faction over another in the "deviant" regimes, called for this reason "despotic" (*Politics* III.6 1279a21). Yet on this issue Aristotle is not a "communitarian" either.

Between the political good (justice) that is here in question and the good that might be referred to as ethical (which concerns the moral subject), Aristotle sees only, but clearly, an analogy: "There are two conditions in which the good is produced for everyone and of these two conditions the first resides in the aim and end of actions being correctly posed, while the second resides in finding actions that concur with that end" (*Politics* VII.13 1331b26–29). Here we recognize the double condition of the morally good act: it is not sufficient to carry out an action well that seeks the sought after end (the perfectly vicious man always succeeds in this), the sought after goal itself must be good. Aristotle views these matters in a similar way when he envisages the double requirement of the constitutionality of the law and of the correctness of the constitution as necessary conditions of what is unqualifiedly just:

> [In all political regimes] there are two things that have to be considered, the first is knowing whether a law's character adequately corresponds to the highest ordinance [that is, if the regime is correct], and the second is whether a law contains something contrary to its basic hypothesis and contrary to the character for which the regime previously was founded for its subjects [that is, if its laws are constitutional]. (*Politics* II.9 1269a30–34)

One can then recognize a certain "morality" in laws conforming to the basic hypothesis of a constitutionally correct regime. But this by analogy, and the analogy amounts to saying simply that there are good cities just as there are good individuals. Good cities are those in which, first, the laws conform to the regime as they were originally intended, just as the moral subject's action conforms to his moral code; and, second, in which this regime itself is correctly oriented toward justice or the common interest, just as the code of the moral subject is correctly oriented toward the good.

The negative result of this is that the just law for Aristotle is not strictly a *morally* just law: that is, it is not a law that an ethically superior norm could justify or render acceptable. And under these conditions the justice that measures positive right and thus establishes it as unqualifiedly just does not seem to imply a jurisprudence inspired by the ethical.

For all that, does justice then imply a jurisprudence that must call upon, like justice or the common interest, an exterior norm, superior to and independent of positive law? My sense is that to pose the question is already to respond to it insofar as serving "the common interest" is tied to the very nature and end of all positive law. With this criterion of the "common interest" Aristotle does not indeed seem to have recourse to any kind of norm that jurisprudence itself would have to seek anywhere else than in the very principle of law, but Aristotle does call upon an end that jurisprudence discovers in the very principle of legislating for a political community. What Aristotle thus proposes for jurisprudence, I think, is a *formal* principle that can distinguish positive law as it is in a correct regime from positive law as it is in a deviant regime. Except for one difference, this jurisprudence is identical to the one at work in the interpretation of laws in their application—that is, in the equitable reinterpretation of other laws and in lawmaking that sets down laws in conformity with the regime or that corrects, by means of law, a defective regime. In all these cases we have seen that the jurisprudence that decides what is just is governed by existing right, with the positive content being determined by the form of the constitution. For its part, the jurisprudence that decides what is unqualifiedly just and distinguishes just laws from unjust laws also is governed by the existence of positive right—but here, abstracting from its content, considers only the principle of all positive law. In this regard, such a jurisprudence is like others in being an empirical operation that takes positive right into consideration; but while jurisprudence thus considers what already has a content determined by right, it also here considers what is formally (by essence or by nature, if you like) a rule of positive right, which is to say a measure of common interest. By definition this step could not call upon any a priori principle exterior to right. Starting from formally positive right, then, we can articulate a principle that seems to escape not only Hume's reproach of confusing what is with what ought to be;

in light of this we also can distinguish, in the content of positive right, just laws from those that are not. The laws of a correct regime (whether, for example, aristocratic or republican) are unqualifiedly just, because in securing the common interest they respond to the very principle of positive right, while the laws of a deviant regime (oligarchy or democracy, for example) are unjust because, in the interests of one faction, they despotically subordinate the interests of another faction within the same community, for which the laws exist.

Let me add a few remarks in conclusion. According to Aristotle, the "deviation" of a regime and its laws can be corrected. But this corrective (which makes an aristocracy from an oligarchy or a republic from a democracy) is a corrective according to the formal principle of right and thus according to the unqualifiedly just, not, as we have just remarked above, a corrective according to a (let us say material) principle of right and thus according to the justice that is relative to the founding hypothesis of an actual constitution. This could just as well serve to transform an aristocracy into an oligarchy, or a democracy into a republic, or again an oligarchy into democracy or the inverse, or an aristocracy into a republic or the inverse, etc. Two considerations in Aristotle's position warrant attention here. First, according to Aristotle, multiple "ameliorations" are possible of a system of laws and of political regimes that are completely indifferent to the requirements posed by a formal principle of right; some among them even lead to instituting or better preserving a system of laws that are unjust in the extreme. On the other hand, it is clear that for Aristotle the formal requirement of right can be fulfilled by very different political constitutions: kingship, aristocracy, republic (see *Politics* III.6). Just as clearly, it means that the formal principle of right, if it is clear (that is, secures the common interest over the exclusive interests of one faction), is a principle that does not allow us to prefer a priori the right of any one of these regimes: the right of a republican regime over that of a monarchy, for example. Now, the ethical principles which bring right into conformity with a moral norm and which deduce a priori the rules of right from universal reason, not only dispose us to a preference but tend to reserve the "right" justice exclusively to that which first asserts the equal freedom of individuals. This elementary principle, which for the ancients already constituted the basic hypothesis of democracies, is according to Aristotle only one among several relative principles of right (I will return to this). In fact it is not even one of the principles of a correct regime, democracy in the strict sense being the regime that sacrifices to the interests of the majority those of the minority. It is sufficient here to note this distinction solely in order to show that freedom for Aristotle is not a formal principle of right but a simple hypothesis serving as the basis of one constitutional regime among others; at best it is a relative principle of right. The importance of this point of view will become clear in our conclusion.

At the end of these opening reflections on what seems to be the formal principle of right for Aristotle, I would like to note that his position could very well be what I stated at the beginning. Indeed, it is in the natural end of right itself and that of positive law that Aristotle seems to find the universal and absolute norm of right. I say *natural* end because it is in the nature of positive law to aim at securing the common interest. And if this is so, it is reasonable to wonder if Aristotle does not fundamentally identify *natural right* with those positive laws that are unqualifiedly just and that accord with any correct regime. These laws would *naturally* be just from the simple fact that they formally comply with the nature of law. This hypothesis resolutely eliminates the idea that a law would be naturally just for some other reasons, in particular the reason that it would set out for human beings an imperative that conforms to human nature or nature in general.

We must, however, verify this hypothesis and address ourselves to the famous passage in the *Nicomachean Ethics* where there seems to be some question of natural right.

NATURAL RIGHT IN ARISTOTLE

In this passage Aristotle speaks of "political justice" (*Nicomachean Ethics* V.10 1134b18). What does this mean? We know that in a certain sense justice is all that is defined by positive laws, and Aristotle elsewhere reminds us of this: "all lawful things are in a certain sense just" (V.3 1129b12). But against this justice "in a certain sense" (that is, relative to the form of a constitutional regime), Aristotle, as we also know, opposes what is "simply" just (that is, without qualification, conforming to the formal requirement of right and assured by the correctness of the constitutional regime that aims at securing the common interest). Now it is to this simple justice that Aristotle assimilates "political justice." He writes, "what we are looking for is also the simply just, political justice" (1134a25–26).[20] Therefore justice is here what defines positive right in a correct regime. It is called "political" in the sense that it governs the mutual relations between citizens; this "political" justice does not apply to relations within the family, those between parents and children, for example, or between husband and wife—relations that for Aristotle are not properly the relations of justice and are only called just "by similitude" (1134a29–30) or analogy with what justice is between fellow citizens. Aristotle indicates twice in the context that what is unqualifiedly just and properly so-called is defined by positive law. The first instance explains what justice properly speaking is: "indeed justice belongs only to those whose mutual relations are governed by law" (1134a30). The second explains that the relations within the family are not of this kind: "there is therefore no question of injustice or political justice there, for this is regulated by law and is found only among those to whom law naturally applies" (1134b13–14).

Consequently when Aristotle later adds, in a disputed passage, "In political justice there is a natural part and a legal part" (1134b18), there is no doubt that such a distinction is one within such positive right as is instituted between fellow citizens in a correct regime. The hypothesis according to which Aristotle would here designate positive right by the expression "legal justice" and would oppose to it a certain natural right as one opposes the particular positively determined to the generally undetermined, is not only a gratuitous hypothesis but a misinterpretation that contradicts the whole context. In this passage Aristotle clearly means to show that positive right, determined and particular, in all correct regimes, contains two types of provisions or conditions.

We will see later on that Aristotle's purpose is to refute the opinion of those who hold that positive right is strictly "legal," that is to say a matter of "convention" (1134b32). Their argument is that "the natural is immutable and everywhere has the same force" (1134b25–26). This is an argument inspired by the model of natural phenomena ("fire burns here as it does in Persia," [1134b26]) suited, according to them, to judge human phenomena. In support of this argument and the obvious observation that right is not immutable ("For they see that just things are changeable" [1134b27]), they draw the conclusion that right is in no way natural. In his refutation of this Aristotle accepts the minor premise, which is evident (right is variable), but he does not accept the major premise which, for his adversary, seems to define the natural by two equivalent traits: (a) being unchangeable and (b) having everywhere the same force. He contests the equivalence a=b, and holds that if a⊃b, the inverse is not necessarily true: b⊃a. The natural which everywhere has the same force is not therefore unchangeable. Having conceded that right "is certainly changing in its totality" (1134b29–30), Aristotle is thus authorized to claim in principle that one part of right is natural because "it has everywhere the same force and is not subject to opinion whether for or against" (1134b19–20), even if it is variable, as is purely legal justice.

We note that in one respect Aristotle admits that the positive right of correct regimes is strictly legal and conventional. And this does not mean that the law it establishes by simple convention poses a precept contrary to nature. Rather this means only that it is naturally a matter of indifference whether the

law is set out in one fashion or another on some points: "as for the legal, it originally makes no difference whether it is one way or another" (1134b20–21).
Aristotle cites some examples ("sacrificing a goat rather than two sheep," etc.)
to which it is easy to find counterparts in actual right (taking the weekly day of
rest on Sunday rather than on Friday, etc.). Curiously, though, at least in
appearance, he does not offer examples borrowed from what he calls natural
right, as if these latter were more evident than the former. Perhaps this evidence
escapes us at first glance. However, I think that the provisions of positive right
that Aristotle believes to be natural, were in fact clear enough to him because
these are by and large all the principal provisions which precisely assure the
common interest in a correct regime. We can understand this by more closely
examining the two criteria, one negative, one positive, by which natural right is
defined.

The first criterion is drawn from what Aristotle asserts about conventional right. If the latter indifferently disposes this or that, it follows that a
provision of natural right for its part could not, in the beginning, go in one
direction or another just as indifferently. To what, then, could it not be indifferent? It is not sufficient eventually to respond "to nature" without specifying
what nature it concerns. If there is not, outside of right, a natural norm to
which the former could be subordinated, we should not for its sake invent subtle explanations that the text does not warrant.[21] For the altogether simple
explanation seems to be that it concerns the nature of right. We have seen that a
provision of right for Aristotle cannot be indifferent, but on the contrary
should be attentive to two things from the beginning: the hypothesis at the
basis of a political regime (in virtue of the principle of the constitutionality of
law), and, above all, the requirement of the common interest (in virtue of the
principle of constitutional correctness).[22] All the textual arguments we have
invoked up to this point to clarify Aristotelian jurisprudence can support this
conclusion. But there is more. We have indeed seen that the formal requirement of right, without which there are no just laws, can be satisfied, according
to Aristotle, under different political regimes, since there are several forms of
correct regimes (monarchy, aristocracy, republic). We have here, then, a fact
recognized by Aristotle that is particularly appropriate to explain why our passage supports the claim that natural right, contrary to nonhuman phenomena,
can be variable and changing. The apparent mystery and discomfort that this
type of affirmation procures are swept aside when it appears that positive right
varies considerably under a monarchy, an aristocracy, and a republic, but
invariably remains in conformity with the nature of right. Here we touch
upon the second criterion that Aristotle uses to characterize natural right.

Natural right, we are told, "everywhere has the same force." No one to my knowledge has questioned the exact meaning of this proposition. Rather, trouble has been taken, though in vain, to find an absolute in a changing nature, taken as a norm external to right. In fact, the expression "having the same force" is one used elsewhere by Aristotle to signify that two different things have the same virtue. Thus, we are told, "the too light [liquid] has the same force as the rare [liquid], or the too thick [liquid] as the abundant [liquid]" (*Generation of Animals* V.1 780b8–9); "every earthly vapor has the force of a thick air" (784b15); "with animals (other than the human) the skin, because of its thickness, has the force of a (fertile) soil" (785b13); "what we call chrysalis (in insects) has the force of an egg (in oviparous animals)" (733b14–15); "sensation (according to the vulgar) has the force of a science" (*Generation and Corruption* I.4 318b23–24); "the courage of a city . . . has the same force as [the virtue of the same name] in each man" (*Politics* VII.1 1323b35) . . . . In each case Aristotle's intention is to indicate that these rigorously different realities, despite their differences, have analogous, if not identical, functions. This idea is evidently that of our passage. Agreeing that the most just right varies from one political regime to another (either in space between two cities or in time inside the same city), Aristotle means to say that despite the variations between a monarchy and an aristocracy or a republic, certain positive provisions of right nevertheless have the same virtue: that of everywhere preserving the common interest.

This judgment of Aristotle allows us to understand how erroneous is the idea according to which "nature" could be for him a norm of right. Two things make such an idea totally inadmissible. First, no "nature" of any kind founds what is called "legal" or conventional right, which is rather an integral part of the unqualifiedly just under a correct regime. Second, there is still reason to believe that the part of right called "natural" could be in some cases perfectly natural without being unqualifiedly just. For we must finally distinguish between the legislative provisions that have everywhere the same force to preserve a regime as it is, and those that have everywhere the same force to preserve a correct regime. None of these provisions is indifferent to the beginning (contrary to conventional provisions which change nothing—either in the basic principle of the regime or in its correctness), but the latter secure the unqualifiedly just, while the former secure only a relative justice. Now these do not seem to be less natural than the others since they everywhere have the same force.

An example of these natural legislative provisions relatively conforming to a formal principle of right is provided by Aristotle when he examines the well–known law of ostracism. This law, as we know and as recalled by Aristotle, is a provision of democratic regimes (*Politics* III.13 1284a17–18), and is therefore, according to him, a provision characteristic of a type of deviant regime. But this law is comparable to analogous measures one finds, he says, in other regimes—tyrannical or oligarchical (1284a33–36). And making significant use of the expression used to define natural right, Aristotle adds, "indeed ostracism has the same force, in a certain sense, as suppressing and exiling eminent citizens" (1284a36–37). Aristotle does not expressly say that this type of provision, intended to save the democratic regime from the threats of those who are excessively superior, exists everywhere. But he asserts that in all known cases of superiority it is better that monarchies also have recourse to a similar "remedy," if the initial legislation could not avoid this problem (1284b13–20). This is as good as saying that universally there are analogous provisions to take, either to save the regime as it is or to "remedy" it such as it ought to be: republican, aristocratic, or monarchical (and Aristotle indicates other safety measures, different, but directed to the same goal, in *Politics* V.8 1308b10ff.). Aristotle can then conclude that "the argument for ostracism promotes political justice in a certain sense" (1284b16–17). According to the formula employed in our passage from the *Nicomachean Ethics*, "political justice" is right properly speaking. The formula is here accompanied by a reservation: it is justice in "a certain sense." This is because between ostracism and other analogous legislative provisions that "remedy" what is imperfect in a regime, there is a well-understood difference: "In deviant constitutions it is clear that they serve a particular interest that from their point of view is just, but it is also altogether clear that it is not simply just," that is to say, unqualifiedly (1284b22–25).

These reflections show that if ostracism, a provision of democracies (deviant regimes) is not as such an unqualifiedly just law, nonetheless the sum of the legislative provisions, which differ according to their regimes and which have everywhere the same force in preserving the safety of regimes or of remedying these same regimes (including the law of ostracism), are natural legislative provisions, some of which are absolutely just and others relatively so. There are therefore cases in which the natural does not correspond absolutely to justice without qualification. In these circumstances it can no longer be a question of taking nature as a norm of right.

The "naturalness" that would be a norm exterior to right, we said in the beginning, should be indicated by the frequency or the repetition of the same juridical provisions from one regime to another. The "naturalness" that Aristotle speaks of seems rather to be bound up with the identity of function that *certain* juridical provisions, *differing* from one regime to another, nonetheless present.

Amongst these natural provisions some are relatively just because they simply maintain the city (without which there is no right), others are unqualifiedly just because they conform to the end of right (securing the common interest to which a correct regime is dedicated).

Far from constituting an obstacle to our conclusions, the idea of a "natural law," to the contrary, confirms them. Aristotle clearly has the idea of a "natural law" that is not a positive law. The latter is called by him a law "proper," while the law seen as natural is called "common." The difference between the two is explained in the following terms: "[I understand] by law proper that which each community has defined for its members, partly written and partly unwritten, and by common law that which follows nature because there really is, as everyone has divined to some extent, a natural justice and injustice common to all men, even if there is no association or contract between them" (*Rhetoric* I.13 1373b4–9). In contrast to positive law, even to unwritten positive law, the common law is undetermined, it is not part of any legal order to which some regime could appeal and by which it governs the relations of its members. As its name indicates, it is shared by all men who have a vague sentiment that a kind of justice should preside over their relations, even when they do not form a community amongst themselves and have not passed any convention between them.

It is probable that Aristotle is here thinking of universal principles similar to those that constitute what later will be called the "law of nations" (*jus gentium*) rather than of rules that may be common to different legislative provisions in use in cities. The universality of natural law is not therefore, in these conditions, the supposedly common trait of all these provisions but the character of all the precepts that govern the conduct of men naturally and spontaneously, independently of positive law. Between this natural law and positive laws there is thus no necessary relation. And nothing impedes certain provisions of positive right from also being called natural (in a different sense than defined above), without reference to this law, for the excellent and evident reason that they do not usually pronounce on the same things. For natural law governs most readily what escapes positive right.[23]

Aristotle knows that jurists can when the opportunity presents itself play on the apparent conflict between common law and the positive provisions of right proper to a political community; he even indicates the way that litigants can take advantage of this conflict—in one instance having positive right on their side, in another avoiding it (*Rhetoric* I.13 1375a25ff.). But aside from the fact that the conflict is occasional (because, most often, the positive right proper to a city does not govern questions that fall under common law), Aristotle does not suggest that common or natural law should prevail over positive right in all cases where there is at least apparent opposition. He teaches litigants that they must call upon common law, "if the written law is contrary to the case" (1375a27–28), but to the written law, "if the written law supports this case" (1375b16); and it is not by coincidence that common law provides a just correction of positive right if, on the first hypothesis, the litigant who claims, with the common law, a right "more equitable" (1375a29) effectively demands a just correction of positive right—which is perfectly possible. For, as we have seen above, equitable jurisprudence dictates right in all cases where positive law seems incomplete and subject to improvement, and this is obviously only in those rare cases when it encounters, in so doing, the authority of common law.

In short, according to Aristotle common law is not the norm for positive right, unless by exception or accident. And when it is the case of an exception, we cannot still maintain that nature provides a norm of positive right, as if the contents of common law were measured by some natural principle, because common law is natural not due to its content, but by reason of its spontaneous and universal character.

Before finishing with these principles given in the *Nicomachean Ethics*, I would like to return to the just "properly speaking," that is to say, to the right instituted by law between fellow citizens. Aristotle tells us that this justice "applies to those who share an existence in pursuit of self-sufficiency and who are free and equal, either proportionately or arithmetically" (*Nicomachean Ethics* V.10 1134a26–28). According to this statement, liberty and (in one way or another) the equality of people are therefore the necessary conditions of right. Yet there is a world of difference between such a statement and those modern ideas bearing on the relation between right and equality and liberty.

The moderns generally make the liberty and equality of people into a norm of right. Deduced a priori from principles of pure reason, as so many principles of nature, they are in the Kantian tradition the conditions without which positive right would not be just. And these conditions are moreover stated as absolutes starting from positive right: human beings are naturally free and equal before the law. We recall that there is nothing like this in Aristotle, for whom the only formal requirement of right and its natural end is securing the common interest. For Aristotle, the liberty and equality of people are not the conditions that measure right but the conditions without which right simply would not apply.

Thus, in a monarchy (a correct regime), right (without qualification) would not apply to the relations between the king and his citizens. The legitimate king, if there is one, is indeed of such superiority over his subjects, both in excellence and political ability, that he seems "like a god among men." Now, legislation applies to equals; therefore for the kings of primitive societies, such as those seen by Aristotle, "there is no law because they are themselves the law" (*Politics* III.13 1284a10–14). On the other hand, the law they promulgate would be applicable to all their subjects, because amongst themselves they are equal; the law would assure the common interest of all subjects and govern their mutual relations for their own interest, exactly as it does under an aristocracy or a republic—where the law, excepting no one, extends itself even to governing, according to either proportional equality or strict equality, the accession of all to power (since there, all the citizens are, in a certain sense, equal).

The second condition for right to apply, which seems even more fundamental than equality, is that people be free. More than the first condition, this violently runs against the modern sensibility. For not only does Aristotle not concede that all are a priori free, he also maintains that some are naturally slaves. For Aristotle, they may not be those who have been reduced to slavery under the law; but for all that, they are human beings to whom right does not apply.

THE NATURAL SLAVE AND RIGHT

This reputedly weak Aristotelian position must be clarified on certain points because, once clarified, it allows us to see better why for Aristotle nature is not a norm of right.

When Aristotle leaves us to understand that the natural slave, just like the slave by law, is not a subject of right, this indicates that a slave is not a subject of "personal" right—because, in fact, in Greek society the slave by law is a subject of "real" right, a possession that can be exchanged, sold, bought, etc. Aristotle does not consider, however, this latter aspect of reality which implicitly results in the slave's lack of personal right. The only thing that interests Aristotle about the right over slavery is the kind of positive provision that institutes that right, and that it was questioned in his time not only by some philosophers but also by some jurists. And it only interests him to the extent that it gives validation to those for whom, "it is the law that makes one man a slave and another free" (*Politics* I.3 1253b21–23). Aristotle writes,

> that they are in a certain way right, is not difficult to see . . .
> because there is also a slave according to the law and a slave that is
> made by the law. For the law is one sort of convention in virtue of
> which one pronounces that those who lose a war belong to those
> who win it. Therefore many legal specialists impeach this right, as

they would an orator, as an illegal measure on the grievance that it would be terrible for him who has the capacity of doing violence and whose capacity gives him superiority to take as slave and subject whomever he has beaten. (1255a3–11)

The argument to which Aristotle thus gives justification is the one that consists in saying that the authority of the master, conferred by this kind of law, "is not just, because it is violent" (1253b22–23).

This concession by Aristotle is not without importance. To the contrary, it amounts to admitting that, as such, the law of slavery is an iniquitous law; as such, it consecrates the right of the strongest and therefore of violence. To sum up and clarify these points, one could say that this law is exactly comparable to the law of ostracism that is used by deviant democratic regimes and therefore, as we have seen, Aristotle maintains that it is just only in functioning as the fundamental democratic principle. The law of ostracism can no more be justified without qualification than can the law of slavery.

Certainly, as ostracism together with other legislative provisions (of which some assure the safety of correct regimes) attest to the existence of something natural in all provisions of this type, so the law of slavery can also be in some way natural. And of this Aristotle is without doubt persuaded as we will see further on. But this conviction does not justify, as such, the law of slavery, any more than the naturalness of ostracism justifies it as such, especially since if the law of slavery may be in some way natural, it is not necessarily so, according to Aristotle, because of the fact that there exists, according to him, a kind of natural slave.

Indeed Aristotle begins by demonstrating that there is a kind of natural slave. Now, before examining this demonstration more closely, it is very important to ask ourselves about its repercussions. Indeed, given that Aristotle defends the naturalness of slavery *independently of the law*, we confront the question of knowing if the law that institutes slavery could, according to him, be just, provided there is correction or if, on the contrary, no positive law instituting slavery could be just (at least unqualifiedly). I know of no interpreter who asks himself this question, yet it is elementary.[24] Everyone, on the contrary, seems to think about the texts as if it were obvious that the first hypothesis corresponds to Aristotle's thought and that he had it in mind to consecrate in right what he finds natural. But this is not obvious. What tells us in fact that Aristotle had in mind the possibility of correcting right so that it will cease to be unjust as it is, and recognize as slaves only those who are so by nature? What tells us that it was, in his view, possible to proceed with this correction? In short, what tells us that

Aristotle did not believe rather in the incapacity of positive right to institute slavery justly?

Perhaps Aristotle thought that a law instituting slavery could be just *if* it applied only to those beings who are naturally slaves. But the condition of such a law is a function of the possibility of having, in practice, a criterion that would distinguish the slave that he calls natural from the one that is not. Now, despite first appearances, concerning this practical possibility, Aristotle is far from touting the assurance that is implicitly attributed to him. As we know, his opinion is that in theory the natural slave is made to obey and the natural master to command. But what, in the eyes of the law, could proclaim the "natural" in these two cases? Aristotle writes that, "from birth, some are distinguished from others *in some cases*" (*enia*: 1254a23). Not only is the reservation significant, but it is not at all certain that, in this context, the affirmation of a distinction of this type concerns the slave and the master rather than, for example, human and beast, who are clearly distinct "at birth" because they are different zoological species.[25] And the certitude that Aristotle does not recognize any possibility of seeing the difference between the free person and the slave at birth is perfectly demonstrable—to which I will return in a moment. Now, without a distinction at birth that would clearly manifest itself at first sight, the distinction between master and slave becomes problematic. In other words, this is what Aristotle emphasizes, precisely because one is a slave only in the soul and starting from a certain moment: "nature as well seeks to mark the difference between the bodies of free men and the bodies of slaves, making some vigorous for a necessary use, the others upright and improper for such work . . . , but the contrary often happens . . . ." And Aristotle concludes: "it is not as easy to see the beauty of the soul as that of the body" (*Politics* I.5 1254b27–30, 32–33, and 1254b38–1255a1). I sincerely do not see how these remarks could not be recognized as a kind of defiance thrown in the face of every attempt to promulgate in right a law that would institute a truly just slavery without enslaving those who do not warrant it. In psychological terms, where the visible signs are visibly deceiving, what law could justly institute slavery?

One should therefore admit, it seems to me, not only that Aristotle displays the severest of reservations about the provisions of right instituting slavery in the terms that he has reported, but also what no one to my knowledge has dealt with, that he displays serious doubts about the possibility of correcting these provisions of right. And this, in my view, helps us to understand that in the final analysis slavery is probably only just, for Aristotle, if it is natural, that is to say, if it is not instituted by law.

Aristotle's fundamental idea, as we have just seen, is that one is essentially a slave in the soul. We must wonder therefore what is, for Aristotle, a "servile soul" which surely betrays no bodily confirmation. He states it briefly in *Politics* I.5 (1254b16ff.), but without his conviction coming to sight, however real it may be, that at birth nothing distinguishes the potential slave from the potential free man. Aristotle confines himself to stipulating, negatively, that the servile soul is a weak soul: the slave is "he who participates in reason to the extent that he apprehends but does not possess it" (*Politics* I.5 1254b23–33). The claim is one of affirming the weakness of reason, but one does not see clearly in what it consists. Now, the fact that this weakness belongs to reason proves, paradoxically, that it is not, for Aristotle, a weakness of birth, nor even a natural weakness in the sense that we understand it. Thus, for Aristotle, reason is a principle that is not given at birth, but that is acquired naturally with age. And this is what Aristotle affirms in the very letter of a passage in the *Eudemian Ethics*—and I am surprised that it has never been related to the issue of the servile soul: "Reason belongs to a natural principle because it will be present in us if growth is permitted and not atrophied—and desire too, because it attaches itself to us and is present in us at birth. On the whole, it is by these two traits that we define the natural: all that attaches itself to us from birth and all that it is possible for us to acquire from the moment that growth has been permitted" (*Eudemian Ethics* II.8 1224b29–34). In Aristotle the servile soul is not therefore a soul deprived of reason at birth; but it is probably not a soul that natural growth has deprived of reason either. On the contrary, the slave was born, like every infant, without reason and, like every infant, he also, according to all appearances, naturally has acquired reason with age. This is why Aristotle protests against those who, in his time, were obviously of a contrary opinion: "they are wrong who deprive the slaves of reason and claim to give them nothing but orders" (1260b5–6). The typically servile soul of the Asian is moreover described by Aristotle as an intellectually gifted soul ("dianetic" *Politics* VII.7 1327b27). In these conditions it clearly seems that if reason is acquired naturally with growth and if the weakness of the slave is after all attributable to reason, then for the slave reason is not absent but deprived of all that age can naturally provide. Briefly, the servile soul is characterized not by a natural defect, but by the defect of all that is not simply natural; this defect is due to the fact that reason in the slave is the simple natural effect of growth and nothing more.

One could be even more precise about Aristotle's thought, but we must for the moment note that the traditional interpretation defends, on this point, a position that seems to take a view opposed to the truth. It supposes that the slave for Aristotle is a denatured man; but in fact, if we have understood properly, on the whole he is the only man in the state of nature in society—a man who reasons and understands what is said to him and carries out his orders well, but not more than this, i.e. he is without this something "more" that is provided by education and which makes one free.[26] It is therefore particularly unfortunate to insult Aristotle by ascribing to him this blindness which would consist in ignoring the fact that nature (except for monstrous failures) makes all men reasonable beings; because this is exactly the conviction that seems to be his. And he also seems to defend the idea that it is the "acquired" more than "the natural" that distinguishes individuals from each other, but with an acuity of analysis and realism that refutes the scope that we grant to the idea of natural equality. Thus, not content to affirm that natural growth gives to each the reason that he potentially has at birth, nor content to note that the differences between individuals are introduced in the soul due to the effects of a certain education, Aristotle still identifies the most significant of these *differences* by opposing the servile soul to the one that is not.

Several differences, in fact, call attention to the servile soul according to Aristotle, one of which, remarkably enough, is engendered by an excessively hot climate which excites the irrational impulse of the soul and thus contributes to docility or to submission.[27] But this character trait, forged by climate, leads only to supporting the authority of a master without rebellion; it does not lead to questioning this authority, without another much more fundamental difference, which is not itself attributable to character: the weakness of reason left on its own, so to speak, and which Aristotle mentions when it is a question of the natural slave. A very simple formula allows Aristotle to characterize the soul where reason is thus abandoned. This soul, he says, "does not have the least deliberative capacity" (*Politics* I.13 1260a12); and the motive for this weakness, which impedes self-determination, is mentioned elsewhere: it is the fact of not having any goal in life.

Here is the passage where this motive is indicated and which no commentator, to my knowledge, has considered in this regard:

> Decision is not found in other animals, nor at all ages, and it is not part of man in every state, because neither deliberation nor the idea of questioning are found there. Certainly, nothing impedes many men from having an opinion about knowing whether he should do something or not, but this is not saying that they can do this by virtue of reason because the deliberative faculty of the soul

is the capacity to see a motive; the end sought, indeed, is a motive; it is the motive which consists in knowing why. . . . As well, those who do not have goals are not capable of deliberation. (*Eudemian Ethics* II.10 1266b21–30)

An implacable logic here underlies the Aristotelian analysis. Deciding in terms of deliberative reasoning demands a goal, an end, a motive for action, which in the end allows for knowing why one decides to do this rather than that. Thus, if the slave does not have any deliberative capacity or, consequently, the capacity for self-determination (as does a free person), it is because of the fact that he personally does not have any goal in life.[28] And this has nothing to do with a strictly intellectual capacity (pure reason). He is perfectly capable, on the contrary, of understanding the goals and motives that are assigned to him, and even of technically deliberating on the means of achieving these assigned goals.[29] As for knowing why some people, some so-called servile souls, do not have a goal that would allow them to be self-determining in existence, it is not hard to guess. For, finally, the goal of existence, in Aristotle's view, is always formally the good—in whatever manner it presents itself. Not having a goal, in this case, is therefore not to have an image of any form of good to pursue in life, and not to have in view any future objectives that determine one kind of conduct rather than another. This is why, by contrast, Aristotle says that the natural master is the one "who has the intellectual capacity of foresight" (*Politics* I.2 1252a31–32). Now this incapacity is not strictly intellectual; it consists effectively in having the power to establish desires only in the immediate, and this betrays the weakness or powerlessness of an education that should fix desire upon a representation of a good to pursue in the future. One can represent this type of good to a servile soul, but his lot, at bottom, is that his soul does not desire this as its own good.

The consequence is that the servile soul thus condemns itself to dependence, which is the mark of its weakness. But "condemns itself" is not the word. For the weakness of the servile soul does not see itself in a negative way; and speaking of the natural slave Aristotle presents him at first and essentially in a positive light. It is not the slave's incapacity that Aristotle first brings to the fore, but his capacities: here his bodily capacity for work (cf. *Politics* I.1 1252a33), there (and more fundamentally) his psychological capacity: "the natural slave is he who is capable of being another's" (I.5 1254b21; see 1254a12–13).[30] That is to say, Aristotle brings to the fore the naturalness of the slave's subjection. This signifies that the natural slave's soul inclines to subjection on its own accord, spontaneously, without constraint or violence. And this is precisely why the man that Aristotle speaks of under the name of natural slave is not him whom the law reduces to the state of servitude.

Aristotle's thought does not limit itself, however, to invoking this sort of unforced inclination so that the condition of some men who completely put themselves under the authority of another may be called natural. His thinking is much more profound and takes into account the equally natural tendency of other men to command, a tendency that would be in vain without the inclination of the former and without the need that the latter have for workers to execute their projects.[31] Thus the tendencies that incline the one to command and the other to obey are, for Aristotle, natural tendencies in the exact sense that we have defined above in our discussion of natural right.[32] In fact, as the different juridical provisions that everywhere have the same force are natural, so too are the different relations (among them the master-slave relations) that everywhere have the same force to bring together ruler and ruled for the realization of the same project. Aristotle says rulers and subjects exist in "several forms" (1254a24), obviously different. The differences are of two orders: sometimes the associates are distinct one from the other (a), and sometimes they are in continuity (b), and further, here the subordination of one to another is properly servile (a'), and there it is not (b'). And in addition to the master-slave relation (a/a'), Aristotle cites several others: the one between soul and body (1254a34)—a collaboration of the type b/a' when it "conforms to nature" (1254a36); the one in the soul between intelligence and the appetites or the passions (1254b5–8)—a collaboration of the type b/b' when it, like the previous one, "conforms to nature" (1254b6-7); and the one between human and beast (1254a26 and 1254b11)—a collaboration of the type a/a'. All these forms of collaboration are different, but all, in spite of their diversity, have the same function, which explains the association of a superior who commands and an inferior who obeys: to carry out a common project. And it is in the universality of this phenomenon, in these different forms, that Aristotle definitively finds the main reason for pronouncing that the union of master and slave is natural.

With this Aristotle claims to prove the existence of a type of master-slave relation that the law does not institute, and probably could not institute justly. But he does not offer thereby the proof that this relation is itself just. The demonstration that there really exists a natural slave is in fact limited to stating a simple fact which itself does not offer a complete guarantee of justice. Certainly the fact that a naturally servile soul spontaneously inclines to subjection disposes of the obvious injustice that constitutes enslavement by violence. But voluntary subjection, which avoids what the law does not succeed in avoiding, is only a necessary condition of justice. It is not a sufficient condition. It does not secure against all forms of injustice to which the subjugated is exposed from the master. The fact that the collaboration of master and slave has something natural about it, since it is a form of universal collaboration without which there could not be the realization of a common project, is not therefore a fact sufficient to prove that this collaboration satisfies the requirements of justice. At best, all these facts inform us only of the necessity which makes one person an instrument of another.[33] At bottom—we can say it without truism—Aristotle's slave is not truly free not to be a slave. But necessity obviously does not make justice, and the handicap which condemns one to being able only to serve obviously does not produce justice with the service that one renders.

However, the slave who does not have a personal goal in life and is satisfied by serving the goals of others thus creates the conditions for a kind of justice to be rendered unto him. And it is here that Aristotle's argument confronts the universal requirements that he has in other regards imposed on the principle of right. What properly justifies the slave's subjection is not the quasi-inevitable character of this subjection, neither is it, even less, the service that he renders to his master; rather it is the advantages he finds there in compensation. The Aristotelian idea that justice demands the common interest is indeed applicable here, not in spite of the instrumental subjection of the slave but because of it.[34] For, in the collaboration of master and slave the interest of the latter is not sacrificed to the interest of the former; according to Aristotle, it is on the contrary secured by the fusion of these interests. Because the slave is a "part" of the master (*Politics* I.4 1254a9–20), his safety and his prosperity are exactly equivalent to those he provides to the master. The analogy of the soul and the body shows this: "it is in the interest of the body to be ordered by the soul" (1254b7–8), because with it, it forms a whole and "the interest of the part and the whole is identical" (1255b9–10). And the slave's interest is to form a whole with the master as the animal's interest is to serve humankind, rather than being abandoned to the perils of savage life, "because it finds its safety there" (1254b12–13).

In conclusion, the justice that Aristotle finds in the slave's state is therefore not due specifically to its naturalness, but to the advantages that the slave can get from it, *if* this state is natural. In Aristotle's view, natural slaves are "those for whom it is expedient and just to be slaves" (*Politics* I.5 1255a3). As a result the Aristotelian thesis on slavery seems to be, in reality, the contrary of what one generally supposes. One generally holds that Aristotle, invoking nature, finds a (bad) justification of a fact consecrated in the right of his time. It is not so. What he thinks, in truth, is rather that slavery can be just only on the condition that it is natural, that is, if it is not established by law. His conclusion is indeed the following: "there is consequently an advantage for the slave and the master, and affection between them, if they naturally feel it should be so; but if their relation is based on law and force, it is the contrary" (1255b12–15). Nothing, perhaps, in Aristotle's philosophy better expresses the fact that nature is not a norm of right. That there are, in his view, men who are naturally slaves is not a fact that justifies the law [*droit*] instituting slavery. To the contrary, justice, which governs the common interest of master and slave, demands that slavery be in no way founded on law [*droit*], but on nature.

Another word regarding this famous law instituting slavery. All of what we have just said does not prevent Aristotle from implicitly recognizing in the positive law instituting slavery, or at least in its principle, something natural—as he does in the law of ostracism. For at bottom, the right of the strongest, as unjust as it is, recognizes in its way the universal authority of the superior that one notices everywhere else. In the controversy that opposes them, partisans and adversaries of the law of force instituting slavery, make in part the same acknowledgment.[35] Their arguments, Aristotle notes in a subtle way, are interchangeable (*Politics* I.6 1255a13). The adversaries who denounce the violence of the law and, at bottom, of all laws, maintain that it is the expression of an elite armed with the means of authority: "in a certain way, the excellence that has the means is also the one that is most capable of violence" (1255a13–14). They thus reply to the argument of the partisans of this law and of every law dictated by authority according to which the strongest, in any domain whatsoever, civil or military, owes his superiority to a quality that founds his right: "the strongest always finds himself in a position of superiority due to something good" (1255a15). Aristotle notes that on either side one recognizes the same fact: "violence implies excellence" (1255a16). Both parties recognize this fact in the legislator, author of the laws, and in him whose conduct the law sanctions. But fact is not right. The adversaries and partisans are thus divided on the question of right, that is, of knowing if violence can *legitimately* function with excellence. The adversaries maintain that this is not the case and that just conduct tied to excellence demands benevolence[36] rather than violence towards others; the partisans, on the contrary claim that, yes, it is just that precisely the strongest govern (1255a16–19). The manner in which Aristotle settles the debate is simple—it amounts to saying that one cannot separate these two arguments from each other and that the strongest cannot exercise his superiority without benevolence. When one separates these arguments, he says, all the others are without value: "it is as if the superior in excellence should not command and be the master" (1255a20–21). It follows that the positive law instituting slavery is defended by the partisans and adversaries who are each partially wrong and par-tially correct precisely because what is at issue is a law that, in one sense, is in conformity with justice and, in another sense, is contrary to it. Now the fact that it in one sense conforms with justice here means only that it secures, as do just laws, the authority of the superior and that in this way, because it has the same force as just laws, it is natural, like everything that secures, in various ways, this authority. The fact that it is in one sense contrary to justice means that this law does not give any assurances, as required by justice, against violent authority. Thus, the positive law on slavery is, when all is said and done, an example of a natural, but unjust, law.

My conclusion is therefore confirmed. Some have sought to find in the Aristotelian theory of slavery an unfortunate attempt to found the right of slav-ery on nature. I believe I have shown, to the contrary, that it is rather a fortu-nate attempt, from the perspective of nature, to question this right. Nothing better than this theory indicates how much nature for Aristotle is not a norm of right. The state of the slave from Aristotle's perspective can be just only on the condition that it is natural. That is, it is not instituted by law but founded on the interest of the weak naturally joined to that of the strong.

I would now like to come back to Aristotle's idea according to which the slave is not the subject of right—and this will allow us to conclude.

CONCLUSION

The Aristotelian idea according to which the slave is not a subject of right or of the just properly speaking, and which governs the relations between equal citizens, does not assert that the law excludes some persons from the sphere of right. This assertion indeed would be valid for the slave declared as such by law. But Aristotle's idea takes into account the natural slave who is not declared to be such by any law and who is consequently not excluded from the rights guar-anteed to more or less equal citizens.

Therefore this idea applies to the situation where one person is naturally dependent on another, as a child is upon its parents. And Aristotle maintains that between this person and the one who is depended upon completely there are not, properly speaking, relations of justice any more than there are between a son and his father. This is not to say, therefore, that relations between them are unjust; it means only that they avoid justice properly so called and that the interests of the slave and the master are in fact secured. They are secured with-out fulfilling the conditions of justice properly so called and of right—which exist, on the one hand, as two clearly distinct partners, and on the other, as the (strict or relative) equality of these two partners. Since the slave is in fact the animate instrument of the master, he is in some ways a part of him, as the child is a part of its parents, rather than a truly distinct being on an equal footing; the slave, therefore, receives from the master as the child does from its parents—the kind of care one accords to a part of himself and therein justice does not rule (*Nicomachean Ethics* V.10 1134b8–13).

But this does not impede man-to-man relations or reciprocal love or friendship between the master and the natural slave (cf. *Politics* I.6 1255b13). Aristotle insists that the love a father accords to his son is not accorded to the slave as such but to the slave "as a man" (*Nicomachean Ethics* VIII.13 1161b4–5). One can very well ask why this common humanity, which for today's egalitarian thought is sufficient to secure equal political rights, does not lead Aristotle to claim for the slave, whom he recognizes entirely as a human being, the same rights as for the master upon whom he depends.

But, in fact, this kind of claim certainly would not have any meaning in a theory of natural slavery, such as Aristotle's, simply because as a human being the natural slave has all the rights of human beings. With regard to the citizens' rights that he does not exercise as a natural slave, these rights are not refused him by right—he himself refuses to exercise them! In fact, the law, if it does not institute slavery, does not deprive the natural slave of any right to which he aspires. If he is not free it is because he is naturally dependent and a stranger to the autonomy of free persons. On this point, Aristotle's thought, which one can acknowledge only with difficulty, has a strict logic. The person who is naturally a slave by definition is not such because of a law that condemns him to slavery and deprives him of the rights of citizens—but rather because of a strictly personal inclination not to share the aspirations of human beings *as* citizens.

Indeed, as we have seen, the natural slave is recognized by the fact that he does not have any goals in life except to survive—comfortably, if possible. Now the very principle of the city, which is the common goal of those who associate as citizens, is not only to live or even to live comfortably—as imagined by "most of the *totally servile* who choose the life of beasts" in search of bodily pleasure (*Nicomachean Ethics* I.3 1095b19–20). On the contrary, the common goal, which is the end of the city and is shared equally by the citizens (and in this they are free), corresponds to the "good life" assured by a total independence: "the end and the highest good is to be self-sufficient" (*Politics* I.2 1252b30 and 1253a1).

This aspiration is therefore above servile inclinations. It is very precisely what one does not share if one is a natural slave. That is, when speaking of justice properly so called, which governs the relations between "free and equal" citizens, Aristotle starts by saying that justice applies to those "who share a life devoted to self-sufficiency" (*Nicomachean Ethics* V.10 1134a26–27). Aristotle's judgment according to which the natural slave is not a subject of right is thus explained. It is not that the law excludes some persons from the right of citizenship; rather some are made such that they do not have any aspirations to be citizens nor do they share the common goals of citizens. Therefore they renounce being subjects of the law that governs the relations of those who share this common goal. Whatever the law is, the citizens' life does not interest them except for seeing in the city the assistance that they need and that they cannot find elsewhere.

Compared to that of the moderns, Aristotle's position thus reduces in the end to this: contrary to the moderns Aristotle does not search for an absolute principle of right outside of the right in human nature; he does not deduce a priori from human nature the equality of human beings, and he therefore avoids establishing as an absolute principle of right an unequally shared desire between men—that desire being freedom (understood as perfect self-sufficiency). What he thus avoids is erecting an absolute a principle of right strictly relative to democracy, freedom and sovereignty of the majority being the basic hypotheses of democracy (*Politics* V.9 1320a28–30).[37] Therefore, judged from an Aristotelian point of view, the moderns' position has the characteristic weakness of making what is contingent universal and of confusing what is the nature of right with what is the necessary condition of its application.

It is up to the partisans of a return to Aristotle, then, to defend this judgment as being in conformity with the truth, and it is up to the adversaries to demonstrate that Aristotle was incorrect in considering that, in fact, democratic right is both relative and perfectly contingent. In order to demonstrate Aristotle's error bearing on this contingency, it does not suffice to establish that justice *properly so called* requires free and equal persons, for it is quite precisely this that he maintains: the freedom and equality of human beings are the conditions without which legal justice cannot be instituted. It must still be demonstrated that justice is entirely satisfied by these conditions and does not require anything more essential than precisely what egalitarian democracy according to its only principle is not adequate to provide—the common interest, that is, what all are equally entitled to which they have the right to desire as equals. Indeed justice is not satisfied by the recognition of equality between persons when it exists; on the contrary, it essentially requires that, *in such circumstances*, an equal interest is secured between persons. If this is the case, if justice resides essentially in allotting to each one's due, then justice may be secured under other laws and in other conditions than those of democratic equality—which are contingent.

At the same time, it will be up to Aristotle's adversaries to demonstrate that it is impertinent to place the justice of democratic laws on the side of a relative right, rather than on the side of a right without qualification (that he calls republican). And to do so, once again it is not sufficient to establish that right properly speaking requires equal and free persons since justice, as we have just seen, also requires that these equals receive their due. Now the typically democratic rule of the sovereign majority is not sufficient to fulfill this requirement. Further, the majority must secure the minority interests as its own. If it is the case that justice essentially requires this common concern, then it *must* be secured by provisions other than those of typically majoritarian, democratic right, and justice can be secured in conditions other than those of republican equality—for these conditions are contingent.

Finally, it is up to Aristotle's adversaries to demonstrate that justice is not satisfied outside of the conditions required by right—which is applicable to free and equal citizens. And to do this they will have to demonstrate that there is absolutely no form of justice possible for the subject of an absolute monarchy, in any time, any place, or outside of right, for the relations between totally unequal persons one of whom is completely dependent upon the other. Now, to this end, it is not sufficient to posit that all persons are equally free before the law, because the law which is disposed to favor all persons and which also requires adult autonomy to have or exercise certain rights, does not imply that the child without these rights is unjustly treated. It therefore would have to be demonstrated that on this issue the law is wrong; and the price to be paid is that Aristotle's thought on natural slavery will be turned against his theory of right. Indeed this thought aims at showing that even without having the rights that are linked to free persons upon adulthood, the natural slave who is in some sense an eternal child, is justly treated.

Adversaries and partisans of Aristotle will have to agree on at least one point: Aristotle is not looking for any norm of right in any nature whatsoever other than the nature of right itself. For Aristotle, there are many things that are natural but not just—at least not unqualifiedly—including a certain number of positive laws (of ostracism or the institution of slavery); but the only things that are natural *and* unqualifiedly just are those coming from positive laws which have everywhere the same force to institute or maintain a correct [*droit*] political regime. Regarding the search for a principle of right in natural reason which comes to each person of age without considering the goals that

are assigned to reason and fixed by a correctly oriented appetite, this idea—
Kantian at bottom—would have seemed to Aristotle as strange as the idea
which would consist in placing in the equal rationality of the virtuous and of
the vicious the norm of the good.

NOTES

1. See in particular, Leo Strauss, *Natural Right and History* (Chicago: University of Chicago Press, 1953); Eric Voegelin, *Anamnesis: Zur Theorie und Geschichte der Politik* (Munich: Piper, 1966); Joachim Ritter, "Le droit naturel chez Aristote. Contribution au renouveau du droit naturel," *Archives de philosophie* 32 (1969): 416–57; Hannah Arendt, *The Human Condition* (Chicago: Chicago University Press, 1958); and Michel Villey, *Philosophie du droit*, vol. 1, 2d ed. (Paris: Dalloz, 1978). I have considered the Aristotelian propositions defended by the first two authors in Richard Bodéüs, "Deux propositions aris-totéliciennes sur le droit naturel chez les continentaux d'Amérique," *Revue de Métaphysique et de Morale* 3 (1989): 369–89, whose conclusions I am here revising. For a more general overview of the renewed interests in Aristotle, particularly in the German tradition, see Franco Volpi, "La rinascita della filosofia practica in Germania," in *Filosophia e scienza politica*, ed. C. Pacchiani, 11–97. (Padua, 1980). (See especially 18–38, "La ripresa di Aristotele.")

2. Aristotle is most often neglected, indeed ignored, by the authors in this move-ment. A critique along these lines, however, can be found for example in Alain Renaut, "Aristote et le droit naturel," *Philosophie du droit*, ed. A. Renaut and L. Sosoe (Paris, 1991), 233–55; and Alain Renaut, *Qu'est-ce que le Droit? Aristote, Wolff, & Fichte*. (Paris, 1992), 59–62 and 77–94.

3. See Ronald Dworkin, *Taking Rights Seriously* (Cambridge: Harvard University Press, 1977). This position corresponds to a theory of natural law understood as a part of morality.

4. This movement is already one of a return to natural right as seen at the beginning of this century; on this subject see Charles Haines, *The Revival of Natural Law Concepts* (Cambridge: Harvard University Press, 1930).

5. Thus, John Rawls, *A Theory of Justice* (Cambridge: Harvard University Press, 1971), who draws from Aristotle (§65) a principle unconnected to his conception of justice.

6. Thus, Michel Villey, *La formation de la pensée juridique moderne*, 4th ed. (Mont-chrétien, 1975), 39, for whom Aristotle has the added advantage of preserving a rigorous distinction between right and morality.

7. Like the Stoics and contrary to the Moderns, Aristotle defended an objective right less exposed to individualism than theories of right founded upon the moral subject; but contrary to the Stoics, he did not take a "cosmic order" as a norm for justice. And it is a mis-take for Luc Ferry and Alain Renaut, *Philosophie politique*, vol. III (Paris, 1985), 49, to ascribe the idea of such a norm to the ancients in general.

8. I will return later to Aristotle's manner of conceiving reason (*logos*) as among the natural principles constitutive of human beings. Here it is useless to recall that the cosmic order or nature, according to him, contains no homogeneous principle (a universal *logos*).

9. The "ideal" justice, as described by Plato (*Republic* V, 479d or VI, 484c) is, to the contrary, taken as the primary target of the Aristotelian critique.

10. On this subject see David Keyt, "Distributive Justice in Aristotle's *Ethics* and *Politics*," *Topoi* 4 (1985): 33; "In Aristotle's political philosophy this situation is reversed."

11. I add that this point is equally taken as accepted in Renaut, "Aristote et le droit naturel," 240, and in Renaut, *Qu'est-ce que le Droit? Aristote, Wolff, & Fichte*, 84. Everyone recognized, finally, that Aristotelian natural right is immanent in positive right.

12. On this subject see Louis Lachance, "Les données permanentes du droit," *Études et recherches. Cahiers de théology et de philosophie* 9 (1955): 96–148, (specifically 136–37).

13. This is a decisive argument in Aristote, *L'Éthique à Nicomaque*, vol II, Introduction, trans., and commentary by R. A. Gauthier and J.Y. Jolif, 2d ed. (Paris-Louvain: Publications universitaires de Louvain, 1970), 391, which identifies natural justice and unwritten universal law.

14. As maintained in Pierre Aubenque, "La loi selon Aristote," *Archives de philosophie du droit* 25 (1980): 145–57, (see specifically 155–57). This latter interpretation argues that for Aristotle natural right would be the convertibility of positive rights. There is a worthy intuition in this interpretation; however, as I indicate later, it is very unlikely that this convertibility is a norm of right for Aristotle.

15. See Renaut, "Aristote et le droit naturel," 248: "As we well know, starting from his conception of natural right Aristotle defended the existence of an inegalitarian positive right authorizing slavery."

16. See Pierre Pellegrin, "La théorie aristotélicienne de l'esclavage : tendances actuelles de l'interprétation," *Revue philosophique* 2 (1982): 345–57, (see specifically 350).

17. This is also the position of a certain notorious Aristotelizing; see, most recently, Julia Annas, *The Morality of Happiness* (New York: Oxford University Press, 1993), 155: "The appeal to nature here falls down in two related ways. One is that the explanation offered for the system . . . is not adequate to explain . . . the functioning of actual slavery . . . . The other failure is that Aristotle infers far too hastily from the thesis that nature is the norm, what happens always or for the most part, to the naturalness of a near-universal institution."

18. In establishing the variability of justice, H. G. Gadamer has submitted these texts to a "hermeneutic" reading. On this subject, see Bodéüs, "Deux propositions aristotéliciennes sur le droit naturel chez les continentaux d'Amérique," 377.

19. On this see Richard Bodéüs, *Politique et philosophie chez Aristote* (Namur, 1991), 131.

20. The manuscripts (except for K[b]) here show: "simple justice and (*kai*) political justice." If this reading is correct, the "and" (*kai*) could have here only an expletive signification (and signify "that is to say"). Nothing, in effect, allows for distinguishing (here or elsewhere) "simple justice" from "political justice" in Aristotelian thought.

21. The best study on this point is to be found in Bernard Yack, *The Problems of a Political Animal: Community, Justice, and Conflict in Aristotelian Political Thought* (Berkeley: University of California Press, 1993), 140–49, which criticizes such interpretations and defends the idea that Aristotle is not seeking a norm of right in nature. Yack concludes that, "Natural Right is thus natural for Aristotle both in its origin and end" (147). This conclusion remains, nevertheless, unsatisfactory: first, because if the origin of right is natural "in the same way that the political community is natural," the positive and determined provisions of right, themselves, are not (but it is these provisions that concern us here); secondly,

because the end of right is in political justice, not in the promotion of "the highest capacity nature gives to human beings," that is, in the development of human nature. Not one text of Aristotle defines justice (even less for natural justice) in this way.

22. The fact that two things are accounted for by law (the nature of the regime and its correctness) poses a problem we will take up later: is there room for the provisions of natural right in a deviant regime that does not establish a justice without qualification?

23. *Nicomachean Ethics* VIII.11 (1159b26ff.), while not making mention of natural law, makes mention of the "just" that is instituted in every community, even temporary ones, as with sailors on the same ship or soldiers in the same company. These forms of justice are eventually secured by particular rules about which the laws governing the political community do not make obvious pronouncements. In VIII.13 1161b6–7, without ever speaking of natural law, Aristotle writes that, "it seems that there is some sort of justice between any man and any other who is capable of participating within law or in an agreement." From this, one can induce that the institution of political law itself develops from a natural if not innate sense to bear justice towards one's fellow human beings. But this tells us nothing about the reasons why some legal provisions would be natural and others not. See my criticism addressed to Yack above.

24. Before William W. Fortenbaugh, "Aristotle on Slaves and Women," in *Articles on Aristotle*, ed. J. Barnes, M. Schofield, and R. Sorabji, vol. 2 (London: Duckworth, 1977), 135–39, there was no modern study that addressed itself to expounding the profound principles of the Aristotelian thesis on slavery. The crux of the matter is found in N. D. Smith, "Aristotle's Theory of Natural Slavery," in *A Companion to Aristotle's Politics*, ed. D. Keyt and F. D. Miller, Jr. (Cambridge: Blackwell, 1991), 142–55. The best approach is found in Malcolm Schofield, "Ideology and Philosophy in Aristotle's Theory of Slavery," in *Aristotele's "Politik,"* ed. G. Patzig (Gottingen: 1990), 1–27, who has not read Smith and concludes, "The theory does not explicitly or otherwise pretend to be a theory directly or indirectly concerned with contemporary slavery" (22). This conclusion brings to light a just enough fact that Schofield only explains with the following reason: "Aristotle surprisingly does not consider it part of his job as theorist of slavery to comment on existing practice." I will try to show further on that the explanation is rather that Aristotle's theory of natural slavery is neither indifferent to practice nor, even less, destined to ground it, but to the contrary, an implicit critique of the practice of slavery founded on right.

25. One might also question this because elsewhere Aristotle very clearly puts the onus for the Asiatic servile temperament and lack of aggressivity on climactic conditions (in this case, too hot) (*Politics* VIII.7 1327b23ff., especially 28–29). I will take up the problem of the difficult conciliation of this text with that of *Politics* I later on.

26. We should here distinguish (what Aristotle does not do explicitly) between the lack of suitable (liberal) education and the resistance of the subject to such an education, a resistance which is better suited to the idea that some are naturally destined to be slaves. But whether it is absence of education or resistance to education, the effects are identical and lead to the same natural subjection.

27. Some have decided—in particular Wolfgang Kullmann, *Il pensiero politico di Aristotele* (Naples, 1992), 76; and note 25—that the text of *Politics* VII is hardly reconcilable with that of *Politics* I; for his part, Eugene Garver, "Aristotle's Natural Slaves:

Incomplete Praxeis and Incomplete Human Beings," *Journal of the History of Philosophy* 32 (1994): 173–95, (see specifically 178–83), considered this text, which stigmatizes the absence of *thumos*, as probably providing the key to the Aristotelian conception of slavery. For my part, I believe that this character trait is of only secondary importance and that, without contradicting Aristotelian thought, this trait is compounded with the lack of liberal education for barbarians in making natural slaves of them.

28. Compare *Eudemian Ethics* I.2 1214b10–11: "Not to have an existence arranged in function of a goal is the sign of a great fault in sagacity."

29. On this subject, see Garver, "Aristotle's Natural Slaves: Incomplete Praxeis and Incomplete Human Beings," 175.

30. This belonging to another, without (legal) right of possession by the other, can only be understood as a spontaneous gift of self, inspired by interest. Aristotle does not, however, elaborate this perspective.

31. "In the first place there must be a union of those who cannot exist without each other" (*Politics* I.2 1252a26–27).

32. The complexity and ambiguity of the notion of "nature" in the *Politics* have recently been elucidated by G. E. R. Lloyd, "L'Idée de nature dans la Politique d'Aristote," in *Aristote. Politique. Études sur la Politique d'Aristote*, ed. P. Aubenque and A. Tordesillas (Paris: 1993), 135–59, who here claims that Aristotle's argument in favor of the naturalness of master-slave relations rests upon "a series of proportional analogies" (141), but without noticing the scope of these analogies. The same deficiency is found in Smith, "Aristotle's Theory of Natural Slavery," 150–55, who denounces in Aristotle the impropriety of the soul-body relations model for explaining and justifying slavery.

33. "He who naturally does not belong to himself, but is another's man, such is the natural slave; yet being another's man is being his possession, even if one is a man, that is, an instrument of execution distinct from the master" (*Politics* I.4 1254a14–17).

34. In other words, the "alienation" of the slave which excludes the application of "commutative" justice (*Nicomachean Ethics* V.8) to its relation with the master, far from ruining the principle of all justice, secures it by the fusion of their interests.

35. From this point on I am commenting on an extremely difficult, and controversially interpreted, passage in Aristotle that has recently been analysed by Schofield, "Ideology and Philosophy in Aristotle's Theory of Slavery," 23–27. My analysis differs from his only on minor points.

36. Here I respect the teaching of the manuscripts (*eunoia*: 1255a17), rather than adopting editors' corrections which are not necessary (*pace* Schofield, 24, n.1).

37. See *Politics* VI.2 1317a40–41 and 1317b2–4): "Now therefore the basic hypothesis of the democratic constitution is freedom . . . . And a principle of freedom is to be ruled and rule in turn, because in a popular regime justice is having an arithmetic equality."

Part Two

Issues in the *Nicomachean Ethics* and *Politics*

CHAPTER 6

The Ambitions of Aristotle's Audience and the Activist Ideal of Happiness

DAVID K. O'CONNOR

Socrates' insistence that the poets be expelled from the best city is a notorious example of the limits of philosophical engagement. People who find themselves in the unfortunate position of being addicted to poetry's charms—whether as performers or audience—simply must leave Kallipolis. We virtuous ones will stop up our ears at the siren songs of these beauty-addicts and sail right by them, or rather set them adrift on the receding tide. This is a harsh teaching, and it is not Plato's final word. But it does bring out a feature of political and ethical discourse that Plato and his Socrates both confronted self-consciously: you can't talk to everyone. In the *Republic*, Socrates could find no starting points with the poets, no common ground on which to force them—or should we say, invite them?—to ascend from their love of images and shadows to fire and light.

Aristotle shares some of this blank puzzlement in the face of the poets and their aspirations. Though his *Poetics* shows that poetry can be made acceptable and even seen as beneficial from the point of view of Aristotelian political science, nothing in this treatise, I think, establishes any continuity between what motivates poets and what motivates statesmen. I know of only two passages where Aristotle says anything at all about the way of life of the poet, so that it could be compared with the three canonical ways of life of the philosopher, the politician, and the hedonist. The most explicit is from the conclusion of Aristotle's discussion of the appropriate type of musical education in the best city (*Politics* VIII.6 1341b8–15):

> On consideration we reject professional [*technikē*] education in instruments and performance. (We mean by "professional education" one aimed at participation in competitions.) For in that sort of education, the practitioner [*prattōn*] is not acting for the sake of his own virtue, but for the pleasure of his audience, and this pleasure is vulgar [*phortikē*]. Thus we judge performance to be more appropriate for the servile class than for the free. And indeed it turns out that performers become low class [*banausoi*].

This reduction of the poet and musician to a species of low-class laborer seems to be confirmed by one of Aristotle's discussions of the claims to happiness of the various ways of life (*Eudemian Ethics* I.4 1215a26–15b1):

> Of the various ways of life, some make a claim to [happiness] but it is as if [*ōs*] they strive for things that are merely necessary: for example, the ways of life concerned with vulgar [*phortikē*] professions and those concerned with money-making and low class professions [*banausoi*]. (I mean by "vulgar" those concerned only with reputation, by "low class" those that are sedentary and wage-earning, and by "money-making" those that involve markets and retail trade.). But there are three ways of life ordered to an undertaking [<*di*>*agōgē*] productive of happiness, pertaining to the three goods previously mentioned as greatest for human beings, namely, virtue and intelligence [*phronēsis*] and pleasure. We also see that these are the three ways of life that all those with unrestricted opportunities [*exousia*] actually choose to live, namely, the political, the philosophical, and the enjoyment-centered ways of life.

Aristotle seems here to be making the same claim as in the *Politics* passage, for though he does not explicitly mention music, he again suggests that some "vulgar" way of life that garners reputation (and what is this if not the life of the professional performer?) is in fact no better claimant to happiness than the lives of bankers or bakers. This dismissal of the poet's life "as if" it were reducible to the lives that pursue mere necessities—to say the treatment is insufficient is to give it too much credit. Aristotle is here simply recording the unintelligibility of the poet's motives rather than offering a real analysis of them. For all their loquaciousness, the poets are people to whom Aristotle could not talk. Aristotle does not exactly expel the poets from his city, to be sure. But he does in effect exclude them from his audience in his ethical discourses, just as he excludes the banker and the baker. With such people Aristotle has no argument; their opinions and their ways of life do not enter into consideration, and Aristotle does nothing to invite them into his investigation. As he would put it, poets lack the starting points necessary in the fit student of political science.

The inability of Socrates to talk to the poets, and the subsequent necessity of expelling them, is a striking illustration of the *existential specificity* of his ethical discourses. Socrates is always talking to particular men (only very rarely to particular women) and seeking some common ground with them. He does not start with an abstract, general theory that he then applies to the particular case at hand. Instead, he tries to appeal to beliefs and motives that are starting points for his interlocutor. Some starting points provide more openings for Socratic ascent than others, and there is no guarantee that Socrates will find a hook in just anyone's aspirations. Plato seems to have been as interested in dramatizing cases where Socrates' invitations were misunderstood or rebuffed as those where they bore fruit and moved the interlocutor toward decency and perhaps even philosophy.[1] But we can say this much: the dialogues usually present Socrates in some specific existential situation with his interlocutor, and the themes he develops and any theoretical machinery he deploys are specially tailored to this situation. What he says to ascetics like Cebes and Simmias is different and has a different existential point from what he says to lusty Phaedrus or to sober Crito. Asceticism, lust, and sobriety do not disqualify one from being Socrates's interlocutor, as being a poet does (at least in the *Republic*; but of course this disqualification is as much a function of Glaucon and Adeimantus as of Socrates). But they do affect what Socrates has to say.

As Aristotle shares Socrates' inability to find common ground with the poets, so more generally he shares Socrates' existential specificity. Aristotle develops and deploys the theoretical machinery of the *Nicomachean Ethics* to address a quite specific existential question: should I devote my life to politics? In other words, Aristotle's primary addressee is a man[2] driven by ambition, an ambition that manifests itself fundamentally if not ultimately in politics.[3] Aristotle issues an invitation to virtue that is aimed specifically at such ambitious men, and it is with them that he seeks a common ground. To interpret this specific invitation as if it were intended to address any adult of sound moral upbringing is a *faux pas* on the scale of bringing all of one's relatives to a wedding when the invitation mentioned only one's spouse. In making this claim, I take myself to be disagreeing with the dominant approach to Aristotle's ethical works in Anglo-American philosophical circles. This approach takes Aristotle's primary addressee to be characterized less by ambition than by a penchant for reflection, and it has a correspondingly different account of the existential question being confronted.

In effect, these Anglo-American interpretations of Aristotle have tended to expel the politicians rather than the poets, and have replaced them with an audience suspiciously like Anglo-American academics, more interested in being reflective than being in charge.

The two tasks of this chapter are to explain what common ground Aristotle hopes to occupy with his ambitious audience, and to consider two challenges, rooted in this common ground, that reject his own favored accounts of the political and philosophical lives. The first section will take up Aristotle's few explicit remarks (in *Nicomachean Ethics* I.3–4) about his intended audience. I offer a *morally minimalist* interpretation of these remarks. The common readings of these remarks make out Aristotle's audience to be much more settled in their convictions and commitments than the passages warrant. I will suggest that we can give a tolerably precise account of whom Aristotle meant to address simply by looking at how he proceeds in the immediate sequel to his reflections on his audience, in *Nicomachean Ethics* I.5. The second section is devoted to Aristotle's articulation (especially in *Nicomachean Ethics* I.5–8) of the common ground he intends to occupy with the ambitious men who are his primary addressees. I call this shared perspective the *activist ideal* of happiness, an ideal that puts engaging in *praxis* at the heart of successful living. As we will see in section three, this ideal seems to expose Aristotle to two challenges: (1) It makes the "hyperactive" life of the tyrant or king look like the exemplar of success (what I call *Simonides' challenge*); (2) It makes the philosophical life look too quiet and idle to be a candidate for happiness (what I call *Callicles' challenge*). The final section will consider Aristotle's response to these challenges, focusing on his identification (in *Nicomachean Ethics* X.7–8 and *Politics* VII.2–3) of contemplation as the highest kind of *praxis*.

ARISTOTLE'S AUDIENCE:
A MORALLY MINIMALIST ACCOUNT

Aristotle points to three qualities he presupposes in his audience. First, they must accept the variety and variability of what counts as noble and just, the subject matter of political science. The young tend to expect a false precision in such things, and this expectation disappears only with some experience in the affairs of the world (I.3 1094b11–1095a4). Second, they must be able to change and control their desires in light of instruction (I.3 1095a4–9). Third, they must not be dazzled by highfalutin accounts of the good or by dialectical sharpness, sticking to their convictions (which Aristotle in the immediate sequel calls "the *that*") sometimes even in the face of arguments to the contrary

(I.4 1095a22–28; see also I.8 1098b9–12). None of these three qualities presupposes much by way of particular moral commitments. Aristotle is primarily
concerned that his audience have developed some judgment and discretion,
and take direction well. There is no reason to think that a man who burns with
ambition and wonders if tyrants can live successful lives, for example, must also
fail to be a good listener, or be unable to put into practice what he learns.

Aristotle then concludes this short discussion of his audience with the
following famous passage (I.4 1095b4–8):

> Therefore, to be a good audience about things concerning nobility
> and justice and political affairs generally, one must have been led
> nobly in forming one's habits. For the starting point is the "that,"
> and if the "that" is sufficiently manifest, there is no further need for
> the "because." A person [who has the "that" but not the "because"]
> has or can easily grasp starting points.

Does this passage shift the center of gravity of Aristotle's remarks, so that
he now requires in the audience a pretty much fully established commitment to
virtue, rather than merely an openness to listen to the case for virtue and a
capacity to be influenced by it? Such an interpretation is extremely common,
shared by commentators who otherwise belong to quite different camps. I will
call it the *moralizing account* of Aristotle's audience.

Insofar as the moralizing account is founded on anything explicitly in
this passage, rather than on general views of Aristotle's project in ethics, that
foundation is Aristotle's suggestion that to be in his intended audience one will
have been "led nobly in forming one's habits." Moralizers take this noble initiation to imply well nigh a fully developed set of ethical commitments. Bernard
Williams expresses this feature of the moralizing account well:[4]

> There is a problem about the way in which Aristotle presents his
> inquiry. Indeed, there is a problem about what he can take ethical
> philosophy to be. . . . He makes it seem as though you might
> review the whole of your life and consider whether it was aimed in
> the most worthwhile direction, but, on his own account, this can-
> not be a sensible picture. . . . [On Aristotle's view,] one becomes
> virtuous or fails to do so only through habituation. One should
> not study moral philosophy until middle age, Aristotle believes,
> for a reason that is itself an expression of the present difficulties—
> only by then is a person good at practical deliberation. But by then
> it will be a long time since one became, in relation to this delibera-
> tion, preemptively good or irrecoverably bad. . . . Aristotle cannot
> reasonably believe that his reflections on the virtuous life and its

role in helping to constitute well-being could play a formative part
in some general deliberation that a given person might conduct.

If the habits presupposed by Aristotle are as determinative of one's values
and way of life as Williams suggests, it is indeed hard to see how there could be
much existential bite in Aristotle's teaching, a point Williams happily concedes
as a piece of his larger thesis about "ethics and the limits of philosophy." Little is
left to do but tidying up one's ethical portfolio, since one is beyond the stage of
considering sinking all one's resources into some new venture. No rich young
man need ever go away disappointed, for he will only be told to follow the
commandments he already more or less knows; the teacher will never say, "If
you would be perfect, go sell all you have and come follow me."

The account of Aristotle's audience shared by Julia Annas and John
Cooper gives a striking illustration of this existential toothlessness. Cooper[5]
characterizes the "point of entry for ethical reflection" (in Annas's apt phrase),
an entry he and Annas agree Aristotle inherited from Socrates, as "the discomfort one experiences when, as a mature or nearly mature person already
having a whole set of evaluative views and fairly settled motivations in line
with them, one begins to do what Socrates had famously urged we ought to
do, and looks to one's life as a whole." But did Aristotle, let alone Socrates,
begin from a "discomfort" common to "mature" persons of "fairly settled motivations" who have become reflective? To be initiated into noble habits, on
this reading as on Williams's, seems to get one more or less all the way to middle age, and Aristotle's auditor so characterized is facing a mild form of midlife
crisis. I instead take the initiation into nobility to have inculcated ambitions
and longings that are still seeking for their proper form of expression. It is the
aspiration itself that is the core of this nobility, and not the more settled commitments to particular virtues we would expect to see in a more mature, fully
formed moral agent. As Cooper and Annas portray Aristotle's audience, they
are characterized by anxious reflection on an ideal to which they are already
committed; I characterize them as restless seekers for an ideal to which they can
commit themselves.

To support this characterization of Aristotle's audience, I propose a
morally minimalist account of the crucial passage. Notice first that Aristotle
begins the passage with "therefore." He seems to think he is not introducing a
new point about his audience, but simply restating the characterization he has
already developed. But this characterization focused on the judgment and
teachability of the audience, not on their moral maturity. Second, the verb he
uses, *ēchthai*, means "to have been initiated/brought up/trained." There is no

presumption in favor of taking this to require anything so robust as the moral closure suggested by Williams. It is true enough that the intended audience must be willing and perhaps even eager to give virtue a hearing, and to act on what they hear. This is already an important kind of moral formation, and I do not take moral minimalism to be equivalent to amoralism. But it is still a long way from closure. Third, it must surely be admitted by all parties that what counts as being "led nobly in forming one's habits" is explicated by the sentence following it: "For the starting point is the 'that', and if the 'that' is sufficiently manifest, there is no further need for the 'because.'" Knowing what "the *that*" is will tell us what sort of habituation Aristotle has in mind here. The first two points show that the crucial sentence may be read in a less moralizing way; the third will, I think, show that it *should* be so read.[6]

I will use a perfectly simple method to determine what "starting points" Aristotle has in mind here, though I do not think it has been exploited often: I will look at what he in fact presupposes about the judgments and attitudes of his audience in the immediate sequel, namely, the comparison of the three lives of pleasure, politics, and contemplation. I will argue that Aristotle seeks common ground with the politically ambitious by emphasizing a noble interest in being active. This is quite unlike the point of entry defined by an interest in being rational or reasonable. The frame of the three lives demonstrates that the centerpiece of the *that* Aristotle presupposed was a tendency to accept aspects of what I will call the *activist ideal* of happiness.

THE ACTIVIST IDEAL OF HAPPINESS

Aristotle starts from the *that* in I.5 as it comes to light in his audience's attitudes and judgments concerning the three lives. He then develops this *that* in the famous "function" (*ergon*) argument of I.7, in the process giving his auditors something of the *because*. Finally, he returns in I.8 to the issues of I.5, now with the vocabulary and conclusions of the function argument in hand. The result is to articulate and develop the strong taste for action that characterizes Aristotle's ambitious audience. Let us consider this in detail.

The famous function argument is primarily intended to get us from the first impressions elicited by reflection on the three lives in I.5 to the more developed and articulated positions of I.8. What is crucial for the mediating role played by this argument is its emphasis on an activist ideal of happiness. This emphasis on activity (*energeia*) is perfectly clear in the function (*ergon*) argument's conclusion (*Nicomachean Ethics* I.7 1098a16–18): "The human good turns out to be activity [*energeia*] of soul in accordance with virtue, and if the virtues are many, then in accordance with the best and most perfect of them." It is true that for an activity to be an activity of the *human* soul it must involve reason (*logos*); but the *ergon* argument is more concerned to emphasize *energeia* than *logos*, which after all the etymologies of the words should have led us to expect. It distorts Aristotle's focus on activity to substitute a focus on reason. The distortion also makes it easier to think that Aristotle's audience is primarily characterized by an interest in reflection rather than in action.

The first "starting point" that comes to light in Aristotle's examination of the three lives is a contempt for sensual indulgence. Aristotle never seriously addresses the man devoted to pleasure and enjoyment. He simply dismisses the enjoyment-centered way of life to focus on politics and philosophy. In effect, Aristotle presupposes that his addressees will share this dismissive attitude. So despite the fact that he includes the life of pleasure in his traditional frame of the three lives, it is not a real competitor. Consider Aristotle's introduction of the enjoyment-centered life (*Nicomachean Ethics* I.5 1095b14–22):

> People reasonably think to grasp the good and happiness on the basis of the ways of life. The many, who are very vulgar, think it to be pleasure, and so they like the enjoyment-centered way of life. (For the ways of life that are most pursued are three: the one just mentioned, the political life, and third the theoretical life.). So the many are manifestly utterly slavish, choosing a way of life fit for cattle; they pick up this account [of happiness] because many people of great power and opportunities [*exousiai*] have passions like Sardanapallus.

The language here is not dialectical, as it would be if Aristotle meant to extend an invitation to further joint inquiry to the hedonist. Instead it is dismissive and abusive. Aristotle has nothing to say to the Sardanapalluses of the world. And he is counting on his audience to follow him.

One might think that Aristotle's rehabilitation of pleasure at the end of the *Nicomachean Ethics* displays a softening of this dismissive attitude. But the basis of the rehabilitation shows that this is a misleading interpretation. Consider the crucial conceptual move Aristotle must make to salvage the respectability of pleasure (*Nicomachean Ethics* X.5 1176a22–29):

> So pleasures that are agreed to be base clearly cannot be said to be pleasures except relative to degenerate people; but of the seemingly decent pleasures, which and what sort should be said to be simply human? Or is this clear from the corresponding activities [*energeiai*]? For the pleasures follow them. So if there are one or

several activities definitive of the complete and blissful man, the pleasures that complete these activities will properly be called human in the definitive sense, while the others will be [human] in a secondary or more derived sense, just as with the activities.

Aristotle is no closer to talking to Sardanapallus here than he was before. To raise pleasure's contribution to happiness to the point where it is worthy of consideration, he has in this passage shifted questions about pleasure to questions about activities (*energeiai*). Far from belatedly listening to the claims of the hedonist, Aristotle has made him completely invisible. It is his audience's interest in the value of activity, not of pleasure, that is presupposed here.

This conceptual shift from the value of pleasure to the value of activity is first broached much earlier in the *Nicomachean Ethics*. In I.8, Aristotle revisits the topic of pleasure, salvaging it in essentially the same way he does in the later passage, linking it up to *praxis* (1099a7–21). We get from the contempt of I.5 to the rehabilitation of I.8 by playing on the second "starting point" that Aristotle presupposes in his treatment of the three lives: a strong attachment to activity (*energeia*) or action (*praxis*). In effect, Aristotle takes a second look at pleasure in I.8, exploiting the perspective that is systematized in the function argument of I.7.

We see this same pattern in all the topics revisited in I.8.[7] The meat of the chapter is a demonstration that all of the things usually sought in connection with happiness are present in the activist ideal. Aristotle enumerates these sought-for things as virtue, intelligence (*phronēsis*) and wisdom (*sophia*), pleasure, and a ready supply of external goods (I.8 1098b22–26). We have just seen how the availability of the activist ideal articulated in I.7 affected the discussion of pleasure in I.8.[8] The movement from I.5's discussion of the second canonical life, the life of politics, to I.8's parallel discussion of virtue illustrates this pattern in more detail. Aristotle appeals in I.5 to his audience's self-conception as "activists" to establish that virtue cannot in itself be what happiness is (*Nicomachean Ethics* I.5 1095b30–1096a2):

> Some take virtue [rather than honor] to be the end of the political way of life, but it too appears too incomplete. It is possible for one who has virtue to sleep or perform no actions [*apraktein*] throughout his life, and in addition to undergo great sufferings and misfortunes. No one would deem someone who lived that way happy except to hold on to a thesis.

His remarks on virtue in I.8 expand on this guiding opinion that virtue as such is too inactive to constitute happiness, but now he can exploit the preferred *energeia* vocabulary, which he established with the function argument of I.7. Notice especially the restatement of the "sleeping argument" in the preferred vocabulary (I.8 1098b30–1099a7):

> Our account [of happiness as activity of soul in accordance with virtue] harmonizes with the people who say the highest good is virtue or some particular virtue, since activity [*energeia*] in accordance with virtue belongs with this. Perhaps it makes no small difference to take the good to consist in possession or in use, or in disposition [*hexis*] or activity [*energeia*]. It is possible for the disposition to accomplish nothing when it is present, as is the case with one who is sleeping or has been otherwise excluded from activity, but for activity [*energeia*] this is not possible, since it is necessarily action [*praxis*], even good action. Just as at the Olympics the finest and strongest are not crowned, but rather the competitors—for the winners come from among them—so in life those from among the finest people who act rightly become successful.

So the activist ideal is presented as the best articulation of the ambition that lies at the heart of the political man's sense of what counts for him as success.[9]

The best opportunity to see the activist ideal at work in Aristotle's more concrete analyses of ethical life comes in his treatment of the tension between benefaction (*euergesia*) and magnanimity. Aristotle's exemplar of virtue on the moral plane, the magnanimous man, prefers actively benefiting others to being passively benefited (*Nicomachean Ethics* IV.3 1124b9–14, 17–18):

> [The magnanimous man] is the sort to be a benefactor [*eu poiein*], though he is ashamed to be a beneficiary [*euergetoumenos*], since superiority belongs to the first, but subordination to the second. He also reciprocates more benefits [*anteuergetikos*] than he receives, so that the one repaid will both owe him something and be the receiver [rather than the agent] of benefaction. Magnanimous men seem to remember the benefits they confer, but not the ones they receive, since the one who receives a benefit is subordinate to the one who confers it, and the magnanimous man wants to be superior. . . . It belongs to the magnanimous man to ask for nothing, or at least to ask with great reluctance, but to give aid eagerly.

So potent is the magnanimous man's attachment to his image of himself as active that he becomes something of an ingrate about the favors he has received, and something of an embarrassment in the favors he lavishes! Aristotle explains these tendencies in his treatment of friendship and benefaction (*Nicomachean Ethics* IX.7 1167b17–18, 1168a5–9):

Benefactors [*euergetai*] seem to love their beneficiaries more than those who receive a benefit love those who do it. . . . Here is the cause of this: Being is choiceworthy and lovable for everything; we have being insofar as we are in activity [*energeia*] (i.e., in living and acting [*prattein*]); the agent of some work [*ergon*] is in a way in activity in that work; and so the agent loves the work as the agent loves his being. This [attachment] is natural, since what the agent is in potency [*dunamis*], the work manifests in activity [*energeia*].

No doubt Aristotle realized that many people are quite pleased to get bigger favors and gifts than they give. But such people are not his primary audience, which consists of those who at least find this ideal of magnanimous agency something to aspire to.

I would like to conclude this section with a suggestion about the Platonic roots of Aristotle's activist ideal, which I hope will buttress my claim about the existential specificity of Aristotle's approach. For this purpose, it is again helpful to contrast my view with Bernard Williams's. Referring to *Republic* 352d, Williams gives the following characterization of the organizing question of Greek ethics:[10]

> It is not a trivial question, Socrates said: what we are talking about is how one should live. . . . 'How should one live?'—the generality of "one" already stakes a claim. ... The implication is that something relevant or useful can be said to anyone, in general, and this implies that something general can be said, something that embraces or shapes the individual ambitions each person may bring to the question "how should I live?"

Williams believes that Socrates, and Aristotle, thought "something relevant . . . can be said to anyone, in general," regardless of his "individual ambitions," in answer to the question "how should I live?" A glance at the passage to which Williams refers shows how unlikely these statements are as characterizations of what Socrates is asking when he says to Thrasymachus (*Republic* 352d), "Whether the just live better than the unjust and are happier . . . must still be considered better: for the argument is not about any old thing, but about the way one should live." This comes after a long series of arguments initiated by Thrasymachus's claim that the *tyrant's* life is the best life (see 344a and 348d). Thrasymachus insists emphatically that he is not talking about garden-variety injustice, but only about injustice on the grand scale, epitomized by tyranny. And so when Socrates refers here to the just and unjust lives, he is considering the quite *specific* existential question posed by Thrasymachus of whether the tyrant's life is the best life, and not the general questions proposed by Williams.

The larger context of Thrasymachus's and Socrates' discussion of tyranny is particularly helpful for seeing the existential specificity of Aristotle's approach, since Aristotle follows Plato closely here. At 351A–E, Socrates argues that a city bent on enslaving other cities—Thrasymachus styles it the "best and most completely unjust city," and it is clearly the analogue of the tyrannical individual—will be capable of engaging in action (*prattein*) only insofar as it does not practice injustice among its own members. He then goes on to suggest that justice will also be required for successful action (*prattein*) by a single man (351e–352a). Though this argument is of dubious validity, it does serve to underscore one way in which justice may be made attractive to Socrates' audience: as the capacity for action, for praxis. Socrates goes on (352d–353d) to develop this link between justice, and virtue more generally, and *praxis*. He argues that the soul has a "proper function" (*idion ergon*) requiring its "appropriate virtue" (*oikeia aretē*) in order to engage in action (*prattein*). These are just the two moves taken over by Aristotle in the *Nicomachean Ethics*, the first linking virtue to *praxis* in I.5 and I.8 the second linking *praxis* to proper function in I.7. Of course, Plato does not develop this focus on an activist ideal of virtue in anything like the thematic way we have seen Aristotle do it. But these passages do seem to be Aristotle's model, and they help to establish the existential presuppositions likely to have been in Aristotle's mind.

A HYPERACTIVIST IDEAL?
THE CHALLENGES OF SIMONIDES AND CALLICLES

Curiously, Aristotle does not discuss in I.8 how his activist ideal harmonizes with the guiding opinion that intelligence and wisdom constitute happiness, even though he explicitly enumerated it among the most important opinions. Since he discusses the other three enumerated opinions, his passing over intelligence and wisdom in silence calls for some explanation. This pointed silence is of a piece with his procedure in I.5. Just when he appears ready to take up the third canonical way of life, the contemplative life, he avoids the discussion (I.5 1096a4–5): "Third [among the ways of life] is the contemplative one, about which we will make an investigation in what follows." The auditor must surely have been surprised to find that nothing "followed" until the tenth book! As with his silence in I.8, he points to the philosophical life while avoiding an examination of it. The first book takes place on the common ground of the activist ideal, which is intended to be shared by politics and philosophy; not until the tenth book (with a sneak preview in the sixth book) does Aristotle make a systematic case on this common ground for the superiority of the philosophical life.

How exactly in *Nicomachean Ethics* I.6–8 does Aristotle develop the common ground of the activist ideal while keeping open a conceptual space for his later argument for the superiority of philosophy to politics? For present purposes, I can only state my position, not defend it. The key passage is Aristotle's explanation of how the term "good in itself" functions (I.6 1096b16–29). He argues against the Platonic notion that only the idea of the good is truly good in itself. Once we acknowledge that such things as thinking (*phronein*), seeing, and certain pleasures and honors are pursued even if nothing comes from them, we also must concede that they are good in themselves even if we also pursue them for the sake of something else. For something to be good in itself is not an all-or-nothing affair, but instead admits of degrees. Something will count as good in itself to the extent that its goodness derives from or is analogous to the paradigmatic cases of goodness. This distinction between what makes something good in itself and what makes it paradigmatic is what allows Aristotle to leave open whether philosophy or politics is in fact the paradigm case of the activist ideal. He can articulate the ideal and show how *both* are good in themselves, presenting both as real claimants to happiness, while he defers the question of which is more paradigmatic. The analogy of the "good in itself" saves the common ground.

I have argued that Aristotle presupposes that his audience has a noble aspiration to be immersed in action, and have shown how he nurtures and articulates this aspiration by developing his activist ideal of happiness. In the process, he has presented this ideal throughout the first book in a way that keeps open the question of whether the philosophical or the political life is a fuller instantiation of the ideal. The great benefit of this approach is that he can keep the ear of his audience by staying on common ground. But there is a high cost as well: Aristotle has so effectively developed the ideal that it can be used to support two positions about politics and philosophy that Aristotle ultimately wants to reject. If one takes the activist ideal to a "hyperactivist" extreme, the life of tyranny and political domination begins to seem attractive. Such a life does, after all, give one unrivaled opportunities to undertake actions. Furthermore, the political man may find the philosophical life to be clearly inferior to his own way of life when both are measured by the activist ideal; perhaps it will look too quiet and idle to be even tolerable for a man of noble ambitions. Both challenges strike at the heart of Aristotle's attempt to defend his own favored positions from within a horizon he shares with his ambitious audience.

Consider first how tyranny appears in light of the activist ideal, or at least of a "hyperactivist" appropriation of the ideal. Xenophon's *Hiero* gives us a splendid illustration of this perspective. Once upon a time, Xenophon tells us, Simonides the poet and Hiero the tyrant had a conversation. When Hiero claimed that the tyrannical life is worse than the private person's life because it provides fewer pleasures, Simonides made this response (*Hiero* II.1–2):

> Well, I believe all these things you are talking about are very small. Many who are believed to be men [*andres*] I see willingly getting less of foods and drinks and delicacies—and sex too, keeping themselves away from it. But it is in the following things that you [tyrants] are very much distinguished from private persons: you make great plans, and accomplish them swiftly; you have many luxuries, and possess horses distinguished in virtue, weapons distinguished in beauty, outstanding ornament for women, the most magnificent houses, and these furnished with things of great value; further you possess a multitude of knowledgeable servants, the best, and you are most capable of harming enemies and profiting friends.

The viewpoint here espoused by Simonides reveals a dangerous risk of the activist ideal: it can produce a person who will be led by perfectly noble motives toward tyranny, not for mere power or the pleasures it provides, but for the chance to undertake the greatest actions.

Simonides' challenge, as I will call this threat, is explicitly recognized by Aristotle. His paradigm case of the man driven to tyranny by such noble motives appears to have been Jason of Thessaly, a fascinating historical figure who, before he was assassinated, was well on his way to the military consolidation of Greece later effected by Alexander the Great.[11] Aristotle quotes Jason to illustrate the least base motive of injustice (*Rhetoric* I.12 31):

> People commit injustice against those toward whom they can then practice many just actions, thinking it will be easy to appease them, just as Jason of Thessaly said he had to do some unjust things so that he would also be able to do many just things.

Aristotle does not dismiss this view of the priority of activity to (what would normally be taken to be) justice. Indeed, in his own discussion of whether the virtue that makes one a good citizen is the same as the virtue that makes one a good man simply, Aristotle sharpens the challenge (*Politics* III.4 1277a23–25, b25–29):

> [On one view,] the same virtue does not belong to the ruler and the citizen, and perhaps for this reason Jason of Thessaly said that he hungered when he wasn't tyrant, as if he did not know how to be a private person. . . . Intelligence [*phronēsis*] is the only virtue specific to the ruler; . . . intelligence is not a virtue of the ruled, but rather true opinion [*doxa alēthēs*].

Jason's "hunger" for a position of political power seems to have a strong Aristotelian justification in this passage, since only ruling gives full scope to the exercise of intelligence.

Simonides' challenge arises purely within the political man's horizon, without any reference to philosophy. Its basic argument is simple: if the happy life is essentially a fully or perfectly active life (thanks to Aristotle for helping us see this!), and if political power provides the most scope for activity, then the life of greatest political power, namely, the noble tyrant's life of domination, will turn out to be the happiest. No real man would settle for anything less if he had the opportunity. Aristotle attempts two different sorts of response to Simonides' challenge. The first tries to stay wholly within the horizon of political action (this compressed paraphrase follows the text of *Politics* VII.3 1325a32–b7):

> Happiness is action [*praxis*], and the actions of the just achieve many noble results. But the partisans of politics are wrong to conclude that the best life would involve maximum political control. They base this conclusion on the belief that such control would make possible the most and best actions, but the injustice of seizing such power would destroy the nobility of the actions undertaken with it.

This is not likely to be an especially effective response to ambitious and noble tyrants like Callicles and Jason. It simply denies Jason's claim that "one must perform some unjust actions in order to be able to perform many just actions." Is it really true, or at any rate is it a truth accessible from the perspective of the activist ideal of happiness, that no actions that flow from an unjust seizure of power redound to the credit of the tyrant? I believe that to challenge more effectively the attraction of maximal political activeness, Aristotle was forced to go outside the political horizon and appeal to the superior activeness of philosophy. An especially striking illustration of this strategy comes from Aristotle's critique of the political proposals of Phaleas of Chalcedon (*Politics* II.7). Phaleas suggested that equality of property would remove the causes of injustice, but Aristotle replied that such equality would not check men of high ambition (1267a10–14): "[If some strive unjustly for power] because they want enjoyment that depends only on themselves, they should seek no cure except from philosophy. . . . People do the greatest injustices for the sake of excess, not necessities: no one becomes a tyrant to get out of the cold."

This appeal to philosophy over politics from within the common ground defined by the activist ideal of happiness is fraught with difficulties. Aristotle tries to respond to Simonides' challenge by showing that philosophy is even more "active" than politics. But when the "real man" first casts his eye beyond politics toward philosophy, he finds nothing there but a childish inactivity. The classic form of this critique of philosophy by the real man is Callicles' great speech in Plato's *Gorgias*. Callicles is responding to Socrates' refutation of Polus's presentation of the life of the tyrant as especially happy (483a–b and 485d–e):

> It is not the part of a real man [*anēr*] to suffer injustice, but of a slave [*andrapodon*]. . . . Even someone who has much natural talent, but who keeps involved with philosophy beyond the appropriate age, must end up without the experience required to become a man [*anēr*] of accomplishment and reputation. . . . An older man [*anēr*] still philosophizing and not giving it up . . . becomes unmanly [*anandros*] and avoids the centers of his city and its public places [*agora*], where the poet says real men [*andres*] achieve distinction . . . and instead lives the rest of his life in obscurity, whispering in a corner with three or four boys, never uttering a word befitting of freedom, greatness, or power.

Callicles' challenge, as we may call this charge against philosophy, dismisses with manly contempt the pretension of philosophy, and insinuates that philosophy is motivated less by intercourse with the gods than by the private pleasures lurking in the shadows with little boys. Real men make it in the *agora*, in public action, not in the retiring little enclaves of the pederast. Aristotle answers this charge by in effect insisting that philosophy, *pace* Callicles, is a paradigm of activeness, not idleness, and therefore also a paradigm of what befits a man. It is an ingenious answer, one that as far as possible preserves the common ground Aristotle has been seeking without sacrificing philosophy to the standards of politics. I also believe the answer is a failure, so that Aristotle is ultimately unsuccessful in his attempt to defend the superiority of philosophy over politics on ground common between them. But here I am interested primarily in showing how Aristotle's argument works rather than in evaluating its success. To this task we now turn.

RESPONDING TO CALLICLES:
PHILOSOPHY AS *PRAXIS*

Aristotle gives similar responses to Callicles' challenge in the *Politics* and the *Nicomachean Ethics*. When he compares the political and philosophical lives, his crucial move is to appropriate for philosophy the mantle of (political) *praxis*. Let us start with the *Politics*, where the key move is more explicit, though also more difficult to justify. Aristotle develops his own position here dialectically from the debate between partisans of philosophy and partisans of politics. On one side are those real men who hold to the position of Callicles; on the other are people who defend a much more retiring and isolationist ideal of philosophy than Aristotle is willing to accept[12] (this compressed paraphrase follows the text of VII.2 1324a25–VII.3 1325a23):

> There is a dispute as to whether the political and action-oriented [*praktikos*] way of life is choiceworthy, or rather that which is divorced from all external things—that involving some sort of contemplation, for example, which some assert is the only philosophical way of life. The partisans of the philosophical life consider despotic rule to be utterly unjust, and nondespotic rule to be an impediment to one's own good; the partisans of the political life believe that the action-oriented [*praktikos*] and political life is the only one for a real man [*anēr*], and that private persons never perform more actions [*praxeis*] in any virtue than persons acting in public affairs [*ta koina*] and engaged in politics. The partisans of the philosophical life consider the way of life appropriate to the free person to be different from the life of the political person; the partisans of the political life argue it is impossible for one who is not at all involved in action [*praxis*] to achieve acting well [*eupragia*], which is after all the same thing as happiness [*eudaimonia*].

Callicles' challenge is easy to hear in this dialectical exchange. The partisan of politics takes an action-oriented approach to happiness, and so explicitly repeats Callicles' charge that philosophy is inactive and unmanly. The partisan of philosophy responds by insinuating that his opponent is really only interested in despotic rule. This dialectical impasse is thus the product of two extreme positions: a "hyperactivist" and excessively macho political ideal, and a "quietist" and excessively separatist philosophical ideal. Aristotle tries to pull both partisan positions back to the common ground of his activist ideal.

Aristotle responds to Callicles' challenge in the conclusion to this passage (VII.3 1325b14–23):

Since happiness is rightly regarded as the same as acting well [*eupragia*], the best way of life is an action-oriented [*praktikos*] one. Yet the action-oriented way of life need not be in relation to others, as some suppose. Nor are only those thoughts action-oriented that occur for the sake of what results from the action. Much more action-oriented are those sorts of contemplation and thought that are complete in themselves; after all, acting well [*eupraxia*] is the end, so that [those sorts of contemplation and thought] must be a kind of action [i.e., since they are clearly part of the end]. But especially [*malista de*] we say in the most defini-tive sense that people are "acting" [*prattein*] who by thoughts [that are complete in themselves] are architectonic of external actions.

This paragraph shows how Aristotle mediates the conflict between the "hyperactivist" partisan of politics and the "quietist" partisan of philosophy. He declares contemplation itself to be an action, a *praxis* in the sense favored by the real men. Not only this, but he goes on to suggest that one type of thinking is the most definitively "action-oriented" *praxis* there is: thinking that, though its own end and complete in itself, orders and produces actions other than itself.[13] The obvious example of such action-oriented yet philosophical thinking would seem to be Aristotle's own *Ethics* and *Politics*.

To say the least, this is a bold move on Aristotle's part. It is as if Aristotle simply rears up at this crucial point in the *Politics* and declares, I too am a real man! This revelation of the philosopher as the paradigm of *praxis*, if not of machismo, seems to me too sudden, too unprepared, to be effective either rhetorically or philosophically. He has done little or nothing to establish enough continuity between the aspirations of philosophy and politics to make his appropriation of *praxis* persuasive.

Aristotle is more subtle when he makes a similar move in the *Nico-machean Ethics* (X.7–8). These chapters are an extended attempt to demon-strate the superiority of the philosophical life over the political life, all from the common ground of the activist ideal of happiness. Aristotle exploits fully the vocabulary of activity we have seen him establish. He sets up a rigorously con-sistent distinction between theoretical activity as *energeia* and political action as *praxis* that is crucial for most of his points:

Theoretical activity [*energeia*] is more continuous, for we are able to be continuous in theorizing more than in any sort of action [*prattein hotioun*]. (1177a21–22)

If in fact virtuous actions [*praxeis*] in politics and war aim at nobil-ity and greatness, the actions themselves will lack leisure and aim at some other end without being choiceworthy in themselves. But the activity [*energeia*] of intellect seems to be of distinguished importance, being theoretical. (1177b16–20)

For virtuous actions [*praxeis*], many external goods or opportunities are needed, and the greater and more noble the actions are, the greater the need. But for the theorizer, there is no need for any such things, at least for the activity [*energeia*] itself. (1178b1–4)

We most of all apply the terms blessed and happy to the gods; but what sort of actions [*praxeis*] should we assign to them? . . . Everything concerned with actions is clearly petty and worthless for gods. But since everyone applies living to them, we will consequently apply activity [*energeia*], since they are not asleep like Endymion. But if action [*prattein*], let alone production, is removed from one who is said to be living, what is left except theorizing? (1178b8–10, 17–21)

In all of these passages, Aristotle uses *praxis* in the restricted way that the real man of politics would use it when he claims that philosophy is not action-oriented (*praktikos*). But then in the concluding paragraph, he makes the same move he made in the *Politics*, dressing theoretical *energeia* in the garb of political *praxis*:

Being human, [the person living a happy life of theorizing] will also need a comfortable amount of external goods. For nature is not self-sufficient for theorizing, but needs for the body to have health and food and other supports. But it must not be thought the happy person will need many and great possessions, even if it is not possible to be blissful without the external goods. For self-sufficiency and action [*praxis*] have nothing to do with excess, and it is possible to perform noble actions [*prattein*] without ruling land and sea. One can perform virtuous actions [*prattein*] with a moderate supply. This is clear to see: private people [*idiotai*] seem to perform virtuous actions [*ta epieikē prattein*] no less than powerful rulers, and even more. So it is sufficient to have just so much, since the happy way of life belongs to the person who engages in virtuous activity [*energein*].

Perhaps Solon too characterized happy people well when he said that they were moderately equipped with external goods, performed the most noble actions [*prattein*] (as he conceived of the noble), and lived temperately—for it is possible to perform the actions [*prattein*] one should with moderate possessions. And Anaxagoras seems to have understood the happy person to be neither rich nor powerful, saying that he would not be surprised

if the happy person appeared quite strange to the many, who only
notice external goods, and judge on the basis of them. So the
opinions of the wise seem to harmonize with the arguments.
(1178b33–1179a17)

If the gods have any concern for human affairs, . . . [they are likely
to befriend those who theorize on the grounds that theorizers] perform actions [*prattein*] rightly and nobly." (1179a24, 29)

The assimilation of activity [*energeia*] to action [*praxis*] here is clear.
Earlier in the discussion, Aristotle had contrasted action's greater need for external goods to activity's very modest needs (1178b1–4); now he says that "one
can perform virtuous *actions* with a moderate supply." Earlier he said that no
actions were worthy of the gods, so that they must be theorizers (1178b8–10,
17–21); now he says that theorizing is the *action* that makes people friends of
the gods.

Most striking, though, is Aristotle's subtle appropriation of Solon and
Anaxagoras. In the *Politics*, his own view of philosophy as *praxis* emerged from
a harsh dialectic between the partisans of macho politics and the partisans
of a retiring and isolationist philosophy. Here the implicit dialectic defined
by Solon and Anaxagoras is less harsh. It is best understood in the context
of Aristotle's claim that we "should not follow the proverb writers, being
concerned with human affairs since we are human, and mortal affairs since
we are mortal, but rather be like gods as much as possible" (1179b31–33).
Anaxagoras would be an enthusiastic supporter of Aristotle's exhortation to be
as godlike as possible; but he is also a model of the aloof partisan of philosophy
that the real men of the *Politics* despised.[14] Aristotle's shift to a *praxis* vocabulary
in this passage allows him to appropriate Anaxagoras's enthusiasm for contemplation while distancing Anaxagoras's apolitical aloofness. To call contemplation a *praxis* in this context is to claim for it a respectability Anaxagoras himself
does not have. Solon, though, is a model of respectability, and so is quite different not only from Anaxagoras but from the macho partisans of politics.
Aristotle clearly has him in mind as one of the "proverb writers."[15] Solon
believed that the gods were jealous of human achievement, and so cautioned
humans not to let their aspirations be too high. From Aristotle's view, this is too
much on the side of the merely human. The modest actions performed with
moderate means that Solon recommended as the path to happiness were not
anything like the "virtuous actions" that Aristotle here claims are available to
"private people" of moderate means, for Aristotle is referring to the same god-
like activity that he has just contrasted to Solon's ideal. But Aristotle wants to
appropriate the moderation of Solon's ideal while escaping its modesty.

Aristotle's move from *energeia* to *praxis*, then, has much the same point as the appropriation of *praxis* did in the *Politics*, but it is less dramatic, primarily because Solon structures the dialectic differently from Callicles. It is not as bold a move for Aristotle to claim a common ground in *praxis* with Solon as it was with Callicles. On the other hand, it is unclear how Aristotle could extend his response to Solon to the more radical appropriation of the activist ideal of happiness of a Callicles or a Jason. But my task in this chapter has merely been to convince the reader that Aristotle does make this move, and that it is central to his presentation in the *Politics* and the *Nicomachean Ethics*. Whether the common ground so claimed can support Aristotle's view of philosophy's superiority is another question.

NOTES

1. Socrates discusses courage with future military failures (*Laches*), moderation with future tyrants (*Charmides*), virtue in general with a duplicitous mercenary (*Meno*), and in the most spectacular case, the need for introspection with the most extravagant extrovert in the Greek world (*Alcibiades I*).

2. As will become obvious, my reading of Aristotle does not take his "sexism" (better: his dialectical engagement with macho conceptions of political virtue) to be a superficial and removable aspect of his overall theory. In this I am in substantial agreement with Stephen Salkever, "Women, Soldiers, and Citizens: Plato and Aristotle on the Politics of Virility," in *Essays on the Foundations of Aristotelian Political Science*, ed. Carnes Lord and David K. O'Connor (Berkeley: University of California Press, 1991), 165–90. By contrast, Julia Annas, *The Morality of Happiness* (New York: Oxford University Press, 1993), 5 n.8, purposely introduces feminine pronouns into her expositions of Aristotle and other ancient philosophers, on the grounds that "the oddity" sometimes produced "is superficial." This difference between my gender-specific reading of Aristotle's primary audience and Annas's gender-inclusive reading is another aspect of the existential specificity of my interpretation.

3. Aristotle's secondary addressee is the man attracted to an Anaxagorean or Platonist perspective, which contemns politics and makes the good something altogether beyond us. Here I focus only on how Aristotle addresses the partisan of politics. My sense of Aristotle's dual audience is very close to that of Aristide Tessitore, *Reading Aristotle's Ethics: Virtue, Rhetoric, and Political Philosophy* (Albany.: State University of New York Press, 1996). But I believe Tessitore characterizes Aristotle's primary audience too much by an attachment to virtue and not enough by ambition. In contrast to Tessitore (see subsection, "A Hyperactivist Ideal? The Challenges of Simonides and Callides"), I claim Aristotle's primary audience are much like Glaucon in the *Republic*: passionate about political leadership, and unsure how to resist the view that tyranny is the completion of their aspirations. Tessitore shares the near universal tendency to moralize Aristotle's account of the necessary starting points of political science. I will take up the question of what Aristotle in fact presupposes in his audience in the next section.

4. Bernard Williams, *Ethics and the Limits of Philosophy* (Cambridge: Harvard University Press, 1985), 39.

5. John M. Cooper, "Eudaimonism and the Appeal to Nature in the Morality of Happiness: Comments on Julia Annas, *The Morality of Happiness*," *Philosophy and Phenomenological Research* 55, no. 3 (1995): 589.

6. It is a very striking fact that *Eudemian Ethics* I.6 has such a similar account of the capacity for judgment and learning presupposed in the audience, and yet says nothing at all to parallel the moralizing reading of *Nicomachean Ethics* I.4. I believe this counts strongly in favor of my morally minimalist reading of that passage. But the point is complicated by the fact that the *Eudemian Ethics* implies quite a different *that* as its starting point. In particular, it does not use the frame of the three lives to establish its perspective. Instead, Aristotle simply introduces, quite abruptly and without the motivation provided by reflection on the

three lives, the notion that happiness must be *prakton* (I.7 1217a30–40). This is just one of a number of differences that indicate how Aristotle rewrote the *Eudemian Ethics* to make more prominent the common ground he sought out with the activist ideal of happiness.

7. The two topics taken up at the beginning of the chapter do not appear in I.5, but they otherwise fit the same pattern. Aristotle demonstrates that the activist ideal fits well with the opinion that goods of the soul are more important for happiness than goods of the body or external goods, since the *praxis* and *energeia* that the ideal identifies with happiness are psychic (I.8 1098b12–20); and with the opinion that happiness is living well and acting (*prattein*) well, since in fact the ideal identifies happiness with these two things.

8. The main point Aristotle makes about external goods is that they contribute to happiness only as the equipment for noble actions, another "activist" treatment (1099a31–b8).

9. Though Aristotle explicitly enumerates intelligence (*phronēsis*) and wisdom (*sophia*) among the things sought for in happiness, along with pleasure, virtue, and external goods, he does not say anything more in I.8 about how they are connected to the activist ideal. I take up this curious silence at the beginning of the next section.

10. Williams, 1 and 4.

11. See Xenophon's account of Jason's career in *Hellenica* VI. Xenophon's *Hiero* also appears to be alluding to Jason and his assassination in its account of the costs and benefits of being a tyrant; see especially *Hiero* IV.5.

12. A fuller account of Aristotle's audience could point out how the retiring philosopher is also a part of Aristotle's intended audience, though less prominently than the ambitious politician. Aristotle wants to energize the potential philosopher as much as he wants to moderate the potential ruler.

13. Translators have obscured this point by rendering *malista de* in lines 21–22 as if Aristotle wrote *alla*, or even *alla mēn gar*, i.e., by translating the phrase by something like "but even" rather than "but especially." (See the versions of Jowett, Barker, and Lord). I cannot see how that can be the sense of the Greek, and the thrust of the passage is that Aristotle is *insisting* on this conclusion, not conceding it.

14. For Anaxagoras as a supporter of divine contemplation, see *Eudemian Ethics* I.4 1215b7–14 and I.5 1216a11–14; for his aloofness see *Nicomachean Ethics* VI.7 1141b3–8 (where he and Thales are paired as exemplars of wisdom [*sophia*] without intelligence [*phronēsis*]).

15. See Herodotus I.32, Solon's interview with Croesus on the subject of happiness.

CHAPTER 7

THE MORAL VIRTUES
IN ARISTOTLE'S
NICOMACHEAN ETHICS

SUSAN D. COLLINS

I seek in this chapter to discuss Aristotle's account of the moral virtues in his *Nicomachean Ethics* with a view to what it teaches us about moral life. My discussion shares many of the concerns fueling renewed interest in Aristotle's political philosophy, in particular the concern to comprehend the connection of the human good to ethics and politics.[1] I diverge from the usual scholarly treatments of Aristotle's presentation of the particular virtues in the attention I give to the substance and order of this presentation. In doing this, I am guided by Aristotle's own prescriptions concerning the investigation of moral virtue. A brief discussion of the significance of these prescriptions for the study of the particular virtues serves to introduce the main subject of this article.

Aristotle clearly indicates that the investigation of moral virtue in the *Ethics* has a practical as opposed to theoretical aim: we are studying virtue not in order to know what it is in a theoretical sense but in order to become good (1103b26–29).[2] In introducing the particular virtues and vices in Book II, Aristotle suggests that it is not enough to give a general definition of virtue, to leave it at saying, for example, that virtue is a characteristic which makes the thing to which it belongs good and able to perform its function well, or that virtue is a mean with respect to two extremes (1106a21–24, 1107a2–3). For the statements that concern the particular virtues contain more truth than do general formulas precisely because actions are concerned with particulars (1107a28–32). One must therefore speak of the particulars, the particular actions, and explain in each case what it would mean to abide by the general rule of virtue that one must act in the way one ought, when one ought, and so forth (1106b18–23, 1109a26–29). A complete understanding of virtue thus necessarily includes a detailed discussion of the virtues possessed by the good person: someone who, having been well raised, has the proper habits or characteristics (*hexeis*). The account of the virtues identifies these good characteristics and their related vices, how many there are, what they pertain to, and how they stand to their respective objects (1115a4–5).

Despite Aristotle's observation concerning the importance of investigating the particular virtues, scholars rarely give their full attention to this part of the *Ethics*. One reason for this neglect is suggested by the observation of a famous Aristotelian that "this part of the *Ethics* presents a lively and often amusing account of the qualities admired or disliked by cultivated Greeks of Aristotle's time."[3] Since Aristotle suggests that the moral virtues are the habits of one who has been well raised, his account of these virtues may be thought to be bound to the conventions of his Greece. Yet a careful examination in fact reveals Aristotle's freedom in this regard. His unconventionality is most evident in the latter half of his account in which he introduces several hitherto nameless virtues and vices.[4] It is further evident in his ordering and ranking of the particular virtues, which do not simply reflect traditional Greek views.

This is not to say, however, that Aristotle takes his bearings from a principle or principles extrinsic to the perspective of moral virtue. As his own observation concerning the practical aim of our investigation indicates, he begins from the assumption that moral virtue constitutes our good. In his account of the virtues, I suggest, he seeks neither to critique explicitly nor to defend directly this assumption. In identifying, ordering, and ranking the virtues, he takes his bearings from principles implicit, if not fully developed, within the moral perspective, and traces in particular the complex interrelation of two fundamental aspects of moral virtue: its connection with nobility on the one hand and with the highest good or happiness on the other.[5] He thus seeks to explicate both the fullness and the limits of the view implicit in the moral outlook that virtue, being both noble and good, is an end in itself and choiceworthy for its own sake (1099a22–30, 1105a28–33). By attending to the details of his account of the particular virtues—their particular perfections, their relations to one another, and the kinds of activities they involve or to which they point—we come to understand more clearly the relation between moral virtue and the human good. The following discussion seeks to contribute to this understanding by sketching the movement and substance of Aristotle's presentation of the particular moral virtues.

Aristotle opens his account of the virtues with a discussion of courage, the proper disposition with respect to the passions of fear and confidence. Yet since courage pertains more to fear than to confidence (1117a29–30), Aristotle seeks first to identify the object of fear with which it is concerned, naming five possibilities: disrepute, poverty, illness, friendlessness, and death (1115a10–11). After eliminating the first four, he establishes that courage is the virtue that pertains to the fear of death, reasoning that the courageous human being is concerned with the greatest of the fearful things—"for no one is more steadfast in the face of terrors"—and that the greatest of the fearful things is death "because it is an end, and for the dead, there seems to be nothing left, neither good nor evil" (1115a25–27).

That death is so unambiguously terrible, and thus the greatest evil, is not obvious if we recall the view to which Aristotle acceded in Book I when he allowed that to some extent good and evil really exist for the dead (1100a18–19). By here taking the strictest view of the matter, however, he disallows the possibility that courageous action may be taken with the hope of a reward extrinsic to the act and for the sake of which one might risk death.[6] Yet the one who acts courageously does not do so simply without hope, for courage is a mean with respect to both fear and confidence. Aristotle establishes how courage pertains to confidence by observing that the courageous man does not appear to be concerned with death in every circumstance but only with the "noblest kinds of death," and these occur in war because war contains the greatest and noblest danger (or risk, *kindunos*) (1115a28–30). By next referring to the honors paid to courageous men by cities and monarchs (1115a31–32), Aristotle indicates the perspective from which he speaks. In war, the welfare of the entire nation is at risk, and this welfare is a good that Aristotle called "nobler and more divine" than the good of any single individual (1094b7–10).

It is in the discussion of courage that Aristotle explicitly establishes that the end (*telos*) of virtue is the noble (1115b11–13). Since courage involves an action in which an individual places his life at risk on behalf of his city or nation, it would seem to be the apparent selflessness of this action to which Aristotle intends to point when he identifies the noble as the end of virtue.[7] Thus, it would also seem that it is the noble selflessness of death in war that arouses the confidence proper to courage.

Yet to leave the matter here would be imprecise, for Aristotle suggests that the confidence proper to courage is aroused not by the prospect of selfless sacrifice but by the opportunity afforded by action in war, namely, that the courageous man may perform some noble action of his own by showing himself to be a real man (*andrizesthai*), either by demonstrating his great prowess or, if it is noble to die, then by facing death in the proper way (1115b4–6). Lacking such an opportunity, Aristotle suggests, a courageous man may well endure death with steadfastness but also with a certain despair (1115a35–b6). Thus, the one who acts out of courage—with the proper disposition toward fear and confidence—also seeks to achieve something for himself: he acts also for his own sake. On the one hand, this corrects what, if left on its own, would be the mistaken impression that courage consists in the selfless sacrifice of one's life for the greater good of the city. On the other hand, it raises the question of how Aristotle can continue to maintain that the courageous man acts for the sake of the noble while at the same time suggesting that he acts for his own sake.

Aristotle resolves this problem through recourse to the principle that virtue is an end in itself which is chosen for its own sake (1105a28–33). He observes that "the end [*telos*] of every activity is the one in accord with the characteristic" and further that "to the courageous man, courage is noble, and thus such a sort also is the end, for each thing is defined by its end" (1115b20–21). The one who acts courageously acts in accord with and for the sake of the characteristic or virtue he possesses. Accordingly, the truly courageous human being's nobility is constituted by his dedication not to something outside of himself but to his own noble virtue: although his action benefits the "nobler and more divine" good of the city or nation (as the honors paid to it testify), it also is its own end, which the courageous man seeks to perform for his own sake. This would appear to resolve at least on one level the difficulty of how his action is both noble and for his own sake. To speak more generally, the virtuous or serious (*spoudaios*) human being views the actions in accord with virtue as noble and good (1099a22–23). Indeed, it is through the activity of virtue that a good person is said to find his happiness (1098a7–18, 1099a24–31).

But to speak more explicitly than does Aristotle, and thus somewhat more crudely, there appears to be a difficulty peculiar to courage with maintaining that the same action is both noble and good. At the end of his account of courage, Aristotle quietly points to the problematic relation between courage and happiness.[8] He does this in the context of addressing what might seem to be, from the virtuous person's point of view, a somewhat lesser difficulty: that courageous action is not pleasant (1117a29–35). In the course of resolving the question of the pleasantness of courageous action, Aristotle observes that "the more a man possesses complete virtue and is happy, the more death will be painful to him, because especially to this sort of man, to live is worthwhile, and he will be robbed of the greatest goods, knowing this, and this is painful" (1117b11–13). Nevertheless, he adds, the courageous man is no less courageous for this, but probably more so, "because he chooses the noble thing in war instead of these things" (1117b13–15). The basis of the view that life is worth living especially for the virtuous human being is the claim made on behalf of virtue itself, the claim that it is our true good, such that the more we possess and live in accord with virtue, the happier our life will be. In light of what courageous action requires, however, we are left with a certain circularity: the one who acts on the basis of courage must forsake his greatest good, his virtuous and happy life, and choose instead to do the "noble thing in war"; yet it is in choosing to do this same noble deed that the courageous human being seeks his true good. In the same action in which the courageous man seeks his true good, therefore, he nobly suffers pain and death and the cessation of his good.

Thus, although it is a part of virtue's claim that virtuous action is choice-worthy for its own sake—it is good for the one who acts—in the case of courage, the same act that promises our good also requires us to endure nobly its loss. This difficulty, inherent as it is in courageous action, cannot be resolved within the sphere of courage. That it remains a difficulty is suggested by Aristotle's strange admission at the conclusion of his discussion that courageous men, who have been identified as possessing the virtue connected with war and battle, are perhaps not the best soldiers. The best soldiers, rather, are those unfortunate souls who, having no other good in life, are willing to exchange their lives "for small profit" (1117b17–20).

In part as a counterweight to the difficulty quietly raised at its conclusion, Aristotle follows his account of courage with an examination of moderation, a virtue which has as its end a clear and unambiguous good. He begins by noting that it is logical to discuss moderation after courage because both are virtues of the irrational parts (1117b23–25), namely, the passion of fear and the desire for pleasure. An intricate discussion of the kinds of pleasures that attach to human actions and passions establishes that moderation pertains specifically to the pleasures of eating, drinking, and sex, and thus to the bodily desires (1118a23–32).

Although Aristotle explains why courage and moderation should be taken up together, he does not explain why the account of moderation should follow rather than precede that of courage. A case might be made for the latter ordering based upon Aristotle's suggestion that while the fear of death is in fact quite rational and proper to a sane human being (1115b7–19), the longing for the bodily pleasures belongs to the "animal part" of our nature and is "boundless and multifold in one who is mindless" (1119b7-9). The two virtues would appear to differ, however, in the reasonableness of their ends. According to Aristotle, moderation, as the virtue pertaining to the bodily pleasures, involves the restraint of the desires with a view to our health or good condition (*euexia*) (1119a16–18). He further observes that if the desires are not restrained, they will constantly clamor for satisfaction, and if indulged, grow to such proportions as to "beat out calculation" (1119b6–7, 9–10). Just as in courage, the aim in moderation is the virtue itself, but since moderation is largely identified with good condition, it leads to our bodily well-being and preservation rather than our harm and destruction. The dedication to such well-being and preservation is hardly noble, but it is, as Aristotle indicates, sensible.

The unambiguous connection of moderation with one's good and its more tenuous connection with nobility is reflected in the fact that Aristotle refers only twice to the noble, the stated end of virtue, in the account of moderation (1119a16–18, b16; cf., e.g., courage, 1115a29–35, b11–24, 1116a10–15). In the first of these references, he says simply that the moderate person will long for the pleasures not conducing directly to good condition only if, among other things, they are not contrary to the noble. This negative formulation of the role played by a consideration of the noble indicates that the concern for nobility is not at the forefront in moderation. In the second of his references to the noble, at the end of his account, Aristotle does state that "the desiring of the moderate person ought to be in harmony with reason, for the target for both is the noble" (1119b15–16). But his very attempt to identify the aim of moderation, good condition, with the noble serves to bring out an important difficulty: whereas courage, in its connection with nobility, would appear to require a dedication to some good greater than one's own, moderation as a virtue is fully and self-consciously directed toward one's own good. Indeed, the contrast of courage and moderation raises one of the most fundamental questions for virtue: is it possible to reconcile that aspect of nobility represented most clearly by courageous action with a concern for or dedication to one's own good without having "the noble" as the aim of virtue disappear? The movement of Aristotle's discussion through the next virtues—liberality, magnificence, and magnanimity—can be seen as reflecting a response to this question from within the moral perspective.

After moderation, Aristotle takes up liberality, noting that it is "next in order" and describing it as a mean with respect to money: the liberal human being is the one best able to use his own wealth well, and this use consists in giving (1119b22–26). The liberal person not only benefits those whom he ought but, in giving of his own things, displays a noble lack of concern for his own good—in particular for his economic welfare—to such an extent that "it belongs to the liberal person to exceed so much in giving that he leaves little for himself, for not to look out for himself is the mark of a liberal human being" (1120b4–6). This noble act of giving, Aristotle also suggests, is made possible in part through the restraint with respect to pleasure provided by moderation. Lacking such restraint, a person will incline toward the more common form of the vice prodigality, giving only to those who flatter him or provide him with some other pleasure, and taking from whom and from where he ought not (1121a30–b10). Of the three virtues Aristotle has discussed—courage, moderation, and liberality—moderation has no specific action or activity as its end (cf. 1119b8–12). Yet as the virtue that involves the restraint of the bodily pleasures, and thus which makes liberality possible, moderation now comes to light as instrumental to another, higher end, namely, noble action.

In the discussion of liberality, Aristotle begins again to emphasize the connection of virtue with nobility or the noble (cf. 1120a13–31, 1120b1–4, 1121a1, 1121b4, 10). It is this connection of liberal action and nobility that appears to inform his decision to discuss liberality after moderation instead of another virtue connected with money. In making his initial point that liberality pertains to money, Aristotle departs from his usual procedure by noting also what liberality does not pertain to: "what occurs in war, what a moderate person is concerned with, and what is involved in making judgments" (1119b23–25). He thus distinguishes liberality not only from the two preceding virtues but also from justice.[9] As Aristotle will subsequently make clear, justice too is concerned with money (1130b1–2). In his account of liberality, he specifically contrasts liberality with justice, observing that "those who give are called liberal whereas those who refrain from taking are praised less with a view to liberality and more with a view to justice" (1120a18–20). In this connection, Aristotle also observes that "it belongs more to virtue to act well than to fare well, and to do noble deeds than not to do shameful ones," and he classifies giving, as opposed to taking, with acting well and doing noble deeds (1120a11–15). Thus, the actions belonging to liberality are more a part of virtue than are those connected with justice, if "the actions in accord with virtue are noble ones and for the sake of the noble" (1120a23–24). Since central to justice are judgments about what is fair or equal, what share of the good is due to different parties, and not, or less obviously, noble action, the movement to liberality instead of to justice allows Aristotle to give the fullest possible expression to moral virtue's connection with noble deeds.

The nobility of liberal action, like that of courageous action, involves incurring the loss of a good, in this case, money (1119b26–27). As the discussions of courage and liberality both indicate, the virtuous person will choose to do a noble deed even though this deed entails a painful loss. The loss suffered

by the liberal man, however, is neither fatal nor, it turns out, of great significance to him, since it is not characteristic of a liberal person to honor money.
He is so easygoing in this respect as to be vulnerable to and even unconcerned
about suffering injustice, and in making expenditures, he is pained more if he
fails to buy something fitting than if he loses money on something useless
(1121a4–7). While it is true that in order to have the means to perform his
noble action, the liberal man needs money, and so cannot afford to be too care-
less with his "household goods," money is still in his view a means and not a
good to be sought for its own sake: unlike "the many," Aristotle tells us, liberal
people are not "lovers of money" (1121b12–16). Stinginess (*aneleutheria*, lit.
"illiberality"), the vice connected with this particular "greediness for gain," is in
fact the extreme most opposed to liberality, though its pervasiveness would
appear to be behind Aristotle's persistent condemnations of it and to make all
the more remarkable the liberal person's choice to suffer the loss entailed by his
action (1121a19–30, 1121b12–16, 1122a13–16). It is with a third and final
condemnation of stinginess that Aristotle concludes the discussion of liberality
and turns somewhat tentatively to the discussion of magnificence.

Magnificence is a virtue also pertaining to money but only to expenditures
and specifically to making a "fitting expenditure on a great scale" (1122a18–24).
Since, as Aristotle noted in his account of liberality, justice also pertains to
money (1119b19–20, 1121a4–5), he might logically have examined justice
next. Yet if we take Aristotle's definition of magnificence as our guide—its connection to expenditure, to what is fitting, and to greatness—it becomes clear
that the difference between liberality and magnificence is essentially a matter of
scale (cf. 1122b10–14, 1125b1–5).

Because magnificence pertains to expenditures on a great scale, it is generally out of the reach of those who do not possess the requisite resources: it is
possible for a man of limited means to be liberal but not magnificent
(1122b26–29). Both the liberal and the magnificent man, however, act for the
sake of the noble, action that "is common to the virtues" (1122b6–7). Yet the
magnificent man surpasses the liberal man not simply with respect to expenditure but also in his aim: the magnificent man seeks to produce a great and
noble work (or product, *ergon*), and "at the *same* expense [as might even be
within the reach of the liberal man], the magnificent man will produce a more
magnificent work" (1122b13–14; my emphasis).[10] In one respect, magnificence is properly understood to be the virtue of the work itself (1122b18),[11]
and in his effort to achieve the greatest and noblest work, which will produce
wonder (or admiration, *thaumastē*), the magnificent man, free from the love of
money Aristotle so vigorously condemned, spares no expense and feels no

twinge of pain over the cost (1122b7–8, cf. 1123a27–31). He is especially concerned to do what is fitting with regard to the "greatest and most honored" expenditures: public expenditures, including most notably "those having to do with the gods (such as votive offerings, buildings, and sacrifices) and the entire divine realm" (1122b19–23).

Coming as it does in the discussion of magnificence, this sole explicit statement in the account of the virtues concerning the virtuous person's attitude toward the gods and the divine alerts us to the omission of piety from the list of the virtues (cf. 1123b18–20). Moreover, Aristotle chooses this context to remind us that the magnificent man does what is fitting not only to the work or object of his expenditure but also to himself, that is, to his own great wealth, reputation or standing, and nobility (1122a25, 1122b23–25). In other words, his magnificent expenditures—his productions—must be understood as expressions or reflections of his own greatness (cf. 1168a6–9). Although this suggestion and the omission of piety do not simply decide the status of the virtuous man as a believer, they do indicate something about the character of his self-understanding and action: his aspiration to do what is fitting to the gods and the divine is commingled with his sense of his own greatness. Even as Aristotle notes in his discussion of private expenditures that "the same thing is not appropriate to gods as to human beings, nor to a shrine as to a tomb," he observes that the magnificent man prefers to adorn his home especially with works that will endure, "for these are noblest" (1123a6–10). In the permanence of these works, the magnificent man seeks for himself and as fitting to himself a permanence akin to, if not as resplendent as, the immortality of the gods.[12]

Aristotle's transition to his account of the next virtue, magnanimity, is seamless. There is no obvious conclusion to the discussion of magnificence because magnanimity, like magnificence, is concerned with great things (cf. 1123a31–35 with 1117b20–22, 1119b18, and 1122a16–17). Aristotle describes the magnanimous man (lit. "great-souled," *megalopsuchos*) as one who both is worthy of great things and thinks himself worthy of them (1123b1–2). The magnanimous man's self-regard arises from the fact that he possesses all the virtues and each to the greatest degree (1123b30–1124a2). Because of his great virtue, he rightly regards himself as worthy of the external good considered to be the greatest, that "which we pay to the gods, for which eminent persons aim, and which is the prize for the noblest accomplishments" (1123b18–20). This good is honor.

Magnanimity requires both that the magnanimous person possess "greatness in each virtue" and that he have the correct regard for his virtue; the honor he pays to himself is simply the natural complement of the magnificent man's attitude toward his works. Yet even though the magnanimous man considers honor to be his just due, the regard he has for his own virtue has a paradoxical effect: it makes him ambivalent toward this greatest of external goods. As a result of the very self-awareness on the basis of which he considers himself worthy, the magnanimous man disdains all external goods, and even honor, as paltry (1124a5–20). This is because nothing is commensurate in his eyes with perfect virtue (1124a8–9), and virtue is the only end to which he is devoted. The perspective of the magnanimous man thus represents the explicit fulfillment of a most fundamental principle of virtue: that it be chosen as an end in itself. Magnanimity accordingly constitutes the peak of an ascent of the virtues from courage. Aristotle calls it the "crown" (or "ornament," *kosmos*) of the virtues, an adornment of the virtues by which they are "magnified" (1124a1–2).

Since the magnanimous man acts only in a manner appropriate to his virtue, he can therefore be expected to reflect his greatness in all his attitudes and actions. For example, he accepts only great honors or those bestowed by serious men, he is equanimous in both good and bad fortune, he seeks to benefit others but disdains requesting or receiving aid as a sign of inferiority, and he never descends to partaking in idle gossip or to being concerned with petty evils or revenges (1124a4–7, 12–16, b9–10, 1125a2–6). In the course of enumerating the magnanimous man's impressive qualities, Aristotle notes also that he will undertake few actions, and then only great actions and risks since these alone are appropriate to his great virtue. Aristotle further observes, however, that "whenever he takes risks, he is unsparing of his life, on the grounds that living is not at all worthwhile" (1124b8–9).[13] The dedication to virtue which issues in the magnanimous man's contempt or disdain for external goods—the same contempt that gives him his admirable and dignified equanimity in the face of good and bad fortune—appears also to influence his view of life itself. Just as external goods pale in comparison to virtue, so even life itself takes on a certain insignificance—Aristotle says three times of the magnanimous man that "nothing is great" to him (1123b32, 1125a3, 15).[14]

By recalling one of Aristotle's most poignant observations concerning the courageous man, we see that a certain transformation has been involved in the movement from courage to magnanimity: whereas the courageous man will lay down his life for the sake of the noble but feels pain in doing so, realizing that he is forsaking his greatest goods, the magnanimous man, because he cares only for virtue and identifies it fully with his own good, apparently feels no such pain. The progression from courage to magnanimity thus refines our understanding of nobility: it consists not in a willingness to forego one's own good in favor of the noble which is not one's good, nor simply in "fittingness," but in "greatness." At the peak of this progression, magnanimity, we have arrived at the most complete and explicit identification of virtue as that end which is both noble and good, in other words, as the highest or most final end.

Yet a difficulty threatens to obtrude. In Book I Aristotle insisted that although virtue is an end in itself, it is also subordinate to the end that is truly most final for human beings: happiness (1097b1–5). Book I suggested that rigorous attention to the question of the highest good entails an express admission of the subordination of virtue to happiness. This admission, however, is in some tension with the principle that virtue must have itself as an end, and these two ends, and their apparent ranking, may well qualify even a serious human being's dedication to virtue. For this reason, Aristotle deflects attention from the subordination of virtue to happiness when he moves to the account of moral virtue: whereas in Book I, Aristotle maintained that "the prize and end of virtue" is happiness, in his account of courage, he identifies the end of virtue as the noble and, in the discussion of magnanimity, honor as the prize of virtue (1099b9–18, 1115b11–13, 1123b35).

Nevertheless, the problem of the relation between virtue and happiness is present even at the peak of the virtues. While a return to Book I shines the clearest light on the inadequacy of the magnanimous man's identification of virtue and happiness, this inadequacy is revealed also in small contradictions in his overall view. Despite the magnanimous man's apparently singular dedication to virtue, he wishes that it be rewarded with a good other than itself, even an inferior good such as he thinks honor to be. Furthermore, although in his dedication to virtue he seeks to be fully self-sufficient and impervious to the reverses of fortunes with which external goods are necessarily connected, he is in fact quite dependent on fortune: his magnanimity depends upon a certain wealth, position, and good birth, and the exercise of his great virtue requires the opportunity for great actions (1125a11–12, 1124a12–16). Indeed, as a result of his wish to undertake only great and renowned actions, he is largely idle (1124b24–26), which has implications for his happiness since happiness requires the activity of virtue (1098b31– 1099a3). Finally, the magnanimous man's concern for happiness or the good life in a broad sense is evidenced by his willingness to accommodate a friend (1124b31–1125a1); he thus seeks friends, who, Aristotle observes in Book IX, are indispensable to our happiness and are thought to be our greatest external good (1155a3–6, 1169b8–10).

By here pressing the question of happiness, we perhaps bring to the account of the virtues an indelicate explicitness with regard to the problematic relation between virtue and happiness, as Aristotle's own efforts to mute the question suggest. Our indelicacy, however, alerts us to an important feature of the discussion to follow: in the movement away from the peak of magnanimity, Aristotle will emphasize less what he identified in the account of liberality as the core of virtue—doing noble deeds—and more those qualities that contribute to the good life broadly speaking. Most significantly, he emphasizes virtues that in one way or another contribute to good relations in our associations with others. This movement culminates in Aristotle's account of the quintessentially political virtue, justice, which constitutes "the use of all the virtues with a view to another" (1129b25–1130a4).

In thus identifying a second complete virtue, Aristotle invites the comparison between justice and magnanimity. It is in fact less indelicate and closer to the surface of Aristotle's discussion to note that magnanimity sometimes falls short when it comes to this other complete virtue. For although magnanimity is said to constitute the possession of all the virtues and each to the greatest degree, the magnanimous man is deficient from the point of view of justice: he does not like to recall his debts (1124b12–15), he overlooks evils (1125a3–5), and he does not act out of a sense of justice but out of a sense of his superiority (1124b9–23). The first step in the correction of the defects inherent in magnanimity, in light of the requirements of justice, is taken in Aristotle's account of ambition.

Described first as the virtue that pertains to lesser honors, ambition (*philotimia*, lit. love of honor) represents in one sense a clear descent from the grand heights of magnanimity. Given the small imperfections in this crown of the virtues, however, the discussion of ambition also represents an advance, which points in particular to the need for a standard or mean by which the proper measure of the love of honor itself can be established (1125b6–8). If we take our bearings from the perspective of the magnanimous man, the question of this standard has been rendered moot inasmuch as he rejects honor as an end to be loved or pursued for its own sake: from this point of view, the love of honor so characteristic of the few who favor the political life is not properly classified as a virtue (1095b22–23). Yet, as Aristotle now insists, we generally praise the one who loves honor "more than the many do" and call him "manly and a lover of the noble" (1125b11–17). Moreover, honor is indeed an object of longing and a good for which human beings vie, as evidenced by the opinion of those who strive after honor, including even the magnanimous man himself (1123b22–24). But while the account of ambition points to the need for a standard by which the competition for this good can be mediated, Aristotle concludes the discussion without establishing any standard, saying only that the mean is nameless and that consequently, "the extremes appear to dispute for it as for something unclaimed" (1125b17–18).

In his discussion of justice, Aristotle will identify honor as one of the common goods, which as such must be apportioned in accord with distributive justice. He will further observe that while distributive justice is established in accord with a principle everyone agrees with—to each in accord with his merit—there is dispute about what constitutes merit: democrats say it is freedom; oligarchs, wealth; others, noble birth; and aristocrats, virtue (1131a24–29). The magnanimous man's claim for honor is thus but one among others and must accordingly establish its worthiness not only to the satisfaction of his own albeit high point of view but also against these other claims (cf. *Politics* 1281a11ff). Although the discussion of ambition may represent a descent from the high perspective of the magnanimous man, then, this is a movement that takes account of the political character of human existence, in light of which Aristotle points to a new peak in justice, the virtue that attends to the demand that each individual be assigned his just share of the good.

He begins his ascent to this new peak by turning next to a discussion of the characteristic pertaining to anger.[15] Strictly speaking, the person who has the correct disposition with regard to anger is one who becomes angry "in the circumstances and at whom one ought, and further in the manner, when, and for as much time as one ought" (1125b31–32).[16] Acknowledging that, like ambition, this virtue has no name, Aristotle chooses to call it "gentleness," a name which actually suggests the virtue's also nameless deficiency and in doing so proves to be quite apt. For the one who is correctly disposed with respect to anger in fact tends toward its deficiency or lack: the gentle person is distinguished as one who "wishes to be calm and to be led not by passion but as reason would command," and is consequently more disposed to forgive than to be moved by the more common desire for revenge and punishment (1125b33–1126a4, 1126a30). Indeed, this disposition toward forgiveness sometimes makes the gentle person an object of blame rather than praise: he is thought to be a fool and slavish, for he appears to endure foul abuse and to overlook his own affairs (1126a4–8). In certain circumstances, not gentleness but harshness, the extreme of anger identified as most opposed to the mean (1126a26–31), is praised: harsh human beings are sometimes praised as manly on the grounds that they are able to rule (1126a36–b2).

In the account of gentleness, we begin to see a divergence of ends within moral virtue itself, a divergence indicated by the fact that gentleness is not always praised. The contrast between the praise sometimes conferred upon harshness and the blame upon gentleness evidences the tension between one of necessities of ruling, punishment or punitive justice, and the forgiveness toward which reason by itself tends. Aristotle's account of gentleness thus suggests that moral virtue itself points to at least two different ends: on the one hand, rule, and on the other hand, away from rule toward something other than political activity. This latter possibility is indicated by Aristotle's observation that gentleness contributes to good relations among friends and associates (1126a25–26, 1126a31). It is explored in the subsequent account of three virtues that pertain in various ways to our associations and the speeches and deeds of our common relations: truthfulness, wittiness, and a virtue Aristotle earlier called friendship (1108a26–28).

In the original list of the virtues, Aristotle had listed friendship after truthfulness and wittiness, and had unqualifiedly identified it as friendship, implying that he meant nothing less than the full scope of associations he discusses in Books VIII and IX of the *Ethics* (1108a26–30). He now chooses to discuss this virtue first, saying, moreover, that it is nameless but resembles friendship because the person who is disposed in accord with the mean is like the one we call an "equitable friend" (1126b19–21). This person is friendly without being a friend because he does not act out of passion or love for those with whom he is associating (1126b22–25). Rather, his friendliness results from his disposition with respect to the pleasures and pains connected with our associations: he is generally complaisant and approving insofar as he does not bring discredit or harm upon himself or his associates; when it is necessary, however, he will express his disapproval even though to do so may cause pain (1126b27–33). His company is clearly preferable to that of his fellows at the extremes: the obsequious man, who praises everything in order to please and opposes nothing, never wishing to pain anyone, and the quarrelsome one, who peevishly opposes everything, never caring whom he pains (1126b11–17).

Aristotle emphasizes that since the virtue and its associated vices are a matter of disposition, the action proceeding from them does not arise out of a specific motive (1126b23–25, 1127a6–10). In his conclusion, he uses this distinction to differentiate the obsequious person from the flatterer, saying that whereas the former seeks to please for no particular reason, the latter does so with a view to his own monetary gain. This is the first time in his account of the virtues that Aristotle has explicitly differentiated among characteristics on the basis of the particular end they serve. That vices or blameworthy traits can be identified in relation to a specific end is not without significance for the question of whether the virtues are means, a question Aristotle addresses directly in his account of the next virtue, truthfulness.

Aristotle begins the account of this next virtue by speaking first of one of its extremes, boastfulness, and by acknowledging that the virtue itself is nameless

(1127a14–15). Both in his present discussion and in Book II, Aristotle offers a kind of apology for taking up largely nameless characteristics. He maintains that one of the reasons for discussing them is to come to see more fully and to trust that the virtues are means, and suggests that to achieve this we must see that in each case, the mean is praiseworthy, and the extremes, neither praiseworthy nor correct but blameworthy (1108a14–16, 1127a14–17). Given Aristotle's general definition of virtue as a mean, it is surprising that this is suddenly in doubt (1106b14–1107a7, 1109a20–26). Nonetheless, truthfulness and its extremes prove to be complicated in this respect.

Aristotle restricts the sphere to which truthfulness and its associated vices pertain to certain speeches and deeds, specifically those that represent a claim concerning what one is or possesses. The truthful person is a straightforward "plain-dealer,"[17] who claims to be nothing more or less than he is. He is flanked on the one extreme by the boaster, who pretends to be greater than he is, and on the other by the person who pretends to be less than he is, and whom Aristotle chooses to call ironic (1127a19–26). Because both extremes involve lying or dissembling, they prove blameworthy when held up against the noble dedication to truthfulness (1127a30–31). Yet their blameworthiness becomes less apparent when Aristotle proceeds to observe that those who boast for the sake of monetary gain—who pretend, for example, to be a prophet, a wise man, or a doctor with a view to their own profit (1127b17–20)—are worse than those who boast because they desire a good reputation or honor (1127b9–13). Thus, although each type of boaster manifests the same vice, blameworthiness is assessed largely on the basis of the particular end each chooses; it is this choice, Aristotle now says, that makes each a boaster (1127b14–15).

Just as the blameworthiness of boasting proves to be more complicated than we might expect, so too does the blameworthiness of the other extreme: irony. Although he insistently maintains that the truthful person acts and speaks truthfully because "this is the sort he is" (1127a27–28, b1–3), Aristotle's hierarchy of boasters suggests that this person's virtue is also connected with a preference for truth over money or repute. In a word, he is what Aristotle calls a "lover of truth" (*philalēthēs*), and his love of truth is appropriate to his virtue since falsehood is wretched and blameworthy, and truth, noble and praiseworthy (1127b3–4, a27–30). Yet Aristotle makes clear that in certain circumstances, truthfulness, the mean, is not praiseworthy: even the truthful person sometimes prefers irony as the more graceful manner of speech (1127b6–9, 22–24, 29–31). Those who employ irony, Aristotle notes, appear refined in character, for they seem to speak not with a view to gain but in order to avoid bombast. Offering a rare example of one who possesses a specific characteristic, Aristotle maintains that "this is what Socrates used to do" (1127b22–26).

To present Socrates as the exemplar of irony, however, does not illustrate the immediate point. Rather, it blurs the line between gentlemanly and Socratic or philosophic virtue, and rescues from its usual reproach the "dissembling" for which Socrates was notorious. By describing the truthful person as a lover of truth, Aristotle has already allied him with the "lover of wisdom" whom he resembles. But though a lover of truth, the gentleman is not yet a philosopher: the difference between the two can be seen precisely in the difference between gentlemanly and Socratic irony. Whereas a gentleman sometimes speaks ironically because it is graceful or noble to do so, Socrates' irony appears to have been a part of a quest for wisdom, a quest often in tension with conventional convictions and authorities. The essential difference between a gentleman and a philosopher can be expressed also as a distinction between the ends to which each is dedicated and for the sake of which each acts: moral virtue, on the one hand, and wisdom, on the other (cf. 1095b17–19). The implication of these different ends for virtue sheds light on Aristotle's willingness in this latter half of his account to raise the question of whether the virtues are means, as well as on his subsequent effort to blur the line between gentlemanly and philosophic virtue.

After praising irony for a second time and reproaching by comparison the other extreme, boasting, Aristotle concludes the account of truthfulness and turns to that of wittiness. Wittiness was classified earlier as pertaining to pleasure in play (1108a23–24). Broadening this classification, Aristotle now recasts wittiness as pertaining to rest, one part of life, and specifically to passing the time (*diagōgē*) in play, a part of rest (1127b33–1128a1).[18] Rest and play, he observes, are "necessary in life" (1128b3–4). He will later make clear that we play for the sake of further activity, noting on the authority of Anacharsis that "we do not play for its own sake but in order to be serious" (1176b33–1177a1). The serious activity of life to which play is ancillary is, for the gentleman, clearly political activity, and the discussion of wittiness thus provides a fitting prelude to that of the next virtue, justice (1177b5). Yet the discussion of wittiness points also in another direction, toward a possibility Aristotle will fully consider only in Book X.

With respect to play also there is a graceful way of conducting oneself, and Aristotle praises gentlemanly wit as a mean between the crude jesting of buffoons, who always strive after a laugh and spare no one, not even themselves, from pain or embarrassment, and the dour humorlessness of boors, who will not abide any kind of fun, either of their own or of others' making. Those who "play gracefully" are both nimble-witted and tactful; as they engage in their amusements, they do not say or listen to anything that would cause another distress or be inappropriate for a liberal and equitable human being (1128a16–19). Such refinement of humor is the basis upon which Aristotle asserts the superiority of the amusements of free and educated human beings over the crude entertainments of the slavish and uneducated, a comparison which also proves the superiority of the New Comedy to the Old, since the former relies upon graceful innuendo (*huponoia*, lit. "understatement") and the latter upon crude language and coarse jokes (1128a19–25). Nevertheless, however graceful gentlemanly wit and the New Comedy may be, they must also be judged. In the midst of his praise of wittiness, Aristotle issues a warning: observing that a joke is a form of slander, he suggests that just as lawgivers forbid slandering certain things, perhaps they need also to prohibit joking about some things (1128a29–31). The need for such legal prohibition is grounded in the power of comedy to effect a certain kind of liberation, for to mock or to laugh at something, and thus to slander it, is to liberate oneself from it. It is precisely this power that prompts Aristotle to make the prohibition of the young from lampoons and comedic spectacles a provision of his best regime (*Politics*, 1336b27–35).

It is curious that Aristotle should choose to distinguish wittiness as the virtue pertaining to rest, especially since he never refers to it in his discussion of rest and leisure in the *Politics* and mentions comedy only to comment on its deleterious effect upon the young. But if laughter and comedy have the liberating power he suggests, then the gentleman, in the very operation of his wit, possesses the capacity to achieve a certain distance and even liberation from law and the regime to which, by his own virtue, he is otherwise dedicated. Indeed, wittiness may rightly be cast as the gentlemanly version of Socratic irony, since both appear to follow a law of their own but employ a kind of understatement out of deference to convention and the authority of the lawgiver. The gentleman's graceful play thus shows itself if not to be ancillary to philosophy then to share in some of the character of the activity or "pastime" that in Book X Aristotle will praise as best (1177a18–1179a32). It is accordingly fitting that Aristotle should choose to single out wittiness as the virtue pertaining to pastime in play and should use the discussion of this apparently minor virtue to praise the virtuous person as being "like a law unto himself" (1128a31–32).

But if, by virtue of its quasi-independence from convention and the regime, the wittiness of the gentleman is the closest he comes to philosophic enlightenment, this is to say that he does not fully achieve it: there are still things he will never say, and some he will not abide even hearing (1128a33–b1). Thus, Aristotle includes tact as a part of the mean because it belongs to the gentleman to heed convention and the lawgiver's prohibitions (1128a16–19), a suggestion Aristotle reiterates in the brief account of the passion of shame preceding the discussion of justice. Shame is not strictly speaking a virtue because the decent (or equitable, *epieikēs*) person will not do shameful things, and whether these things are shameful in truth or only by opinion does not matter (1128b21–24). To put this suggestion in its best light: while the gentleman is "like a law unto himself," he is never lawless, which is appropriate to his virtue, and especially to his justice.

Having completed his consideration of the three virtues that pertain to our associations and the speeches and deeds of our common relations, Aristotle turns finally to his lengthy discussion of justice. We can gain some sense of the distance we have traveled from the one peak of magnanimity to this other complete virtue by briefly contrasting magnanimity with the three virtues that precede justice. Whereas the magnanimous man's sense of his own superiority causes him to treat his equals with a certain haughtiness and his inferiors with ironic condescension, and to be unwilling to accommodate another except a friend (1124a20, b5–6, 26–31), the friendly human being seeks to make our "living together" pleasant. He is thus less solitary and more sociable than the magnanimous man, and his nobility consists less in greatness and pride than in his conformity with a mean between two obviously unpleasant extremes. Whereas the magnanimous man speaks truthfully or frankly because he disdains the timidity he associates with dissembling (1124b24–31), the truthful person directly associates truth with nobility, and prizes truthfulness not as an extension of magnanimity but as a praiseworthy characteristic in its own right. Finally, the quickness and playfulness for which Aristotle praises the one who possesses a refined wit stand in contrast to the deliberateness and seriousness typical of the actions and speech of the magnanimous man (1125a12–16). Although the particular virtues are never simply incompatible with each other, as Aristotle's insistence that the virtues are all parts of a whole suggests, the status of each within that constellation reflects different aspects of moral virtue. That moral virtue has different aspects is captured in a broad sense by the fact that there are two complete virtues: magnanimity, or virtue in relation to oneself, and justice, or virtue in relation to another.

But for Aristotle's efforts, the grandeur of magnanimity and the nobility or brilliance of other virtues such as courage and magnificence might cause us to overlook the otherwise nameless and apparently minor virtues pertaining to the speeches and deeds of our common relations. The consideration of these very characteristics, however, has proven to be an integral part of our investigation of the good life in a complete sense.[19] On the level of the moral virtues, this investigation culminates in the discussion of justice, the comprehensive virtue which looks to the happiness of the community as a whole. By changing the order of the three virtues pertaining to social relations and consequently omitting friendship from our present consideration, however, Aristotle suggests that an account of our living together or of our associations also demands the fuller treatment provided in Books VIII and IX of the *Ethics*.[20] If, as is thought, friends are the greatest external good and indispensable to our happiness, the discussion of moral virtue cannot be the last word on the question of the best life. Moreover, Aristotle indicated in his account of wittiness, and will later make explicit, that a full consideration of the best life cannot be completed within the limits of the moral perspective: there exists an alternative that does not simply share that perspective.

As Aristotle moves to his discussion of the final moral virtue, however, he does so with the understanding that the political community, and consequently justice, are of signal importance for human beings: the political community adjudicates those goods we desire and must share in common; it has the authority for the corrective and punitive actions necessary to rule; and it is the original educator. While acknowledging its singular importance, we may nevertheless confine the examination of Aristotle's lengthy discussion of justice to determining how justice is a characteristic like the other virtues. In doing so, we start from the foundation Aristotle uses to establish an "outline" for what will proceed: that "everyone means by justice the sort of characteristic on the basis of which people are made fit to do just things, act justly, and wish just things" (1129a6–9).

In order to proceed, Aristotle must first clarify the different meanings of justice, since, as he has already acknowledged in Book II, we speak of justice in more than one sense (1108b7–8). We mean by an unjust man, Aristotle observes, both one who is a lawbreaker and one who is unfair (lit. "unequal," *anisos*) and grasping (or takes more than his share, *pleonektēs*) (1129a31–33). Since we regard one who breaks the law as unjust, he argues, "it is clear that all the lawful things are somehow just" and thus, in one sense, we mean by justice the pronouncements of the law (1129b11–12).[21] Further, the law is comprehensive, and, having as its aim the establishment and preservation of the happiness of the political community, it commands all the virtues and prohibits every wickedness (1129b14–24). This justice is, therefore, "complete virtue," though not simply or unqualifiedly. Because the acts of virtue and abstention from vice commanded by the law are commanded with a view to our relations with others, justice is complete in constituting the use of all the virtues with a view to another (1129b19–27). This is why, Aristotle observes, the saying of Bias that "ruling will show the man" is thought to be apt, for directedness toward another and especially toward the community is intrinsic to ruling (1130a1–2).

Yet complete justice is not what we seek to investigate but justice as a particular virtue within the whole of justice. A "sign" such a characteristic exists is that while an apparently unjust action may issue from a wickedness other than injustice—a man may commit adultery, for example, as the result of desire—we call such an action unjust only if it is performed for the sake of gain—another man, for example, may commit adultery for the sake of profit (1130a24–28). When a man acts unjustly with a view to his own profit, we call him grasping or unfair, for he seeks to acquire more of those goods human beings pray for and pursue (1129b1–4). According to Aristotle, then, partial justice is a characteristic pertaining to the love of gain or profit concerning specifically honor, money, and safety (1130a32–b3).

Having insisted that a particular justice exists which is a part of the whole of justice, though "both have their power in our relations with one another" (1130b1–2), Aristotle turns to identifying its mean. Partial justice has two forms—distributive and commutative—each of which pertains to certain terms and parties, and constitutes the mean or proportion that correctly fixes the relations among them. Distributive justice pertains to the distribution of the common goods of the regime, for example, honor and money, among parties on the basis of merit. Commutative justice seeks the rectification of a loss incurred in a voluntary or involuntary transaction or exchange, and involves the restoration of the mean between two parties considered as equals (1130b30–1131a9).

In concluding his discussion of partial justice, however, Aristotle describes just action itself as a mean between suffering injustice, or receiving less than one's share, and doing injustice, or taking more than one's share (1133b30–31). It is not necessary to press Aristotle's description of this mean too hard to begin to see that it raises a difficulty for his original claim that there is a particular justice which is a characteristic like the other virtues. For whereas the other virtues, as means with respect to an excess and a deficiency, are also then associated with two vices, the same cannot be said of justice: receiving less than one's share or suffering injustice, the one extreme, is hardly a vice.[22] Indeed, Aristotle's attempt to distinguish justice as a particular characteristic or virtue is problematic from the beginning. For he has already identified a specific virtue pertaining to each of the three goods he explicitly connects with partial justice: honor, money, and safety. As magnanimity, liberality, and courage respectively constitute the particular perfection and mean pertaining to these goods, it is not clear how justice adds to this perfection or constitutes a separable characteristic with respect to gain.[23] Despite Aristotle's efforts to portray justice as a characteristic like the other moral virtues, then, it emerges more clearly as a disposition to act in accord with the mean established by law or, to use Aristotle's terms, "to choose the just share" over "the *choiceworthy*" (1134a1–6; my emphasis). Unlike the other virtues, therefore, its moral status is intrinsically bound up with obedience to law.

The difficulties attendant in defining justice as a characteristic and its clearer connection with obedience to law point to the problem inherent in justice: the tension between choosing the just share or obeying the law and the concern for one's own good or what is choiceworthy. It is this difficulty that most distinguishes justice from the other virtues. For as characteristics, the other virtues are considered good not because they pertain to actions directed toward the good of another but because they are good for the person who possesses them. Even courage, the virtue that entails risking one's virtuous and happy life and thus one's greatest good, involves a nobility the courageous man cherishes as good. By comparison, justice is the most problematic of the virtues precisely because, as Aristotle acknowledges, "justice, alone of the virtues, is thought to be the good of another" (1130a3–4).

Yet in contrast to the famous attack on justice by Thrasymachus in the *Republic*, an attack that blames justice because it is the good of another, Aristotle's treatment of this difficulty is the picture of discretion. For in addition to insisting that justice is a characteristic like the other virtues, he emphasizes that because justice is directed toward the good of another, it is "often thought to be the greatest of the virtues, and more wonderful than the evening or morning star" (1129b27–29). Furthermore, Aristotle maintains that "the best man is not the one who uses virtue with a view to himself but the one who does so with a view to another," and reiterates that justice is hard (1130a7–8). The aspect of justice that makes it hard is essential to why we admire it; while Aristotle acknowledges that justice is the good of another, he also suggests that this is a part of its greatness. Moreover, speaking in accord with the proverb, Aristotle asserts that "in justice, every virtue is summed up in one" (1129b29–30). Since justice in this complete sense finds its expression in law, our deference to law is not simply an acknowledgment of our citizenship in the community but also an expression of our desire to become good. In the best case, the law aims to educate citizens in order that they may live the best life, which, from the perspective of moral virtue, consists in noble and good actions on behalf of the city and friends. In seeking to make us virtuous, therefore, the law seeks also to make us happy. It is in this spirit that, early in his account of justice, Aristotle admonishes us not to pray for and pursue the "goods of fortune" but to become such that these goods will be good for us (1129b1–6). He thus also concludes that doing injustice is a greater evil than suffering it since the former involves complete vice (1138a31–35).

With the discussion of justice, we come to the end of Aristotle's account of the moral virtues. Especially in the latter half of this account, Aristotle has indicated that there is more to be said on the question to which our inquiry has been directed: how to become good. In the discussion of justice itself, he suggests that the question remains open, yet forestalls discussion of it, saying:

> That which is productive of the whole of virtue are the laws that have been established with a view to the education of a good citizen, but as for the education of the individual, in accord with which he is a good man simply, whether this is a part of the political art or of another, must be determined later. For perhaps this is not the same thing for a good man and for every citizen. (1130b25–29)

As Aristotle's postponement of the discussion of this possibility suggests, the question of whether moral virtue fully constitutes our good is not properly at the forefront of our present study.[24] Indeed, to investigate the virtues with a view to knowing what virtue is in the most radical sense—to press from the start, in other words, the question of their rationality—is to begin from an already sophisticated position which is bound to obscure the complex goodness of the virtues. More precisely, such sophistication will obscure the important fact that the goodness and choiceworthiness of moral virtue is bound up in a complicated way with what Aristotle identifies as its end: the noble.[25]

By tracing out the principles implicit in moral virtue, and especially its connection with nobility, and by adhering to the rule that we will better know what good action is once we study the particular virtues, Aristotle allows moral virtue to come into its own. He thus draws a portrait of the moral life that captures how the particular virtues perfect human action, speech, and relations by gracing them with nobility, decorum, greatness, gentleness, wit, and justice. If even in his discussion of justice, the culmination of his investigation of the virtues, Aristotle points to the possibility that moral virtue may not fully constitute our good, the awareness of this possibility did not cause him, nor must it cause us, to be blind to the richness and goodness of the life in which moral virtue finds its activity. On the contrary, the study of his account of the virtues allows us to reflect upon the impressiveness and choiceworthiness of the moral life and its superiority to less impressive and less choiceworthy alternatives. And while moral virtue may not constitute the activity of soul Aristotle himself holds to be the highest and best, he suggests nonetheless that it points in the direction of this activity and that the particular virtues in one way or another may reflect it. These virtues thus prove themselves worthy not only in their own right but also from a still higher point of view.

NOTES

1. Although the list of "neo-Aristotelians" is long, a few recent articles have managed to survey the field. See, in particular, John R. Wallach, "Contemporary Aristotelianism," *Political Theory* 20 (1992): 613–41; Peter Simpson, "Contemporary Virtue Ethics and Aristotle," *Review of Metaphysics* 45 (1992): 503–24; and Gregory Trianosky, "What is Virtue Ethics All About?" *American Philosophical Quarterly* 27 (1990): 335–44. Peter A. French, Theodore E. Uehling, Jr., and Howard K. Wettstein, eds., *Midwest Studies in Philosophy*, vol. 13, *Ethical Theory: Character and Virtue* (Notre Dame: University of Notre Dame Press, 1988), is devoted to the study of virtue in ethical theory and contains a number of representative articles.

2. Citations of the *Nicomachean Ethics* are to the standard Greek edition of Ingram Bywater, *Aristotelis Ethica Nicomachea* (Oxford: Clarendon Press, 1894). Translations are my own.

3. David Ross, Aristotle, 6th ed. (London: Routledge Press, 1995), 209. Consider also H. H. Joachim, *Aristotle: The "Nicomachean Ethics"* (Oxford: Clarendon Press, 1951), 111: "This portion of the *Nicomachean Ethics* contains Aristotle's analysis of the 'best life' as it was lived in his time—as it was manifested in the speculative and political (social and moral) ideals and achievements of the Greeks." The exception to this neglect is the tradition of the commentaries, but for reasons I will note, even the commentaries do not always undertake a systematic study of the virtues.

4. As R. A. Gauthier and J. Y. Jolif, *Aristote: "L'Éthique à Nicomaque,"* 2d ed. (Louvain: Publications Universitaires de Louvain, 1970), 155, observe, Aristotle himself points out that the existing language is insufficient, making it necessary for him to invent his own vocabulary (1107b30, 1108a16–19).

5. Cf. Joachim, *Aristotle: The "Nicomachean Ethics,"* 114, where he seems to contradict his earlier judgment of the conventionality of Aristotle's account by observing that "the order in which Aristotle discusses the moral virtues in Books III and IV seems to depend on some kind of psychological theory." While allowing that certain principles of order apply in Aristotle's discussion, Sir Alexander Grant, *The "Ethics" of Aristotle* (New York: Arno Press, 1973), 55, rejects the idea that Aristotle is taking his bearings from principles of psychology: "It must always be remembered that [Aristotle's] *Ethics*, while tending to advance psychology greatly, are not composed upon a psychological system." The order of the virtues and the exhaustiveness of the list are necessarily issues for students of the *Ethics*. Perhaps the most systematic treatment of the virtues is found in Thomas Aquinas, *Commentary on the "Nicomachean Ethics,"* trans. C. I. Litzinger, 2 vols. (Chicago: Henry Regnery Company, 1964), (see especially par. 333–57 of his commentary). In brief, he contends that Aristotle discusses first the virtues and vices pertaining to internal passions, then those pertaining to passions connected with external goods, and finally those pertaining to external actions. Aquinas, of course, seeks to transform Aristotle's political philosophy in such a way as to make it amenable to Christianity. Harry V. Jaffa, *Thomism and Aristotelianism: A Study of the Commentary by Thomas Aquinas on the "Nicomachean Ethics"* (Chicago: University of

Chicago Press, 1952) discusses the difficulties with this effort and with Aquinas's presentation of the virtues. Jaffa confronts also the traditional problem of the relationship between the *Nicomachean* and *Eudemian Ethics* as it bears on the question of the coherence of the former, and discusses the development of the discussion in the *Nicomachean Ethics*. In contrast to Aquinas, Ross, *Aristotle*, 211, rejects any suggestion that the virtues and vices are systematically ordered, arguing, "No attempt is made at an exhaustive logical division of either feelings or actions. The order is haphazard; two of the cardinal virtues are treated first and in considerable detail (the other two being reserved for treatment in Books V and VI); the other virtues are taken up just as they occur to Aristotle's mind, one no doubt suggesting another as he proceeds." Grant, *The "Ethics" of Aristotle*, 55–56, interprets the logic of the order more strictly: "He seems to have taken up first the most prominent and striking qualities, according to the common notions in Greece—Courage, Temperance, and Liberality. Liberality suggested to him Magnificence—Magnificence, Great-souledness; and from this he proceeded to distinguish the more ordinary quality of Ambition. He then added, what had hitherto been omitted, the virtue of regulation of the temper; and pointed out that in social intercourse three excellent qualities are produced by bringing the demeanour under the control of the law of balance . . ." See also J. A. Stewart, *Notes on Aristotle's "Ethics,"* 2 vols. (Oxford: Clarendon Press, 1892), 213, who sides generally with Grant; Gauthier and Jolif, *Aristote: "L'Éthique à Nicomaque,"* 153; and especially W. F. R. Hardie, *Aristotle's Ethical Theory* (London: Oxford University Press, 1968), 116–120, who takes up several of the arguments regarding the order and exhaustiveness of the list of the virtues and who finally sides with Ross. I am not offering here a full account of the order of the virtues, but in accord with other scholars, I would suggest that the logic of Aristotle's discussion can be uncovered only by attending to the concrete details of this discussion. In principle, I follow MacIntyre's suggestion that "a philosophic theory of the virtues is a theory whose subject matter is already implicit in and presupposed by the best contemporary practice of the virtues," (Alasdair MacIntyre, *After Virtue: A Study in Moral Theory* [Notre Dame: University of Notre Dame Press, 1981], 148), though I diverge from MacIntyre's historicism. Concerning the relation of philosophy or theory to "prephilosophic political life," see also Leo Strauss, *The City and Man* (Chicago: University of Chicago Press, 1964), 11–12, and "Classical Political Philosophy," in *What is Political Philosophy* (Chicago: University of Chicago Press, 1988), 94.

6. Aquinas's efforts to transform Aristotle's view are evident at the conclusion of his commentary on courage: "We must consider, however, that to some virtuous men death is desirable on account of the hope of a future life. But the Stoics did not discuss this, nor did it pertain to the Philosopher in this work to speak of those things that belong to the condition of another life" (Aquinas, *Commentary on the "Nicomachean Ethics,"* par. 590). Cf. Jaffa, *Thomism and Aristotelianism*, 33.

7. It is precisely in the context of his commentary on this passage of the *Ethics* that Aspasius anticipates Aristotle's later identification of the end of virtue with the noble. See Gustavus Heylbut, ed., *Commentaria in Aristotelem graeca*, vol. 19, *Aspasii in Ethica Nicomachea* (Berlin: G. Reimeri, 1889), 81 (hereafter cited as Aspasius).

8. The immediate tension between courage and happiness prompts Sir Alexander Grant, *Aristotle* (London: William Blackwood & Sons, 1877) to observe that "the most

moral of the virtues here named, from a modern point of view, is courage, on account of the self-sacrifice, the endurance of danger, pain, and death, which it implies" (107–8).

9. Burnet observes that "Aristotle speaks as if *dikaiosyne* had already been treated in its natural place along with *andreia* and *sophrosyne*" (John Burnet, *The "Ethics" of Aristotle* [London: Methuen & Co., 1900; reprint Salem, N.H.: Ayer Company Publishers Inc., 1988], 164).

10. Arguing that Aristotle intends here to distinguish magnificence from its own excess and deficiency and not from liberality, Burnet maintains that "the whole sentence is intended to show the likeness of the *eleutherios* and the *megaloprepēs*" (Burnet, *The "Ethics" of Aristotle*, 175). But given that the suggestion arises in a passage devoted primarily to distinguishing liberality from magnanimity, it is less innovative to understand this particular sentence as consistent with that effort.

11. With Muretus, Burnet brackets *megaloprepeia* as a gloss, so that the sentence reads "the virtue of a work lies in its greatness" (Burnet, *The "Ethics" of Aristotle*, 176). Rackham (Aristotle, *Nicomachean Ethics*, trans. H. Rackham [Cambridge: Harvard University Press, Loeb Classical Library, 1934]); and Gauthier and Jolif, *Aristote: "L'Éthique à Nicomaque,"* do the same. Zeller, Susemihl, Bekker, Bywater, and Apelt all retain it (see Gauthier and Jolif, 268). *Megaloprepeia* appears on three manuscripts (although its place shifts) and is consistent with Aristotle's indications here that magnificence is as much a part of the work or product as it is of the one who produces the work. He has in fact just noted that the magnificent man produces a "more magnificent work." Aristotle also likens the magnificent man to a "knower" (*epistēmōn*), saying that "he has the capacity to comprehend what is fitting and is able to spend great amounts with grace" (1122a34–35). Aristotle's contention in Book II that the virtues, in contrast to the arts, depend upon habit rather than knowledge in the strict sense suggests that magnificence is closer to the arts than are the other virtues as a result of its connection to a work or product (1105a26–b5).

12. Consider again Aquinas, *Commentary on the "Nicomachean Ethics,"* par 719: "The gentiles . . . worshipped not only gods, i.e., certain separated substances, but also demons whom they held to be intermediaries between gods and men. Therefore, [Aristotle] adds that everything expended on the worship of any demon whatsoever belongs to this same classification. The Philosopher speaks here of a heathen custom that has been abrogated by the plain truth. Hence if someone now spent any money on the worship of a demon he would not be munificent but sacrilegious." Cf. Aspasius, *Commentaria*, 106.

13. The phrase I have translated as "the magnanimous man will be unsparing of his life on the grounds that living is not worthwhile" can also be translated in the way Martin Ostwald, for example, chooses: the magnanimous man will not spare his life in the midst of great risks, "aware that life at any cost is not worth living" (Aristotle, *Nicomachean Ethics*, trans. Martin Ostwald [New York: Macmillan Publishing Co., Library of Liberal Arts, 1962], 96). I have chosen the former translation for two reasons: first, it better explains why Aristotle says that the magnanimous man will have, literally, a reckless disregard (*apheidein*) for his life, and second, the Greek recalls Aristotle's statement in his discussion of courage that especially for the virtuous human being, "to live is worthwhile" (1117b11–12). Regarding this latter point, it is also instructive to consider Aristotle's statement regarding the pain the courageous man experiences in having to forsake his life.

The suggestion that life itself takes on a certain insignificance for the magnanimous man is buttressed by Aristotle's observation in Book IX that the serious man "would prefer to experience intense pleasure for a brief time than quiet pleasure for a long time, and to live nobly for one year than an ordinary existence for many, and to do one great and noble deed than many small ones" (1169a22–25). In addition, see Aspasius, *Commentaria*, 112, who also interprets the magnanimous man's willingness to take great risks as a sign that "he does not hold living to be a great thing."

14. Compare Aspasius, *Commentaria*, 108.

15. Given that the object of gentleness is anger, a passion, it is at first puzzling that Aristotle does not discuss it along with courage and moderation. Grant observes, "Had the *Ethics* been composed on a psychological plan, what is said here might have been arranged under the head of *thumos*, and would have been connected with the relation of *thumos* to courage which is discussed above" (Grant, *The Ethics of Aristotle*, 81).

16. In an effort to capture something of this definition of *praotēs*, some translators and commentators offer an alternative translation: Burnet suggests "patience" and "good temper" (Burnet, *The "Ethics" of Aristotle*, 188); Thomson, "patience" (*The "Ethics" of Aristotle*, trans. J. A. K. Thomson [New York: Viking Penguin, 1976], 160); Welldon (Aristotle *Nicomachean Ethics*, trans. J. E. C. Welldon [Buffalo: Prometheus Books, 1987], 129); Apostle (Hippocrates G. Apostle, *Aristotle's "Nicomachean Ethics,"* Grinnell, Iowa: The Peripatetic Press, 1984], 70), and Ross (Aristotle, 96), "good temper"; but Ostwald (*Nicomachean Ethics*, 100) and Rackham (*Nicomachean Ethics*, 231) prefer "gentleness."

17. Welldon's suggestion for *authekastos*.

18. This is the first mention of *diagōgē* in the *Ethics*. It is an important term which is difficult to translate. "Passing the time" or "pastime" suits the context here, but *diagōgē* also has other meanings—a way or course of life, a course of instruction—which express better the activity or *diagōgē* Aristotle will praise as best in Book X. Cf. 1171b13, 1176b12, 14, 1177a9, 27.

19. Compare Ross, *Aristotle*, 211; Grant, *The "Ethics" of Aristotle*, 55–56.

20. That Aristotle wishes to draw our attention to this omission is indicated also by his distinction between the virtue of "friendship" and friendship, a distinction he did not make when he first enumerated the virtues, and by his reiteration at the end of the account of wittiness of the original order of the three virtues. Cf. Gauthier and Jolif, *Aristote: "L'Éthique à Nicomaque,"* 153.

21. The meaning of Aristotle's qualification here is of course controversial. Cf., e.g., Aquinas, *Commentary on the "Nicomachean Ethics,"* par. 901; Gauthier and Jolif, *Aristote: "L'Éthique à Nicomaque,"* 339; Burnet, *The "Ethics" of Aristotle*, 207; Jaffa, *Thomism and Aristotelianism*, 181.

22. Gauthier and Jolif, *Aristote: "L'Éthique à Nicomaque,"* 406–8, recount various scholarly views of the problem of justice as a mean and of the question raised by Aquinas in particular regarding the relation between external acts and internal passions (or dispositions). That suffering injustice is not a vice is, as they observe, later noted by Aristotle himself (1138a34–35).

23. One might hold, as Gauthier and Jolif apparently do, that Aristotle is able still to make a distinction between partial justice and these other characteristics (Gauthier and

Jolif, *Aristote: "L'Éthique à Nicomaque,"* 344–45, 406–7). But it would nonetheless remain a merely formal distinction.

24. The full implications of this postponement are lost if, like Burnet, *The "Ethics" of Aristotle*, 212, one resolves the problem by saying that the good man and the good citizen are the same not in all regimes but in the best, aristocracy (Burnet cites *Politics*, 1293b5). To accept this as Aristotle's definitive resolution is to overlook many of his equivocations in the *Politics* concerning this question (1267a15–1277b32), but also in particular to forget the terms of the question: whether the education of the good human being is even a part of politics.

25. This is a difficulty, I would contend, even with such important efforts as those of Martha Nussbaum and William Galston to return the discussion of virtue and the human good to a central place in moral and political philosophy. See, for example, Nussbaum's "Non-Relative Virtues: An Aristotelian Approach" in *Midwest Studies in Philosophy, Volume 13* and "Aristotle on Human Functioning," *Political Theory* 20 (1992): 202–46, and Galston's *Justice and the Human Good* (Chicago: University of Chicago Press, 1980). Galston himself expresses a reservation concerning what he calls "the instrumental view of virtue" (54).

CHAPTER 8

ARISTOTLE ON THE QUESTION OF EVIL

DAVID BOLOTIN

I have been asked to discuss Aristotle's views on the question of evil, political evil in particular. To do this I have chosen to concentrate on the *Nicomachean Ethics*, which is the introduction to Aristotle's political teaching as a whole, and I will refer to the *Politics* only to elaborate on a few suggestions that are made in the *Ethics* but which the *Ethics* itself does not pursue in any detail. A fuller discussion would of course also have to consider the *Politics*—with its treatment of tyranny, for instance—more directly.

Although Greek has no word that quite corresponds to the English word "evil," Aristotle speaks clearly enough of what we have in mind when we say that Hitler and Stalin were evil. What he calls it is injustice (*adikia*). In the *Rhetoric* he defines "doing injustice" (*to adikein*) as "doing harm voluntarily (and) contrary to the law" (a law that need not be the written law of a particular community, but may be an unwritten one that is, or is regarded as, universal [*Rhetoric* 1368b6–9]). In the *Ethics* he says further that the man who does injustice is himself unjust if the harm he does, in addition to being voluntary, is also the result of deliberation and choice (1135b19–25). Now it is those who do such actions, and in such a manner, whom we would call evil. And it is those who choose to do such actions on the largest scale whom we tend to regard as the most evil, at least in the political realm.

Aristotle does, of course, discuss the theme of evil, or injustice, in his political writings. But he gives it a much less prominent place than we might have expected from a study of Thucydides or Plato. Thucydides' *Peloponnesian War* focuses on the threat and the challenge from injustice, in particular the injustice of Athens's empire and her imperialism. The bulk of Plato's *Republic* is a response to Glaucon's admitted difficulty in choosing between the just and the unjust lives. By contrast, Aristotle's political writings *presuppose* the clear superiority of justice to injustice, and their addressees are apparently free enough from war, or the threat of war, to concern themselves instead with articulating their vision of the noblest and best life. Evil or injustice, Aristotle seems to suggest, does not raise the most serious questions for a gentleman. Even the *Politics* pays relatively little attention to injustice as such. And in the *Ethics*, moreover, whose central theme is the virtues, in their relation to happiness, justice itself is treated as only one of eleven moral virtues. It is discussed, to be sure, at greater length than any of the others, but not at the beginning of the book, and not nearly so extensively as friendship. Not only, then, does Aristotle seem less inclined than Thucydides and Plato to dwell upon *in*justice, but justice too seems to have a less significant place in his thought.

The suggestion, however, that injustice, or even justice, is not so important to Aristotle as to Thucydides and Plato needs to be qualified, and for the following reason. When Aristotle begins to speak thematically about justice, which he had initially listed as but one of the moral virtues, he surprises us by saying that justice, in one sense of the word, comprises all the virtues, or is "complete virtue," and that the injustice corresponding to it is not a part of vice, but rather the whole of vice (1129b25–1130a10). He makes this claim on the grounds that the just, in the broadest sense, is identical with the legal, and that the law commands us to live in accordance with each virtue and forbids us to live in accordance with each vice. Aristotle helps clarify the perspective from which the law can be said to enjoin each virtue and to forbid each vice, by noting that the law aims at what is advantageous in common for everyone, or at least for the preponderant part of the community. Acts of cowardice in war, for example, are clearly harmful to the political community, and they are accordingly forbidden by the law. Even acts of immoderation tend to be destructive of families, and therefore also of the whole community, and they too are prohibited by the law. Since, then, all the actions that follow from moral vice tend to the community's harm, they are regarded as unlawful, or in other words, unjust. That the moral virtues are parts of justice in the broadest sense, as the vices are of injustice, means that virtue is something we owe not merely to ourselves, but also, and perhaps more importantly, to the others with whom we live. Or in Aristotle's words, justice is "complete virtue, because the one who has it is able to exercise his virtue also in relation to another, and not only as it concerns himself" (1129b31–33). Accordingly, Aristotle's entire moral teaching can be seen as a teaching about justice and injustice.

Aristotle does, however, also speak of justice in a narrower sense as one of the virtues that make up virtue as a whole. Corresponding to this there is a more limited form of injustice. This second form of injustice does not involve transgression in general, but more particularly greed, or seeking gain for oneself at the expense of others. Injustice in the comprehensive sense can have all sorts of motives, as many motives as there are for the various vices. But injustice in the more limited sense is motivated by the desire for the pleasure that comes from gain (1130b1–5). We should note, however, that what Aristotle means in this context by gain is not limited to those goods, like honor or wealth, that we would ordinarily speak of as such; gain can also include the satisfaction of some passion, such as the passion to kill or the passion for revenge. It is not always easy, therefore, to determine whether or not a given unlawful action falls within the sphere of particular injustice (1132a6–14; b11–16; 1137a1; contrast 1130a22–27 with 1131a6).

For there to be genuine instances of someone doing injustice, in either sense of the word, the actions must of course be voluntary; they must be in that person's power to do or not to do, since otherwise he could not be held responsible for them. Now the question had been raised, by Socrates among others, as to whether the unjust man or evildoer knows how he ought to act and, if he doesn't, whether his action is not an involuntary one, something for which he can neither be held responsible nor justly punished. But Aristotle replies that ignorance of how one ought to act, as distinct from ignorance of the particular circumstances surrounding one's action, is not a cause of involuntariness, but rather of wickedness (1110b28–1111a1). And he further observes that men punish those who are ignorant of what is in the laws, which people ought to know and which is not difficult to know, on the assumption that it was in their power not to be ignorant (1113b33–1114a3).

If we bring together Aristotle's two senses of the word injustice, we are led to his definition in the *Rhetoric*, that doing injustice is doing harm to others voluntarily and contrary to the law. Aristotle begins, then, from this common sense awareness of evil as evil, of evildoing as doing harm to others in such a manner that one is justly punished by the law. This awareness is presupposed by him. It is not something he has to recover, as we seem to have to do, against the background of a prevailing view of man that would leave no room for genuine evil.

I should mention in passing that Aristotle also speaks of those the unnaturalness of whose pleasures, or the extremity of whose folly, cowardice, licentiousness, or harshness, puts them in a different category from that of the morally vicious. Among his examples of such people he includes some who were horribly cruel, such as a woman who was said to have cut open the wombs of pregnant women and eaten the infants, a man who sacrificed his mother and ate her, and other cannibals. But he also includes such people as those who would fear the sound of a mouse, those who engage in homosexual practices, and those who eat coal or bite their nails. All such people, he says, are either brutish, i.e. their natures are depraved, or else they are diseased, for instance they might be insane (1148b15–1149a12). Aristotle adds, with regard to brutishness, that it is a lesser and less destructive thing than vice, since in brutishness the better part of a human being, or his rational principle, is not merely corrupted, as it is in those who are vicious, but absent (1150a1–8). The implication, then, is that those who are brutish are not responsible for their actions in the way that normal human beings are; though some of them, those who are brutishly cruel, might have to be treated like enemies by all civilized people, they lack the freedom to deserve being condemned as truly evil.

To return, however, to evil or injustice, the obvious response to it would appear to be to resist any temptations to it within oneself and to oppose it in others who intend harm, especially when they intend harm against one's own political community. And if one is unable lawfully to prevent such acts of injustice, then one would be obliged to help try to punish the evildoers, at least in the case where they are fellow citizens. Moreover, as Aristotle says in the *Rhetoric*, a good man would not be pained, but he must even rejoice, when a parricide or other serious criminal receives the punishment he deserves (*Rhetoric* 1386b25–32). Rejoicing at such deserved punishments is an aspect, according to Aristotle, of righteous indignation, which he defines primarily as being pained at others' undeserved prosperity, and which he speaks of as a sign of good character (1108a35–b7; compare *Rhetoric* 1386b8–12).

Now to say, as Aristotle does, that we must respond to great evil with righteous indignation is only to say what decent political men normally feel. And yet Aristotle compels us to raise some questions about this response, for despite his praise of indignation in the *Rhetoric*, he explicitly distinguishes it, in the *Ethics*, from the moral virtues. Although he treats it, like the virtues themselves, as a mean between two extremes—in this case between enviousness and spitefulness—he speaks of it merely as a passion, rather than a virtue. He is unwilling, apparently, to consider it even as a part of the virtue of justice. But why is he unwilling to include it among the virtues? Let me suggest, as a preliminary answer to this question, that he sees political life as being incompatible with full satisfaction, and even the full expression, of the indignant man's hope for justice. In order to show this, I will begin by examining more closely the discussion of particular justice.

There are two forms of particular justice, traditionally known as distributive justice and commutative justice. Distributive justice is meant to govern the distribution of honor, or wealth, or the other goods that can be divided among those who share in a regime. It directs the distribution of equal shares to those who are equal, and unequal shares to those who are unequal. Commutative justice, on the other hand, is meant to direct the transactions that take place among the members of the community, both the voluntary transactions, such as buying and selling, and the involuntary ones, such as stealing or killing. This second form of particular justice has as its principle that equality of goods or of losses between those involved in the transaction be preserved or restored, and it disregards the quality of the men themselves. "It doesn't matter," says Aristotle, "whether a good man has robbed a bad man or a bad man a good one, nor whether the man who has committed adultery is good or bad. But the law looks only at the difference in regard to harm, and it treats the men as equals, [examining] if the one does injustice and the other is injured, and if the one did harm and the other has been harmed" (1132a2–6).

Now there are difficulties with each of these notions of justice. As for distributive justice, the difficulty concerns, at least primarily, the application of the standard. For even if we agree that honors are to be assigned in proportion to excellence, how precisely are we to decide who is most excellent? Since, in particular, to hold ruling offices is one of the greatest honors in any community, how are we to decide to whom these offices should be assigned? This question is not discussed at any length in the *Ethics* itself, but it becomes a guiding question of the *Politics*, where considerations such as the following are raised. Are the various kinds of relevant superiority commensurable with one another, so that the relative strength of the competing claims could be measured and judged? It seems that the only way to make these claims commensurable is to determine which kinds of men contribute, and in what degree, to the purpose or purposes for which the community was formed. But the excellences that most contribute to the political community may not be the truest excellences (see *Politics* 1282b31–1283a3). This difficulty may be alleviated if we say, with Aristotle, that the political community exists for the sake of the good life, the life in which men exercise the moral and political virtues. But Aristotle has to admit that the city comes into being for the sake of mere survival, which continues to be among its chief concerns, and that the sheer strength of numbers contributes greatly to survival in war, whereas the men of excellence are everywhere quite few. So is it even just, in an unqualified sense, for a political community to distribute its ruling offices in strict proportion to true excellence? (Compare *Politics* 1252b27–30 with 1278b15–30 and 1280a25–35ff.; compare 1279a37–b4; 1281a28–34 and b21–30; 1301b40–1302a2.)

As for commutative justice, there is an obvious difficulty, not merely with the application of the standard, but with the standard itself. Is it simply just that the criminal law considers only the particular actions that are before the court, and not the overall character of the individuals involved? Furthermore, Aristotle's own example, which I quoted above, suggests that a good man—and such a man he had earlier characterized as having nothing to be ashamed of— might in some circumstances even commit adultery (1132a2–6; compare 1107a9–17; 1128b20–25). Yet Aristotle takes it for granted that adultery is a violation of commutative justice. We are thus led to wonder whether commutative justice, with its demand to treat all men as equally entitled to what is said to be lawfully their own, does not in some cases forbid actions that are compatible with virtue.

There is a further difficulty with commutative justice, even in voluntary transactions, and this arises in connection with the application of its standard of equality of goods or losses. The exchange of goods—and thus also every city, which remains together, according to Aristotle, in part because of such exchange (1132b31–1133a5)—requires that the various goods be treated as commensurable in value. But is there any genuine answer to the question, say, of how many beds are equal in value to one house? The value of all goods to be exchanged is measured, says Aristotle, in terms of need. But we must wonder about the validity of this standard of value. To take one example, is it a valid standard even when one group of people has acquired a monopoly over some resource that is necessary for life? Still more important is the following difficulty, which Aristotle explicitly raises. For a community of exchange to exist, exchange must be possible even when the two parties are not simultaneously in need of one another's goods. In these circumstances the one without immediate need will not voluntarily relinquish his goods unless he is confident that whatever he would have exchanged them for, if he had then been in need, will be available to him when the need arises. It is for this reason that money was established, by agreement, as a token that a man may receive in place of goods, and that he may exchange in the future in order to satisfy his future need. Now money, according to Aristotle, exists not by nature, but rather by convention or law, since it is in our power to change its value or to make it useless (1133a30–31). In other words, money only exists as such so long as the members of a community keep their promise to give in exchange for it as much, or roughly as much, as they would have given for the goods that it was originally exchanged for. Now we may assume that such promises will generally be kept, at least for as long as those who made the first exchange continue to be in need, and to roughly the same degree, of one another's goods. This reciprocal need will continue to hold the community together so that it remains, in Aristotle's words, "like a single being" (1133b7). But the fact remains that every such community, and this includes, to repeat, the political community, is held together in part by virtue of a fundamental convention—however useful that convention may generally be—and not simply by nature. Accordingly, Aristotle concludes his discussion of exchange by saying that commensurability among the different goods to be exchanged is impossible "in truth," although it is "sufficiently" possible in relation to need. And this means that commutative justice, and the equality that it requires, cannot be precisely determined without some degree of arbitrariness.

Now these difficulties, although they are discussed by Aristotle in connection with his treatment of merely particular justice, have important implications for legal justice, the justice that had appeared to comprise all the virtues. For despite appearances to the contrary, commutative and distributive justice cannot be regarded merely as subclasses of legal justice. To some degree, at least, they are standards in terms of which the various codes of law must themselves be judged. If there are difficulties regarding these standards, these difficulties affect law or justice as a whole. Indeed, the lawgivers themselves acknowledge that there are such higher standards by their very claim that the law is just, for they also say that the common good is [what is] just (1160a11–14; compare 1129b12–25). Now for obvious reasons Aristotle is reluctant to dwell on the difficulties that surround legal justice, but he does call attention to them, even in the *Ethics*. In the passage where he does so most explicitly, he first reminds us that what is just in the truest or fullest sense of the word is the politically just, which exists only among those who share in a single political community, and whose life together is regulated by law. But he then distinguishes, as subspecies of the politically just, the naturally just, on the one hand, and the conventionally or legally just, on the other. The naturally just is said to have the same power everywhere, a power that does not depend on opinion. By contrast, the conventionally or legally just enjoins actions that are not intrinsically superior to alternate ways of acting, i.e. they are not superior except for the fact that they have been established as lawful. Now it is true that the rules of what is naturally just will presumably be codified, more or less explicitly, in the laws of all political societies. Nevertheless, Aristotle's distinction between the naturally and the legally just raises questions about the status of at least some laws.

Even the naturally just itself, moreover, is not regarded by Aristotle as a simply valid standard, for he acknowledges that it is changeable in its entirety, at least among mortals. This acknowledgement seems to mean, as Aristotle suggests by his illustration, that there are extreme circumstances in which every city can, as perhaps it must, disregard the rules of natural justice without suffering the harmful consequences that would follow from a more frequent disregard. It is largely for this reason, I believe, that Aristotle speaks of this kind of justice as the naturally just, or naturally right, rather than as a natural law (1134b18–35). The rules of what is naturally just, moreover, are apparently so broad or indeterminate that they need to be supplemented by more particular laws that are merely conventional or positive. And these laws, as distinct from what is naturally just itself, are not the same everywhere, "since neither," as Aristotle says, "are the regimes" (1134b35–1135a5). By this brief reference to regimes, Aristotle touches upon a theme that he will develop at much greater length in the *Politics*, namely that the laws in force everywhere are derivative from the regime, or from the character of the ruling class, i.e. from the particular society's answer to the central question of distributive justice, the question of who should rule (*Politics* 1283b4–8; 1289a10–22). Now we have already seen some of the difficulties that stand in the way of any attempt to achieve true distributive justice. Still, Aristotle does say that despite the variety of regimes, there is "one alone that is everywhere the best according to nature" (1135a5). From parallels in the *Politics*, this best regime according to nature appears to be the absolute rule of a single man who is superior in virtue to all the others in the community, even when they are taken collectively (*Politics* 1284a3–15; 1284b25–34; 1288a15–29). It is according to nature, apparently, for everyone else in the community to submit voluntarily to this man's rule, and not to presume to restrain him by any law. And yet even if such an outstanding man were to arise, it is hard to believe that the rest of the community would willingly yield to him as an absolute ruler. Indeed, Aristotle suggests that they would even have reason not to by pointedly failing to speak of such rule as being advantageous, i.e., advantageous for the community as a whole. (Compare 1288a15–29 with 1284b37–40, 1285b37–1286a1, 1287b37–1288a2, and 1288a30–32.) The best regime according to nature, then, is rather a standard for criticizing all possible political regimes, insofar as they cannot simply defer to superiority in virtue, than it is a vindication of any of them. And if all legal codes are, as Aristotle says in the *Politics*, derivative from the regimes, the element of arbitrariness in political regimes cannot help but call into question the authority of the laws themselves. Indeed, from the perspective we have now reached, we can perhaps understand why Aristotle compares the differences among positive laws to those in weights and measures, which tend to be larger where people buy and smaller where they sell. What he seems to imply is that all positive laws, while they are advantageous for some or most members of the community, are more or less disadvantageous for others. No wonder, then, that Aristotle had qualified his initial statement that identified justice in the broad sense with law by saying, in his repetition, that "everything lawful is *in a sense* just" (1129b12, emphasis mine). And we are now prepared for Aristotle's statement, toward the end of his discussion of justice, that what the laws command is only accidentally just at best (1137a9–12 and context).

By denying the existence of any simply authoritative law, Aristotle raises obvious questions about the meaning of evil, and about the status of punishment. And if even the best of all possible political regimes is incapable of distributing honor and other goods in genuine accordance with desert, we can perhaps better appreciate Aristotle's unwillingness to encourage indignation, at least to such an extent as to call it a part of virtue. Someone might object, however, that the mere inadequacy of law, and even of all possible political regimes, to achieve a truly common good should not blind us to the existence of those who owe their success or power to great and manifest injustice. Isn't it a part of human virtue to respond to these men, and to their undeserved prosperity, with righteous indignation? Aristotle's grounds for denying that this is the case are still not sufficiently clear. We must, therefore, look further into his account of justice and injustice.

In his early statement that the bad man's ignorance of how he should act does not absolve him of responsibility, Aristotle says, "It doesn't want to be called involuntary if someone is ignorant of what is advantageous" (1110b30–31; compare 1114a31–b5 ff.). Now what is most striking about this remark is that Aristotle doesn't blame the bad man for choosing to pursue his own advantage, but merely for his ignorance of what it is. This is especially surprising, since Aristotle characterizes the unjust man, in one sense of the word, as a man who is greedy for his own advantage. When we look more closely, however, at what Aristotle means by greed, it turns out that he is not being inconsistent in approving of a certain kind of self-seeking. For what he says, more precisely, is that unjust men are greedy for the goods of fortune, which are good in an unqualified sense, but not always good for the individual. And he goes on to say that instead of doing what people in fact do, which is to pray for and to pursue these goods, "they ought to *pray* that the goods in an unqualified sense be good for *themselves*, but they should *choose* what *is* good for themselves" (1129b1–6, emphasis mine; compare 1134b11–12; 1136b6–7; 1136b20–22; 1159a12; 1169a17). In other words, the greed that he disapproves of is not, at bottom, the pursuit of more than others have, or more for oneself at the expense of others, but rather the pursuit of a certain kind of good even when it is not is truly good for oneself (compare 1137a26–30).

Aristotle's approval, however, of a certain kind of self-seeking is still surprising, especially since he had said that the man of moral virtue is one who chooses to do virtuous actions for their own sake, and not, presumably, for the sake of any ulterior end (1105a28–33). Yet this initial characterization of the way in which the morally good man acts turns out to be quite incomplete. Indeed, the very fact that Aristotle speaks of *choosing* what to do indicates, in the light of his own analysis of choice, that all morally good actions must be looked at, if not as mere means to some further end, at least with reference to some more ultimate or comprehensive good. Now except for his somewhat ambiguous discussion of happiness at the beginning of the *Ethics* (compare 1094b6–10 with 1097b1–5), along with a few other scattered remarks (e.g. 1119a16–17; 1126b28–1127a5), it is in this thematic account of justice that Aristotle indicates for the first time at least one of those further ends in relation to which the goodness of morally good action is to be understood. This end, as we have noted already in our account of justice, is the advantage or happiness of the political community. In keeping with the political end of justice, and of all the virtues insofar as they are encompassed by justice, Aristotle's thematic discussion of justice never says that the just man must choose to do just actions for their own sake. Now the suggestion that moral virtue is directed toward the community's good is surely an intelligible one. Indeed, the consideration of some such end is indispensable for a precise understanding of moral virtue. How can one distinguish, for example, whether a particular action is brave, rash, or cowardly without considering its likely contribution to the community's well being? But if the directedness of justice, and of moral virtue altogether, toward the political good is to make sense, doesn't the well-being of the community have to be something higher than mere peace and prosperity, something superior, indeed, to even the noblest actions of moral virtue? Yet is the political community capable of any such activity (compare *Politics* 1323b40–1325b32, especially 1324a19–23)? And especially if, as we have argued, no political community can achieve a good that is truly common to all those with a claim to citizenship, a thoughtful man may be led to wonder whether his own advantage—if only in the sense of the good of his own soul—must not be his ultimate goal. Now if a man's answer to this question is "yes," it does not follow, of course, that he will choose to abandon the practice of morally good actions. Aristotle argues emphatically and often that the practice of virtue is indeed in our own highest interest. But to make such interest one's ultimate goal is to have transcended justice, or the sphere of moral virtue altogether, insofar as one's just or morally good actions will be chosen, not for their own sake, nor even for the sake of the community, but rather for their contribution to one's own truest well-being.

Aristotle endorses, I believe, the limited critique of the moral horizon that I have just outlined. For he argues at length in the last book of the *Ethics* that the moral or practical life as a whole is inferior, and from the perspective of the individual's happiness, to the life of theoretical wisdom. Moreover, the assumption that Aristotle endorsed this critique of the moral horizon offers us the most intelligible explanation of why he did not consider indignation to be a part of virtue (consider also 1109b9–11). If a man's own happiness, the happiness of contemplation, is the highest goal of all his actions, indignation at the evil in the world must necessarily have a lower status than it would otherwise.

In the course of Aristotle's discussion of the theoretical life, he calls attention to the unfortunate lack of leisure that characterizes the military man and the statesman in their struggle against the evils that threaten their communities. On the other hand, he seems to admit that their actions are the noblest and greatest of all virtuous actions (1177b16–17). Especially important, among such actions, are those of the statesman who is also a lawgiver. For whatever the deficiencies of law, and its posture toward evil, it remains true that when separated from law and justice man tends to be the worst and most dangerous of all living beings (see *Politics* 1253a31–37). Moreover, Aristotle observes that education to virtue is difficult, if not impossible, apart from a political order that has good laws. Only law, as distinct from mere paternal command, has the compulsory power to engender the good habits that must precede the acquisition of true virtue (1095b4–8; 1103b22–25; 1179b4–1180a24). Accordingly, Aristotle concludes the *Ethics* with a transition to the *Politics*, in which he will offer guidance to statesmen and legislators toward the performance of their noble and necessary tasks.

NOTE

This study was written at the request of Allan Bloom for the conference "Theoretical Perspectives on the Problem of Evil in Twentieth-Century Politics," which was held June 19–21, 1987 at the John M. Olin center at the University of Chicago.

CHAPTER 9

FRIENDSHIP AND SELF-LOVE IN ARISTOTLE'S *NICOMACHEAN ETHICS*

LORRAINE SMITH PANGLE

In the *Nicomachean Ethics*, Aristotle sets out to account for all of the important moral virtues and show that together these virtues constitute the core of happiness. By the opening of Book VIII, the serious reader will be both impressed and troubled: impressed with Aristotle's rich and compelling portrayal of the virtues, but struck also by certain problems Aristotle reveals with the moral man's outlook and self-understanding. Virtuous action seems to be supremely choiceworthy in itself, yet at some level the virtuous man expects to be honored or rewarded, as a compensation or at least recognition for the noble sacrifice he has made of his own good. Virtue and happiness do not fit perfectly together, and this problem appears acutely at the two major peaks of moral virtue, greatness of soul and justice. The great-souled man has all the virtues in the highest degree, but his life is less a flurry of joyful activity than a patient search for actions and honors that are worthy of his great dignity, and that he is unlikely to find unless fortune favors him with rare opportunities. Justice, also, gathers all the moral virtues into one, and as Aristotle says, shines more brightly than the evening star and the morning star, yet justice is also thought with good reason to be "the good of another" (1129b27–30, 1130a3–4; all translations are my own). Can a life spent pursuing justice answer our longings for happiness, or is justice mainly good because it secures the peace and order that lay the groundwork for happy lives? The discussion of moral strength, moral weakness, and pleasure in Book VII further underscores the question of whether the demands of duty are not, all too often, in conflict with the things that promise happiness.

In light of these problems, friendship now comes to sight as a third and perhaps highest and most satisfying summit of the moral life, on which virtue and happiness may finally be united. True friendship (unlike the social grace of *philia*, discussed in Book IV) is either a major virtue itself or at least an occasion for the most honorable and delightful exercise of the virtues. If the life of a great-souled man lacks clear content, if putting himself in the service of his inferiors seems slavish, and actions aimed at winning honor from them seem undignified, the pursuit of serious friendship is a worthy outlet for his energies and talents (see 1125a1). Friendship likewise completes and goes beyond justice, or even renders justice unnecessary (1155a27). And good deeds of all kinds are especially praiseworthy when done for friends, Aristotle says. Paradoxically, acts of friendship seem both more truly generous and more conducive to one's own happiness than acts done strictly because they are right or noble. Acting for the sake of what is right or noble means having primary regard not for the good of the beneficiary, but for one's own virtue or the good of one's soul. Yet spontaneous acts of friendship tend to be more pleasant than impersonal acts of virtue not only for the recipient, but also for the doer.

And if the noblest acts of friendship are more pleasant than most other noble acts, Aristotle argues, the ordinary give-and-take of friendship is pleasant and good for us in all sorts of ways. He says that friendship is so choiceworthy in itself that no one would wish to live without it, even if he had all the other good things (1155a5–6). He argues that friendship is necessary for security, prosperity, and virtue, and that the sociability we have in common with animals gives a natural basis for family and political bonds and for a broader sense of humanity as well. In the process, he shows that friendship is a growth with diverse and tangled roots, that our natural sociability runs deep in us, and yet that it is not altogether to be counted upon, for men consider it necessary to praise those who love their fellow men and who are good friends.

The high praise Aristotle accords friendship in Book VIII.1 implicitly raises two fundamental questions about friendship. First, to what extent and in precisely what way is friendship noble? Will we find in friendship the true selflessness or self-overcoming that we initially think of as constituting friendship's nobility? Will friendship be noble in some other way that is not ultimately self-denying? Or will it prove on close inspection to be a more or less complicated, more or less disguised pursuit of the good for oneself? Second, to what extent and in precisely what way is friendship delightful and fulfilling? Is it, as Montaigne argues, the essential kernel of true happiness, so precious that the lifetime he spent in pleasure, comfort, tranquillity, and the active use of exceptional faculties, when compared with the few short years he had together with a true friend, seemed to be "nothing but smoke, nothing but a dark and tedious night?"[1] Does the healthiest, happiest human being still have a neediness that only friendship can satisfy, and if so, what is the nature of his need for friendship?

THE THREE KINDS OF FRIENDSHIP

Because friendship has such diverse origins, Aristotle begins his inquiry by distinguishing the different types of friendship and their different sources. He says that there are three types of objects that are loved or lovable: the good, the pleasant, and the useful. The good that we love is not precisely the good simply, but what seems to each man good for himself. By the good simply, Aristotle means the things that are judged so by a good man in a flourishing condition, for he is the proper measure of what is good, as of what is noble (see 1113a24–b2). Everything that is truly good will seem good to the healthy soul, and hence potentially lovable, but to actually love it one must also find it good for oneself. For loving another being implies need and a thirst for happiness that cannot be simply fulfilled by one's own inner resources.

At the same time, loving someone does not make that person a friend, Aristotle says, in the first place because we want friends to love us back. The centrality of reciprocity in Aristotle's account of friendship indicates the importance of our concern with our own good. But in the second place, friendship is distinguished from other loves, especially loves for inanimate objects, by its rising above an exclusive concern for our own good. "People say that we ought to wish for the good of a friend for his own sake" (1155b31–32). Aristotle terms this unselfish disposition goodwill. Here, then, is the paradox of friendship as Aristotle presents it: in seeking and choosing friends, we seek the good for ourselves, and apparently we love another only if and only so long as he is good for us, yet we are persuaded that we are not real friends unless we wish one another's good apart from what is good for ourselves.

Aristotle then offers a preliminary definition: to be friends, men must feel goodwill and wish the good for one another, with one another's knowledge, on the basis of one of the three lovable qualities he has enumerated (1156a3–5). But this definition is problematic. Do pleasure and utility in fact give rise to the love of another for his own sake? Aristotle has already said that the useful is lovable not for itself but only as a means to something else, and later, at 1167a13, he states unequivocally that pleasure and utility are not the basis of goodwill. Goodwill, he suggests there, is a response to virtue or excellence of some sort. It is a desire for those who seem good to us—whether brave or beautiful or excellent in some other way—to prosper. If we admire a living being, perhaps it is inevitable that we should wish it well, at least so long as its good and ours do not conflict. Goodwill is thus a natural and reasonable source of the wish to see virtue rewarded; it wishes that good men might prosper not because virtue needs a reward but because our sympathies are naturally with those we admire.

Now if goodwill arose only in response to excellence, those who loved one another for their pleasantness or utility would feel no goodwill, and hence their associations would not meet even the minimal test of friendship. But Aristotle seems to acknowledge that in fact they do involve some goodwill, when he says that in friendships of each of the three types, people wish the good for their friends with respect to the quality that they love (1156a8–9).[2] Drinking companions truly wish one another to have a good time, and business associates wish one another to prosper, and not just as a means to their own continued pleasure or profit. This goodwill is based perhaps on elements of virtue in each partner, such as wittiness or fairness, but perhaps simply on a sense of kinship and fellow-feeling between them, which Aristotle does not mention as a source of goodwill. Throughout his discussion of friendship, Aristotle tends to understate the extent to which goodwill and affection can arise for reasons other than the virtue of the two parties. He paints friendship as being more akin to virtue, more supportive of and demanding of virtue, than it really is.

However, Aristotle shows that in a friendship of pleasure or utility, if the goodwill of each friend is true and generous, it is also weak, and not in itself a sufficient motive for continued exertions on the other's behalf. For when the other ceases to be useful or pleasant, the friendship dissolves. Such friendships are weak and unstable, Aristotle explains, because the friends love one another not for their characters but for something that is incidental to their characters. What people find pleasant and useful is bound to change, depending on their passing tastes and enthusiasms and needs (1156a9–23). There is no deep and essential connection between the ways in which such friends are intrinsically good and lovable (if indeed they are at all) and the ways in which they are pleasant and useful to one another. Therefore, in friendships of pleasure and utility there is nearly always some degree of confusion or mutual self-deception. Each partner acts generously and believes his and his friend's generosity to be based on goodwill and affection, yet in fact each troubles himself about the other only so long as the time he invests brings a good return in pleasure or other benefits.

Of these two defective forms of friendship, that based on utility is clearly the furthest from perfect friendship, for such friends do not necessarily even enjoy or spend much time in one another's company (1156a27–28). Friendship based on pleasure is characteristic of the young and is extremely unstable, but as long as it lasts it is warm and heartfelt. Among the lower forms of friendship Aristotle classes erotic love, which he characterizes as an exchange of pleasure for pleasure or pleasure for other benefits, and he says it is especially unstable because the lover and beloved take pleasure in different things (1156a32–b6; 1157a2–10). Aristotle does not present eros, as Aristophanes does in Plato's *Symposium*, as "finding one's missing half"—finding one who in a lasting way complements and completes what is lacking in one's soul. Virtuous people, he suggests, can be whole in themselves, and it is those who have such wholeness who can be the best friends.

Aristotle draws a sharp contrast, then, between the two lower forms of friendship, "friendship for the sake of the useful" and "friendship for the sake of pleasure," and the higher form, "friendship of the good." Friendships of the good are not formed in order to secure some good for the two partners that is distinct from the friendship itself, not even a high-level good such as moral virtue or knowledge, for then they would merely be friendships of utility with a higher good as the end. In friendships of the good, Aristotle says that the partners love one another for what they are in themselves (1156b6–12). Loving another for himself means delighting in the existence of the other, wholly apart from how that existence affects one's own life. Does such affection constitute an exception to Aristotle's assertion that men love what is good for themselves?

Apparently not, for Aristotle says the good are *also* good, pleasant, and useful to one another in addition to being good in themselves; their friendship is in fact the perfection of all three types of friendship. But if their affection depends upon their being good for one another, is it not a little absurd to say that a good man loves his good friend strictly for what he is in himself, and truly for his own sake . . . and yet only if the friend also happens to be good for him? Or is there such an intrinsic connection between a virtuous man's being good in himself and his being good for his friend that somehow his very goodness (and not any benefit accruing from this goodness) *constitutes* his being good for his friend? Aristotle will ultimately give a fuller account of why the good are good for each other, but he provides part of the answer here in explaining why they are pleasant for one another. When a strong and healthy soul sees other strong and healthy souls in action, it is naturally moved not only to feel goodwill but to take delight in contemplating them, as beings that are both good and akin to itself (1156b14–17). Perhaps this appreciation or contemplation is the core of good men's loving one another, and each is good for the other simply because it makes men happy to see and to contemplate what is good and akin. This, then, would be a love almost without need, and perhaps as close as is humanly possible to come to loving another simply for the other's sake.

We may still wonder, however, whether such love of another for his character is the core even of the best friendships, though it is surely present there, and far more enduring there than elsewhere. For if it is the heart of friendship, and friendship is essential to happiness, why do good men not cherish most their love for the best people they know or even the best they know of, whether alive or dead? Why do even virtuous people care so much about reciprocity? Why does Aristotle stress the time that virtuous people must spend and the trust they must build before they can become friends? The true core of friendship seems not to be this cherishing of the other for himself so much as an active, mutual exchange of pleasure and benefits that takes place when two spend their days together, and each has much to offer that the other desires.

Aristotle continues, however, to denigrate friendships that turn upon pleasure and especially mutual assistance, and he even says at 1157a15 that people in a friendship of utility are not friends of one another at all but only of their own advantage. Yet however defective these two types are, he is unwilling to exclude them from the class of friendships altogether. For, as we shall see, a very large number of friendships, even of decent men, will turn out to be in crucial respects friendships of utility, and pleasure will prove to be in some ways as important for friendship as virtue is.

At 1157b7ff., Aristotle draws a distinction in friendship—which he says also holds for the virtues—between the underlying disposition (*hexis*) and the full and active exercise of this disposition. The full activity of friendship comes through living together, and even the disposition to be friends, which involves goodwill and the friendly regard that remain when friends are asleep or separated for a time, cannot persist indefinitely without opportunities for active intercourse. As a result, Aristotle's first definition of friendship as mutual goodwill mutually known and resting on one of the three lovable qualities now proves inadequate. Goodwill is not enough, because friendship in its full sense involves desire, mutual enjoyment, and common activity. By the same token, it now becomes clear that the goodness of two people does not in itself assure that they will or can become friends, for they must also be capable of pleasing one another and of taking pleasure in society. Even unusually virtuous men can still be prickly, vain, cranky, and infirm in all sorts of ways that make their company unpleasant and keep them apart. Aristotle gives a powerful statement of the importance of pleasure and ties it to what is fundamental in our nature: "most of all nature appears to flee what is painful and to aim at what is pleasant." No one can pass his days with someone who is unpleasant to him, but "nothing characterizes friends so much as living together" (1157b17–18 and 19–20). The pleasure of friends' company is not a consequence of a deficient state, and those who are prosperous or blessed are if anything the least inclined to live alone.

Friendship, then, is like the virtues in consisting in both a disposition and an activity. It is not one of the virtues because pleasure is essential for friendship in a way that it is not for moral virtue, and because friendship rests as much upon the spontaneous *pathos* of affection as it does upon good character and good judgment. It might be argued, however, that the elements of spontaneity and pleasure in friendship make it better than the moral virtues, which can be hard and painful. Can friendship or love plausibly be seen as the peak of the virtuous life, the supreme good to be sought, and the greatest part of happiness? Or is friendship a lesser good, partly an end in itself but more important as a means or support to other things that matter more?

THE RANK OF FRIENDSHIP

In the course of an examination of unequal friendships, Aristotle indirectly reveals his judgment that friendship and its virtues are neither the highest nor the best things in life. He says that in friendships between unequals, the superior partner should receive more affection in proportion to his superiority (1158b25–26). This affection, like the honor that is given to heroes and parents, does not repay a debt, but simply acknowledges it. Feeling affection does not make one deserving of the friendship of a superior, but virtue makes one deserving of affection. Thus affection, the proper virtue of friendship (1159a35), is a lesser virtue, appropriately a response to virtue or excellence taken as a whole, and it should be found especially in the inferior party in an unequal friendship. Likewise, Aristotle indicates, affection is not our greatest good. If it mattered to us most of all, we would cherish most the person most capable of love, and never relinquish a friendship no matter how much inequality arose between us and a friend. But in fact, when there is a wide disparity between two people, "they are no longer friends or even expect to be friends" (1158b33–34). Because such differences preclude friendship, we would not wish for our friends the greatest of goods, which Aristotle says would be to become god, for then we would lose them as friends, and "each man wishes for his own good most of all" (1159a13–14). But presumably we would wish for divinity for ourselves, even at the expense of our friendships. Aristotle thus indicates that what we most would wish for is not friendship but rather divine self-sufficiency.

Now there is something in virtually everyone—something serious and good—that resists Aristotle's suggestions that we all care most about our own good and that friendship is neither the highest nor the best thing in life. Aristotle is aware of and acknowledges the force of this contrary position. As he says, everyone recognizes that affection is simply good in itself to receive. Aristotle contrasts the intrinsic goodness of affection with the derivative goodness of honor, which he says is sought either as a promise of other good things to come or as support for a sense of self-respect that lacks perfect confidence (1159a18–25).[3] We all sense that giving affection is also intrinsically good, for as Aristotle says, it is central to the good thing that we call friendship (1159a27–28). The intrinsic goodness of loving and that of being loved are connected: both are rooted in the simple, irreducible human desire for companionship, for kindred souls, for others that are truly one's own.

Aristotle now brings this other side of friendship powerfully to the fore by bringing up its most vivid expression, the love of mothers. Mothers love their children not because they are good, pleasant, or useful, but because they are their own, which is as close as human beings ever come to loving without cause or loving unconditionally. What is especially impressive about mothers' love is that it seems not dependent upon the mothers' good being served. As Aristotle says, mothers may deprive themselves of contact with their children if this seems to them best for the children, and they will go on loving them without return (1159a28–32). It is striking that love comes closest to being perfectly selfless when the object of the love is most fully and indisputably one's own, both similar to oneself and formed by oneself. Such love, which as Aristotle points out, tends to exceed the love children feel for their parents, seems to be noble, and not at all the mark of an inferior. Indeed, acts of great devotion are perhaps the most moving and inspiring of all acts to witness, and seem to be the sign of the highest virtue.

The most powerful case that friendship and its chief virtue of loyal, steadfast devotion are intrinsically the highest and best things in life is made by Montaigne. In his essay "On Friendship," Montaigne shows what one would have to maintain to argue that friendship is simply the peak of human life. Like Aristotle, he says that virtue in both parties is a prerequisite of perfect friendship. "In this, where a man deals from the very bottom of his heart, without any manner of reservation, certainly it is necessary that all the springs be perfectly clean and true" (70). According to Aristotle, in the best friendship each loves the other because he is good in himself as well as good for his friend. But to love for a reason is not to love for the sake of loving; it is to take the other's virtue and capacity to benefit us as constituting a standard by which we determine whether a friendship is worth pursuing and worth maintaining.

Montaigne, in contrast, suggests that one chooses a virtuous man for a friend because such a man has the greatest capacity for faithfulness and intimacy, but that his particular virtues by no means exhaust or capture the divine, mysterious reasons why one loves him. Montaigne sees that to give any reason at all for the love is to point beyond and away from the friend to something else as our highest concern.[4] Therefore he refuses to say that he chose La Boétie for any quality or combination of qualities. "If anyone should press me to say why I loved him, I feel that this cannot be expressed except by answering, "because it was he, because it was I" (65). Montaigne therefore places great importance upon the freedom of the choice of a true friend, the freedom of both parties to stay or go at will throughout the course of a friendship, and the freely chosen submission of each to the will of the other. The friends recognize no higher authority than one another, and the friendship is not in the service of anything else, any good or benefit to the partners or to anyone. It is, in itself, the highest good.[5]

The question is whether Montaigne can be consistent in maintaining this bold position. He certainly does not flinch from confronting its corollary: that the truest friend would do anything for his friend, and would even commit an act of impiety or sedition if the friend commanded it. But Montaigne immediately pulls back, adding that for true friends such as Blossius and Gracchus, or himself and La Boétie, an evil command is impossible and unthinkable, because the partnership is guided by reason and the character of each is absolutely pure. He thus never requires himself to explain why friendship seems so noble, if the reason is not the friends' devotion to virtue. He seems to find its nobility in the selflessness of the friends vis-à-vis one another: "each of them above all things seek[s] to be useful to the other," but he scorns to take mutual benefits of any sort, even regarding virtue or wisdom, as the goal or rationale of the friendship. If devotion to another does not take virtue as its standard, and does not seek above all to support the other in virtue, but simply seeks to serve his pleasures, is it still noble? What Montaigne cannot bring himself to do is to consider a friendship between men who are neither rational nor virtuous, and claim that this friendship is noble.

Aristotle seems right, then, to suggest that friendship is not the highest thing, and that friendship's virtues, devotion and loyalty, are not the highest virtues. Love had seemed to promise to solve the split between virtue and happiness by bringing together inclination and duty. It does indeed sometimes do so, and as Aristotle stresses, good friends can make it easier and more pleasant to be brave, generous, and so on. But once we consider the cases where loyalty and virtue do diverge, it becomes clear that friendship is only a fine and good thing to the extent that it is limited by an independent and higher commitment to virtue taken as a whole. If moral virtue does not make sense on its own terms, as the core of the finest and happiest life, a concern for friendship may just as soon worsen the tragic split between duty and happiness as heal it. Aristotle is rather quiet about the possible tensions between virtue and friendship. He stresses instead their convergence, and the ways in which cultivating virtue and rendering affection in proportion to desert can make friendship more lasting (1159a34–b10). For he recognizes that friendship looks more unambiguously good to most people than does virtue, and that the longing for companionship is extremely strong.

Aristotle also seems right, however, to deny that companionship by itself is the thing we most want. If we imagine a friendship between people who could never assist one another in their neediness, never comfort one another in their sorrows, never teach each other anything new, however long they conversed together, how could such a friendship still be considered supremely good? Friendship's capacity to provide for the separate goods of each friend would only become irrelevant if it were possible, as Montaigne claims, for the good of two friends to become a seamless whole, in which all considerations of "mine" and "thine" would cease to apply. Perhaps Aristotle's strongest argument that union itself can never become so perfect as to fully satisfy each partner is his observation that every friendship requires equality or at least balance, so that each is satisfied with what he gets out of the friendship (1158b28–34). The happiness of both friends must be attended to, and attended to more or less equally, and that means that if the good of each has become part of the good of the other, it is never the whole or even the heart of it, for then the good of either would suffice for both.

ETHICAL FRIENDSHIP

At the end of Book VIII, Aristotle delves into the problems and complaints that arise when people believe that a friendship has become unfair. He thereby mines a vein of richly revealing behavior, from which we can begin to understand the limits of human selflessness. The overt theme is friendship of utility, since it is here, Aristotle says, that complaints and reproaches chiefly

arise (1162b5–6). But in the interstices of the discussion, problems with virtuous friendships become evident as well.

To be sure, what Aristotle says explicitly is that in friendships of virtue
there are no complaints or quarrels. These friends are so far from quarreling
over who will get the greater benefit from the friendship that they actually compete to do good to one another, and the beneficiary of a good deed "retaliates"
by doing good in turn. But by using the language of competition and retalia-
tion, Aristotle shows the problem. Even or precisely when men are most concerned to act nobly, they engage in a subtle kind of assault upon or attempt to
get the better of one another. They will not complain when they get less benefit, but problems do arise in their efforts to get the greater share of the noble.
Can these problems be solved by recognizing the ultimate selfishness and
unseemliness of such contests, and taking nobility a step further by allowing
the other to pick up the tab, do one a favor, or run a greater risk? This is something of a solution, and surely the noblest, most cultivated friends will not be
ostentatious and quarrelsome in their attempts to do good. But on some level
the competition must necessarily remain, if only in the form of an infinite
regress of noble self-denials. Nor is it clear, apart from the absurdity of an infinite regress, that this sort of self-denial is congenial to noble souls. Passive
acquiescence in the benefaction of others seems unlikely ever to satisfy their
longing to cultivate excellence and do good in a splendid way.

Complaints also are unlikely to arise in friendships of pleasure, Aristotle
says, but they are common in friendships of utility, since each person is in these
friendships for his own advantage and measures what he thinks he deserves in
the light of what he wants (1162b13–19). Aristotle has accustomed us to think
of friendships of utility as vulgar, crabbed affairs between calculating old men,
scarcely meriting the name friendship at all. But to the extent that people quarrel in any friendship, they reveal the fact that they see the friendship as an
exchange of goods in which the current balance of accounts is unfavorable to
themselves. It is important to preserve a distinction between friendships that
are based on true affection and "friendships" of strict utility in which partners
care nothing for one another as human beings and come together only for
profit. However, when people quarrel over the affection or attention they think
they deserve, affection itself becomes, as it were, an object of exchange. When
we consider utilitarian friendship broadly, as including the full range of what
people seek for themselves from one another, most human friendships turn out
to be in some degree friendships of utility.

Friendships of utility are of two kinds, Aristotle says, one "ethical" and
the other "legal" or based on fixed terms (1162b22–23). The second class is

further divided into cash transactions and transactions made on credit, which introduce the more friendly element of trust. Ethical friendships, by contrast, do not rest on fixed terms, but instead their premises are slippery and submerged. One begins by giving a gift or favor to another "as to a friend" (1162b32), and one ends by expecting an equal or greater return, and complaining if one does not receive it. Such friendships are ethical inasmuch as they involve a concern both to act generously and to secure justice, but these two moral concerns are at odds. The reason for the tension and the slippage in ethical friendships, Aristotle says, is that "all or most men wish for what is noble, but choose what is beneficial" (1162b35–36). A weak attempt to be noble quickly collapses and the friendship shifts grounds, because one or both of the friends lack self-knowledge and clear-sightedness. They can wish for something noble and choose something beneficial because they actually wish for the latter even more, but without fully acknowledging it to themselves. Aristotle leaves it ambiguous whether this contradiction characterizes everyone or just most human beings. At any rate, he indicates that the treachery of ethical friendship, which at first seemed to be only the higher form of the lowest type of friendship, utilitarian friendship, is in fact likely to play some part in virtually all human friendships.

Aristotle gives sound advice as to what one should do when inexplicit expectations erupt into open complaints: return the favor, if you can, as if it were not a gift but a loan, and measure what is owed by the real benefit derived from the thing that was given, and not the effort that it cost to provide it, which may or may not have been as substantial as the benefit. For in a friendship of utility what matters is the benefit each derives. In a friendship based on virtue, by contrast, the return that is owed should be measured by the virtuous choice or intention of the giver, since choice is the decisive factor for virtue and character (1163a2–23). It follows that in these cases, one will normally owe more than the cash value of the gift or favor one receives, because the benefit was given in a generous spirit, and generosity calls for both a return and gratitude. Aristotle reiterates that in such friendships people do not complain when their good deeds go unreturned; they are too noble and cultivated for that. But does their cultivation stop them from silently registering debts in the backs of their minds? Is anyone so noble and self-sufficient as not to feel hurt by ingratitude?

Thus vulgar ethical friendships shade over into more refined ethical friendships, and these in turn give way gradually to friendships of virtue, in a single continuum. In the low form of ethical friendship, one only pretends to give as a friend, and then demands a return. In the more high-minded form, the giver genuinely believes himself to be a friend and to be acting nobly and generously, but then he demands an equal or greater return, equal if he now decides the gift was really a loan, greater if he still considers himself to have been nobly generous and to deserve a reward as well as a return. The virtuous friend will never demand a return, but he may still have a sense of entitlement, and precisely because he never claims the return and the gratitude to which he feels entitled, perhaps all the greater a sense of entitlement.

Of these three types, the first is deceitful but not confused, and the second is clearly confused as to whether he is engaged in a profitable partnership or an act of noble generosity.[6] People in friendships of virtue do not suffer from this confusion; they do not see themselves as engaged in a profitable partnership. But are they wholly free of confusion? The fundamental confusion in ethical friendships turns on the question of whether a good deed is choiceworthy for its own sake or whether it needs to be rewarded. If an unsolicited good deed is done *for the sake* of a reward, it seems that no reward or even return is really owed, although as Aristotle says, a decent man will make some return. People who clean windshields uninvited and then hold out their hands for change are called hustlers and have no just claim on the drivers, although many people will pay them anyway, in New York because they are afraid, but in Toronto because they are nice and do not want to be stingy. High-minded ethical friends are not like squeegee-pests; they are not acting only for a reward, but in some sense they see a fine act as good in itself, and they may be prompted by affection as well. But to the extent that they feel betrayed when their good deeds meet with no gratitude and return, they reveal that they have in fact acted *in expectation* of a reward. Shutting one's eyes to one's expectations at the time of acting does not make the action disinterested, but only confused.

There seem to be two possible ways to choose a virtuous action clear-sightedly. One would be to choose it in the recognition that it is a sacrifice, bad for oneself and one's own happiness, but noble and therefore choiceworthy in and of itself altogether apart from any reward. We may wonder, however, whether such a disposition towards virtue and one's own happiness is humanly possible. Can love make it possible? If one has a great enough love, can one sacrifice one's own good for the sake of another and his happiness, and truly expect nothing back? To be certain that such a person is not secretly motivated by the hope for a reward, we would have to see how he would respond if his sacrifices were met with ingratitude and cold indifference. Could he accept this disappointment without feeling angry or betrayed?

The second way to escape confusion in the performance of noble actions is to choose them as both noble and good for oneself, and this seems in fact to be the outlook of everyone who is truly noble-minded and not secretly mercenary. All such people seem to say, "I am not in the final analysis depriving myself of what matters most; a pure soul is worth more than diamonds." It is this outlook, this choice of virtue entirely for its own sake, or both for its own sake and the sake of its beneficiaries, rather than for extrinsic rewards, that we admire as genuinely noble and deserving. Here then, is the great paradox of the noble: it is only when one can be truly indifferent to any reward that one seems to deserve it. But is anyone so perfectly pure in motive? Clearly many think that they are, that not only have they not acted for the sake of a reward, but that their happiness does not require that they be paid off after the fact, and that the universe is not evil or tragic if they are not. But may there not be a lingering but powerful hope even here, a hope that precisely their willingness to forego a reward makes them especially worthy of reward, and that somehow the universe will come through for them? Could they bear it if noble people routinely fared worse than evil people and routinely were laughed at? Could they say that this adversity is trivial compared with the great good of having a noble soul, and the laughter is the laughter of fools?

But perhaps these questions imply too strict a standard for perfect virtue. After all, it is not only heroes but all decent observers who wish for virtue to be rewarded, and who believe that the virtuous man's beneficiaries are indebted to him. If this is the outlook of a decent onlooker, is it not natural, even unavoidable for the virtuous man himself to consider his beneficiaries to be in his debt? Thus the question arises whether a virtuous man could not choose virtue for itself and yet still be consistent and unconfused in maintaining that generosity ought to be returned and virtue rewarded, as a simple matter of justice. Does this belief create a subterranean sense of entitlement and expectation that necessarily contaminates the purity of his motive? Or may he say with perfect consistency that while his beneficiary is indeed indebted to him, he himself does not need any reward, although he welcomes it as a kind of icing on the cake?

The question to be asked here is: Why is any debt incurred, if indeed the act is good for the virtuous man and he is made happier by performing it? Does every freely given benefit require a return, or only those that involve sacrifice? A camper who runs out in a midnight thunderstorm to bring in everyone's clothes from the clothesline puts his friends in his debt, because it is better to have dry clothes without getting a midnight soaking than with one, but the camper who entertains his friends around the campfire with lovely music does not make them feel indebted in the same way, because creating beautiful music is even more pleasant than merely hearing it. If his friends "owe" him anything, it is only thanks, and only owed in the sense that a good person will *want* to express his pleasure and warm regards to one who has delighted him. Such thanks, for the musician who plays for the love of it, will indeed be nothing more than icing on the cake. But is most noble action so unambiguously good as making beautiful music? When we believe the beneficiaries of virtuous action truly owe a substantive return, it is because we perceive the benefactor to have made a sacrifice that needs a reward. But this judgment suggests that we are unsure of whether virtuous action truly is good in itself, or we consider it good to do, but not as good as benefiting from it.

But if this is the outlook of virtuous men, can they truly choose virtue for its own sake? Can they be content endlessly to accept the lesser of two goods, endlessly to be on the less advantageous side of all their transactions with others, and not to be rewarded? If not, they are to some extent, out of the corner of their eyes, acting with a view to a reward, and to that extent they are confused. In the next chapter, Aristotle argues that no one is willing always to have the smaller share (1163b10–11), and this unwillingness becomes especially clear in unequal friendships. Men who are superior in virtue or usefulness think that their superiority entitles them to more, he says, and a friendship ceases to be a friendship at all and becomes a *leitourgia*, a public service or charity, if a man does not get out of it any fair return. But why would one shrink from continual public service if the best of all things is to act nobly? Why would one not precisely seek out decent and needy men to be one's friends, so that one could confer benefits on them, since, as Aristotle has said, good deeds are especially noble when done to friends? But instead, people seek an equal return in friendship as in political life, and Aristotle says that in both cases the superior party who performs great services must be rewarded.

However, the argument at the end of Book VIII has as its premise that virtue needs a reward; it therefore does not apply to the true lovers of virtue, who find noble actions completely good and satisfying. Aristotle seems to have left such people behind, but they will reappear in Book IX. These men, the only clear-sighted and consistent of noble men, would take a view of noble action rather different from the common view, which honors dying for a cause as the peak of virtue. To them, virtue at its best and fullest would have to be something less stern and resigned, and altogether more joyful and satisfying than our customary conception of it.

SELF-LOVE AS THE STANDARD OF FRIENDSHIP

Aristotle turns in Book IX to his deepest inquiry into the relation between friendship and self-love. Love, Aristotle says in chapter 4, is defined by our relations with ourselves: the standard of love at its best is that one cares for another and his welfare as one cares for oneself. A friend, he says, is considered to be one who (1) wishes for and does what is good or seems good for his friend for the friend's own sake; (2) wishes the being and life of the friend for his own sake; (3) enjoys spending time with his friend; (4) enjoys or prefers the same things; and (5) shares the sorrows and joys of his friend (1166a1–9). All of these elements, Aristotle argues, are found above all in a decent man's relationship with himself, and virtually all are absent in the wicked. He takes up the same five characteristics of friendship in the same order at 1166a10–29 and again at 1166b7–26, except that each time he begins with the fourth: a good man is of one mind with himself and desires the same things with his whole soul, whereas the wicked are divided, desiring one thing and wishing another, judging one thing as best but doing something else. Inner harmony is one of virtue's greatest rewards and inner dissension or self-hatred perhaps the worst consequence of vice and moral weakness. At the same time, if perfect harmony or unity of choice and purpose is the mark of friendship, friendship will necessarily always be an imperfect approximation of what a good man can realize completely in his own soul, for friends have separate bodies and, invariably, separate desires. By bringing the issue of unanimity to the fore, Aristotle points to this crucial limitation of friendship.

Taking up next the first characteristic of friendship, Aristotle says that a good man wishes and does what is good for himself for his own sake. He acknowledges that everyone wishes his own good, although only the best accomplish it. Others seek the wrong ends by failing to grasp what is truly good, or know in a sense what is best but lack the moral strength to do it. In considering the sense in which we wish the good for ourselves, Aristotle shows dramatically that men's fundamental concern is not a disinterested love of the good but a love of their *own* good. "No one would choose to become someone else and for that being to have everything good (for as it is the god has the good), but only being whatever he is; and each person seems to be or to be most of all that by which he thinks" (1166a21–23). No one, in other words, could wish that he might disappear and be replaced by some better and happier being, for such a being already exists, but that does not suffice to make *him* happy. And the part of us that must remain in order for us to remain ourselves, according to Aristotle, is our mind. We can wish for different bodies and even different, more orderly passions (e.g., we can wish we were not afraid of snakes), but we cannot wish our considered judgments regarding what is good, bad, dangerous, etc. to be anything other than what they are. Even wishing to be wiser is only wishing that we had more of the intelligence that we already have and that we already love. And without our memories and hopes we would not be ourselves at all. Passions can overwhelm us and lead us astray, whereas having self-control means having one's mind in control, and it is our rational acts that we consider most fully to be our own acts, autonomous and voluntary (1168b33–1169a2). If we are most of all our minds, then the most important virtue will be clarity of mind, and the highest form of self-love will be the love of a philosopher for his own mind.

Second, Aristotle suggests that only the good man wishes for his own life and preservation, and he says that extremely wicked people even do away with themselves. But surely this is a morally edifying exaggeration. By arguing that no one would trade in his own existence for that of a better being, Aristotle implicitly concedes that virtually everyone, good and bad, not only wishes for his own good but loves his own existence. Third, the good man wishes to spend time with himself, Aristotle says, since he has good memories, good hopes, and ample subjects in his mind for thought, whereas wicked men shun solitude and seek to forget themselves in the company of others. Does this mean that our sociability is directly tied to our defects, that in seeking out friends we are above all fleeing the chaos or the poverty of our own souls? Or is it rather the case that we are meant by nature both for society and for solitude, and that the best man will be best suited for both? Aristotle does not deny that good men love society, but he does show that a powerful root of our sociability is a neediness that the best man would not feel.

Finally, the good man shares his own joys and sorrows, in the sense that he experiences them fully and simply, without inner divisions, vacillations, or regrets. By setting up freedom from regrets as the standard of true virtue and inner harmony, Aristotle suggests how rare such virtue and harmony are, since even most very decent people have regrets. To escape them entirely, one would have to have an almost superhuman degree of self-understanding. All potential inner conflicts must be resolved with such clarity and certainty that there is no room for wavering, and every decision must be made with such wisdom that it cannot be regretted. If one might in retrospect have chosen otherwise in some instance, one would still have the peace of knowing that one chose the best course in light of everything one knew or could reasonably have been expected to know at the time. Virtue and inner peace require, in short, being philosophic.

These five elements are considered the components of friendship, Aristotle says, because the good man is disposed in these ways towards himself, and he has the same attitude towards his friend as towards himself, for a friend is another self. Men know of no better way to treat another than the way they wish to be treated and seek to treat themselves: friendship is derivative from, because it is an extension and reflection of, each man's concern with himself. But how satisfactory is this image of the friend as another self? The juxtaposition of "other" and "self" is at the very least paradoxical, since for each of us our own identity and consciousness is utterly unique. Perhaps Aristotle intends this formulation to represent a kind of limit case, the never fully attained perfection at which friendship aims.[7] But even leaving aside the fact that each consciousness is separate, is it true that the best friend is most completely similar to oneself? Why, then, would we not be best friends with our own echoes and reflections? An absolutely identical friend, who did the same things and thought the same thoughts at all the same moments as oneself, would seem to be unhelpful and uninteresting. Differences and complementarity can make friends more useful and pleasant to each other, and this complementarity will be more important the more limited and needy each friend is, but if true friendship turns on sharing experiences and loving others for what they are, as a good man loves himself, similarity in virtue will matter most. However, no degree of similarity can erase the ultimate separateness of two individuals. The paradox of the phrase "another self" points to the fact that even if a friend were identical, he would never be interchangeable with oneself, since the pain of personal catastrophe can never be obliterated by knowing that there is someone else who is still faring well.

THE LOVE FELT BY BENEFACTORS

How does a friend come to be another self to the extent that one feels an intense affection and desire and willingness to make sacrifices for him? How does the natural warmth and goodwill we feel for those who seem good and akin to us turn into deep devotion? One clue can be found in the affection benefactors feel for those they help. Aristotle notes the somewhat puzzling fact that benefactors seem more attached to their beneficiaries than the reverse (1167b17–19). He rejects the common explanation that the benefactors take an interest in their beneficiaries as creditors do in their debtors, out of a desire to get something back from them. He concedes that some such concern may often be at work, since most people prefer to have good done to them than to do it. But this fact does not account for the genuine affection that benefactors feel. The true cause of this affection lies deep in human nature, in our love of life. The affection of benefactors is like the love of craftsmen for their work, poets for their poems, money-makers for their money, and mothers for their children. Each loves what he or she produces, because "existence is for everyone an object of choice and of love, and we exist in activity, in living and acting, and in his activity the maker is, in a sense, the work produced" (1168a6–8). Or, as Aristotle says in the next sentence, the work reveals in actuality what the maker is in potentiality. In one sense, the product we love, especially if it is an inanimate product like a pot, is one step removed from the being or living that we love most of all. We exist fully in activity and only secondarily or by extension in the product that remains when our work is done. But in another sense, the finished work is the realization of what its maker was only potentially before he made it: the finished work is not just a relic of his activity but the final cause or defining purpose or true meaning of his activity. Since the best thing in life is being fully in action, and activity done for the sake of a product is subordinate to that product (1094a5–6), the most choiceworthy thing of all will be activity that is done for its own sake, including activity that is shared with friends. But second best will be the efforts we make for the sake of friends, not for money or for lifeless objects.

The more of our thought and energy and trouble we invest in someone, the more that person seems to be an extension of or a realization of our own life, and so, loving our own existence, we find his existence precious to us also. This is a major reason why time and familiarity build affection, especially between good people: each person's efforts on the other's behalf increase his affection, and greater affection makes him care more and trouble himself still more for the other. Thus Aristotle shows that the love of one's own, a source of so much prejudice, skewed judgment, and resistance to serious inquiry, has a thoroughly natural and even sensible root. If what we truly, deeply love is life, and if we are more alive the more we have in hand and the more we love and accomplish, then as Aristotle stresses, it is natural that we should especially love our own actions and friends and beneficiaries as part of our own fully realized existence. But inevitably, the activity of the present and the prospect of more such activity for a finite span of years does not satisfy all that we yearn for. We begin to look and hope for something more, something to compensate us for our mortality, something lasting and meaningful to make sense of our suffering. And this concern for what is noble both reinforces and distorts the natural love of our work and of its objects or beneficiaries.

Aristotle says that one reason the benefactor is more pleased by his act than is the beneficiary is that to the former it is noble, whereas to the latter it is at most useful, and what is useful is less pleasant and lovable than what is noble (1168a9–12).[8] Now this statement is both troubling and puzzling. First, if in most benevolent activity what is noble to the giver is only of passing utility to the receiver, if it does not usually change his soul in a lasting way and make possible his own virtuous activity, then Aristotle indicates that such benevolence is problematic in putting the high in the service of the low. Second, this statement seems to contradict the statement Aristotle has just made (at 1167b28) that most people prefer to have good done to them than to do it, which is to say, they prefer the useful to the noble. The explanation comes in the immediate sequel. What is noble is more pleasing and lovable than what is useful for everyone *in retrospect*. Hence even vulgar people will love their beneficiaries, feeling pleased with the good deeds they have done, and they will prefer the memory of good deeds to the memory of useful ones whose profits have long since been spent. But what matters most for our happiness, Aristotle gently reminds us, is not memories or anticipations but present action (1168a14–15), and so noble action cannot be counted as altogether good if it is not best and most choiceworthy at the moment of acting as well as afterwards.

Therefore, when life's sweetness is elusive or insufficient and one hungers for something splendid and lasting, when one's focus is on sacrificing for others because it is noble, when one throws oneself into charitable or political work not out of love for others or for the activity itself, but out of a cold sense of justice or a hope for fame or reward, one tends to live for one's memories or one's hopes. One's attention is drained away from the present that matters most, away from joyful, active life, to settle instead on thoughts of permanence. And these thoughts are likely self-deceiving. Although the concern for permanence can lead to a clear-sighted pursuit of lasting truths, or a clear-sighted interest in posterity, it also creates a strong temptation to imagine that one can live on in one's work after death much more than one actually can. It is true that to some extent Shakespeare is still alive in his plays and Lincoln in his speeches. Their spirits and thoughts persist enough that we can come to know them and love them. They are alive for us, then, but they are not alive for themselves. Therefore, if Shakespeare, in writing his plays, took pleasure in the present imagination of the pleasure he would give to us, and even took pleasure in feeling affection for thoughtful readers he would never meet, this was a solid pleasure that enhanced his inherently happy activity of writing. But if he imagined that fame would somehow give him a happiness that would go on after his death, he was deceived. If the most important thing is living and being in the activity of the present, not hopes or memories, then to be the best thing in life and the core of happiness, virtuous action must not be a sacrifice for the sake of something else beyond the action itself.

What place will helping others have, then, in the best possible life? Taking activity for its own sake as the goal, we can establish a hierarchy of activities that involve helping others. Lowest would be that which aims at helping the body and that one does for pay. Higher would be activity that seeks to help the soul, especially that which is prompted by love and which needs no reward. Best of all is that which helps and is delightful to both partners—the engaging discussions of teacher and student that educate the student while pushing the teacher to greater clarity, or the trip to a skating pond of mother and child, in which the mother takes pleasure in seeing the child awaken to the discovery of something new and wonderful, and each person enjoys both the company of the other and the activity itself. But every such apprenticeship ultimately makes sense only as aiming beyond itself to a mature partnership in excellent, joyful activity.

SELF-LOVE AND NOBLE SACRIFICE

In chapter 8, Aristotle provides the capstone of the argument he has been building that the best friend is not another but oneself. He thereby demonstrates that the most important thing for happiness is not to have a good friend in another but to have the right stance towards oneself and the capacity to secure what is good for oneself, especially for one's soul or mind. Aristotle does not bend his efforts to making the case that all men in fact love themselves most of all, although he clearly implies that they do. For showing that all the actual men that we know love themselves most would not prove that the rarest and best man, leading the best possible life, might not love others more. Instead, Aristotle makes the more radical contention that decent people *should* love themselves most of all, and that the greatest self-love is characteristic of the very best people, even or especially in their moments of seemingly greatest self-sacrifice.[9]

Aristotle begins from the obvious truth that self-love is almost universally an object of reproach. Giving this disapproval its due, he nevertheless contends that the "facts" do not agree with the speeches or arguments that the best men put others first and neglect their own good for the good of their friends (1168a36–b1). But curiously, the facts he adduces on the other side are not human beings' actual behavior but more speeches or arguments. To prove that loving oneself most is right and good, Aristotle must show not only that good men in fact love themselves most, but also that people and especially serious people reveal in their speeches and beliefs a recognition of the supreme goodness and nobility of a certain kind of self-love. Furthermore, Aristotle must show that this somewhat obscure recognition, when brought to light and clarified, leads to a more comprehensive and satisfying understanding of the phenomenon of self-love than the blanket condemnation that is usually expressed.

The relevant facts are, then, the common beliefs that one should love one's best friend above all, that the best friend is one who truly wishes a person's good for his own sake, and that this goodwill is most to be found in a man's regard for himself (1168b1–5). The love of self and the love of another are not different in kind, one basely seeking to acquire the good and the other nobly indifferent to it. Both aim at the good and take their bearings by what promotes human happiness. If it is good to seek the good of another, how can it be bad to seek the good of oneself? If it is right to love the benefactor that one has in another, how is it wrong to love the even greater benefactor that one has in oneself? Aristotle identifies the element of truth in the common criticism of self-love: "Those who blame self-love call men lovers of self who assign to themselves a larger share of money and honor and bodily pleasures: for these are the things which the many set their hearts upon and zealously pursue as the greatest goods, and thus they are objects of contention" (1168b15–19). What the majority blame in others largely because they want it for themselves, Aristotle blames because it is bad to set one's heart on a lesser good rather than on the greatest good, and everyone somehow sees this too. Those who zealously pursue money, bodily pleasures, and even honor, he says, are gratifying their desires and passions and in general the irrational parts of their souls. These are the many, and their self-love is bad both in leading them into conflict and injustice and in keeping them from what is truly best.

The higher form of self-love, in contrast, impels one to try to outdo everyone else in virtue and to secure the greatest possible nobility for oneself. The man who is characterized by this form of self-love gratifies and obeys the dominant part of himself, his mind, in everything. But if the mind which a virtuous man gratifies most is most truly himself, more truly than are the pleasures and passions that drive the vulgar, then the virtuous man loves himself more than anything, and his is the greatest self-love. This form of self-love is good for everyone concerned. Obeying and gratifying one's true self means doing what one should, choosing virtue, because "intelligence always chooses what is best for itself" (1169a17).

Now the force of this argument is not at first glance fully apparent. Why does obedience to reason necessarily mean loving one's own mind or one's own virtue more than one loves those one wishes to benefit? It is, after all, perfectly conceivable that one might obey reason in everything, and yet one's reason would be such that it would unswervingly pursue the good of others (or at least put the good of friends on a par with one's own). In what way is Aristotle's claim that intelligence always chooses what is best for itself more than a bald assertion? To substantiate this claim, he must show that virtuous men are not like thinking bees, who would obey their minds in always serving the good of the hive. And this proof comes in Aristotle's account of the spirit in which noble-minded men choose their actions. Immediately after making his claim that intelligence chooses what is best for itself, Aristotle gives a vivid account of all the generous and courageous acts of sacrifice that morally serious men will make for their fellows (1169a18–b2). He thereby provides reassurance that choosing the best for oneself or one's mind does not by any means entail neglecting the good of others. At the same time, he demonstrates that morally serious men do love themselves most of all, and he reveals a problem with their outlook.

In all that he does, the morally serious man acts so as to secure what is noblest for himself. But acting nobly means first and foremost acting by deliberate choice. If one's overwhelming concern were really the welfare of one's fellows and not one's own character or nobility, it would not make a great difference whether one served it through deliberately chosen action or otherwise, so long as its good was secured. But in fact, for human beings, the difference between serving others voluntarily and doing so involuntarily is the greatest difference in the world. The same man who would consider it supremely honorable to lay down his life for the fatherland would find it a horrible outrage if his fellows simply seized him and sacrificed him as a passive victim to appease the enemy. The noble-minded man will give up wealth, honor, and everything that men fight over, including life itself, but he will not give up what he loves more than mere existence: his own rational judgment and moral integrity, his autonomous power of choice and action. He would never submit himself blindly to the will of another, although he might choose to trust one who in his judgment is better and wiser than he is. The virtuous man, in making a sacrifice, is hence different from a thinking bee in two respects. First, it is crucial that it be *his* sacrifice, deliberately chosen; and second, he must be able to understand this sacrifice as ultimately best for the best part of himself, his rational soul, or at least consistent with its good. He may face death believing that his soul is about to be extinguished, but if he chooses this death for its nobility, he will do so with the judgment that a brief moment of great glory is better than a lifetime of mediocrity, or of shame at his cowardice in the crucial test. He would be horrified at the thought of sacrificing his highest good, and becoming base, vile, foolish, or weak-willed for the sake of someone else.[10]

But Aristotle has now deftly pulled away the curtain and shown that acts of apparent noble sacrifice, made by those who understand nobility as the highest good, really are not acts of sacrifice at all. What at first seemed to be a sacrifice is in fact (or at least is judged by the one choosing it) an exchange of lesser goods for greater goods. And sacrifice of the greatest goods—one's mind and integrity—would be morally repugnant. The question is whether, when such noble acts are so clearly seen for what they are, they can still make sense as the epitome of virtue and the highest purpose of a virtuous life. Is there not something absurd and distasteful about trying to get the better of everyone else by giving up the most for them? But if so, we must reassess what makes a generous or apparently selfless act noble.[11] If nobility is a great good that the most virtuous men are eager to secure for themselves, its essence cannot lie in sacrifice, or in the magnitude of what is given up. Rather, a generous deed must be noble because it is the rationally chosen act of a strong soul, able to see clearly what is good, to love friends who are good, to marshal great capacities to benefit those one cares about, and to pursue one's highest concerns with enlightened, unwavering self-command. And if the essence of nobility does not lie in sacrifice, then the most clear-sighted virtuous person will not compete for the opportunity to make sacrifices, although he will still willingly make them if necessary.

How, then, will a wise person balance his concern for his own good with a concern for the good of others, and how would the balance he finds compare with that of the common run of people and that of the somewhat confused high-minded gentleman? The paramount concern for the most noble-minded and wisest human beings, and in varying degrees important for everyone, is the mind's concern for itself, for rationality of choice, clarity of understanding, and integrity. For the noble-minded gentleman, a central part of the integrity he cherishes is the principle of putting others first. He thinks incoherently that noble actions can be true sacrifices, making him worthy of honor or of other rewards, and at the same time that they are best for the highest part of himself. For the wisest person, the mind's concern with itself is not primarily a concern to act nobly in this sense, but a concern to act virtuously and intelligently, in pursuit of good ends, and with a proper grasp of the relative rank of those ends. But is this overarching concern the mind's only concern? When Aristotle says that intelligence chooses what is best for itself, is this the same as saying that intelligence chooses what is best for *oneself*? Does intelligence, then, never pursue the good of others when this conflicts even in a minor way with one's own good, and are all benevolent actions really chosen only for one's own happiness, understood either as pleasure or as securing the noble for oneself or as some such thing? Perhaps, but it seems truer both to Aristotle's analysis as a whole and to the phenomena to say that a healthy soul has a wide range of wishes and concerns, both for oneself and for others, that are the true ends of action. The satisfaction of all one's wishes would be perfect happiness, but this fact does not prove that everything one does is for the sake of one's own happiness: such an argument would be a mere tautology. Our happiness consists both in our good narrowly understood and in the good of others, and although the happiness of a loved one pleases us, it is putting the cart before the horse to say that we benefit him in order to make ourselves happy. Instead, when we act out of goodwill, we benefit him because we love him, and because we love him, it makes us happy to see him happy. Thus, although the mind's concern with itself is paramount, it is not the decisive concern behind every action.[12] In most situations there are various possible courses of action that might meet the demands of both integrity and rationality, depending on one's *other* concerns. Staying up late to comfort a distraught friend may conform to one's overriding concern to act rationally and virtuously, but one does not necessarily do it because it is noble or even because it pleases one; one may do it simply because one loves one's friend.

It seems, then, that one can pursue the good of others in three possible ways. First, one may find the action inherently rewarding as a contribution to a common good, an interesting challenge, a source of pleasant interaction with those one cares about, or an opportunity to learn and to improve one's own abilities. Here there is no sacrifice of personal good, and no felt need for honor or reward. Second, one may choose the act for its nobility, perceiving it as a sacrifice and incoherently believing that this is what makes it choiceworthy. One may then compete for the opportunity to make the sacrifice, but one will also consider oneself entitled to gratitude, honor, or some other reward as a result. Third, one may choose the act out of love, seeing with perfect clarity that it is a sacrifice of one's personal good, but preferring it anyway because of one's affection for another. Now if, as Aristotle says, everyone loves his own good most of all, a clear-sighted person will not set aside his own good to secure a good of equal magnitude for his friend, but he may well do it to secure a greater good for his friend. He will prefer having a good day to knowing that his friend has had a good day, or hearing Itzhak Perlman to knowing that his friend has heard Itzhak Perlman, but he will gladly give a concert ticket to his friend if he knows it will mean more to him than it would to himself. Such a clear-sighted friend will not compete for the opportunity to die for the other, but he may nonetheless choose to do so, just as Socrates did, who preferred to give up a few uncertain years in exile and in decline, so that philosophy might win renown, and so that his young friends like Plato, who had as yet written almost nothing, might prosper.

We asked earlier whether, out of love, one can truly sacrifice one's own good for that of another, and truly be content to do so without expecting a reward. Our answer now can be a qualified yes. Such a thing can only be done by one who is perfectly clear-sighted, so that confused expectations do not muddy his motives. He will not rush to embrace the sacrifice, but if the reasons are compelling enough, he will make it. It will not in the strictest sense be a sacrifice of his happiness, because the good of his friend is a part of his happiness (hence it will not need a reward), but it will be a sacrifice of his personal good. He will not be free of disappointment if his friend shows no gratitude, because friendship matters to him, the virtue of his friend matters to him, and a good man does feel affection and gratitude to his benefactor as a matter of course. He will feel disappointment, then, at ingratitude, but no sense of betrayal or outrage, since his choice was not premised upon the expectation of a return. Thus it turns out that the wisest man is the one most capable of both the truest self-love and the truest friendship, for only he has a mind that is perfectly good and lovable, only he can love what he is without inner conflicts, and only he can love another without illusions, without competition over the noble, and without surreptitious expectations of reward.

But if the very best friends will not see their sacrifices for one another as either the peak of nobility or the core of their friendship, what will the focus of the friendship be? Precisely at the same point at which Aristotle shows the self-contradiction of competing for the noble, he introduces the concern that can lead to the truest common good: the love of reason (1169a2–5). In wisdom there is a nobility that is rare but not scarce. Thoughts can be truly shared, unlike money and honors and power and all the bodily goods, which can only be divided. From this point on, then, Aristotle will bring philosophy increasingly to the fore as a focus for the best friendships and the best life.

THE GOODNESS OF FRIENDSHIP

In Book IX.9, Aristotle offers his final reflections on why friendship is important in the best life. Aristotle, who has been examining friendship all along from the perspective of the moral gentleman, now brings his discussion onto a new plane in this chapter. He mentions happiness for the first time in Books VIII and IX, and mentions it repeatedly. In connection with the new focus on happiness, two other themes come into bold relief—the theme of nature and the theme of the philosophic life.

Aristotle, a champion of friendship, puts the question of why a happy man needs friends in the mouths of those with the most vulgar outlook. Friends are good for getting us what we need, these people think, and so if someone already has everything good, what use are friends? To this question, Aristotle replies first of all that it would be strange to assign all good things to a happy man and not friends, which are considered the greatest of external goods (1169b3–7). Now Aristotle has said elsewhere, at 1123b18–20, that honor is the greatest of external goods. Honor is truly an external good and dependent on the whims of chance; it can come and go like fortunes in a casino. Who are the people who think of friends as such external goods? Ordinary people who are not so crude as to think of friends as tools may still consider them as possessions. They imagine a happy man to be one blessed by fortune with money, good looks, a splendid sports car, beautiful women, a stable full of polo ponies, and rich, famous, glamorous friends. But of course friendship is not a possession but an activity and a disposition of soul.

A more thoughtful and moral reason why the happy man will need friends is that noble activity needs an object for its beneficence. But we have seen that a happy man will spend as much time as possible in activities that are ends in themselves, as opposed to activities that, however noble they may be, would never be chosen unless they promised to cure some evil. Thus it is something of a problem for the virtuous man if he needs the company of people who have problems for him to solve (see 1177a28–32). After mentioning noble deeds, Aristotle continues his ascent to the highest constellation of reasons for the importance of friendship in the happy life, and he mentions nature for the first of many times in this chapter. Companionship is irreducibly good because man is a political being, intended by nature to live with others of his own kind. Although Aristotle mentioned this natural sociability at the beginning of Book VIII (1155a17–22), he has since left it in the background, but it is the essential foundation both of goodwill and of affection. Indeed, a sympathy for and attraction to those who are like us is perhaps even more important than admiration in creating goodwill, and it explains why wishing another well for his own sake so often goes hand in hand with desiring him as a friend for our sake.

Against the view of the vulgar, Aristotle now makes his three most serious arguments. First, Aristotle says that if good activity that is one's own is inherently pleasant for the good man, good activity of his own friend will be pleasant in a similar way as both good and his own, especially since we are better able to observe our neighbors and their actions than ourselves and our actions (1169b30–70a3). After much discussion of the ways in which friends help one another and provide opportunities for one another, Aristotle now gives full due to that essential marrow of friendship of the good, the cherishing of the other for what he is, altogether apart from any benefit that he gives oneself. Such cherishing is naturally pleasant because its object is good and naturally good because it constitutes one of life's finest pleasures, a pleasure of the soul that is not the replenishment of a deficiency but simply sweet. But Aristotle seems to overstate the case for the goodness of this aspect of friendship, drawing in questionable premises to bolster his argument. Delighting in the contemplation of a friend's activity would be supremely good for us if the friend's activity is truly more easy to observe than our own, and if at the same time it is somehow truly our own. Granted, most of us, especially at the outset, can learn more from observing (and reading about) a wide variety of people than simply from considering ourselves, and granted that the actions of our own friends, especially if we have helped to form them, are *somehow* our own. But does the happy man have a blind spot with respect to himself? Would he not know himself best of all? Is not a friend's activity always ultimately his and not ours, so that the pleasure of contemplating it will always be a somewhat passive and vicarious pleasure? Is there not a tension between saying we can see his activity better than our own and saying it is our own? We see again the problem that first arose in the discussion of VIII.3, the problem that cherishing seems at once to be the core of what it means to love a friend for himself, and yet too passive to capture what is best in friendship; and soon we shall have the resolution to this problem.

Aristotle now shifts his sights slightly to take up the second argument. What is supremely good for us is not, after all, our friend's activity but our own activity, and however good and pleasant good activity is, it seems that it is also hard to keep oneself going at it all alone. It is a great human defect that we flag easily even in the activities we care most about, and need prods to keep us going—most commonly prods of fear or of extrinsic rewards, but in the best case, the spur provided by an excellent companion in the activity who can infect us with his enthusiasm, inspire us with his accomplishments, and confirm for us the validity of our own thoughts and accomplishments. Now for everyone, even the wisest, company in activity makes that activity more pleasant, but in Book X Aristotle will argue that the very wisest souls do not need company in order to remain active in the best activity, which is philosophy (1176a32–b1). The advantages of friendship in helping us see ourselves indirectly and in helping us stay active seem to apply especially to the friendships of young or imperfect individuals, and the fact that Aristotle includes such factors in his final statement on the goodness of friendship suggests that perhaps the very most important friendships are to be found on the ascent to the best life, and that friendships at the summit itself will be somewhat more tranquil and less intense.[13]

Finally, Aristotle turns to his profoundest account of the necessity of friendship in the happy life, an account based most emphatically on nature and stressing most explicitly the importance of thinking for happiness. Friends are good to the good man above all because what is good by nature is intrinsically good and pleasant to him, and the life of a good man is good by nature, and so it will be good to him (1170a12-b19). Now we all think we know without any need for argument, as surely as we know anything, that life is good and death is bad, but Aristotle makes an argument for life's goodness that calls the comn. understanding into question. Aristotle argues that life is not, as we think, good absolutely. It is good because it is definite, i.e. it has a definite end and purpose, which is to realize fully in action what is best and most distinctive about us, our capacity for perception and thought. Living well for Aristotle means above all thinking well, and only the life of a good man, as long as is not spoiled by suffering, is truly good.

It is pleasant to observe the life of a good man, but to take part in that life is even better, and to the extent that the best lives consist especially in thought, these are the lives most capable of being shared. Through conversation each friend can enter into the life and existence of the other, and so enjoy that existence more fully than he ever can simply by observing it. Through sharing the activity and especially the thought of a friend, one's interests are expanded and one's activity of thinking is intensified, enriched, clarified, and made more pleasant: one therefore becomes more fully alive.[14] Thus the vital sap of friendship is found in living together, and as Aristotle says, living together for human beings means above all conversing together, not feeding in the same place, as it does in the case of cattle. In posing the two extremes of rational conversation and feeding together as the possible meanings of living together, Aristotle is silent about noble acts of benefaction. These are still necessary in misfortune, as Aristotle will reiterate in chapter 11, but they are not what we live for, not what friendship truly turns upon. And everyone somehow sees this. As Aristotle says in closing, friendship consists above all in sharing those activities that seem good to each person, whether they be drinking, dice playing, sports, hunting, or philosophy (1172a3–6); but the truest, most characteristic activity of friendship is conversation.

We began the investigation of friendship wondering whether friendship might not be the peak of noble virtue and of the human good, able to make us both happy and worthy of happiness. Can we be so nobly devoted to others that we love them more than ourselves? Can such devotion give meaning to empty and unhappy lives, making us whole and somehow saving us from the abyss of our mortality? Aristotle has shown that friendship is neither so lofty nor so powerful. Can we truly love and care for others, pursuing their good for their own sakes and not as a mere means to our happiness? Absolutely, and such love is indeed noble, though not quite in the sense that we all at first imagined it to be. Is friendship a central and integral part of the happy life? Certainly. But friendship is fundamentally good because it magnifies life, expanding our concerns and activities and intensifying our joys: friendship makes better what is already good in life. What matters most of all for happiness, then, is not the companionship that friendship brings but the pleasures and good activities that it augments. In Book X, Aristotle will make the case that the best of all pleasures and good activities is philosophy. In philosophic conversation we find the full realization of our natural ends both as social beings and as rational beings. The best human being will therefore be, if not the most passionate friend, still the one best suited to friendship, and so we may conclude that the best of all friendships will be that of fellow-friends of wisdom.

NOTES

1. Montaigne, Michel de, "On Friendship," in *Selected Essays*, Charles Cotton and W. Hazlitt, trans.; Blanchard Bates, ed. (New York: Modern Library, 1949), 71.

2. The question of whether the two lower forms of friendship involve true goodwill is a vexed one. Following John A. Stewart, *Notes on the "Nicomachean Ethics" of Aristotle* (Oxford: Clarendon Press, 1892), 2: 274, A. W. Price argues in *Love and Friendship in Plato and Aristotle* (Oxford: Clarendon Press, 1989), 148–54, that they do not involve goodwill, and that a friend of pleasure or utility wishes one's friend pleasure or prosperity not for *his* sake but instrumentally, for one's own sake. It is hard to see, however, how such instrumental well-wishing differs from the desire for one's wine to keep, which Aristotle emphatically says is not friendship. In contrast, John M. Cooper, in "Aristotle on the Forms of Friendship," *Review of Metaphysics* 30 (1977): 619–48, argues that Aristotle attributes true goodwill to all forms of friendship, but perhaps he makes Aristotle more consistent in this regard than the text warrants. Suzanne Stern-Gillet, in *Aristotle's Philosophy of Friendship* (Albany: State University of New York Press, 1995), 38, and A. D. M. Walker, in "Aristotle's Account of Friendship in the *Nicomachean Ethics*," *Phronesis* 24 (1979): 180–96, also see goodwill in the lesser forms of friendship, but in a qualified way and in response to something that is peripheral to the friend's true character. For a radical interpretation that denies goodwill to all forms of friendship, see A. W. H. Adkins, "Friendship and Self-Sufficiency in Homer and Aristotle," *Classical Quarterly* n.s. 13 (1963): 30–45.

3. It therefore follows, incidentally, that the great-souled man, who is concerned especially with honor, is not the highest type, and is less admirable than the most self-sufficient human beings.

4. Compare Plato *Symposium* 210a–212a. Price, in *Love and Friendship*, 103–8, articulates well the problem that loving someone for his virtues means having primary regard for those virtues and not for the friend's utterly unique identity. But in attempting to resist Aristotle's suggestion that virtue is properly our highest concern, Price makes the remarkable claim that Aristotle is "idiosyncratic" in equating "loving someone for himself" with "loving him for his character." This dissatisfaction is shared by Julia Annas, in "Plato and Aristotle on Friendship and Altruism," *Mind* 86 (1977): 532–54.

5. Stern-Gillet suggests that the emphasis on freedom of choice and spontaneity, as opposed to loving another for his virtues, has come to characterize modern friendship altogether, and it is this focus upon the "contingency and capriciousness" of friendship that has caused the topic "to drop out of the philosophic agenda" (*Aristotle's Philosophy of Friendship*, 8).

6. On this confusion, see also Cooper, "Forms of Friendship," 639, and Price, *Love and Friendship*, 155–57.

7. Stern-Gillet argues that, to the extent that friends are truly "other selves" to one another, the friendship can be seen less as an external good and more as an outgrowth of the friends' own souls. Hence such friendship is an appropriate part of the happiness of complete and self-sufficient beings (Aristotle's *Philosophy of Friendship*, 14–15; but compare 131).

8. Compare Price, *Love and Friendship*, 115–16.

9. As Vasilis Politis points out, in "The Primacy of Self-love in the *Nicomachean Ethics*," Oxford Studies in Ancient Philosophy, no. 11 (Oxford: Clarendon Press, 1993), Aristotle is really making two separate arguments here: first, that one ought to love one's true self as much as possible, and second, that one ought to love oneself in preference to all others. He will provide a fuller proof of the first assertion than of the second.

10. Although Aristotle has given some reasons for the naturalness and reasonableness of loving oneself most, his examples in this chapter suggest that the primacy of self-love over love of others is at bottom an irreducible fact of human nature, as such neither noble nor base. In contrast, having as much as possible of the right kind of self-love is good and noble. By blurring his account of the way in which men in fact love themselves in preference to others with an account of the way in which they ought to love themselves as much as possible, Aristotle softens the harshness of his teaching about the primacy of self-love.

11. Price gives a clear account of the contradictions involved in noble self-sacrifice according to Aristotle, but he places the blame on Aristotle for having "stumbled into self-contradiction" (*Love and Friendship*, 110–14). Unfortunately, he never offers an alternative account of the moral self-understanding that avoids this contradiction. Stern-Gillet tries at least to soften the contradiction by insisting that the man who makes a noble sacrifice is not in any sense acting with a view to getting the best for himself; his own acquisition of nobility is just an unintended by-product, as it were, of his disinterested love of virtue (*Aristotle's Philosophy of Friendship*, 70–71). This interpretation flies in the face of Aristotle's whole analysis in IX.8 and makes Aristotle a Kantian. Politis argues more persuasively that Aristotle is indeed denying the possibility of moral self-sacrifice and doing so with perfect consistency ("Primacy of Self-love," 170). Politis, however, perhaps gives insufficient weight to the importance of sacrifice in the common understanding of what makes virtuous action noble, even as Aristotle presents this understanding. Thus we have in IX.8 a major reinterpretation of the character of nobility.

12. For a discussion of whether our happiness is or should be our exclusive goal, see especially Sir David Ross, *Aristotle* (London: Methuen and Co., 1949), 230–31; Dennis McKerlie, "Friendship, Self-love, and Concern for Others in Aristotle's *Ethics*," *Ancient Philosophy* 11 (1991): 85–101; and C. Kahn, "Aristotle on Altruism," *Mind* 90 (1981): 20–40.

13. Compare *Nicomachean Ethics* 1177a27–b1; Stern-Gillet, *Aristotle's Philosophy of Friendship*, 133–37 and 141–42; and John M. Cooper, "Friendship and the Good in Aristotle," *Philosophical Review* 86 (1977): 310–15. Stern-Gillet struggles somewhat unsuccessfully to resist the conclusion that friendship will be more important for the less fully developed than for the most self-sufficient. Cooper notes that Aristotle's arguments for the necessity of friendship all point to human weakness, but he doubts that such weakness is ever overcome, even by the best men.

14. This interpretation of Aristotle's third argument is a slight extrapolation from the text. For an interesting discussion of the problems with this argument as read quite narrowly, see Cooper, "Friendship and the Good in Aristotle," 290–302; also see McKerlie, "Friendship, Self-love, and Concern for Others," 93–101.

CHAPTER 10

SOCRATES IN ARISTOTLE'S "PHILOSOPHY OF HUMAN AFFAIRS"

ARISTIDE TESSITORE

This chapter examines Aristotle's remarks about Socrates in the *Nicomachean Ethics* and *Politics*, two works that together comprise Aristotle's "philosophy of human affairs" (*EN* X.9).[1] Although the larger Aristotelian corpus includes several important statements on this topic, I focus on these works because of their explicitly political character. The chapter traces what might be called Aristotle's political presentation of Socrates; that is, the manner in which he is made to appear to readers whose primary interest lies in the realities of politics.[2] Despite current scholarly preoccupation with the historical Socrates, I address this issue only obliquely.[3] Indeed, the effort to distinguish the historical Socrates from the persona we encounter in the works of Plato, Xenophon, and Aristotle would appear to be of limited value since it is the latter—a figure who no doubt bears some resemblance to the original—who is of greatest interest to students of philosophy.

Nevertheless, there is one historical fact that is crucial for an understanding of Socrates: namely, his trial and subsequent condemnation on charges of impiety and corruption of the young. About this fact, however, there can be no doubt. I cite it here because the significance of his trial and condemnation figures prominently (whether explicitly or implicitly) in all subsequent accounts of Socrates. That significance might be stated in a general way as follows. In the historical figure of Socrates the fundamental tension between the life of the philosopher and the requirements of life in the city was brought into sharpest possible relief; the life of radical inquiry was summoned to the tribunal of political justice and found wanting. Socrates the philosopher was condemned to death because his activity in some way undermined the deep although vulnerable guarantors of public order—the shared beliefs of citizens concerning the gods and the noble. In some important and disturbing way Socrates refused to take his bearings from those beliefs considered most authoritative and praiseworthy by his fellow citizens. If this activity was not subversive in intent it was in effect and combined with his own apparent intransigence, it elicited the severest possible penalty.

These well-known facts concerning the trial and death of Socrates are inseparable from his influence on later generations of students. Perhaps one might say that Socrates, more than any other philosopher, personifies the public face of philosophy, that is, philosophy as it confronts and is confronted by the exigencies of political life. If later generations of philosophers were to gain even partial acceptance among their fellow citizens, the life and death of Socrates was an event to be reckoned with. This theme is obvious in the writings of Plato and Xenophon, several of which are explicitly apologetic in character. It is also present in the writings of Aristotle, particularly in his moral-political works. Although an additional generation had intervened since the execution of Socrates, religious and political charges against philosophers were not a thing of the past as Aristotle's own forced exile to Chalcis made all too clear.[4]

If philosophy were ever to be accepted by the city, that acceptance would require as a constitutive element a new attitude toward its hero-victim; those who had once condemned Socrates for his often outlandish and galling manner would have to see him in a new light. If Plato and Xenophon had begun the task, they had not completed it. Could the "gadfly of Athens" come to be regarded as the city's greatest benefactor as the Platonic Socrates gratingly claimed (*Apology* 30c–e; 36d–e)?[5] In what follows I hope to show that Aristotle sought to extend the circle of those who might acknowledge the truth imbedded in this Platonic assertion. Although it may prove impossible to mitigate entirely the disruptive consequences of philosophy for civic life, the apologetic character of Aristotle's political writings is suggested by the extent to which they reveal how philosophy is able to offer respectful and substantial clarity regarding matters of vital importance for those who bear primary responsibility for the city. In the course of Aristotle's "philosophy of human affairs" he attempts to bring readers to some positive, if critical, appreciation for Socrates' life and teaching.[6]

ETHICS

Socrates is mentioned by name seven times in the *Ethics*. These seven references are embedded in four thematic treatments: (1) courage (1116b3–5), (2) truthfulness and irony (1127b25–26), (3) prudence (1144b17–19; 28–30), and (4) incontinence (1145b23–26; 1147b14–17).

COURAGE

Socrates makes his first appearance in the *Ethics* within the context of Aristotle's account of courage where he is associated with the second mistaken or imperfect understanding of this virtue. Courage is defined as a mean with respect to the emotions of fear and confidence, and is displayed especially with reference to that which is most fearful—namely, death. However, even death does not in all circumstances afford an equal opportunity for courage. The fullest measure of this virtue is exhibited on the battlefield where soldiers are called upon to defend their country nobly or die in the effort. That death in battle provides the standard is, Aristotle observes, supported by the fact that public honors are conferred precisely on this basis. Although it is possible to be courageous in the face of illness or a storm at sea, courage in the full sense (*kuriōs andreios*) is found midst the perils of war.

The second major emphasis in this treatment is Aristotle's insistence that the courageous person acts with a view to the noble. If the formal cause of virtue is best explained as a mean between excess and deficiency, its final cause is attachment to the noble. Although courageous individuals sometimes experience fear, they do so in the right manner (*hōs dei*) and as principle (*logos*) dictates on account of the noble (*tou kalou heneka*) (1115b11–13).

Two observations are appropriate at this point. First, courage is essentially a political virtue; it is exhibited by one who nobly confronts death on the battlefield. Secondly, Aristotle's initial elaboration of the noble is presented within this same civic horizon. The kind of courage that one might exhibit in confronting a fatal disease (although it might also be borne as one ought, according to principle, and for the sake of the noble) fails to provide the full measure of courage because, Aristotle asserts, the noblest kind of death involves sacrifice for one's country.

The second part of Aristotle's account takes up five qualities that bear some resemblance to courage but do not constitute the virtue in the proper or most authoritative sense. The five "types" of courage discussed are (1) political courage, (2) experience, (3) spiritedness, (4) cheerfulness, and (5) courage based on ignorance.

The second mistaken or imperfect type of courage identifies it with confidence as it results from experience in the face of some particular danger (1116b3–23). It is here that Aristotle first speaks of Socrates, asserting that this view was at the origin of Socrates' supposition that courage is knowledge (*epistēmē*) (1116b3–5). Aristotle explains that this type of courage is exhibited most clearly by professional soldiers. Due to their superior experience, professional soldiers are able to distinguish false alarms from the real thing and so often appear courageous owing to the ignorance of fellow soldiers regarding their true situation. Moreover, the greater experience of professional soldiers makes them adept at fighting, for they know how best to use their arms and possess the best quality arms both for attack and defense. Generally, the superior experience of professional soldiers makes them like armed men fighting against unarmed, or trained athletes competing with amateurs.

Despite their superior fighting ability, Aristotle explains that professional soldiers possess less courage than those citizens who act on the basis of political courage. The reason for this is that professional soldiers rely on their superior strength whereas citizen soldiers are constrained by the fear of disgrace. Hence, whereas citizen soldiers prefer death to safety procured in a shameful way, professional soldiers prove to be cowards when the danger imposes too great a strain or when they are at a disadvantage in numbers or equipment. Aristotle concludes that the type of superiority shown in this case is only incorrectly understood as courage in the proper sense of the word.

Several aspects of Aristotle's initial statement about Socrates warrant further comment. The first and most obvious point is that, from Aristotle's point of view, Socrates' understanding of courage was inadequate; the identification of superior experience or knowledge with courage is mistaken. Secondly, Aristotle's analysis suggests a similarity between the Socratic understanding of courage and the kind of courage exhibited by professional soldiers.

A few tentative comparisons suggest themselves. In the first place, like professional soldiers, Socrates did not appear to be especially attached to the *polis*, at least not after the fashion of those citizen soldiers whom Aristotle has just finished discussing. Moreover, if, as the context makes clear, Aristotle is speaking of foreign mercenaries (*xenoi*), this does not seem an altogether inappropriate way to introduce Socrates who must have seemed like a "foreigner" or "stranger" to many of his fellow Athenians (see *Apology* 17d). Second, although Aristotle indicates that professional soldiers do not possess the virtue of courage, he does acknowledge their superiority in fighting. As Aristotle points out, the most courageous are not necessarily the best fighters. If this second point is applied to Socrates it suggests that he may exhibit a real superiority, although it is a superiority that cannot be understood in terms of courage—at least not as it is defined by Aristotle and exhibited by civic-minded soldiers. This second observation points to a third, one that bears on a major point in Aristotle's discussion. The superiority of professional soldiers derives from their experience, something that results in a greater knowledge of war (Aristotle specifically mentions the ability to distinguish false alarms from real ones) as well as a more extensive and specialized training in the art of fighting. Does this description of the superior experience and consequently superior knowledge of professional soldiers find any analogue in Socrates?

Even those not attracted to Socrates would probably have been impressed by his unwavering refusal to beg for mercy or plea bargain at his trial. Might this Socratic courage be based on an ability to distinguish between false and true alarms? Perhaps, as Socrates maintained at his defense, death, at least in some circumstances, is less to be feared than acting in a way that does not befit a superior man (cf. *Apology* 29a–b and 34c–35b). Socrates claimed that the philosopher does nothing other than spend his whole life dying and preparing to die (*Phaedo* 64a5–6). We might wonder whether Socrates' unusual way of life did not in fact provide him with the best possible training and arms as he faced death, ostensibly at the hands of the Athenian *demos*.

Whatever we make of these particular comparisons, Aristotle indicates that neither the teaching of Socrates nor the example of professional soldiers reveals the virtue of courage in its most authoritative sense. Moreover, despite Socrates' strange detachment from the civic standards that govern the lives of most Athenians, Aristotle's remarks suggest that he may be characterized by a real superiority which, although not properly understood as courage, is in some way based upon knowledge or experience.

IRONY

After a consideration of courage and self-control in Book III, Aristotle takes up liberality and magnificence as he begins an ascent to one of the high points of the *Ethics*, his account of magnanimity in Book IV. The magnanimous person possesses all the virtues to a great or extraordinary degree. In the latter part of Book IV, Aristotle descends from this peak in order to consider several qualities that, although lacking proper names, are part of human excellence as a whole. He discusses ambition, gentleness, agreeableness, truthfulness, wittiness, and a sense of shame. It is within the context of Aristotle's discussion of truthfulness and, not surprisingly, within the more specific context of irony, that he turns for a second time to the figure of Socrates.

Aristotle begins his account of truthfulness (1127a13–b32) by explaining that he is speaking of a virtue that manifests itself even when nothing is at stake because it is the result of a fixed disposition (*hexis*). Boasters pretend to praiseworthy qualities they do not possess, whereas ironic or self-depreciating individuals disclaim their praiseworthy attributes. The mean is found in the straightforward person (*ho authekastos*) who acknowledges the truth without exaggeration or understatement. The individual who possesses this quality is considered morally good (*epieikēs*) and even praiseworthy because one who loves truth (*ho philalēthēs*) even when nothing is at stake is likely to be even more truthful when something is.

Aristotle indicates that both excess and deficiency (boastfulness and self-depreciation) may be pursued with or without an ulterior motive. Those who pretend to more than they deserve with no ulterior motive are considered more foolish than bad. If, however, someone's pretensions have glory or honor as their aim, such an individual is subject to censure (although not severe censure). It would be more disgraceful (*aschēmonesteros*) if the object of one's striving was money or something that would get money.

In contrast to boasters, those who understate their merits possess a more gracious or beautiful (*chariestereos*) character since they are not motivated by gain but by a concern to avoid ostentation. Persons falling into this category sometimes deny or reject the most generally accepted and highly praised opinions (*ta endoxa*). Aristotle cites Socrates as his example before going on to speak of those who disclaim insignificant and obvious qualities. These, he maintains, are appropriately despised. This latter sort of self-depreciation might even be understood as a kind of boastfulness, for both excessive attention and extreme negligence bespeak an element of pretense. However, those who employ (*hoi chrōmenoi*) understatement in a measured way (*metriōs*) regarding things that are not commonplace or obvious appear to be gracious (*charientes*) (1127b29–31).

Several points deserve mention in this account of an apparently minor moral virtue. To begin once again with the most obvious point, Aristotle praises individuals of straightforward character because they embody a virtuous mean between boastfulness and self-depreciation and because a love of truth that expresses itself in small things will naturally embrace greater things as well. It bears noting, however, that the same word that Aristotle uses to describe the straightforward person also describes someone who is blunt or plain (*ho authekastos*). Although these latter qualities would not incur moral blame, one might wonder if the type of character that comes closest to the mean is in every case superior to the one who uses irony in a measured way—the person whom

Aristotle twice refers to as "gracious." Could it be that Aristotle wishes both to recognize the decency of straightforward persons and to direct readers to some appreciation for the more gracious and certainly more complex character of Socrates?

As we have seen, Aristotle indicates that one may be characterized by boastfulness or irony with or without any ulterior motive. Since the only examples of acting from an ulterior motive pertain to boastfulness, the reader is left to wonder what kind of motive might lead one to use irony. Indeed, the only indication furnished by Aristotle in the present case is his reference to Socrates who is clearly placed into the category of those who use irony in a measured way to speak about things that are not obvious or easily seen. If straightforward persons reveal their love of truth (*philalēthēs*) in small matters of no consequence, might Socrates' love of the truth lead him to use irony in matters of great import?[7] Does Socrates use irony because the truth requires it or is best approached in this manner?

A second and related reason for using irony emerges from the larger context provided by Book IV as a whole. In his account of magnanimity, Aristotle indicated that individuals possessing this virtue reveal their greatness toward persons of position and fortune whereas they are measured (*metrion*) in dealing with those of moderate station because it is vulgar to lord it over the weak (1124b17–23). Moreover, when addressing the many, they speak with ironic self-depreciation (*eirōneia*) so as not to call attention to the sharp difference in character that separates a superior individual from an ordinary one. In fact, Aristotle describes the magnanimous person as one who is marked by a curious combination of truthfulness or candor (*alētheutikos*) and irony (1124b26–31).

We have already noted that Aristotle's discussion of the minor virtue of truthfulness takes place in the shadow of his account of magnanimity. By recalling this earlier peak, the present discussion is caste in a new and striking light. Most pertinent in this regard is the fact that irony—that trait for which Socrates stands as Aristotle's sole exemplar—cannot always be understood as a deficiency but is sometimes employed in a measured way by those who embody the highest human excellence.

PRUDENCE

The third and fourth references to Socrates occur within the context of Aristotle's consideration of the relationship between prudence and moral virtue as a whole. This treatment (1144a6–1145a11) might be likened to a revolving door that can be entered from either of two sides. On the one hand, prudence requires moral virtue, since it furnishes the good at which a prudent person aims. The good only appears as such to the morally serious person, and its absence means that the good for which one strives will be defective. Whereas such individuals may be clever in the choice of means to attain their ends, they cannot be called prudent unless the end at which they aim is given by moral virtue. On the other hand, moral virtue cannot exist without prudence. Although the dispositions for particular moral virtues are somehow already present by nature, even good natural dispositions (*hai phusikai hexeis*) can be harmful without the interior sight provided by prudence. Just as a man with a powerful frame takes a particularly hard fall when deprived of sight, prudence supplies "moral vision" for one with a strong natural disposition to virtue. If someone possessing natural excellence (*hē phusikē aretē*) acquires prudence, the disposition that previously only resembled virtue becomes virtue in the full or authoritative sense (*hē kuria aretē*). Hence, if it is true that prudence requires moral virtue, it is also true that moral virtue cannot exist without prudence.

After offering this helpful, if circular, account of the relationship between prudence and virtue, Aristotle amends the opinions of others on this subject. He speaks first of Socrates, maintaining that his line of inquiry was right in one way but wrong in another. He was mistaken in thinking that all virtues were forms of prudence, although he spoke well in maintaining that they cannot exist without it (1144b17–21). Socrates conceived of the virtues as rational principles (*logoi*), supposing all of them to be forms of knowledge (*pasas epistēmas*) (1144b28–30). If this overstates the relationship between reason and virtue, Aristotle's contemporaries understate it. They maintain that virtue is a disposition determined in accordance with right reason and that right reason is what is meant by prudence. Aristotle again offers a slight modification. Virtue does not merely conform to right reason as to something external (*kata ton orthon logon*), rather it is "with" right reason (*meta tou orthou logou*) (1144b25–27). The rational principle from which virtue takes its bearings does not exist outside virtuous persons, it is rather something within them.

Aristotle adopts a middle position between the Socratic and contemporary views and we do well to grasp something of the differences separating these positions. Aristotle's Socratic references appear to be taken from the *Meno*,[8] which begins with Socrates' confession of complete ignorance about the nature of virtue (71b). This statement startles, not to say scandalizes, Meno and understandably so since it flies in the face of conventional civic education as well as the common experience of decent persons, both of which lead most to assume that they know what virtue is. Socrates is, however, undaunted by Meno's ridicule and adds to his initial admission of ignorance that he has yet to meet *anyone* who knows what virtue is (71c). One could hardly describe this manner of inquiry as conciliatory. Indeed, in light of this latter remark, Socrates' confession of ignorance begins to sound like a boast. At the very least, his remarks are intended to challenge or provoke Meno to take up an investigation of something that he believes he already understands.

In the *Meno* (as in other dialogues), Socrates' insistence on knowing and subsequent confession of ignorance are shown to have a direct bearing on his own way of life. As long as one cannot claim to know what virtue is, the most important activity would seem to be the attempt to discover what it is (something that Socrates is not very successful in getting Meno to do precisely because and to the extent that Meno remains unconvinced of his own ignorance). Such an activity, one could argue, properly takes precedence over the effort to conform one's actions to the admonitions of famous teachers, great statesmen, or even the laws of the city itself. Perhaps the life of inquiry should be regarded as the only truly "virtuous" life whereas all others, to borrow from the final image of the *Meno*, are merely lives lived among shadows.

In contrast to Socrates' jarring and provocative approach to the question of virtue,[9] Aristotle sheds light on the common but complicated experience of decent persons and only gently suggests the limits of that experience. At the outset of his study, he had warned that the mark of a well-educated person is to expect only that degree of precision of which a subject matter admits (1094b12–27). By deemphasizing the problematic question concerning the precise relationship between knowledge and virtue, while at the same time bringing an appropriate rigor to his treatment of virtue as a whole, Aristotle is able to acknowledge the dignity of moral virtue without, however, offering final clarity or precision about the nature of the good. Perhaps we should understand Socrates' inquiry as an expression of his uncompromising desire for precise knowledge of his subject matter. Whether or not this is so, in contrast to the impression conveyed by the surface of the Platonic dialogues, the life of moral virtue as it is practiced by morally serious persons is not presented by Aristotle as a shadowy kind of existence, but as a way of life that is intellectually serious and capable of substantial happiness.

The disagreements between Aristotle and Socrates on this issue should not, however, obscure a deeper agreement. The well-known conclusion of the *Ethics* explicitly teaches that a life devoted to the practice of moral virtue is not the best or happiest way of life. Moreover, we should also bear in mind that what Aristotle does recommend to his readers as a serious, if secondary, way of life is the practice of moral virtue as it has been elucidated and amended by Aristotle the philosopher. In the present context, he modifies the contemporary view of virtue by moving closer to the Socratic one; he insists that virtue

requires the active presence of some guiding principle (*logos*). The major difference between Aristotle and his contemporaries on this question is the shift
away from those norms that exist outside an individual toward those that come
from within. Aristotle's subtle emendation rules out the possibility that the
standard for human excellence could be provided by one who simply obeys the
laws of the regime. Such an individual might be a good citizen but should not
be considered a simply good human being (cf. *Politics* 1276b16–1278b5, esp.
1277b25–29 and 1278a40–1278b5).

The fuller significance of this distinction is suggested by Aristotle's concluding remarks in this section. If it is true that authoritative virtue (*hē kuriōs
aretē*) cannot exist without prudence, prudence does not possess more authority (*kuria*) than wisdom nor does it govern the better part of the soul. To maintain otherwise would be like asserting that political science, since it governs
everything in the city (including religious festivals), also wields authority over
the gods (1145a6–11). Whereas prudence qualifies one to rule in the city,[10] wisdom constitutes a higher and more authoritative human excellence. Even if the
wise are de facto subject to the political authority of those who rule, Aristotle
has managed to present a famous, even strident, Socratic teaching on this topic;
namely, those who rule, indeed, the city itself, should be subject to the greater
authority of the wise.[11]

INCONTINENCE

Aristotle's final references to Socrates occur within the context of his discussion of continence/incontinence.[12] His general consideration of this theme
is divided into three parts. Aristotle lists a variety of opinions on the subject
(1145b8–20), brings to light six puzzles (*aporiai*)[13] entangled in those opinions
(1145b21–1146b8), and then attempts to disentangle them (1146b8–
1152a36). The first of the puzzles raises a question about the kind of "right conception" characteristic of those believed to act incontinently (VII.2 1145b21–
1146a9). This problem was focused most sharply by Socrates who thought that
it would be strange if, while knowledge was present, something else could over-
power it and drag it around like a slave (1145b23–24). In fact, he used to com-
bat this view altogether. Socrates maintained that no one acts contrary to what
is best while knowing that what one is doing is bad; actions falling short of
goodness are due instead to ignorance. The most jarring aspect of this Socratic
teaching is that it denies the existence of incontinence (1145b25–27), and in so
doing raises a question about the nature and extent of moral culpability.[14]
Aristotle's formulation of the puzzle expresses sympathy for those who experience Socrates' outlandish position on such an important matter with some-

thing like frustrated indignation. The Socratic view, Aristotle asserts, is clearly at odds with things that appear most manifest (*tois phainomenois enargōs*) (1145b27–28).

Aristotle's thematic treatment of Socrates' teaching is divided into a preface and four (difficult and abbreviated) arguments leading to a final evaluation (1146b24–1147b19). It is sufficient for our purposes to summarize the conclusions of each of these arguments, noting especially their bearing on Aristotle's final evaluation of Socrates.

After a preface in which he dismisses the argument of those who adhere to the Socratic thesis in a modified form, Aristotle offers three dialectical (*logikos*) arguments. The first concludes with the assertion that it would not be surprising if someone were to act against knowledge possessed but not currently in use, although it would be strange (*deinos*) if one acted against knowledge while actively beholding (*theōrounta*) it. Aristotle's second argument amounts to a technical rendition of the first. It would not be strange if one knew both universal and particular propositions in a habitual way but, in a particular case, considered only the universal and not the particular. (For example, one might know that dry food is healthy, but fail to realize that the food before one was dry.) Aristotle adds, however, that it would be astonishing (*thaumaston*) if the individual in question knew in the sense that both universal and particular propositions were apprehended as concrete particulars. Aristotle's analysis thus far differentiates different ways of knowing. However, he has not joined the issue since it is only the last kind of knowing that is involved in incontinence; namely, when one undertakes a particular (that is, concrete) action which is in some sense known to be wrong.

In his third argument Aristotle speaks of the kind of knowing that characterizes someone who is asleep, mad, or drunk. This type of knowing is likened to young students who correctly reel off formulae but without understanding the significance of what they are saying. The incontinent fail in the same way. They may act against what they know but that knowledge is in some way defective for it has not yet "grown into them" (*sumphuēnai*) (VII.3 1147a22). While each of these arguments explains how it is possible to act against what one knows to be right (in opposition to the Socratic view), it should also be observed that each of these arguments points to another way of knowing—perhaps the kind of knowing that Socrates sought—that, Aristotle says, it would be surprising, even astonishing, if one were to oppose by one's actions.

Aristotle's final argument addresses the Socratic paradox from the viewpoint of the natural philosopher (*phusikōs*). He describes a physiological state in which rational control is temporarily overcome by passion or pleasure, a state comparable to that produced by drunkenness or sleep. One acting under the influence of passion or pleasure either does not possess knowledge or possesses it in a defective way, much like drunken persons who repeat the sound moral maxims of Empedocles without altering their behavior in the least. Aristotle's conclusion is striking: "We seem to be led to the position that Socrates sought to establish—it is not knowledge in the authoritative sense (*kuriōs epistēmē*) that is overcome in an incontinent act, nor is such knowledge dragged about by passion" (1147b14–17).

For all the difficulty of Aristotle's particular arguments in this section, their overall effect is clear. In opposition to the Socratic paradox, Aristotle maintains that incontinence both exists and is intelligible. However, Aristotle also points to a kind of knowing that cannot be overcome by emotion. While disagreeing with Socrates about an all-too-familiar aspect of human experience, Aristotle begins to suggest the proper way to understand a much-less-familiar Socratic maxim by pointing to the existence of the rare and authoritative kind of knowledge that was the object of Socratic investigation. The arguments in this section address the question of moral goodness from the perspective of both dialectic and natural philosophy. Within this broader horizon of inquiry, Aristotle brings his readers from an initial frustration with the patently outlandish character of Socratic inquiry to some appreciation for the less than obvious truth to which that inquiry was devoted. In effect, Aristotle's justification of the Socratic paradox provides readers with a greater appreciation for the requirements of knowledge in a strict sense, that is, the kind of authoritative knowledge sought by the wise (see 1141a16–20 and 1145a6–11).

POLITICS

Aristotle's references to Socrates in the *Politics* fall into two major categories. The first (*Politics* I.12–13) in some sense continues Aristotle's treatment in the *Ethics* and focuses on Socrates' teaching on moral virtue.[15] The second group of references all pertain to Socrates' more explicitly political teachings in the *Republic* and *Laws*. These are addressed thematically in Book II with brief additional comments in Books IV, V, and VIII.

VIRTUE, FAMILY, AND POLITICS

Book I of the *Politics* culminates in a discussion of the household which focuses on relations between male and female, and parents and children (chs. 12–13). A consideration of the character, virtue, and education of the family is essential for an examination of politics since, as Aristotle notes, women comprise half of the free population in the city and children (at least male children) constitute the next generation of political leaders (1260b13–20). Aristotle's consideration of the household is undertaken with a view to his primary concern for the *polis*. Although his views on the relation between the sexes and their respective forms of excellence are offensive to contemporary sensibilities,[16] an accurate assessment of that teaching must begin with a recognition that this analysis is governed by the political realities within which members of the family live.

Rule within the family differs fundamentally from mastery since wife and children are free whereas slaves are not. The kind of rule that a husband exercises over his wife is "political" in contrast to rule over children which is "kingly" (1259a36–59b1). Political rule is characterized by an alternation of ruler and ruled since all are on an equal footing (1259b4–6). Aristotle does not, however, apply this to the marital relationship, claiming instead that the male is more expert in leading than the female. Whereas both women and children share in the virtues of character, they share in them in a way that corresponds to their work (1260a14–17). For this reason Socrates was wrong to suppose that the moderation, courage, and justice of men and women are the same. The most relevant difference is that, while both men and women share in the deliberative faculty, women lack authority (*akuron*) (1260a13). Aristotle bolsters this claim by quoting Sophocles to the effect that silence is a crown for a woman but not for a man. Indeed, Gorgias was more correct than Socrates on this point insofar as he maintained that there were different virtues for men, women, children, and slaves (1259b27–31).

How should we understand Aristotle's initial critique of Socrates in the *Politics*? Was Socrates wrong to seek a single understanding of virtue that would apply to all human beings regardless of their political circumstances? Despite his stated preference for Gorgias's approach, Aristotle does not articulate different versions of moderation, courage, or justice for men and women in his thematic treatment of these virtues in the *Ethics*. What seems to have changed is that the political realities that furnish the background horizon for the *Ethics* have moved into the foreground in the *Politics*. The gist of Aristotle's criticism of Socrates in the present context is directed against his apparently blithe disregard of political circumstances in his single-minded pursuit of the idea of virtue. At the very least, Aristotle criticizes Socrates for failing to take into account the lack of authority that characterized women in Greek society.

It is not at all clear, however, that Aristotle fully subscribes to this conventional fact of Greek political life. The one example he gives to support his distinction between male and female virtue is taken from Sophocles' *Ajax* and it is hard to avoid the conclusion that this citation is highly ironic. Praise for the crowning female virtue of silence is directed at Tecmessa by the crazed warrior hero, Ajax. Ajax's madness has destroyed whatever deliberative capacity he possessed and his wife's sober attempt to calm him reveals an unambiguously superior state of mind. If the lack of authority accompanying female speech makes it easy for Ajax to ignore her good counsel, this dismissal comes at the cost of the destruction of Ajax himself. Aristotle's reference to this well-known heroic legend calls into question the justice of those traditional standards that, notwithstanding their limitations, profoundly shape the realities and possibilities of political life.

Socrates' mode of inquiry may not have given sufficient weight to those conventional distinctions that in large part determine the specific character of any given society, but Aristotle's quotation from Sophocles' play also suggests that he does not think such conventional distinctions fully adequate. In particular cases it may turn out that women embody a fuller degree of virtue than men; indeed, possess the kind of deliberative excellence that defines political virtue itself. Nevertheless, the possession of virtue is never fully apparent and the lack of authority characteristic of a woman's social condition inevitably impedes a fair evaluation of those virtues she does possess. Socrates' neglect of this political fact of life, whether willful or not, effectively diminishes the usefulness of his inquiry for those whose primary interest lies in the rough and tumble of politics.

POLITICAL IDEAS: ARISTOTLE'S CRITIQUE

As we might expect in a work devoted to the study of politics, the remainder of Aristotle's references to Socrates are directed to the political teachings attributed to him in Plato's *Republic* and *Laws*.[17] Aristotle's assessment of Socrates' political ideas proves to be relentlessly critical. A succinct enumeration of his major points follows.

Socrates' fundamental presupposition, that it is best for a city to be one as far as possible, is defective since a city is by nature a multitude. An excessive concern for unity, even if it were possible, is not desirable because it would destroy rather than preserve the political association. Moreover, the particular means proposed by Socrates to establish unity are deeply problematic.

With respect to his proposal for a community of wives and children, Aristotle points to several difficulties: (1) What belongs to all in common is in fact accorded the least care. (2) Inevitable physical resemblances make this schema impractical. (3) Even worse, outrages, involuntary homicide, and incest would be increased. (4) Affection among citizens would be diluted to the point of nonexistence. (5) The pesky problem of transferring children between classes is never worked out.

The case for holding possessions in common fares no better. (1) Common property leads, not to unity, but to resentments. (2) Rather than increase, it would decrease virtue since moderation and liberality presuppose some degree of private ownership. (3) Given Socrates' insistence on the importance of education, his reliance on ordinances rather than an appropriate combination of habit, philosophy, and law is especially odd. (4) The mode of organization of the regime as a whole is never made sufficiently clear although it appears to result in two opposed cities—a ruling class and laborers (farmers and artisans). (5) Not only is it dangerous to have the same persons always ruling, but Socrates even goes so far as to destroy the happiness of the ruling class itself.

In light of the sketchiness of Socrates' remarks in the *Republic*, Aristotle turns to the *Laws*. Although this teaching is intended to be accessible to the everyday world of politics, Aristotle complains that it is gradually brought around toward the implausible regime of the *Republic*. In addition to the problems already indicated, (1) the city is too big and (2) insufficiently attentive to the requirement of arms. (3) Socrates is too vague about the extent of possessions; (4) the equalization of property is unconnected to the size of the population; and (5) the separation of housing sites is problematic. (6) He is also unclear about the specific character of the rulers.

Aristotle's subsequent references to Socrates in the *Politics* all refer to the *Republic* and are no less critical. (1) He fails to be sufficiently attentive to the importance of the military element (IV.4); (2) his discussion of the devolution of regimes is inadequate (V.12); and (3) he is mistaken in his recommendations about the type of music most appropriate for education in the best regime (VIII.7).

POLITICAL IDEAS: PERPLEXITIES

Several aspects of Aristotle's Socratic critique are perplexing. Most striking is the inclusion of the following affirmation midst seemingly unyielding criticism. "All the discourses of Socrates, are extraordinary: they are sophisticated, original, and characterized by keenness of inquiry" (1265a10–13). What are we to make of this combination of criticism and praise?

The first point to be noted is the incomplete character of Aristotle's presentation. Not only is he silent about the famous "third wave" of reform in Book V (philosophic rule), but he makes no attempt to do justice to the sophisticated and extraordinary character that he attributes to Socratic inquiry.

Indeed, what we are told leads to the opposite impression: Socrates was wrong in the aim he assigned to the city and in the novel means he invented to achieve that aim. Not only are his ideas impractical, they would destroy the very unity he most wanted to establish; in fact, they would destroy the city itself. Although Socrates' proposals (concerning communism of women and posses-sions) may appear attractive (*euprosōpos*) and humane (*philanthrōpos*) to some, especially in light of the lawsuits, perjury, and flattery that typically prevail (1263b15-22), Aristotle is emphatic in his insistence that they are doomed to fail in the real world of politics.

Might the "attractive appearance" of Socrates' ideas explain something of the harshness of Aristotle's criticism? Despite their outlandish and utopian character, communist schemes have been attempted throughout history and were not unknown in the ancient world. Aristotle mentions upper Libya as a place where the communism of women was practiced (1262a21–24). Although some may be tempted to enact Socrates' proposals (the possibility of a regime modeled along the lines of the *Republic* is acknowledged at 1261a4–6), Aristotle's analysis is intended to explain why such arrangements are impossible to sustain (1261a11–14; 1261b30–32; 1263b28–29; compare 1265a1–2).

Whereas communism of wives and property might be attempted, rule by philosophers (at least explicit and direct rule) is considerably less likely, as Socrates himself acknowledged in making this proposal. The closest approxi-mation to this Socratic idea is found in regimes where philosophers, or at least philosophically informed individuals, are responsible for the laws. This may explain why Aristotle turns to the *Laws* of Plato, instead of discussing philosophic rule. Aristotle later adverts to the view that law in some way functions as a political substitute for *nous* (1287a28–30).[18] Could it be that Aristotle speaks in Book II especially of those aspects of Socrates' proposals which, because of their appealing and humane appearance, might actually be attempted but with disastrous results? Aristotle's sober criticism of Socratic ideas, offers a compelling, if not always heeded, account of their utopian and politically dangerous character.

Thoughtful readers of the *Republic* have doubted the prescriptive charac-ter of Socrates' teaching, and we might well wonder about Aristotle's position on this still controversial issue.[19] In Book II, Aristotle gives special attention to three individuals who had something to say about regimes. But unlike his con-siderations of Phaleas and Hippodamus, Aristotle's analysis of Socrates con-cludes with the singular and, in its immediate context, unexpected praise quoted above. What are we to make of this endorsement in light of the fact that, as we have seen, all of Aristotle's references to Socrates in the *Politics* are critical, sometimes devastatingly so? At the very least, Aristotle recognizes that there is more to Socrates' teaching than he is willing to acknowledge in the present context, something that leads to a further question. Is Socrates' extraordinary brilliance to be sought elsewhere or might there be another and better way to understand the proposals recorded in the *Republic* and *Laws*?[20]

The latter alternative gains some plausibility from a second peculiar aspect of Aristotle's treatment—his complete silence about what is arguably Socrates' most consistent trait. Socrates' irony was notorious and Aristotle's failure to account for it is especially odd in light of his earlier use of Socrates as the sole exemplar of irony. Socrates is presented in the *Ethics* as one who disowns accepted or highly regarded opinions. The fact that some find Socrates' (first two) political reforms "appealing and humane," does not, of course, obviate the possibility that they are intended ironically. There is, at least, substantial evidence for this interpretation in the *Republic* where Socrates expects that each of his proposals is to be met with laughter, and finally acknowledges their impossibility (592a–b).

We are left with the following possibility regarding Aristotle's paradoxical combination of criticism and praise for Socrates' political ideas. If one were to take the most attractive aspects of those proposals out of context and read them without any appreciation for Socratic irony, one is confronted with the kind of schema that Aristotle relentlessly criticizes as utopian. On the other hand, by concluding his thematic consideration of the *Republic* with an affirmation of Socratic brilliance nowhere in evidence in the foregoing analysis, Aristotle indicates that Socrates should not be dismissed as easily as his own critique suggests. Aristotle effectively cuts off a false and politically dangerous reading of Socrates' political ideas while leaving open (without explaining) the sense in which their brilliance might be properly detected. Despite the impractical appearance of Socrates' proposed reforms, Aristotle's commendation of Socratic inquiry might entice some to take a second look. Read as an exploration of the possibilities and limitations of justice, Socrates' political ideas may prove to have more in common with those of Aristotle than first meets the eye.

CONCLUSION

The aim of this chapter has been to suggest that Aristotle's presentation of Socrates in his "philosophy of human affairs" is both more careful and more sympathetic than is often acknowledged. More typical evaluations regarding

Aristotle's repudiation of the Platonic Socrates as well as his culturally determined understanding of human excellence, do not do justice to the suppleness
of Aristotle's mode of inquiry in the *Ethics* and *Politics*.[21] It is by taking seriously
the apologetic dimension of Aristotle's political writings that both his awareness of the limitations in the understanding of morally serious persons and his
appreciation for the Socratic mode of inquiry assume their full and proper
force. I have attempted to show that in the course of these writings Aristotle
seeks to bring his readers to some positive appreciation for Socrates' life and
teaching. On the one hand, he corrects the most politically disturbing aspects
of that teaching, approaching them in a way that reflects his own concern to
preserve and foster the best sensibilities of civic-minded readers. On the other
hand, he directs readers to an appreciation for the seriousness of Socratic
inquiry, however outlandish and galling it might initially appear. Without trying to persuade his readers that the "gadfly of Athens" was in fact the city's
greatest benefactor, Aristotle's double appreciation for the dignity of politics
and the life of radical inquiry is uniquely suited to bring his audience to a new
and positive appreciation for the Socratic way of life. For Aristotle, as for Plato
(although in a way that differs from Plato), Socrates continues to personify the
public face of philosophy. Aristotle's prudent and intriguing assessment of the
exemplar *par excellence* of the philosophic life can be understood as part of his
larger effort to secure an at least partial acceptance for the place and importance
of philosophy in the city.

Notes

I wish to thank the *Earhart Foundation* for their generous support during the preparation of this chapter. An earlier version of portions of this essay appeared in *Interpretation*.

1. Hereafter *Ethics* refers to the *Nicomachean Ethics*. Standard abbreviations are used throughout. Translations, though indebted to Rackham, Irwin (*Ethics*), and Lord (*Politics*), are my own.

2. Although I believe it is wrong to presume that Aristotle neglects the concerns of philosophically minded students in these works I hope to show that his presentation of Socrates belongs to what, from the most obvious point of view, might be called the dominant horizon of these books—his concern to foster and in some way shape the best sentiments of civic-minded readers. I address the question of Aristotle's audience thematically in *Reading Aristotle's "Ethics": Virtue, Rhetoric, and Political Philosophy* (Albany: State University of New York Press, 1996), esp. ch. 1.

3. The work of Gregory Vlastos has been most influential in pushing the search for the historical Socrates to the forefront of the contemporary scholarly agenda. See especially his final book, *Socrates, Ironist and Moral Philosopher* (Ithaca: Cornell University Press, 1991).

4. After the death of Alexander the Great in 323, Eurymedon indicted Aristotle for impiety (Diogenes Laertius, *Lives* V.5). Aristotle decided to leave Athens before the matter came to trial, lest, as one tradition reports it, he give the Athenians a second opportunity to sin against philosophy.

5. The incompleteness of the apologetic task as it was undertaken by Plato is further suggested by the following Socratic statement (among others): "Now the men who have become members of this small band [philosophers] have tasted how sweet and blessed a possession it is. At the same time, they have seen sufficiently the madness of the many, and that no one who minds the business of the cities does anything healthy. . . ." *Republic* 496c.

6. This thesis runs contrary to some of the prevailing views on this subject. Alasdair MacIntyre, for example, contends that the *Ethics* contains "a systematic repudiation of the morality of Socrates" and that Aristotle's references to Socrates in the *Ethics* evidence "none of Plato's respect." *A Short History of Ethics* (New York: Macmillan, 1966), 67–68. Werner Jaeger's influential study seeks to establish a chronology for Aristotle's writings based on the extent to which they evidence a rejection of the Platonic Socrates: the more Aristotle "developed" as a thinker, the more he repudiated the views of his teacher. *Aristotle: Fundamentals of his Development*, trans. Richard Robinson, 2d ed. (Oxford: Clarendon Press, 1948).

7. At the outset of the *Apology*, Socrates ironically acknowledges that he is a clever speaker but, unlike his accusers, he speaks cleverly with respect to the truth (17a–b). In fact, Socrates is initially presented in the *Apology* as an unusual combination of *ho authekastos*, who will speak plainly in his accustomed manner, and *ho eirōn*, who acknowledges his ability to speak cleverly. In the defense that follows, the Platonic Socrates proceeds to give a remarkable demonstration of great subtlety clothed in simple, straightforward speech.

8. In the *Meno*, Socrates undertakes an investigation of virtue. Socrates' paradoxical identification of virtue and knowledge emerges in the course of this dialogue, where it takes the particular form referred to by Aristotle in the present context: namely, the identification of virtue with prudence (88a–89a).

9. It may be appropriate to recall that the frustrated Meno likens the effect of Socratic argument to that of the torpedo fish that numbs anyone who comes into contact with it (80a–d). The dialogue also includes Anytus's thinly veiled threat of political retribution. Not inappropriately, Anytus construes Socrates' remarks to be critical of leading Athenian statesmen past and present (94e–95a).

10. Aristotle's example of a prudent man was Pericles who is said to have possessed the ability to discern the good both for himself and for humankind. Aristotle maintains that this capacity characterizes one who is capable of managing both households and cities (1140b8–11).

11. As we shall see, Aristotle's thoroughgoing critique of Socrates' proposals in the *Republic* does not include a criticism of his proposal that philosophers should rule.

12. There is no suitable translation for *akrasia* and *enkrateia*. I retain the traditional *incontinence* and *continence* simply because none of the alternatives seem better.

13. *Aporia* can also be translated by "dilemma" or "antinomy" and is likened by Aristotle to a knot or tangle which binds the intelligence (*Metaphysics* 995a27ff., cf. *EN* 1146a21–27).

14. The radical character of Socrates' denial of incontinence is even more evident in light of his explanation of what actually occurs. Socrates' analysis of incontinence leads him to assert that there is no good apart from pleasure and that virtue consists in knowing how to choose the greatest pleasure. See *Protagoras* 351c–361c, esp. 357a and 358b. The harsh implications of the Socratic consideration of incontinence are not only unacceptable but even antagonistic to the best sensibilities of decent person. Although regrettable, it is not surprising that Socrates' mode of inquiry eventually elicited the condemnation of his fellow citizens.

15. As in the *Ethics*, Aristotle appears to have the *Meno* in mind.

16. For those primarily interested in gender equity, Aristotle is typically regarded as a villain. See, for example, Susan Moller Okin, *Women in Western Political Thought* (Princeton: Princeton University Press, 1979), esp. ch. 4. For a more balanced assessment, see Arlene Saxonhouse, *Women in the History of Political Thought: Ancient Greece to Machiavelli* (New York: Praeger Publishers, 1985), ch. 4.

17. Vlastos denies that references to Socrates in the *Republic* reflect the views of the historical Socrates.

18. Michael Davis makes a similar observation in *The Politics of Philosophy* (Maryland: Rowman & Littlefield Publishers, 1996), 40. We should note, however, that Book III of the *Politics* concludes with a dialectical consideration of the relative advantages of rule by law or the one person of outstanding virtue, a discussion that in some way addresses the problems raised by Socrates' "third wave" of reform (*Politics* III.15–17).

19. The former position is advanced by Leo Strauss, Alan Bloom, and Mary Nichols (among others). It has been questioned by Martha Nussbaum and Bernard Yack.

20. At the beginning of his critique of the *Republic*, Aristotle writes that the end proposed by Socrates is "impossible; but how one should distinguish [a sense in which it is possible] is not discussed" (1261a11–14). Lord translation (University of Chicago Press, 1984); compare Simpson translation (University of North Carolina Press, 1997).

21. Consider, in addition to MacIntyre, *Short History*, and Jaeger, *Aristotle*, John Randall who identifies Aristotle's teaching on human excellence with "the values, norms or ideals of Greek culture . . . the ethic of an upper class in a slave society" (*Aristotle* [New York: Columbia University Press, 1960], 248).

CHAPTER 11

ARISTOTLE ON NATURE, HUMAN NATURE, AND JUSTICE

A Consideration of the Natural Functions of Men and Women in the City

JUDITH A. SWANSON

INTRODUCTION

Aristotle's views are often characterized as dogmatic. The sixteenth-century skeptic Montaigne called Aristotle "the prince of dogmatists."[1] Contemporary critics claim that Aristotle is especially dogmatic about the difference between men and women and between their roles in the city. According to those critics, Aristotle believes that women are both biologically and politically inferior to men, and that, while the function of women is to reproduce and keep a household, the function of men is to govern and defend the *polis*. I would like to suggest that any dogmatism that characterizes Aristotle's views about men and women is meant both to reveal and to conceal truths about nature. By way of his dogmatism, Aristotle impresses upon his audience the considerable extent to which human beings cannot escape the political implications of the physical and intellectual strengths and weaknesses nature gives them. While that dogmatism discourages political challenges to the natural order in the name of progress or freedom, it encourages philosophic investigation of the natural order in the name of truth. Aristotle's dogmatism is meant to induce the attentive or philosophic members of his audience to consider the purpose of his dogmatism, and to recognize that its purpose is not only to stress nature's inescapability, but to conceal from the less reflective and more politically ambitious members of his audience nature's changeability, which is a truth equal to the truth of nature's inescapability, but one more vulnerable to abuse by those who measure political success in terms of change and innovation.

This chapter is divided into three main parts: in the first part, I explain why Aristotle's conception of nature is the unapparent key to the unity of his thought; in the second part, I analyze Aristotle's biological, psychological, metaphysical, and political findings about the natures of men and women, with a view to illustrating the complexity of his understanding of nature; and in the third part, I consider the political implications for men and women of Aristotle's notion of political justice, which I follow up with concluding remarks.

THE WHOLE OF NATURE AND THE UNITY
OF THE ARISTOTELIAN CORPUS

Discussion of the problem of nature in Aristotle must begin with an appreciation of why nature is indeed a problem, and not an obvious concept, in Aristotle's corpus.[2] Nature is a problem because, by virtue of its usage in all of Aristotle's works—his works on biology, physics, logic, metaphysics, politics, ethics, and rhetoric, and by virtue of Aristotle's characterization of it as a plurality—it appears not to meet the requirement of knowability that Aristotle himself establishes in his logico-metaphysical works, namely, categorizability or classifiability. That which forms a class or category or a one is knowable. Classes or categories of things (*genē*) are knowable or comprehensible because they each preserve distinctive forms or species (*eidē*). Because classes preserve different species, they constitute separate subjects of study or bodies of knowledge and thus require separate methods (*hodos*) or sciences to be known: "things which differ in genus have no means of passing into each other, and are more widely distant, and are not comparable" (*Met.* 1055a6).[3] As an unclassifiable plurality, nature seems to lack a science of its own and thus seems hopelessly unknowable, incomprehensible.

On the other hand, the very fact that Aristotle refers to nature (*phusis*), often frequently, in his various sorts of works, induces consideration of the nature of the natural plurality; for it appears to comprehend, join, or relate in some way the various branches of study. At least four features of the natural plurality provide grounds for relating or joining the various branches of study to one another: (1) its teleology or purposiveness, (2) its integration of form and matter, (3) its anthropocentricity, and (4) its relation to unity.

First, Aristotle's view that nature ordains a purpose or end to each living thing is the basis on which he relates the generic branches of knowledge by analogy.[4] As is well known, he illustrates in the *Politics* how the city—that which of all things would appear to be altogether conventional—is natural. Like any living organism, such as an acorn or a puppy, the city has a natural end, which is also, like the acorn's and puppy's ends, its most developed, mature, and self-sufficient form. Political self-sufficiency is at least analogous to biological maturity, and the findings of the human or political sciences, on the one hand, and of the physical sciences, on the other, are accordingly analogous.

A second feature of the natural plurality, connected to its purposiveness, that appears to provide common ground for separate branches of study, is its composition by form and matter. If nature ordains purposes to living things, then it gives them principles or forms by which to realize those purposes. Forms, as the intelligible principles of material things, are immanent in matter. Matter and form as such have no antecedent reality; they exist together, by necessity. The form or intelligible principle immanent in the human body Aristotle calls soul (*psuche*). If, as Aristotle observes in the *Nicomachean Ethics* (I.13), the human soul is not only part reason and part desire, but part vegetative or bodily, then is not the study of the habits or functions of the body—namely, biology, relevant, and not merely analogous to, the study of the habits of the soul—namely, ethics? If body and soul are one, then the habits of the "body" must affect, and reflect, the habits of the "soul," and vice versa. The "body" cannot be in good condition or healthy unless the "soul" is too, and vice versa.

A third characteristic of the natural plurality that would appear to join the human and physical sciences, and to confirm a link especially between biology and ethics, is its identification of man as the pinnacle of the hierarchy of living things. Since active reason characterizes only the human soul, man is a model of intelligibility in the realm of living things; if the intelligibility of all living things is relative to man's, then the attributes of nonhuman animals are not merely analogous, but comparable to, those of human beings.[5] In his *History of Animals*, Aristotle illustrates that the psychological traits, in particular, of nonhuman animals are comparable to man's; like man, they too have such qualities of character as courageousness, compassionateness, and deceptiveness. The resemblance between the ways of the soul of man and those of animals suggests that the ways of the soul—the subject of ethics—are not simply products of human culture or nurture—not simply acquired or cultivated—but also to some extent given, in bodily nature. Indeed, if there is a bodily soul, then its study would seem to be most fittingly characterized not as ethics, but as bioethics, which the *History of Animals* seems to be.

A fourth feature of the natural plurality that provides grounds for relating the branches of study is its paradoxical relation to unity. In the same text in which Aristotle explains the principle of classification, which principle separates the bodies of knowledge, he also seems to explain indirectly the paradox of nature that would unify those branches. At the beginning of *Metaphysics*, Book X, he notes that all sets of contraries can be reduced to the primary or generic contraries of unity and plurality (1054a21–1055b29). Unity and plurality are contraries, or opposites, because unity is indivisible and plurality, divisible. The phenomenon of contrariety results from deprivation. Just as vice or badness is a privation of virtue or goodness, so odd is a privation of even. Thus, if unity and plurality are contraries, then plurality must be a privation of unity.

The privation of a category or class can result either in a contrary that forms a continuum with it, as virtue forms a continuum with vice, or in a contrary that constitutes a different class, as odd does from even. In the case of contraries that form a continuum, they share a substrate or common ground (*Met.* 1056a31–1056b1).

If nature is many, or indeed just two, then it is a plurality and the opposite of unity. That which is not one is a plurality. That nature is in one sense many is obvious, but also obvious according to Aristotle is that the substrate of nature is not one but two. Nature's duality is apparent from our own human constitution, which combines matter and form, the nonrational and rational. We are made aware of nature's duality by both our frustrations and our aspirations; the recognition that we are neither beasts nor gods, but rather in-between beings, gives rise to the perception that nature as we experience it is a privation of form, which is rational, from matter, which is nonrational. In that reflection itself, we glimpse the whole of nature; the truth about nature which lies in the realm of thought alone.

Indeed, Aristotle himself must have glimpsed the whole of nature in order to make the claim in the *Nicomachean Ethics* that the natural is that which has everywhere and always the same force or power (1134b19–20). If the intellect can grasp or intuit the whole of nature, then the substrate or unity of nature must be a kind of intelligibility.

If nature as a whole is intelligible, if in other words the unity of nature is noetic, then surely the various branches of study—the biological, psychological, political, ethical, and metaphysical, which focus independently on the physical, the human, and the divine—must be in some way intelligible to and thus relevant to one another. By subsuming under the concept of nature not only the physical or the empirical, as does post-Enlightenment thought, but also the human and the divine, Aristotle suggests that the physical, human, and divine sciences are mutually relevant.

It seems, then, that nature does have its own appropriate method or science; if the whole of nature is knowable at all, then it is evidently so through that activity which apprehends both the demonstrable and the indemonstrable, namely philosophy.

The following review of Aristotle's biological, psychological, metaphysical, and political analyses of the natures of men and women is meant to suggest both the independence or distinctiveness of each sort of analysis, and their mutual relevance. Together they lead to the conclusion that, contrary to the accusations of Aristotle's contemporary critics, nature, perhaps especially as manifested in the natures of men and women, is far too complex to dictate the political roles of men and women. For a city to accommodate or even address such complexity, which can be apprehended only philosophically, it would have to be ruled by philosophers, which is unlikely. If nonpolitical nature does not let itself be ignored by politics, however—if in other words the biological, psychological, and metaphysical or logical findings about men and women are not entirely irrelevant to their own and every city's well-being and functioning—then those findings must somehow be reflected or accommodated by cities. The reflection or accommodation of such natural truths by cities not governed by philosophers requires the comprehension of those truths by ordinary citizens. Thus Aristotle, the teacher of future politicians, presents the truths of nature dogmatically, as if nature did prescribe clear and definitive roles for men and women.

THE COMPLEXITY OF NATURE: THE BIOLOGY, PSYCHOLOGY, METAPHYSICS, AND POLITICS OF THE NATURES OF MEN AND WOMEN

THE BIOLOGY OF MALE AND FEMALE

According to Aristotle's analysis of the generation of animals, a male animal differs from a female in three primary biological ways: the epithets "male" and "female" designate not only (1) the outwardly visible sexual parts and (2) the observable reproductive function of an animal, but also (3) its principle (*archē*), which is situated in the heart (*Generation of Animals* 766a31–b4). The principle of an animal determines its sex even before the appearance of sexual parts. As if anticipating the modern chromosomal theory of sex differentiation, Aristotle concludes that the principle is the cause, and sexual parts and reproductive functions only manifestations, of maleness and femaleness.[6] He observes nonetheless that an animal "really is male or female" only after the appearance of sexual parts, as if anticipating another modern discovery—that embryos, whether chromosomally coded male or female, appear to be the same until seven weeks after conception (766b5–6). Conversely stated, an embryo is not really male or female until sexual parts emerge. If male and female principles are undetectable, then their ambiguity or combination is possible. Aristotle goes further in declaring the essentiality of biological androgyny: "things are alive in virtue of having in them a share of the male and of the female" (732a11–12). He thereby illuminates his earlier claim that, "although male and female are indeed said in referring to the whole animal, it is not male or female in respect of the whole of itself, but only in respect of a particular faculty and a particular part" (716a28–31). The fundamental biological androgyny of human beings explains why "a boy actually resembles a woman in physique, and a woman is so to speak an infertile male" (728a17–18).

Aristotle explains how, although essentially androgynous, males and females come to be. Form, in semen, and matter, in menstrual blood fuse, producing a male offspring when form dominates matter, and a female when matter dominates form (766b15–17). Since form, which Aristotle associates, if not equates, with the principle of movement and soul, ranks higher in nature than body or matter, this understanding of genesis is said by some modern commentators to be "misogynistic" on two counts: (1) the male animal provides, through his semen, the better procreative part, and (2) the domination of soul over matter characterizes males, not females. The details of Aristotle's (dispassionate) analysis show, however, that the charge of misogyny is inappropriate.[7]

As to the first charge, that semen provides soul, the superior procreative element, Aristotle explains that the male provides only sentient soul, the part of the soul that endows living beings with sense perception, which functionally defines bodily parts and makes them responsive and active (736b14–27, 741a13–14). Indeed, sentient soul "cannot be separated from the body" (De Anima 413a3–5). Although without sentient soul human beings would, if they had any bodily definition at all, be lifeless, with it they are not thereby endowed with *pure* form or reason. Reason enters into the procreative process through semen, but is generated not from the male himself but from "outside" and is thus "partly separable" from matter (GA 736b30–39, 737a8–12). "Reason alone enters in, as an additional factor, from outside, and alone is divine, because bodily activity has nothing to do with its activity" (736b27–29). In short, inasmuch as sentient soul cannot exist without matter, just as matter cannot live without sentient soul, it cannot be said that the male's contribution to procreation is decidedly superior to the female's.[8]

As to the charge that Aristotle's genetic science is misogynistic because it attributes femaleness to the domination of matter over soul, it should be noticed that this domination occurs, *and repeats itself in*, the reproductive tract. "The female is so to speak a deformed male" *because*—Aristotle explains in the next clause—"the menstrual discharge is semen, though in an impure condition; i.e., it lacks one constituent, and one only, the principle of soul" (737a27–30). In other words, a female offspring results when a relatively inferior reproductive system results. Relative to males whose semen contains sentient soul, the female, whose menstrual blood is unconcocted matter, is *reproductively* deformed. Moreover, to go to the mat with Aristotle's critics, one could point out that not even the female's menstrual blood is pure matter, which Aristotle admits by identifying it as impure or unconcocted semen. Indeed, that all matter is to some extent "informed" indicates the androgyny of all tangible existence (see 740b19–22).

That the domination of matter occurs in the female's reproductive tract means that it does not occur in her constitutive soul. The part of the soul that makes a human being human is the rational part, the part that enters into the procreative process from outside, and Aristotle gives no indication that the amount or kind of reason or intellectual virtue that enters varies according to the dominant sex of the embryo. Hence he grants that the constitutions of the male and female souls are the same inasmuch as they both possess nutritive and sentient soul and reason (741a7–8).[9]

Aristotle thus resolves his apparently contradictory claims that male and female are fundamentally opposites, fundamentally mixed together, and fundamentally the same. "Male" and "female" are opposite principles, the one being of movement, the other of material cause. But they are complementary opposites, in fact compelled to unite since neither has antecedent reality. United, one dominates, yielding, in the procreative process, either male or female parts. The unification or mixture of principles yields maleness or femaleness because "mixing is the coming to be one of what is mixed as they are changed."[10]

Consistent with that conclusion, Aristotle maintains that male and female human beings are one in *genos*, since "things that are one in *eidos* are all one in *genos*" (*Met.* 1016b36). According to Pierre Pellegrin, within the biological corpus, *genē* are related not by analogy but "according to the more and the less." In *Parts of Animals* Aristotle states:

> For those kinds [*genē*] which differ by degree, i.e. according to the more and the less, have been linked under a single *genos*, while those which are analogous have been separated. I mean, for example, that a bird differs from another bird by the more and the less,

i.e., by degree (one has the wings longer, another shorter), while a
fish differs from a bird by analogy (for that which is feather in one
is scale in the other). (644a16)

Accordingly, male and female differ not by analogy as do a bird and a fish, but
by degree, according to the more and the less, as does one sort of bird from
another. But male and female differ with respect to that which makes male and
female both same and different—that is, their respectively combined maleness
and femaleness or androgyny.

Pellegrin notes that not only is *genos* characterized by the fact that it
admits within it a difference according to the more and the less, or according to
excess and defect, but in the Aristotelian conception, fixing the categories or
levels of generality of the more and the less, or of excess and defect, is *logically*
impossible.[11] Thus it is impossible to determine logically or a priori the degree
to which males and females differ in their androgyny.

THE PSYCHOLOGY OF MALE AND FEMALE

In *History of Animals*, Aristotle observes that the characters or ways of life
(*ta ēthē*) of animals are more evident the more developed or intelligent and the
longer-lived they are (608a11–13). In the same context he makes the remarkable
observation that female animals across the species tend to have certain characters
or ways of life, and male animals across the species tend to have others. Thus, he
writes: "in all kinds in which there are the female and the male, nature has established much the same difference in the character of the females as compared
with that of the males. But it is most evident in the case of humans and of the
animals that have some size and of the viviparous [live birth] quadrupeds"
(608a22–25).

He then identifies the character that females tend to have, and that that
males tend to have (608a25–b19). First of all, the character (*to ethos*) of
females tends, in comparison to that of males, to be softer, gentler, or milder
(*malakoteros*). The female character is also "quicker to be tamed, and more
receptive of handling" (608a25–27). Evidently, females are easier than males
to control; they are more easily induced to follow.

The character of females is also "readier to learn [*mathēmatikoteros*], for
example, the female Laconian hounds are in fact cleverer than the males"
(608a27–28). Their willingness to follow and their eagerness to learn may thus
complement each other.

In addition, "all females are less spirited [*athumotera*] than the males,
except the bear and leopard: in these the female is held to be braver [*andrei-*

otera]" (608a33–35). In the *Politics*, Aristotle says that spiritedness (*thumos*) is "the part of the soul or complex of passions [extending to anger, ambition, arrogance, and affection] connected with man's sociality" (*Politics* VII.7).[12] Spiritedness becomes enraged at unjust treatment in particular because it is "expert at ruling and indomitable" (*Politics* 1327b38–1328a5). That women are less spirited than men would appear to mean then that they are less able than men to rule with justice.

Subsequently in the text, Aristotle not only repeats that females tend to be softer, but adds "more vicious, less simple, more impetuous, more attentive to the feeding of the young" (*HA* 608a35–b3). Capable of being vicious or hostile but also of caring for their families, females appear to be more inclined to go to the extremes of loving and hating. This trait would also seem unsuited to the political realm, which is sustained not by extreme and intense emotions, but by affection or friendship that is "watery" or diluted, and defined in terms of justice.

By contrast, males are simpler socially than females. They are not only "more spirited [*thumodestera*]" and "wilder" but also "less cunning" (608b3–4). While the wilder nature of men would seem to make them unsuited to the confinement of the household, their lesser ability to deceive might make them more trustworthy citizens than women.

Aristotle in fact closes his comparison of the male and female characters by noting respective qualities that would make the male not only a better citizen but a better comrade and soldier. Although "a wife is more compassionate than a husband and more given to tears, . . . [she is] also more jealous and complaining and more apt to scold and fight." The female is also more dispirited, despondent, less inclined to move, and more afraid of action than the male, while "the male is a readier ally and is braver than the female."[13] In any case, if male and female characteristics "are more evident in humans," then a woman's character is decidedly different from a man's (608b4–19).

THE METAPHYSICS OF MALE AND FEMALE

According to Pierre Pellegrin, "there is no line of demarcation between Aristotle's logico-metaphysical work and the biological corpus. Of course biology is distinct at least in terms of its *object*, which gives it a certain *de facto* autonomy, but it remains a branch of *physics*, in Aristotle's system of the *theoretical sciences*."[14]

Thus, although key terms in Aristotle's biology have a properly biological *usage*, they do not have a properly biological *sense*; in his biological works, such terms refer to concepts which Aristotle defines more formally, that is, in a way more disengaged from the constraints of particular material, in his logico-meta-physical works.[15] The terms *genos* and *eidos*, for example, which are usually translated respectively as genus and species, each have various connotations that complicate their normally implied distinction. Consequently, Aristotle's claim in the *Metaphysics* that men and women do not differ in *eidei*—in species (1058a30–31) needs consideration.

Just several lines before the claim that men and women do not differ in *eidei*, Aristotle states that "difference in *genos* [is] the otherness which makes itself an other" (1058a7). Apparently, as Pellegrin notes, "the *genos* is character-ized simultaneously by identity and by difference," and is thus "a *unity of con-traries*." In the first of particular senses of *genos* given in the *Metaphysics* (V.28), *genos* is the manifestation of a lineage, and *eidos*, the identity or sameness that characterizes that lineage. Thus a given reality can be *genos* or *eidos* according to the point of view from which one considers it—whereas the concepts of genus and species cannot be so applied, and *genos* can refer to sameness of different degrees of generality: the *genos* of living things as opposed to that of nonliving, the *genos* of human beings as opposed to that of birds, the *genos* of birds as opposed to that of fish, the *genos* of sparrows as opposed to that of eagles.[16]

While *genos* sustains sameness or identity, it necessarily accepts difference or otherness by way of the genesis that occurs within it; "the *genos successively* includes contraries which transform into each other . . . [it] includes in itself the *diaphora* . . . 'specific difference.'" Accordingly, as Pellegrin explains, "that which differs within the *genos* can differ to the extreme limits of difference, pro-vided that it continues to relate itself to a 'same,' which implies that the *diaphora* is not a pure otherness." As Aristotle himself says,

> Difference is not the same as otherness. For the other and that which
> it is other than need not be other in some definite respect . . . , but
> that which is different is different from some particular thing in
> some particular respect, so that there must be something identical
> whereby they differ. (*Met.* 1054b23, tr. Ross)[17]

Thus whatever else "male" and "female" signify, within the *genos* of human beings, they clearly signify only a difference and not an otherness.

Otherness or "the real *diaphora*," Pellegrin observes, "can be attributed only to two things which have between them a contrariety in their essence (their *logos* . . . *Met.* 1058b1), and not to those whose contrariety is accidental or produced by the material. Thus a concrete man, whether black or white, would be specifically different from a horse no matter what its color, because the *logoi* of man and horse have a specific difference. But on the one hand a black man will not be specifically different from a white man, although white and black are contraries, and on the other, the difference of the sexes, in that it is (according to Aristotelian doctrine) produced by movements of material, will not be *diaphora*."[18] As Aristotle says, women differ from men not as footed from winged animals but as white from black swans. Male and female of the same species differ merely physically; their essence or formula, their *logos*, is the same (*Met.* 1058a31–37, b7–10, 21–24).[19]

Thus, Aristotle's biological, psychological, and logical accounts of the sexes issue different conclusions. While men and women are biologically androgynous, and the same kind of living being according to logical categories, they exhibit distinct psychological characteristics. If these findings are all politically or normatively relevant, their combined normative significance is not obvious. Should we infer from the biological similarity and logical indistinguishability of the sexes that they ought not to be differentiated politically, or should we infer from their divergent psychological tendencies that women are suited to the household and men to public life? To learn if Aristotle means for us to take political instruction from nature in any sense, we need to consult his work on politics.

THE POLITICS OF MALE AND FEMALE

After observing at the beginning of the *Politics* that the union of two partnerships, that of the male and female for the sake of reproduction, and that of the master and slave for the sake of preservation, gave rise to the institution of the household, Aristotle states:

> The first partnership arising from [the union of] several households and for the sake of nondaily needs is the village. . . . The partnership arising from [the union of] several villages that is complete is the city. It reaches a level of full self-sufficiency, so to speak; and while coming into being for the sake of living, it exists for the sake of living well. Every city, therefore, exists by nature, if such also are the first partnerships. For the city is their end, and nature is an end; what each thing is—for example, a human being, a horse, or a household—when its coming into being is complete is, we assert, the nature of that thing. Again, that for the sake of which [a thing exists], or the end, is what is best; and self-sufficiency is an end and what is best. (*Politics* 1252b15–16, 28–1253a1)

Whereas according to Aristotle's ancient predecessors the city is ordained by the gods, and according to his modern Enlightenment successors the city is

ordained or authorized by consent, according to Aristotle the city is ordained by nature. The city is natural for two reasons: (1) because it grows out of natural associations—male and female, master and slave, households, and villages, and (2) because it is the end of the other associations. Natural associations *mature* or *grow* into the city. Since maturity is superior to immaturity and causally first in nature, the city is more natural than any of its earlier associations which are chronologically first in nature.[20]

As a contemporary scholar, Wayne Ambler, has pointed out, the first account of the genesis of the city does not make note of and explain the fact, confirmed in the second account, that the household and its partnerships—unlike the village—continues to exist even after the city comes into being.[21] While the village dissolves into the city, the household maintains its institutional integrity. By ignoring in his first account of the genesis of the city the continued existence of the household, Aristotle establishes the uncompromised authoritativeness of the city, as if to advise citizens to obey and serve their city.

If that is his advice, he nonetheless proceeds to complement it with the argument, characteristic of Enlightenment political thinkers, that *the city* should serve *its citizens*. Going beyond the Enlightenment perspective, Aristotle says more exactly that the city should perfect man (1253a2–4, 26–29).[22] Man is by nature a political animal. A man without a city is either a beast or a god. An individual paradoxically needs a city to become self-sufficient, or complete.

The city's perfection of man requires speech, because "speech serves to reveal the advantageous and the harmful, and hence also the just and the unjust." Speech that makes moral distinctions occurs, however, not only in the city proper—in the political assembly—but also in the household, in private. Both the city and the household are institutions concerned with identifying what is good and bad and just and unjust for human beings (1253a14–18).

The city must allow households to exist apparently because they assist the objective of perfecting human beings by helping to cultivate their moral character or judgment. The city is not, then, unique in this effort; it does not improve the character of human beings by itself.[23]

If human beings move toward their natural end in the household, then they are by nature not only political animals, but domestic ones. In fact, Aristotle explicitly states in the *Nicomachean Ethics* that human beings are domestic or pairing animals (1162a16). According to him, human beings are not merely political animals, but "dualizers."[24]

Concern for the good for man, which Aristotle says is the concern of politics, thus turns out to include concern for the preservation of the household.

Preservation of the household requires preservation of the proper functions of its parts or members.

Aristotle observes that the differences between men and women enable the household to function. Although he initially, in the first chapter of the *Politics*, connects male and female to the function of reproduction, in the third chapter he indicates that reproduction is just one of a few functions—such as mastery (*despotikē*), marital rule (*gamikē*), and fathering (*patrikē*)—that the man and woman in a household need to perform (*Politics* 1253b3–7).

Aristotle does not however merely identify the tasks of household management, but addresses how households *should* function; the activities or rule of the master, the marriage partners, and the father "must be investigated to determine what each is and what sort of thing it *ought* to be" (*Politics* 1253b7–8). Accordingly, he appears in the *Politics* to describe a norm, a pattern typical of households, and also to suggest an ideal, thereby indicating that the point of empirical analysis is to draw normative and prescriptive conclusions. Why this must be the point becomes apparent if one recognizes that nature both ordains or prescribes ends *and* gives human beings the power of choice. Human beings can apparently impede and promote the fully functioning existence or ordained end of other human beings and living things.

After discussing (in chs. 4–11) slavery and the production and acquisition of wealth, things necessary to physical existence, Aristotle returns in the last two chapters of Book I of the *Politics* to the subject of household roles, as if to discuss the *morally necessary* functions of the household. He discusses in particular expertise in paternal rule (*patrikē*) and expertise in marital rule (*gamike*). He observes that "the male, unless constituted in some respect contrary to nature, is by nature more expert at leading than the female" (*to te gar arren phusei tou thēleos hēgemonikōteron, ei mē pou sunestēke para phusin*) (1259b1–3). The observation would fully explain the assumption that husbands rule over wives, if husbands always have male natures, and wives always have female natures. If husbands and wives are ever constituted contary to the norms of maleness and femaleness, respectively, then marital rule in those instances would not be characterized by the husband's superior leadership, but by the wife's equal or superior leadership ability.

The possibility that husbands and wives do not always conform to the norms of maleness and femaleness, and thus that husbands are not always the better leaders, appears at first to explain Aristotle's claim that wives are or should be ruled politically—rather than, for example, despotically or monarchically (*Politics* 1259a39–b1).[25] Yet Aristotle qualifies the term "politically" in such a way as to indicate that he does not believe that husbands and wives are equal or even approach equality. He says that he does not mean here by "political rule" what is usually meant—namely, the alternation of ruler and ruled, which is the practice when the parties "tend by their nature to be on an equal footing and to differ in nothing" (1259b4–6). What he means by political rule is nonetheless what happens even when the parties are equal and do take turns ruling: "[the ruling party] seeks to establish differences in external appearance, forms of address, and prerogatives, as in the story Amasis told about his foot-pan" (1259b6–9). In a political relationship, the transformation of a subject into a ruler is like the molding of a gold footpan into a gold idol—only the image, not the substance, changes.[26] If, however, Aristotle denies that husbands and wives are equal, which seems to be the basis for his not sanctioning their sharing of power or their taking turns at ruling, then by advocating that a husband rule a wife politically Aristotle cannot mean only that a husband should assume the *image* of a ruler, and can mean that in part only if he means that a husband should display or show off his natural superiority in leadership.[27] Furthermore, he says that "the male (*to arren*) always stands thus in relation to the female (*to thēlu*)" (1259b9–10). Husbands, if constituted according to nature, are not only naturally better at leading than wives, but always want to appear to be better leaders and to be looked up to.

Aristotle next argues that there are different ways to rule and be ruled, at least amongst human beings, because the ruling and ruled parts of the soul are present in different ways in human beings (*Politics* 1259b21–1260a14); "the free person rules the slave, the male the female, and the man the child in different ways." Accounting for their different treatments are the natures of the souls of the slave, the female, and the child: "the slave is wholly lacking the deliberative element; the female has it but it lacks authority; the child has it but it is incomplete." A ruler should evidently rule according to his subject's capacity to reason for himself or herself.

If a woman's deliberative capacity lacks authority, then does it (1) lack authority in her soul, over her emotions, or (2) only among men in the city, or (3) lack authority in her soul and among men? Since the term for "without authority," *akuron*, was a biological and medical term implying inadequacy of capacity, and also a political term implying lack of legitimate authority, all three interpretations are plausible.[28] On the one hand, since Aristotle is considering the virtues of the ruling and ruled parts of the soul in order to discern the virtues of the political ruler and politically ruled (*Politics* 1260a4–7), it would appear that the description of a woman's deliberative capacity lacking authority refers to its ineffectiveness in her soul rather than merely among male citizens. If all women are by nature overly emotional, however, then they would tend to be immoderate and unjust, not to say licentious and cowardly, which does not accord with Aristotle's conclusion about the virtues of different kinds of souls, namely that "the moderation of a woman and a man is not the same" (1260a20–24).[29]

In fact, the conclusion that a woman may be moderate induces a reader to notice that Aristotle says that it is the *female* (*thēlu*) not the woman (*gunē*) whose deliberative capacity lacks authority. When a female becomes a woman, which was in ancient Greece usually synchronous with her becoming a wife (*gunê* can mean either woman or wife), her deliberative element may immediately acquire authority, or the respect or interest of men, if only because one of their kind has chosen to marry her, live with her, and make her the mother of his sons. Indeed, in Aristotle's time wives were valued at least as potential mothers of male heirs.[30]

Although it appears from the *Politics* that women would fare best as wives in households, and men would flourish as active citizens in the *polis*, *should* that be the case—is that a *just* and *good* arrangement according to Aristotle? To answer that question, we need to consult his explanation of political justice.

POLITICAL JUSTICE AND THE ROLES OF MEN AND WOMEN IN THE CITY

According to Aristotle, political justice is part natural and part legal. The part that is natural is universal, inasmuch as it has the same force or applicability over time and place. In other words, whatever was politically just for Athens in the fourth century B.C.E. had just as much a natural or necessary element as whatever is politically just for Boston at the end of the twentieth century. The part of political justice that is natural or necessary is thereby obligatory. In every time and place, in every human community, there are naturally right responses to the political problems at hand. It is the duty of communities to enact those responses because they are naturally right.

If there are naturally right solutions to political problems, then there are naturally wrong ones. Aristotle's detection of moral standards, guidelines, or restrictions in nature seems, from the post-Enlightenment point of view, rather like a willful infusion of morality into nature or a conflation of nature and morality. According to Hobbes, Locke, and Rousseau, for example, the only moral cue nature gives human beings is the desire for self-preservation or self-interestedness, while according to Kant morality transcends nature altogether.

Although Kant and Aristotle certainly agree that moral standards are not arbitrary, they disagree as to why; according to Kant they are not arbitrary because they issue from practical reason which, being a human attribute, operates independently of nature the demands of which are not always regular and predictable and, whether regular or irregular, are not intrinsically moral. The reliability or constancy of practical reason is due precisely to its ability to resist or overcome nature. According to Aristotle, moral standards are not arbitrary and are objective because they are—in contrast to Kant's view—grounded, or perhaps more accurately, elevated, in nature; the natural objectivity of morality makes it compulsory.

Many people, Aristotle observes, do not believe that nature contains or intimates any moral guidelines at all because they infer from the physical laws of nature that nature always operates uniformly, and they see that human laws, institutions, and practices differ from community to community. All nations do not establish the same penalties for murder, but all over the world fire burns wood, rivers flow to oceans, and objects fall downward. Noting the uniformity and regularity of physical laws, many people cannot imagine how political justice, which has always varied, can have any natural basis.

It is true, Aristotle affirms, that part of political justice is merely conventional, and thus arbitrary prior to its establishment. Nature is apparently indifferent to the execution of many particular matters related to justice, such as the tallying of votes, the payment of debts, and marriage rites. Nonetheless, the varying practices of human communities do not disprove the existence of natural justice any more than varying opinions about the shape of the earth disprove its sphericalness. Just because people do not perceive natural justice does not mean that it does not exist.

Nor does the changeability of natural justice disprove its existence. The whole of nature does not conform to the standards of uniformity set by the physical laws of nature, as attested not only by natural justice but also by nature's furnishing human beings with the capacity for choice-making. If political justice combines natural justice, which is changeable, and convention, the outcome of choice-making, then politics is not directly derivative from physics.[31] The practical cannot be reduced to the theoretical. Nature issues no timeless maxims, precepts, or laws for human beings to follow, as it issues such laws for the physical world.

Human beings cannot thus avoid the responsibility of making choices. The reasoning capacity that nature gives us to make choices asks us not to make them arbitrarily. That is to say, according to Aristotle, nature wants us to live reasonably—indeed, even well and nobly. Paradoxically, that may require us to go beyond what nature immediately gives us. By giving us reason, nature invites us to improve upon the immediately given. Aristotle likens the human ability to improve upon the given, which is naturally right or just in that sense, to the human ability to change our natural righthandedness into ambidexterity. Although nature generally makes us favor our right hands, which serves us, with effort we can become ambidextrous, which serves us better.

What Aristotle does not further illustrate in his account of political justice in Book V.7 of the *Nicomachean Ethics* are the restrictions natural justice imposes on us. If such justice is not arbitrary, then it must circumscribe our moral license. Apparently, we cannot endlessly improve upon or perfect nature; at some point, our effort to make our world more just will backfire, and yield perversion or corruption rather than perfect justice, as the experiment of the city-in-speech in Plato's *Republic* illustrates. Better to warn against political idealism in speech, as Plato does, than to let its dangers be realized in practice. What Aristotle does not say, in other words, but what he must mean, metaphorically, is that although we can with effort become ambidextrous, we cannot with effort become three-handed; or at least if we do, we have produced not excellence but monstrosity.

Although the restrictions natural justice imposes cannot be determined a priori, their essence, which makes them restrictions for human beings, is knowable. It is knowable because it is ontological, and one of the human intellectual faculties, which Aristotle calls *nous*, can intuit the ontological. In other words, while the content of natural truths is unknowable a priori, their necessariness, or obligatoriness, is knowable. Because the variability of natural truths, the first principles of ethics, does not deny their naturalness or ontological basis, it does not deny their knowability as such, either. Those select human beings who have the faculty of intuition or *nous* can apprehend that in ethical matters human beings are obliged to heed certain truths; just as there are physical facts of nature, so too there are ethical facts of nature.

The natural or ontological element of justice makes it not only obligatory but also nonarbitrary or objective inasmuch as it is part of the ordered cosmos. What is right by nature for human beings, however, not only harmonizes with the cosmos, but becomes manifest only in the concrete. Part of what makes natural justice right for human beings is its inseparability from the particular. Aristotle offers no hypothetical vantage point, such as John Rawls's "original position," from which we can ascertain a theory of justice. We must continually discover the limits of natural justice by way of prudent assessment of given situations.[32]

Human beings can realize natural justice by way of deliberate and conscious means, on the one hand, such as law and education, and by way of habitual and unconscious means, on the other, such as custom and social practices.

The divine principle of nature works through the judgment of wise men who perceive the whole of nature and thus both the potential and the restrictions nature places on human beings, and who may influence law and education. Nature may also make that wisdom imperfectly available in the time-tested practices of custom.[33]

CONCLUSION

Although Montaigne called Aristotle a dogmatist, he also conceded that "we learn from [Aristotle] that knowing much gives occasion for doubting more."[34] I have tried to suggest that it is in fact Aristotle's knowing much—in particular about nature and human nature—that induces him to present some of his insights dogmatically. His dogmatism means to conceal an elusive teaching about the changeability of nature from those in his audience whose political ambitions might lead them to misconstrue and abuse that teaching.

Aristotle's dogmatic doctrine of functionalism is directed at political men as such; men who are or will be in positions of power, and for the sake of power or gain. He does not trust them to discern simultaneously the potential for change and the resistance to change inherent in human nature. Anticipating that such men will instead make laws according to their arbitrary will, Aristotle instructs or advises them to heed the simple functionalism that physical nature apparently dictates, and that custom more or less ordains, and to abstain from decreeing or legislating changes that violate that politically effective functionalism. Because the preservation of cities depends on the preservation of both the political realm and the household, it depends on the preservation of the traditional roles of men and women. Aristotle gives permission only to good and wise rulers to move the city beyond traditional and politically functional arrangements and ordain those that are good and just in a higher or complete sense.

Although Aristotle's dogmatic doctrine of functionalism appears to reveal a distrust of politicians or political leaders, it is in fact based on an insight into the nature of politics, its nature especially in a democracy. The tendency of politicians to fixate on the potential for change and ignore nature's restrictions derives from the character of politics, which tends to regard common opinion as authoritative to validate itself. Common or popular opinion maintains that the purpose of politics is progress (in the name of freedom), which is assumed to be in opposition to the preservation of the status quo. In other words, although political or practical activity can preserve what exists, its purpose is more commonly thought to be change, innovation, or progress.

Aristotle exposes and criticizes the popular equation of good politics with innovation in Book II of the *Politics*, after his defense of the naturalness of the city in Book I. In Book II, he critiques the political proposals in Plato's *Republic*, and those of Phaleas, and Hippodamus, all of which aim to effect radical political change. By way of his various criticisms, Aristotle implies that these proposals do not reflect an understanding of nature as a whole, and are consequently naive. Furthermore, change in politics is not like change in the other arts, such as medicine, because politics depends on the compliance of citizens to laws, which compliance will not be forthcoming if laws are frequently changed (esp. *Politics* 1267b22–30; 1268a6–8; 1268b22–1269a28).

In sum, the doctine of functionalism is Aristotle's second sailing in the realm of political philosophy; that is to say, it is the doctrine on which the city must rely or fall back if it is led by men whose primary concern is not the good for human beings, but power or gain. Should a city ever become so fortunate as to have political leaders whose primary concern is the good for human beings, then and only then will it have both the means and the moral license to improve upon the politically functional arrangement that nature gives us. Then and only then should politics aspire to make both men and women ambidextrous.

NOTES

1. *The Complete Essays of Montaigne*, trans. Donald M. Frame (Stanford: Stanford University Press, 1958), 376.

2. The Greek editions and translations of Aristotle's texts cited throughout are *Politik*, ed. A. Dreizehnter (Munchen: Wilhelm Fink Verlag, 1970); *The Politics*, trans. C. Lord (Chicago: University of Chicago Press, 1984); *Ethica Nicomachea*, ed. F. Susemihl (Leipzig: B.G. Teubner, 1903); *Nicomachean Ethics*, trans. W. D. Ross (Oxford: Oxford University Press, 1925); *History of Animals* and *Generation of Animals*, trans. A. L. Peck (Cambridge, Mass.: Loeb, 1963 and 1965); *Metaphysics*, trans. H. Tredennick (Cambridge, Mass.: Loeb, 1933); *De Anima*, trans. D. W. Hamlyn (Oxford: Clarendon, 1968). In a few instances, I modify these translations and emphasize words.

3. See also Pierre Pellegrin, "Logical Difference and Biological Difference: The Unity of Aristotle's Thought," in *Philosophical Issues in Aristotle's Biology*, ed. Allan Gotthelf and James G. Lennox (Cambridge: Cambridge University Press, 1987), 321–22.

4. See also Pellegrin, "Logical Difference," 321–22.

5. Ibid., 330.

6. Aristotle was the first to place the origin of sex determination at the very beginning of embryonic development, and made other substantially modern and profoundly influential claims in the field of embryology. See Joseph Needham, *A History of Embryology*, 2d ed. (New York: Abelard-Schuman, 1959), 37–60.

7. Among the scholars making this charge are Maryanne Cline Horowitz, "Aristotle and Woman," *Journal of the History of Biology* 9, no. 2 (1976), 183–213; Eva C. Keuls, *The Reign of the Phallus: Sexual Politics in Ancient Athens* (New York: Harper & Row, 1985); G. E. R. Lloyd, *Science, Folklore, and Ideology: Studies in the Life Sciences in Ancient Greece* (Cambridge: Cambridge University Press, 1983); Nicole Loraux, *Les enfants d'Athéna: Idées athéniennes sur la citoyenneté et la division des sexes* (Paris: Francois Maspero, 1981); and Susan Moller Okin, *Women in Western Political Thought* (Princeton: Princeton University Press, 1979). For a response to Horowitz and to the charge of sexism in Aristotle's biology, see Johannnes Morsink, "Was Aristotle's Biology Sexist?" *Journal of the History of Biology* 12 (1979): 83–112.

8. Although the male's contribution of sentient soul to procreation is naturally superior to the female's contribution, because sense perception—a sort of knowledge—is categorically superior to matter, it is not evident that, as some critics argue, that superiority implies or translates into a political-ethical superiority, such that the father is the more important of the two parents. Keuls, for example, believes that Aristotle is claiming that a father is more a father than a mother is a mother, just as Apollo argued in his defense of Orestes. Nonetheless, if that is the implication of Aristotle's argument, it would hardly seem to deserve Keul's characterization as chauvinistic inasmuch as it reduces the importance of being a mother. See Keul's *Reign of the Phallus*, 145, 405–6.

9. Although Aristotle uses *nous* at *GA* 736b27 ("Reason enters in . . . "), the context suggests that he means all forms of reason or intellectual virtue. On the various forms, see *EN* VI; on Aristotle's three different usages of *nous*, see Terence Irwin's glossary in his translation of the *Nicomachean Ethics* (Indianapolis: Hackett, 1985), 429.

10. Stephen R. L. Clark's paraphrase of *On Generation and Corruption*, 328b22. He observes that "the metaphysics of form and matter perverts, but does not quite obliterate the theory of mixture" (*Aristotle's Man: Speculations upon Aristotelian Anthropology* [Oxford: Clarendon, 1975], 208).

11. Pellegrin concludes: "None, then, of the classificatory concepts of Aristotelian biology is taxonomic, because none of them defines a constant level of generality to which a taxonomic construction, in fact or even in intent, could refer." Because "the doctrine of the more and the less as applied in biology does not legitimate the view that this branch of knowledge can be held to account for peculiar concepts . . . we must consolidate the bridge which we have stretched between the logico-metaphysical usage and the biological usage of the concepts of *genos* and *eidos*" ("Logical Difference," 328–33).

12. Lord, *The Politics*, 280.

13. A note by D. M. Balme, the translator, explains that this is to be assumed from the earlier statement at 608b3 that the male is "more spirited" (*HA*, 219).

14. Pellegrin, "Logical Difference," 313–14.

15. Ibid., 314, 318.

16. Ibid., 318–19, 323–24.

17. Ibid., 319.

18. Ibid., 321.

19. Thus the text does not support the contention that Aristotle shared and promoted the ancient Athenian view, generated by Greek myths, that women are as different a species from men as birds are from fish (see Loraux, *Les enfants d'Athena* [Paris: Francois Maspero, 1981], 76–81, 91–92). Further accounting for the phenomenon of difference, though, Aristotle says that "just as a number does not possess the more and the less, neither does the substance in virtue of the form [*kata to eidos*], but if it does possess the more and less, it is substance with the matter that does so" (1044a10–11). Thus, while Socrates cannot be more or less male than Alcibiades in virtue of the form (*kata to eidos*), he can be more or less male than Alcibiades in virtue of their both being substances with matter and thus embodying in different ways the male characteristics they each have (1033b24–26, 1035b28–32, 1037a5–7, 1042b9–11, 22–35); see Pellegrin, "Logical Difference," 321, 332–37. See also James G. Lennox, "Kinds, Forms of Kinds, and the More and the Less in Aristotle's Biology," in *Philosophical Issues in Aristotle's Biology*, esp. 345–46. Lennox offers this synopsis of relevant statements in the *Categories, Metaphysics*, and *Parts of Animals*: "For two individuals to differ in degree, they must both be the same general *sort* of thing. With respect to that sort they do not differ in degree. But the general sort is constituted of *features with range*—any sub-kind may have those features exemplified by different specifications of that range." Lennox characterizes his interpretation of Aristotle as "non-typological, teleological essentialism" (346, 340 n. 4).

20. See Wayne H. Ambler, "Aristotle's Understanding of the Naturalness of the City," *The Review of Politics* 47, no. 2 (April 1985): 168–69.

21. Ibid., 169.

22. See also ibid., 169–70.

23. See also ibid., 171.

24. See A. L. Peck, Aristotle, *Historia Animalium*, vol. 1 (Cambridge: Harvard University Press, 1965), lxxiii–lxxv and Carnes Lord, "Aristotle's Anthropology," in *Essays on the Foundations of Aristotelian Political Science* (Berkeley: University of California Press, 1991), 55.

25. There is a lacuna in Dreizehnter's text; Lord supplies the meaning that one *ought* to rule a wife in the following way (*The Politics*, p. 248 n. 31).

26. The anecdote about Amasis is in Herodotus II.172, noted by Lord, 248 n. 32.

27. Arlene W. Saxonhouse suggests that the basis for the husband's rule is acquired conventional accoutrements of power more than it is an ability or virtue bestowed by nature on the male ("Family, Polity, and Unity: Aristotle on Socrates' Community of Wives," *Polity* 15 [1982], 205–6). R. G. Mulgan also proposes this interpretation but does not think that Aristotle is committed to it since he presents the household as arising out of natural differences (*Aristotle's Political Theory: An Introduction for Students of Political Theory* [Oxford: Clarendon, 1977], 46–47).

28. For example, W. W. Fortenbaugh maintains the reading that women are by nature overly emotional ("Aristotle on Slaves and Women," in *Ethics and Politics*, vol. 2, *Articles on Aristotle*, ed. Jonathan Barnes, Malcolm Schofield, and Richard Sorabji [London: Gerald Duckworth, 1977], 138–39); Saxonhouse seems to grant more credence to the reading that the deliberative capacity of women is not respected by men ("Family, Polity, and Unity," 208); and Horowitz argues that women lack men's respect according to Aristotle because they are overly emotional ("Aristotle and Woman," 207, 211).

29. Nor does it accord with his comment in the *Rhetoric* that women have the virtues of moderation and industry (*Politics* 1361a3–7).

30. See W. K. Lacey, *The Family in Classical Greece* (Ithaca: Cornell University Press, 1968), esp. 23–24. See also Sarah B. Pomeroy, *Goddesses, Whores, Wives, and Slaves: Women in Classical Antiquity* (New York: Schocken Books, 1975), 60.

31. See also Ambler, "Aristotle's Understanding," 177.

32. As Eric Voegelin explains, "What matters is not correct principles about what is right by nature in an immutable generality, nor [even] the acute consciousness of the tension between the immutable truth and its mutable application . . . but the changeability, the *kinēton* itself, and the methods to lift it to the reality of truth. . . . The *kinēton* of action is the *locus* where man attains his truth. The truth of existence is attained where it becomes concrete, i.e., in action" ("What is Right by Nature?" in *Anamnesis*, trans. and ed. Gerhart Niemeyer [Notre Dame: University of Notre Dame Press, 1978], 63).

33. As Voegelin also explains, the divine principle (*archē*) of the cosmos can use human instrumentalities of reason, knowledge, and habits of virtue, or it can take a short cut directly to human action. "The normal case is not that of the fortune-favored unwise, but rather that of the wise man. . . . Insofar as . . . [the wise man's] knowledge is the instrument used by the divine to attain truth in the reality of action, ethics itself is a phase in the movement of being that ends in the *kinēton*, and its creation is a labor of serving the

unmoved mover. The philosophical achievement of ethics has its dignity as a part of the divine movement that leads to the truth of action" (ibid., 64).

34. *The Complete Essays of Montaigne*, 376.

CHAPTER 12

ARISTOTLE AND THRASYMACHUS ON THE COMMON GOOD

────────────

WAYNE AMBLER

INTRODUCTION

It is frequently noted that Aristotle wrote at a time when political authority was under attack. If the Greek *polis* in its heyday enjoyed the fulsome support of its citizens, unchallenged by powerful or at least by open criticism, the same was not true in the late fifth and fourth centuries. Natural philosophers, sophists, and Socrates himself doubted orthodox views about the gods and justice, making it less clear for precisely what reasons men should put their fortunes and their lives at their city's disposal. Aristotle was not distracted from fundamental questions by the contemporary crisis of the Greek city, but his *Politics* addresses some of these questions in light of that crisis. He was certainly no simple conservative who tried once again to claim divine support or descent for cities or their rulers, but his ringing declarations of the naturalness of the city and the political nature of human beings were clearly part of an attempt to reestablish political authority on grounds which were at once more persuasive and more amenable to reason. Also serving in Aristotle's defense of political authority are his elevated doctrine that the city exists to cultivate virtue and his presentation of the common good as an "absolutely just" foundation which supports three correct (*orthai*) regimes. While this chapter will focus narrowly on the issues raised by Aristotle's most prominent discussion of the common good (*Politics* III.6–7), it does so in the belief that this particular discussion provides a helpful illustration of the way in which Aristotle attempts to strengthen and guide political authority.

A philosophic defense of actual cities may also bring advantages to the one who makes it and to the activity from which it proceeds. If political authority was under attack, many must also have sensed that it deserved or needed a strong defense of its justice. By offering a powerful new defense for a threatened but still vital cause, Aristotle could not but win allies for another project still more in need of support. For if the reputation of political authority had suffered in the last century, neither was the reputation of philosophy as yet securely established in the face of varying degrees of indifference, suspicion, and hostility.[1] We shall investigate below one small way in which Aristotle made progress not only toward a philosophical politics but also toward a politic presentation of philosophy. The main features of his attempt emerge more clearly when set in the context of the debate between Thrasymachus and Socrates.

The main teachings and tenor of the *Ethics* and *Politics* bespeak a general posture completely opposed to that of Thrasymachus. Aristotle's recurring seriousness about nobility; about such ethical virtues as moderation, magnanimity, and liberality; about the political nature of human beings; about cities devoted to virtue and just cities; and his occasional but intransigent defenses of the contemplative life, all suggest that he is guided by principles wholly opposed to such cynical views as those proclaimed by the likes of Thrasymachus and Callicles. That Aristotle parts company from Thrasymachus on many issues surely helps confirm his position on each, and the reader distressed by Thrasymachus's assaults on justice and decent politics will find support throughout Aristotle's political work. It is nonetheless helpful to zero in on some one main disagreement in order to see better the way Aristotle goes about explaining and defending his more elevated view of men and cities. Since Aristotle's doctrine of the common advantage is a direct rebuttal of Thrasymachus's claim that justice is the advantage of the stronger, since Socrates refutes Thrasymachus without appealing to the common advantage, and since the common advantage is an issue which remains central to contemporary political discourse, a focus on this issue has the added benefits that it illuminates a point on which Aristotle appears to part company with Socrates and which speaks to us with unusual directness. Thus our study of Aristotle will be introduced by a study of the Thrasymachus section of Plato's *Republic*.

Aristotle's teaching that just regimes pursue the common advantage is in one respect like his teachings that the city's purpose is the cultivation of virtue, that the city exists by nature, and that natural right exists. Each of these teachings is sufficiently striking and sufficiently emphasized by Aristotle that it has come to be associated with his name; none would be omitted from summaries of his political thought. But it is also true that the direct discussion of each of these issues is confined to relatively short and isolated passages. That these short passages defy simple analysis poses one sort of problem; that their familiar theses are elsewhere neglected or complicated poses another sort of problem.[2] But this feature of Aristotle's writing has at least the advantage that one knows where to begin: briefly mentioned in several places, the common advantage is an explicit theme only at *Politics* III.6–7. It is here that Aristotle divides all regimes into two main kinds, the correct and the deviant. His basis for doing so is expressed in the following lines:

> It is manifest then that as many regimes as aim at the common advantage are correct regimes according to what is absolutely just, while those which aim only at the advantage of the rulers are all in error and are deviations from the correct regimes. (1279a17–20)

The distinction between the common advantage and the rulers' private advantage takes center stage in Aristotle's assessment of the justice of the different regimes. The challenge of better understanding this distinction will take us in two directions: the first will lead us to look at the discussion which issues in Aristotle's invocation of the common advantage. The second will lead us to look at Aristotle's use of the common advantage once invoked. But let us first recall the argument to which Aristotle's doctrine is such a fitting response.

The main theses of Thrasymachus, Socrates, and Aristotle are easily summarized and invite simultaneous investigation. The first declared that rulers rule and are right to rule in their own interest, the second that they rule and are right to rule in their subjects' interest, and the third that they should but do not always rule in the common interest. Aristotle puts the common advantage at the center of his defense of justice whereas Socrates does not. On the contrary, its existence or importance is tacitly denied by Socrates as well as by Thrasymachus. Since Thrasymachus's position is familiar and clear enough to need little discussion, I'll begin with Socrates' response. Consideration of this response will do nothing to diminish our eagerness for a civic-minded rebuttal of Thrasymachus's thesis, and thus will lead us to Aristotle.

SOCRATES AND THRASYMACHUS ON THE COMMON GOOD

At the outset of his most probing inquiry into Thrasymachus's account of justice, Socrates not only shows that Thrasymachus has made an error in logic (as was the case previously, 339a5–340c9), he also gives the impression of presenting a rival teaching of his own about how rulers ought to rule and at least sometimes do rule (341c4–342e11). This particular argument shows that Socrates is not merely a skilled practitioner of the art of words who refutes but never teaches (as charged at 337c); it also suggests that Socrates' teaching is a noble one in sharp contrast to the depraved view of justice and political life advanced by Thrasymachus. Its conclusion is a forceful reminder of this argument:

> So then, Thrasymachus, I said, no one else in any rule whatsoever, insofar as he is a ruler, either considers or enjoins what is his own advantage but what is advantageous for the ruled and for whatever it is that he serves as a public servant; and looking toward what is advantageous and fitting for it, he both says everything he says and does everything he does. (342e6–11)

Socrates seems, then, to advance a position diametrically opposed to that of Thrasymachus: the true ruler is not the expert in exploiting others for his own benefit; he is a public servant through and through, and he thinks not at all of himself. Socrates appears to offer something like an extreme version of the common moral exhortation to unselfishness, and this appearance helps throw Thrasymachus off course, for he thinks Socrates is guilty of errors he has heard many times before. But while Socrates' emphasis on selfless rule certainly is preferable to Thrasymachus's enthusiasm for exploitative rule, it neglects to lead us to look for a common advantage that links stronger and weaker, ruler and ruled. Its focus is entirely on the advantage of the subject, and it forgets momentarily the interest of the ruling group or individual.

Thrasymachus does not see this as a particularly cunning argument but as one steeped in naiveté. He does not now assault Socrates for being unfair in the way he argues (contrast 340d1–341c3); he appears to think that Socrates, whatever his intellectual gifts in the abstract, is a mere babe in the woods when it comes to the tough stuff of actual political life (343a3–4, d2). Like Callicles, he is outraged that Socrates seems neither to have seen the outrages that the strong inflict upon the weak nor to have inferred from them that one ought to join the strong in inflicting them.[3] Thrasymachus's outrage is of course made possible in part by his misunderstanding of what Socrates has in mind.

Thrasymachus's mocking counterattack fails to intimidate Socrates into the admission that perhaps some rulers do advance their own interests when they rule. Indeed, when he advances his next thesis, that rulers do not rule voluntarily, Socrates momentarily seems to move still further away from

Thrasymachus's views. Since he has noticed that many are hungry for the benefits of ruling, Thrasymachus not surprisingly responds to the new thesis by
denying it emphatically (345e2–4). But while Socrates never openly concedes
anything to Thrasymachus and never changes any of his own positions, his
explanation of how it is that men do not rule voluntarily puts his previous argument in a very different light and helps us to understand it better. This new
light helps defend Socrates against the charge that he is naive and shows that he
has not forsaken the politics of this world in favor of another. Socrates' account
of why men do not rule voluntarily is based especially in his description of the
wage-earning art (*misthōtikē*), and it is this art which seems to turn his position
upside down.

From his account of the unselfishness of the true ruler, Socrates might
well have seemed to be some sort of amiable simpleton who did not understand
why shepherds fatten sheep. Or, as a sympathizer might see it, he might be
thought to have willingly forsaken the defective rulers of the world we know
and to have concerned himself with rulers who live only in speech. But neither
of these views is correct. After he explains the thesis that men do not rule voluntarily, for they demand a wage in return for what they do, we see more clearly
that this account of the true ruler does not at all require us to believe that the
men who rule are unconcerned with their own interests. On the contrary, it
freely suggests or rather insists that men—including the best men—are so concerned; they are willing to rule only because of the wage they derive thereby
(347a3–d6). Socrates thus separates himself unmistakably from the thesis that
Thrasymachus had thought he was advancing, that the human beings who rule
can and should be completely unselfish, and he detects in all men that their
actions are guided by their desire for a wage: he has not forsaken this world and,
unlike Thrasymachus, he is not even outraged by it. Socrates' surprising or
shocking charge that even the best men seek wages for their actions is softened
by his distinction among different kinds of wages, for he certainly does not
mean that good men rule for wages of money or even of honor. In the end, however, neither he nor Thrasymachus argues here that men ought to subordinate
their own best interest to that of others. Indeed, the conclusion to Socrates'
remarks on the wage-earning art is anything but naive or moralistic:

> The result is that everyone who knows what's what would choose
> to be benefited by another rather than to have the trouble of bene-
> fiting him. (347d6–8)

The ruler as ruler looks after his subjects, but a sensible man will not forget
himself. And, the best men are sensible.

Socrates' discussion of the wage-earning art, whose practice accompanies that of all other arts, shows that he does not dispute Thrasymachus's position by moralistic arguments which preach selfless devotion to the interests of others. Most arts may in some sense be at liberty to neglect their own advantage and consider the advantage only of that over which they preside (342a1–b8), but this is not yet to say—though at first it seems to say—that the human beings who exercise these arts are or ought to be as indifferent to themselves as are their arts. Socrates' remarks on wage earning leave intact the thesis that most arts are selfless, but they turn its apparent moral teaching topsy-turvy. In teaching that men are not primarily selfless artisans (for they are willing to practice the arts only in order to earn a wage) and by showing no attachment to the view that men ought to be simply selfless artisans (for the best men are no less eager for their wages than are others), Socrates shows that he does not hold the view for which Thrasymachus had such contempt.

The introduction of wage earning shows Socrates' position to be less elevated, but it also holds out the prospect of making it more solid, for it leads us to consider the interest of the ruler along with that of the subject. If it should be advantageous for rulers to promote their subjects' advantage, we could with more confidence count on them to do so. Socrates certainly disagrees with Thrasymachus about what the most profitable life is (compare 338a5–7 with 347b1–9); but here, at least, he does not disparage the profitable by appeal to such justice or nobility as may be indifferent to the advantage of the individual.[4] Thrasymachus not unreasonably thought that Socrates was arguing out of great naiveté, but the latter's introduction of the wage-earning art shows that Socrates too is prepared to take a hard look at the respective "earnings" of rulers and subjects. But while Socrates' comments invite an examination of the relationship between the interests of rulers and ruled, he does not direct such an investigation here, and he certainly stops short of concluding that it is not the common advantage of both groups that the one rule and the other obey. Indeed, the implications of his remarks point to obstacles to the attainment of a strictly common advantage between political rulers and subjects.

Socrates' brief sketch calls special attention to the case of good men (*hoi beltistoi*, 347a10; *hoi agathoi*, b6; *hoi epieikeis*, c6). It is reassuring that he implies quite firmly that the best men will not use political authority to prey upon their subjects, but he also alludes to nothing in them that resembles public spirit: if not compelled to rule, they won't. Either cities must suffer by lacking the rule of the best, or the best must suffer by being compelled to rule.[5] Much might be said to try to solve, deny, or mitigate this problem but here, at least, Socrates chooses to force it upon us. If the best life for the best men is not a life of ruling, and if

cities benefit most from the rule of the best men, then there would indeed be
barriers to attaining a strictly common advantage in this case.

Socrates' discussion of the wage-earning art has a bearing also on the
question of the character of actual political life. Thrasymachus leveled the cynical and still familiar charge that the strongest political group makes the laws in
its own interest and calls this justice (338d7–339a4). Socrates had no trouble in
showing that if rulers misunderstand their interest, Thrasymachus's view is
open to the objection that it is not clear whether justice is their true or only
their imagined interest (339b7–340c9). This is a triumph for Socrates, but it
does not begin to establish a more civic-minded view of actual political life. In a
sense, it deepens rather than mitigates the indictment of actual rulers, for it
casts doubt on their intelligence without denying their selfishness. Perhaps in
part for this reason, Socrates goes on to attack more directly the substance of
Thrasymachus's view of the "ruler in accurate speech," and his account of the
unselfish art of ruling may appear to paint a more noble picture of actual rulers
as well. Nevertheless, the hollowness of this appearance becomes evident by
noting Socrates' care in distinguishing between the art of rule and the men
who happen to wield political power. Socrates does not offer here anything
like a general assessment of the character of actual rulers,[6] but it is worth noting that far from rebutting Thrasymachus on this point, his few words on the
subject are not flattering to actual rulers. Just as his later account of the true
city indicts rather than defends actual cities, so Socrates' comments on ruling
and on the way good men conduct themselves suggest the faultiness of most
of those who wield political authority. By Socrates' most unusual standards,
the very desire to rule is the sign of a defect, and yet he notes that in actual
cities men commonly fight to become supreme (347d). There is nothing sneer-
ing or cynical about Socrates' tone, but it is not too much to say that he does
not rebut Thrasymachus's general characterization of rulers as men who
above all are hungry to advance their own perceived interests.

Socrates certainly shows that he is worlds apart from Thrasymachus on
questions of the greatest importance (Why rule? Just how advantageous are such
wages as money and honor? Is justice simply what the stronger say it is?). But the
massive importance of Socrates' disagreements with Thrasymachus ought not
obscure those points which he leaves uncontested. As noted above, Socrates does
not deny that actual rulers seek to advance their own interests or that their interests are in important respects in conflict with those of their subjects. Socrates
even goes beyond this point, for he does not claim that the men who rule
should seek to model themselves on the idea of the true ruler and prefer their
subjects' interests over their own. It is true that the ruler as ruler should care for

his subjects; but the ruler as man is a wage earner, and good men are presented as taking care of themselves. Finally, and most importantly for present purposes, Socrates agrees that there is an important opposition of interests between rulers and their subjects. Socrates treats ruling as bad, Thrasymachus treats it as good; but both imply that, be it bad or good, it is a source of tension between rulers and subjects (347d2–9). Although it is certainly not denied that there are some goods that can be good for all, there is no hint here of a common advantage between rulers and subjects on the question of who should rule. It is especially in this regard that Aristotle's treatment of the issue appears most promising.

THE PROMISE OF ARISTOTLE'S POSITION

Thrasymachus maintained that there is a dominant group in every city and, further, that every dominant group rules in its own interest and against the interest of its subjects. Aristotle begins his most thematic treatment of justice in the *Politics* by agreeing with Thrasymachus's first point while disputing the second: there is everywhere an authoritative or dominant group, the *politeuma*, but its rule need not be exploitative, need not be for the advantage of the ruler and at the expense of the ruled.[7] Aristotle tacitly challenges the core of Thrasymachus's position and teaches instead that while rule is sometimes for the ruler's sake, it may also be directed toward the advantage of the subjects or toward the common advantage.[8] He does this first by distinguishing three different kinds of rule and next by distinguishing six different kinds of regime (III.6–7). At the center of both classifications is the question of who benefits from the rule, and both classifications suggest that rule is sometimes—perhaps half of the time— for the common advantage. Aristotle's classifications volunteer that slave masters rule selfishly, but they deny that fathers do; and such familiar regimes as kingship, aristocracy, and polity are presented as being devoted not to the interests of the rulers alone but to the common advantage. If he is right on this, then Thrasymachus is wrong, and the prospects for justice in a serious sense and in actual political life are much brighter than the latter allowed. These prospects have helped to win for Aristotle and perhaps even for philosophy more generally the helpful reputation of being politically responsible, and it is they which turn our attention to the *Politics* and, especially, to III.6–7.

UNSELFISH RULE AND ACCIDENTAL ADVANTAGES

It appears that there are these three main kinds of rule: despotic, familial, and political (1278b30–1279a17). Despotic rule is said to be directed toward the advantage of the ruler, and familial toward the advantage of the ruled. These two kinds of rule recall the two opposed descriptions of the true ruler as presented by Thrasymachus and Socrates, all the more so since Aristotle follows Socrates in using the selflessness of the artisan (as artisan) to illustrate selfless rule. But whereas Socrates and Thrasymachus seemed so radically at odds, with one saying that all true rulers exploit their subjects with a view to their own advantage and the other responding that all true rulers think only of their subjects and not at all of themselves, Aristotle makes distinctions: despotic rule is directed toward the interests of the ruler; familial rule is directed toward the interests of the ruled. He also makes selfish rule less repugnant, at least for the moment, by confining it to a more or less accepted sort of subpolitical rule; and he makes Socrates' emphasis on unselfish rule more believable by associating it with the father's rule over the family. Surely this example is well chosen to suggest that Thrasymachus's cynical portrait of rule cannot be true in all cases. Even unsupported by evidence, Aristotle's example will persuade all fathers that unselfish rule exists, and not only in speech.

Thrasymachus implied with some force that ruling groups pursue their own interests at the expense of their subjects. He did not so much argue this point as illustrate it with the powerful image of shepherds fattening sheep. To insist on the selfishness of rulers seemed to him to show also the harmfulness of their rule for subjects. Socrates lets on that he knows that rule may have effects quite apart from what it intends (346b1–6), but his emphasis on precise speech leads or allows him to focus on the object of rule rather than on its effects. It is thus left to Aristotle not only to deny Thrasymachus's claim that rulers seek only their own interest but also to show that selfishness need not result in exploitation, unselfishness in sacrifice. He does this by his teaching on the incidental or accidental advantage (*to kata sumbebēkos sumpherōn*). Rule and the arts have intended beneficiaries but they also have accidental consequences. The Athenians might have explained this simple point by expressing their regret to the defeated Melians that ruling in their own interest had the accidental consequence that it sometimes happened to harm others; but it is characteristic of Aristotle's main emphasis that he notes instead that rule intended to benefit only one group may have the accidental consequence that it also benefits another. He shows that selfish despotic rule has accidental advantages for its subject, and unselfish familial rule may have accidental advantages for the father who practices it. Thus a kind of common advantage, although Aristotle does not call it such, may be effected in both kinds of rule even though it is not intended in either.[9] Showing this helps Aristotle win for himself the reputation for good sense and moderation, for his point is well-taken and serves as a barrier against the false inference that what is good for the rulers must be bad for subjects, and vice versa.

Aristotle undertakes to show the importance of the accidental consequences of rule in regard both to the selfish rule over slaves and to the unselfish rule over the family. He reminds us that in the case of natural master and natural slave, there is an identity of interest, but he now adds that this identity is effected even though the slave master rules exclusively with a view to his own interest (1278b33–37). The slave's interest just happens to be promoted because it is a condition for the fulfillment of the master's interest. In this happy case, apparently, the slave master could do nothing more to benefit the slave if he should try. It seems at least from these lines that Aristotle wants to present what is accidentally advantageous as being, potentially, quite advantageous indeed. His use of the example of familial rule may be better suited to persuade us of this, at least if we tend to confuse natural with conventional slavery. Devoted parents rule for their children's sake, not for their own, and yet there must be rewards for so doing. Aristotle strengthens this thought still further by noting how unselfish artisans may nonetheless benefit from helping those to whom they minister or over whom they preside (1278b37–1279a7).

We note in passing that Hobbes, for example, who could not take seriously the notion of disinterested public service, thought he saw an identity between the interests of a monarch and those of his subjects. The monarch could, like Aristotle's slave master, be counted on to pursue his private interest; and the public interest, like that of Aristotle's slave, was certain to prosper if only accidentally.[10] There is nothing unfamiliar about the attempt to weave together the interests of self-interested men or, especially, those of self-interested rulers with their less-powerful subjects, for how else is one to secure decent government if there is indeed a "defect of better motives" in those who rule. But, although Aristotle deems it important to consider the accidental consequences of rulers' actions, it is clear that he is not as sanguine about their effect as is Hobbes, who is in other respects not inclined to a rosy view of things. Even as Aristotle introduces the importance of the accidental consequences of rule, he alludes to their limits; he does this in the case of slavery and even in the more promising case of familial rule.

If certain aspects of Aristotle's discussion stress the great extent to which accidental advantages may happen to accrue to the ruler or ruled, others call our attention to the limits of such advantages. Aristotle does mention that the slave's advantage is identical to that of the master, but he confines his comment to the case of natural slavery, for which the standards are so high as to make us wonder whether they are ever met (1254b16–20, 1255b4–15). Moreover, when he goes on to explain how and why the interests of rulers and ruled coincide in the case of despotic rule, he goes no further than to say that masters who let their slaves die cease to be masters. This consideration may help save the lives of men in truly desperate circumstances, but it stops well short of suggesting that servitude is in other respects good for the enslaved. If our political circumstances are never other than desperate and always recommend submission as a way of securing ourselves, we have others to thank for this teaching, not Aristotle. Remarkably, servitude has advantages for the slave, but Aristotle does not exaggerate their depth or scope.

Aristotle's treatment of the accidental advantages that accompany the unselfish rule over the family is also sensitive to conflicts of interest between the ruling and ruled members of the association: surprisingly, he stops short of using the family as a model for an association whose rule is directed toward the common advantage of all its members. Aristotle has already said or implied that the coupling of male and female is natural (1252a26–30), that the household is "in accord with nature" (1252b13), that the relationships within the family deserve to be called friendships (*EN* VIII.12), that man by nature is more a coupling or conjugal animal than a political animal (*EN* 1162a17–18), and that children are a common good which help to bind husband and wife together (*EN* 1162a28). It would seem but a short step, or rather no step at all, to say that rule in the case of the family exists for the sake of the common advantage, or for the best interests of all its members. And, in fact, Aristotle begins to take this step, but he immediately steps back again. His retreat in no way challenges the nobility or decency of rule in the family; it presents the head of the household as being utterly unselfish, like Socrates' ruler insofar as he is a ruler, and thus as being the exact opposite of the utterly selfish slave master. Here is what he says:

> The rule over children and wife and the whole household . . . is either for the sake of the ruled or for the sake of some [advantage] common to both; in itself it is for the sake of the ruled, just as we see also in the arts, such as medicine and gymnastic, but accidentally it could also be for their sake. (1278b–79a)

Aristotle thus does not deny that the head of the household could profit from his rule; but he does distinguish between rule for the sake of the ruled and rule for the sake of an advantage common to ruler and ruled alike, and he describes familial rule as the former of the two types. This distinction could turn out to be of practical importance if accidental advantages should be more limited or precarious than strictly common ones. Moreover, Aristotle's reticence to proclaim that the family is knit together by a single and supreme common advantage should help discourage us from being too easygoing about the question of the common advantage in the city, an association that Aristotle presents as being larger and less unified than the household (1261a17–20). If the division between rulers and ruled is a stumbling block to the common advantage in the case of the family, what is to be expected in the case of the city?

In the absence of a strictly common advantage, accidental advantages could come to the unselfish head of the household. Aristotle explains this "could" on the basis of two examples from the arts and surprisingly says nothing directly about the special naturalness, wholeness, or intimacy of the family. He thus appears to try to establish the less doubtful by the more doubtful case, and the very relevance of the latter to the former he does not argue. But notwithstanding that it is a curious procedure,[11] perhaps a closer look at how artisans might profit from practicing unselfish arts will establish that accidental advantages are indeed likely to arise for the unselfish ruler of the family.

Socrates explained the practice of unselfish arts by the additional practice of selfish art, the art of wage earning. Aristotle avoids recourse to this sort of compensation and instead shows advantages that are more directly linked to the practice of the unselfish art itself. While such advantages contain the hope of allowing us to drop Socrates' unseemly emphasis on the wages necessary to encourage men to rule, they appear to be uncertain. Aristotle's formulation is cautious: "For nothing prevents that even the athletic trainer himself might sometimes be among those who exercise, just as the ship's pilot is always one of the sailors" (1279a2–4). The pilot who thinks only of his crew is nonetheless carried to safety along with them; and the trainer may, in a roughly similar fashion, enjoy the benefit of his art, if he exercises along with his trainees. But Aristotle is even more terse here than usual, and he does not pause to examine the bearing of his examples on the rule over the family. They do show ways in which some artisans or rulers are also the patients and thus the beneficiaries of their arts, but Aristotle calls attention to the difference in this regard between the arts of the pilot and the trainer, and his raising but dropping of the example of medicine illustrates a case in which the artisan cannot always be his own patient and thus does not profit so directly from his own art. Aristotle has implied that fathers may benefit from their selfless rule as artisans do, only to mention three different arts which suggest three different relations between ruler and ruled. And he then leaves the issue without drawing a conclusion or otherwise clearing the matter up. We may infer that since the father is like the pilot in being always a part of the group over which he presides, Aristotle means to teach that the father is always a beneficiary of his own rule, even though that rule is unselfish in its intention. But even if the purpose and composition of the family were as simple and uniform as the simplified example of the ship implies, this example—and all three examples from the arts—would establish no more than that artisans or rulers benefit only insofar as they are also subjects or patients; they note no advantage for the ruler as ruler and hence point to no reason to accept the burdens of ruling or of practicing the other arts. This problem is thus like the problem noted in the case of despotic rule: Is it good to be a slave because the lives of slaves are useful to and therefore generally protected by their masters? Is it good to exercise unselfish rule over a group because, as a member of this group, one will oneself enjoy some benefit from this rule? The thesis that there are accidental advantages that bind ruler and subject has potential as a way for weakening Thrasymachus's implied claim that what is good for the stronger is bad for the weaker, but Aristotle's support for this thesis is to this point reserved. Aristotle has so far resisted the temptation to pronounce that the family is united by a strictly common advantage, and his comments about how it "could be" united by accidental advantages invite one to consider also cases in which it is not.

POLITICAL RULE

Aristotle's treatment of the third kind of rule appears to be more encouraging regarding the mutual satisfaction of the interests of rulers and ruled than were his treatments of despotic and familial rule. Only in this case, the case of political rule, does Aristotle use the phrase "the common advantage," which he now substitutes for the weaker phrase, "the accidental advantage." But if the very notion of the common advantage is by itself an attractive and powerful one, Aristotle gives it still further emphasis by putting it at the very center of his schema of the six different kinds of regimes. Unmentioned in Socrates' refutation of Thrasymachus,[12] the common advantage is used by Aristotle as the basis for singling out those regimes which are "correct in accord with what is absolutely just." Those which consider only the advantage of the rulers he calls "in error and perversions of the correct regimes" (1279a18–20). While the use of the phrase "absolutely just" (*haplōs dikaion*) is not unprecedented, it strengthens the view that rule for the common advantage meets all moral objections.

But while the common advantage is central to Aristotle's classification of six different kinds of regime and is therefore at least an implicit theme in the many passages which discuss these regimes, Aristotle's treatment of the issue is brief and curious, and this complicates the question of what he means by it. His discussion is curious in the first place because so little preparation has been made for this dramatic entrance of the common advantage as a way of distinguishing among regimes. Now, suddenly, we have a major tool for distinguishing just government from unjust, but where did it come from? The immediate context for the introduction of the common advantage showed remarkable caution about using the phrase. Aristotle briefly raised the possibility that rule in the family might exist for the common advantage (1278b39), only to state that it aims only at the advantage of the ruled. Distinguishing between accidental advantages and the common advantage strictly so called, Aristotle detected only the former as a tie between rulers and ruled in the family. Nor did Aristotle use this idea in such previous discussions as would seem to have welcomed it. For example, in Book II Aristotle discussed and assessed three actual and four proposed regimes but never praised or blamed any of them in relation to the common advantage. Indeed, Aristotle's assessment of these regimes is remarkably silent about justice in general. (He says the three actual regimes are "justly praised" [1273b25–26], but he does not evaluate the regimes themselves in regard to justice.) Further, when Aristotle discussed the schema of regimes in the *Ethics*, he did so in a way very similar to the presentation he is about to make in the *Politics*; one striking difference, however, is that while the schema in the *Politics* is centered upon the common advantage, that in the *Ethics* makes no mention of it (1160a31–b22). The common advantage is a memorable feature of Aristotle's political teaching, but it gains its prominence only in the *Politics* III.6–7. And once gained, this prominence is then quickly lost: the common good or common advantage is a theme in the central chapters of Book III, but this phrase does not occur in the final five books of the *Politics*.[13] The common advantage serves as one of Aristotle's most prominent and most promising ways of defending political authority; but, as we have begun to argue, it does not carry the main burden of this defense.

To see better just what part of this defense is provided by the common advantage, we turn to his introduction of this standard as a way of distinguishing among regimes. Here are the lines in question:

> Therefore, also in cases of political rule, wherever it has been established in accord with the equality and similarity of the citizens, men think it proper to rule in turns. They previously did this in the natural way, each thinking it proper to serve and then that someone else aim at his good in turn, just as he who ruled previously aimed at the good of the other. But now men wish to rule continuously because of the benefits from what's common and those from ruling, just as if it always happened for whoever was ruling, if sick, to become healthy. For it is in this fashion, perhaps, that they would pursue office.

> It is manifest, then, that those regimes which aim at the common advantage happen to be correct in accord with what is absolutely just, while those which aim only at the advantage of the rulers are all in error and are deviations from the correct regimes. For they are despotic, but the city is an association of the free. (1279a8–21)

The general drift of this statement is not difficult to follow. It in effect uses the two kinds of subpolitical rule as models for two kinds of political rule. "Ruling naturally" practices the unselfishness of familial rule, contemporary rule the selfishness of despotic. These in turn establish the standards by which the six kinds of regime are divided into two groups, correct and deviant, the former of which is described as pursuing the common advantage. This passage of course looks favorably upon the unselfish rule that aims at the common advantage and implies that Aristotle is disgusted with the greediness of contemporary rulers. As an alternative to the corruption of modern times, Aristotle describes the rotation through office of equal men who all rule unselfishly, who all share equally in their city, and who all benefit from it.

This is a very attractive picture or model of a kind of rule, but one is entitled to ask about its relation both to actual politics and to the standard which it introduces, the common advantage. Aristotle himself addresses the former question by implying that the standards of "ruling naturally" as here described have been met only in the past, a distant or mythical past. At least in these few lines Aristotle seems to concede that contemporary rulers rule as selfishly as had Thrasymachus charged. He does imply, as did Socrates, that rulers of this sort misunderstand their own interests (see *Republic* 339c1–3), that the profits from their exploitation are not nearly so valuable as they think, and he does not deny that a ruler's selfishness might have accidental advantages for his subjects; but while this is important in other respects and certainly does not suggest the thesis that justice is simply the interest if the stronger, it is an unattractive picture of actual political life and keeps us from accepting uncritically the apparent implication of the conclusion of the passage, that the common advantage is often the goal of actual rulers.

If contemporary political life is described as failing to meet the standards here set forth, it is also to be asked how far these standards are an appropriate basis for judgment. It is not easy to see that "ruling naturally" is political rule in the fullest sense. As is clear from the bulk of the *Politics*, but especially from the sequel to the passage before us, Aristotle presents political life as being beset not simply by the problem that human beings are often selfish but especially by the problem that we comprise different groups which are moved by different notions about whose rule is just. The goal of having a succession of men who rule unselfishly, each awaiting the benefit of his successor's rule, may be reasonable in the case of the chairmanship of a fortunate academic department; but, by the standards of what Aristotle says in upcoming chapters, it is unpolitical in the sense that it abstracts from the fundamental controversies that divide one political group from another. Aside from these controversies, it is believable that equal and similar men could even out the disadvantages of ruling by taking turns; but taking turns would amount to permanent revolution in cases in which, say, the poor, the rich, and the well-born are in contention for political power. Aristotle's brief picture of natural rule addresses the problem of opposed interests in equal individuals, but it does not yet indicate that the main contenders in actual political life also have very different ideas about what justice is. The common advantage as depicted here is thus advanced as a solution before all the problems which beset it are fully developed, and its simple fulfillment through the "natural rule" of equals could not be proposed after the complex discussion of distributive justice in chapters 8–13.[14] We can summarize this point by saying that Aristotle's brief picture of natural rule shows an attractive solution to the problem of just rule so long as men view ruling as a burden to be avoided. The sequel of his *Politics*, however, stresses that this condition does not apply in actual political practice.

Moreover, even this happy picture of selfless rulers does not quite imply that there is a perfect conformity between the interests of rulers and ruled. To the contrary, Aristotle does not now speak directly of the common advantage; and he drops the claim that was made in the case of natural despotic rule, and made indirectly in the case of familial rule, that there are accidental consequences of rule that make it advantageous even for those who are not its intended beneficiaries. Surely there must be, but Aristotle now seems to imply that in natural rule, citizens benefit only when they are not ruling. The good of being ruled by others might be distributed equally over time, but it cannot be simultaneously enjoyed in common. It is remarkable that in the text most filled with promise about the common advantage as both a moral and practical standard for judging regimes, Aristotle stops short of suggesting that this advantage is so common as to embrace simultaneously rulers and subjects alike. Even as he notes that master and slave share interests, that the head of the household and his family share interests, and that some artisans and the beneficiaries of their arts share interests, this discussion stops short of suggesting that there is a strictly common advantage between the political ruler and his subjects. Along with interests they may share is the question of who will rule and who will be ruled; and at least on this issue, interests diverge. In this one respect, Aristotle presented the interests of natural masters and slaves as meshing more readily together (1255b4–15).

These few problems do not, however, mar the impression of a happy picture of political life. Since these men are said to be equal and similar, and since they do not fight to win the advantage of never ruling, their selfishness and the tension of interests between rulers and subjects do not work any harm. The very happiness of the picture makes it difficult to press the question of the identity of the common advantage.

Aristotle hesitated to pronounce that there was a common advantage in the family not because he was secretly protesting domestic oppression; he did so because he was being strict about the idea that there may be some interest that is truly common and deeply good, so that ruling with view to it, the head of household would simultaneously foster both his own best interests and those of all other members of his family. He was at this moment not yet prepared to speak of the common advantage as being common only to a part of the family, to the ruled only, for example;[15] nor would he have been content to note that family members share some particular good in common, such as a house, for example, if this good was, all things considered, not of such importance as to overwhelm such other interests as might divide them. It is because he here is exploring what it would mean in its most complete sense that Aristotle steps back from declaring that the head of the household can rule toward the common advantage: the common advantage strictly so called must be something truly common and deeply advantageous for the entire group in question. It is important that various goods can be shared by different people and that accidental advantages can link the interests of those not quite bound by the common advantage in the strictest sense, but Aristotle does not fail to consider again the possibility of a still more complete and essential linking of interests (recall 1253a19–29).

What is meant by the common advantage is hence equivocal in two main ways, in the extent of its commonness and in the depth of its goodness. If in his treatment of the family Aristotle reserved for the common advantage its richest meaning and hence declined to apply it even in this case, he succeeds in using it to define the correct regimes only by diluting its meaning.[16] In particular, the common advantage which is introduced by Aristotle's description of "ruling naturally" is not strictly common to rulers and ruled alike. As we noted just above, the rulers in the case of "ruling naturally" profit from ruling only when they are not ruling. Socrates had also presented rulers as being excluded from the benefits of their own rule, and it is helpful that he dramatized this problem by describing the amusing picture of a city of good men who fight to avoid having to rule (347d2–8). Neither Socrates nor Aristotle describes in these passages an actual political situation; both are directing our attention to the division of the city into rulers and ruled as the major stumbling block to be overcome if there is to be a strictly common good. Moreover, both do so initially in backwards fashion, as though having to rule were the great evil of political life. They thereby avoid promoting such cynical views of politics as do Thrasymachus and so many others, while they also suggest that there is a rich private life superior to the life of ruling.

Aristotle's dilution of what is meant by the common advantage becomes more clear in his first definition of the three correct regimes. The correct regimes pursue the common advantage, while the deviations pursue only the advantage of the rulers (1279a17–21). But this is as much as to say that the advantage of the rulers is not part of the common advantage, at least not entirely.[17] Whereas Aristotle previously had looked for some advantage which embraced the entire family, he here employs the term even while implying that it does not include the interests of those who rule. Rulers are still to be blamed if they put their own interests ahead of their subjects', but the character of their error, and our prospects for reforming them, are different if rulers must neglect or hurt themselves in order to benefit their subjects. It is at first surprising that Aristotle invokes the common advantage in the case of the city immediately after having hesitated to do so in the case of the family, for the former would seem to be, and was previously said to be, a much tighter community than the latter. Our surprise is diminished in part by noting that the common advantage as applied here to the correct regimes is narrower in scope: it is common to the ruled, but not to their rulers.[18]

This conclusion is also in accord with the schema of regimes as it was presented in the *Ethics*. The interests of rulers and ruled were there distinguished; there was no claim that they are united by some common advantage (*EN* 1160a31–b9). If it was striking at first that the *Politics* speaks of the common advantage in a passage which is otherwise closely modeled on one in the *Ethics*, it turns out that the meaning of the phrase is restricted and does not introduce a fundamentally new teaching. It is helpful to recall, however, how the passage in the *Ethics* addresses the problem posed by the division of the city into rulers and ruled. Aristotle there calls the monarchical ruler who promotes his subjects' advantage a king and says that he must be self-sufficient, superior in all goods, and in need of nothing (*EN* 1160b2–7). Such a man, if there is such a man, is free to rule with a view to the advantage of his subjects. But by setting the requirements for unselfish rule so high as, in effect, to require divine kings to meet them, Aristotle invites us to doubt that we will witness it. Hence he solves the problem of just rule in theory, but he does so again in such a way as to under-score another of its difficulties in practice. Or, to change the emphasis, I wonder whether he is willing to teach us the problem only in a context in which he miti-gates it by the addition of a purported solution.

But if it is too much to ask of the common advantage that it be deeply good and truly common between rulers and ruled, Aristotle has already noted that accidental advantages often bind ruler and ruled. Such accidental advan-tages may go a long way toward substituting for the strictly common good from which Aristotle distinguishes them. Surely it is part of statesmanship, as Madison implies in *Federalist 51*, to arrange things as much as possible such that the interests of different men and groups can be advanced together. Beyond this, it is important to emphasize again that, where there are conflicts of interest between rulers and ruled, strong and weak, the main effect of Aristotle's work is to teach that just rule is directed toward the advantage of the subjects. And per-haps to help encourage rulers to act properly, he does not stop short of calling the advantage of the subjects "the common advantage."

We find ourselves in this situation: against Thrasymachus's attack on actual cities Aristotle offers a potent concept which Socrates had neglected, the common advantage. His doing so seems part of the more sober or political character of his teaching, for he does not invoke the common advantage in defense of a heavenly regime presided over by philosopher kings; he does so in defense of regimes which go by the familiar names of kingship, aristocracy, and polity. Defending political authority in this way tends not only to strengthen it but also to encourage that it be used well, and not for the narrow interests of any one party or class. Moreover, to the extent that this promising teaching becomes associated with a or even *the* philosopher, it is bound to improve the reputation of philosophy among those who have felt the need to strengthen political authority against its many detractors, some of whom may themselves have been associated with philosophy. But while Aristotle's generous invocation of the common advantage is memorable and attractive to all friends of political authority, it occurs in a passage that also proves on examination to be remark-ably sensitive to the actual disharmony of interests between ruler and subject. It is not too much to say that Aristotle's main discussion of the common advantage presents it as a fundamental problem, not as a simple solution. Further, this dis-cussion quickly gives way to a debate over distributive justice in which the con-clusions of the schema of six regimes is thrown into question, and the focus on the common advantage as a nonpartisan standard of justice is blurred or lost. This observation helps us notice after the fact that Aristotle's two previous ref-erences to the common advantage in the *Politics* were to uses of the phrase by others, and in both cases Aristotle implied that he doubted that its use was justified.[19] The common advantage enjoys a prominent place in the language of actual politics, and Aristotle helps to cement and guide its prominence. He does not, however, allow its prominence to protect it from doubts about its ability to bind together rulers and subjects in either actual cities, where ruling is itself perceived to be good, or in imaginary ones in which ruling is to be avoided if possible. Justice must preside over the distribution of an authority which cannot be held simply in common.

NOTES

1. Plato, *Republic* 487c–d; Plutarch, *Nicias* 23.

2. By neglected I mean, for example, that after raising our hopes by presenting an account of natural right in *EN* V.7, Aristotle then fails to refer back to it when he discusses the different kinds of regimes in the *Politics*. To the elusiveness of his teaching in the first place is added the problem that it is not pursued in contexts which would seem to invite it.

By complicated I mean, for example, that while Aristotle does call for the city to encourage virtue, he also teaches that Sparta was virtually alone among ancient regimes in her attempt to do just this (*EN* 1180a24–30, 1102a9–12); and, more to the point, he teaches elsewhere that Sparta was grossly mistaken about what virtue is. Indeed, she made men bestial while thinking she made them courageous (*Politics* 1338b9–19, 1333b5–35, 1334a40–b4). Aristotle teaches boldly that virtue is at risk when neglected by cities; he shows one complication of this emphasis by indicating that the rare city which cares about virtue does not know what it is.

3. Even though he attacks justice and says he asks for no favors (341b9–10), Thrasymachus becomes angry at the way Socrates argues (338d3–4, 340d1, 341a7–9). He seems unable to live by the amoral argument he tries to make. Plato's Callicles is similarly incapable of ridding himself of a passion or concern for justice (see esp. *Gorgias* 511a5–7, b6).

4. That Socrates thinks it important to defend justice and nobility as profitable is made clear not only here but elsewhere as well (cf. 444e7–445a5, 367d3–5).

5. This problem has a later history in the *Republic*, of course, when Socrates says that for their city to become perfect, some necessity must constrain philosophers to rule (499b).

6. See, however, 487e–489c. The *Gorgias*'s attack on actual rulers, which is extended to include Athens's great political heroes, is presented in terms similar to those used here in the *Republic* (*Gorgias* 502d–503d, 515c–517a).

7. Another kind of response would be to deny or downplay the importance of the distinction between rulers and ruled. Aristotle takes this route in his initial response to conventionalist doctrines such as those of Thrasymachus. Consider *Politics* 1253a1–5, 19–29, and note that Book I in general does not yet acknowledge that the city is divided into rulers and ruled. His later emphasis on the citizen, who both rules and is ruled, also has this advantage. Thrasymachus and Socrates, by contrast, never mention "citizen," and both refer often to rulers and ruled as distinct groups.

8. Aristotle alludes to Thrasymachean attacks on justice and the city in other places as well (1252b30ff, *EN* 1130a2–3, 1134b5). In still others he shows the influence of Socrates' counter-arguments (*EN* 1134b4–7). That he does not state Thrasymachus's position at length or even mention his name (apart from *Politics* 1305a1) may be out of a sense of the present and potential influence of this position more than out of the view that it is unimportant. Thrasymachus had his hearing in the *Republic* and, as Glaucon and Socrates noted, justice was already widely thought to lack intrinsic goodness for the one who practiced it, so

Aristotle could well have thought that he should address these views without giving them the benefit of still another powerful statement.

9. Socrates' discussion of wages is similar to Aristotle's discussion of accidental consequences in that both begin to account for the way the interests of different parties may be linked. One important difference is that Socrates' account puts man's concern for his own interest always in the forefront.

10. *Leviathan* II.19. Hobbes makes this still more general claim in *De Cive* X.2: ". . . for all the profits and disprofits arising from government are the same, and common both to the *ruler* and the *subject*."

11. The more likely argument also has its disadvantages. If Aristotle should emphasize the special intimacy of the family as a basis for establishing that it is united by a common advantage, we would run the risk of implying that there can be no such common advantage in the absence of the family's bonds. Similarly, if he should stress that a parent's love makes irrelevant the question of his interests in ruling the family, he would again run the risk of underscoring the problem of rule in the city, where parental love is not present. But this is not to say that his treatment of the family here is governed entirely by the needs of his argument about the city.

12. The phrase "common benefit" (*ōphelian koinon*) occurs at 346a6–7, where Socrates denies that there is any art which produces such a benefit.

13. The *Politics* contains eleven direct references to the common good or advantage (*to koinon agathon, to koinon sumpheron, to koinon lusiteloun*). Nine of them are in chapters 6–13 of Book III. The other two are in paraphrases of political remarks that might be made by others (1268b31, 1276a13); they are not part of Aristotle's own teaching (except to show with what carelessness the phrase is commonly used).

14. Let me try to identify one manifestation of this complexity. Whereas the chapters which present the schema treat the common advantage as a standard above partisan controversy (for the six regimes are assessed directly on this basis), the chapters on distributive justice (chs. 8–13) indicate more clearly that the identity of the common advantage is itself a matter of partisan dispute. Aristotle does bring "the common advantage of the citizens" forward as a way of solving a controversy between the better and the more numerous citizens; but he at once indicates that this hardly settles the issue, for "the citizen is different in each regime" (1283b36–1284a3). As the definition of the citizen changes, so does the scope and identity of the advantage which is common to all citizens.

15. In this first reference to the common advantage in the *Ethics*, Aristotle makes it plain that upon hearing the phrase "the common advantage," one must ask, "Common to whom?" (*EN* 1129b14–17). See also *Politics* 1283b40–1284a3. I think he also asks, "How advantageous?"

16. Let me note again that Aristotle never says of any particular city, whether actual or among the best regimes in speech, that it fulfills or promotes the common advantage. He introduces the three correct regimes as doing this, but his comments on particular kingships, aristocracies, and polities do not refer to the common advantage. See above, note 13.

17. Surely there are various advantages that unite rulers and ruled, but if there are also separate and opposed interests, then one must weigh the two in relation to each other.

As noted above, we seek not any common interest but one which is more important than such various opposed interests as individuals may have.

18. We often speak of "the public interest" in this way, without presuming that it is in the interest of rulers to promote it. Hence they claim to be public servants, and we look for indirect ways to encourage them to promote this public interest. For example, we try to make ambition counteract ambition.

19. 1268b31, 1276a13. The former of these passages uses the term common good (*koinon agathon*). I have not seen evidence that Aristotle uses this broader term to overcome such problems as he raises in the case of the common advantage.

CHAPTER 13

COMMUNITY AND CONFLICT IN ARISTOTLE'S POLITICAL PHILOSOPHY

BERNARD YACK

The shared sentiments and commitments which constitute a community are often the source of its deepest conflicts. Anyone who has lived in a family rather than merely longed for a home knows that all too well. A stranger may cheat you, but only a brother, a comrade, or a colleague can betray you. In the end, distinctive and ugly forms of distrust are part of the price one pays for community.

Aristotle understands the tensions characteristic of community life very well. Political community is for him a conflict-ridden reality rather than a speculative alternative; he expresses none of the *Gemeinschaftsschwärmerei* which his concept of political community so often inspires in modern critics of liberal political theory and practice. The core of the *Politics*, Books III–VI, focuses instead on the kinds of conflict peculiar to political communities. The existence of these conflicts bespeaks the presence, not the absence, of political community for him.

Only an extremely selective reading of the *Politics* could support the claim, affirmed even by one of Aristotle's most assertive contemporary champions—Alasdair MacIntyre—that Aristotle fails to recognize "the centrality of opposition and conflict in human life."[1] Yet MacIntyre's view epitomizes a widespread understanding of Aristotle's concept of political community, an understanding which I challenge in this essay. Like MacIntyre, most of the scholars who have championed Aristotelian political concepts since World War II have disconnected Aristotle's analysis of political community from his analysis of political conflict.[2] Hannah Arendt, to take the most influential among these scholars, concentrates solely on the distinction between political and household communities made in Book I. As a result, she develops out of that distinction an understanding of "political" action which differs so much from Aristotle's that she would have to deny that the battles over distributive justice, analyzed at such length in Books III–IV of the *Politics*, represent political phenomena.[3] Joachim Ritter, to take another influential example, also develops an interpretation of Aristotle's concept of political community without considering whether it explains or contradicts his treatment of political life in the later books of the *Politics*.[4]

The tendency of most contemporary readers to ignore the connections Aristotle makes between political community and political conflict may result from their familiarity with liberal political theories. In the light of liberal justifications of political institutions in terms of individual calculation of interest and obligation, Aristotle's statements about the logical priority of the community to the individual in Book I of the *Politics* stand out and attract the greatest attention. Likewise, the analyses of political argument and conflict in the later books generally receive less attention since they do not contrast as sharply with widely accepted principles of liberal political thought.[5] Such a perspective distorts our understanding of Aristotle's concept of political community by making political community seem to be a form of identity and political conflict a divergence from political community. This may be the way in which some of Aristotle's antiliberal admirers understand political community. But it is not, as I shall attempt to show in what follows, the understanding of political community developed in the *Politics*.

THE POLITICAL ANIMAL AND
THE POLITICAL COMMUNITY

The first sentence of the *Politics* begins: "Every *polis* is, as we see, some form of community." Politics, the political things, concern what goes on in a particular kind of community (*koinōnia*). *Koinōnia* is, in Aristotle's usage, a far less exclusive term than its closest English equivalent, *community*. Wherever individuals hold something in common (*koinon*), whether it be a home, a contract or a goal, Aristotle sees community.[6] He thus suggests that even business partners or travelers on a ship form a community. (*Nicomachean Ethics* 1151a; afterward, *EN*)

That man is a social, or communal, animal (*zōon koinōnikon*) (*Eudemian Ethics* 1242a23; afterward, *EE*), Aristotle apparently deems too obvious to need proof. When he argues, in the first pages of the *Politics*, that man is by nature a political animal, he is not attempting to prove that human beings are by nature social beings, beings who satisfy their needs and establish their goals only through interaction with each other.[7] Rather, he is interested in examining the character of a particular kind of community found among some human beings: the political community.

Community among human beings alters in character, for Aristotle, with the particular kind of thing they share. Aristotle does not view community as the equivalent of identity or simple unity, and thus does not measure different communities by the degree of identity they contain. Indeed, he ridicules Plato for measuring the worth of political communities in this way, suggesting that for Plato the true community would be a single individual (*Politics* 1261a). Heterogeneity is as essential a component of the phenomenon Aristotle tries to capture with his concept of community as some form of shared identity. Both components taken together, nonidentical individuals and/or groups holding something in common, form a community. The kind of thing shared by heterogenous individuals and/or groups provides him with the basis for distinguishing among the different kinds of community.

Aristotle's first concern is, therefore, to describe and account for the particular kind of community we call political. Although he can expect his Greek readers to have identified political life with life in a *polis*, he proceeds to do so, not through observation and analysis of life in the *polis*, but rather through reflection on the capacities for different kinds of community held by animals with the specific nature of human beings. It is with such reflections, of course, that Aristotle loses the sympathy of most contemporary social theorists. If his insistence on the different character of community in different settings draws him closer than one might first expect to much of modern social theory, then his teleological reasoning sets him apart once again.

At the same time, however, it is precisely the argument from human nature which keeps Aristotle's concept of political community alive in contemporary debates. For it allows us to ask whether that concept might be relevant to the understanding of our own political communities. If he had derived his concepts from observation and generalization, that question would hardly be worth asking, given the vast differences in size, religion, and social structure between our communities and the *polis*. Instead, his argument in Book I of the *Politics* continues to inspire suspicions that there is something in human life captured by Aristotelian political concepts which has escaped modern social theory. In order either to confirm these suspicions or finally put them to rest, we first need a clearer and less metaphorical understanding of the insights supporting Aristotle's political teleology than his interpreters have heretofore provided.

What then does Aristotle mean by calling man a political animal by nature? What kind of community does nature prepare human beings for and how does she so prepare them? Aristotle's answer to these questions are a little confusing, since he uses two different definitions of "political animal" in his works, each suggesting a different understanding of political community. The first, found in his *History of Animals*, is, despite its location, as influential as the second, placed at the beginning of the *Politics*.

In the *History of Animals*, Aristotle classifies political animals as a subclass of gregarious animals. Gregarious animals live socially, in herds or swarms. Those, like bees and ants, which work toward a common end he describes as political animals, as opposed to animals, like cows, which pursue only individual ends in their herds. Man, Aristotle suggests here, is peculiar among political animals, so defined, in that he uses his community for both common and individual ends (*History of Animals* 488a). The definition of political community suggested by the *History of Animals* classification focuses on the subordination of individual to common ends. At least since Rousseau, modern intellectuals, offended by what they perceive as the low opinion of the human race implied by liberal, individualist theories of social interaction, have often turned to Aristotle for a celebration of community defined in this way.[8]

But this understanding of political community is not that which guides Aristotle's study of political life. If Aristotle accepted this definition of political community in terms of sacrifice of individual to common ends, then he would have had to conclude that man is an imperfectly political animal, since the measure of "politicality" would be the degree of devotion to the common good. Bees and ants would be much more "political" in their behavior than human beings. But Aristotle argues precisely the opposite in the *Politics*: "man is more a political animal than bees or any other gregarious animal" (1253a8). If man is "more political" than bees and ants, then political community must have some other meaning than devotion to a common end. There must be some other kind of sharing in which human beings surpass all other creatures.[9]

It is our capacity for reasoned speech (*logos*) which demonstrates to Aristotle that we are more political in our behavior than bees. Our specific difference leads in some way to a kind of community among us which no other animals share.

> The mere voice, it is true, expresses pain and pleasure . . . but speech is designed to indicate the advantageous and the harmful, and therefore also the just and unjust; for it is the special property of man that he alone has perception of good and bad, just and unjust, and all other such things, and it is community in these things that makes a household or a *polis*. (1253a)

This account of the character of political community suggests a number of troubling questions, the most important of which is: How does one get from the account of a natural capacity to the definition and explanation of a particular kind of community which exists among us? The teleological reasoning usually attributed to Aristotle in response to this question—that since the human capacity for a just and virtuous life can be perfected only in community, there must exist, by nature, a community devoted to the good life—is especially unsatisfying for most modern readers. And so it should be, for it rests on taking a biological analogy literally. To accept this reasoning as an explanation of the existence of political communities, we would have to think of the political community as an organism which grows out of our natural capacities in the same way that an oak grows out of an acorn. Unless one takes the analogy to organic growth literally, the organic analogy merely tells us that whatever process takes us from our capacity for reasoned speech into political communities is, in some way, *like* organic growth. We are still left with the problem of identifying and accounting for that process.

Aristotle makes use of organic analogies in the opening pages of the *Politics* (1253a20). But he does not let those analogies take the place of an explanation of the nature of political communities. Rather he suggests that when individuals come together out of need in particular circumstances, their human capacity for reasoned speech compels them in some way to share in something more than need, to share something having to do with the just and unjust. Much of Aristotle's reasoning in the opening pages of the *Politics* is not made explicit. To try to bring to light his implicit reasoning, I shall try to examine the opening pages of the work in the light of the analysis of political regimes he introduces in Book III.

Individuals come together out of need, Aristotle suggests, but end up living for the sake of the "good life" in political communities (1252b31). He starts by considering communities brought together by physical need, the family, the clan, village. A larger community of need, a community which goes beyond kinship and neighborhood, develops, he suggests, as individuals seek a self-sufficient community, one which will have all the means of satisfying their needs within its direct control (1252b28).

Why does the capacity for reasoned speech compel such individuals toward sharing in a community which goes beyond need to justice and notions of good and bad? "Mere voice," Aristotle answers, "it is true, indicates pain and pleasure . . . but speech is designed to indicate the advantageous and the harmful, and therefore also the just and unjust" (1253a). Other animals have the capacity to communicate pain and pleasure, need and satisfaction. But *logos* gives human beings the capacity to calculate and communicate advantage and harm, the consequences which may follow from any given action, as well as the ability to communicate pain and pleasure. This capacity gives rise to the possibility of argument among human beings. For we can agree and disagree about the consequences of an action; we cannot argue about whether another person feels pain or not. The rational animal is therefore an argumentative animal, a conclusion implicit in the Greek expression, "animal possessing *logos* [speech, reason, argument]." Individuals coming together out of need will argue about the advantageous and the harmful.

The key to Aristotle's political teleology lies in his suggestion that the capacity for reasoned speech leads human beings to argue about "the advantageous and the harmful, and *therefore also* the just and unjust" (emphasis added). What reasoning lies behind that "therefore also"? One suggestion might run as follows. We cannot determine advantage and harm without implicit hierarchies of ends, and such hierarchies become explicit in argument about advantage. Political communities would then be based on sharing in argument about general standards of justice and goodness, shared standards brought to light and registered in some way in what Aristotle calls the *politeia*, the political regime. As is well known, this Aristotelian concept refers to the moral as well as the legal constitution of a political community. The *politeia* is both the sense of justice which is "the order of the political community," and "the ordering of ruling positions" (1253a37, 1290a8). The democratic regime represents the democratic *ethos* or way of life, as well as a particular distribution of political office and honor. Following such an interpretation we could say, with a more modern conceptual vocabulary, that a political community's constitution registers its mores, *Geist*, or political culture.

Joachim Ritter, in his influential article on "The Civic Life," interprets Aristotle in this way. He sees in Aristotle's argument about the connection between reasoned speech and man's political nature the suggestion that it is only through argument and action in a free political community that we come to know our rational nature. The ethical character and standards of human rea-son only become "actual," that is, existing concretely "for us," in the public standards of the political community.[10] However interesting this interpretation may be to modern readers, the Hegelian language of self-actualization which Ritter uses should make us wonder whether his interpretation represents an accurate reconstruction of Aristotle's implicit reasoning. In this interpretation, the standards of the political community become a text with which to interpret the spirit of its people. Political standards are indeed important, but only because they focus for us the underlying ethical and spiritual standards of the community.

Such a derivation of the standards of political justice from broader social, ethical, and linguistic standards corresponds to the orientation of most contemporary social theorists, but reverses Aristotle's in Book III of the *Politics*. There, Aristotle moves from the ordering of offices to the broader *ethos* of the community. He argues that just as the regime defines the political community, so the ruling body (*politeuma*) defines the regime (*politeia*); "for in all things the ruling body is supreme over the *polis*, and the ruling body is the regime" (1278b11). His analysis of political regimes in Book III thus suggests that Aristotle has a much more specifically political sense of justice in mind when he argues in Book I that our capacity for reasoned speech leads man to argue about "the advantageous and the harmful and therefore also the just and unjust," and in so doing, makes us political animals. An examination of that analysis might help us to tease out the meaning of this argument.

Aristotle classifies regimes in Book III according to the makeup of the ruling body. But though he uses the number of rulers—one, few, or many—to derive the names of the different regimes, it is their claim to rule which he uses to distinguish the character of different regimes. To make this point clear he chooses to *begin* his discussion of the six different regimes with a paradox about oligarchy (1279b), a paradox which would otherwise appear to represent little more than a pedant's delight in ambiguity. He argues that although the com-mon definition of oligarchy is the rule of the few rich, a regime in which the many were rich and held power would still be an oligarchy, for what defines oli-garchy is the claim of wealth to rule, rather than merely the number of rulers in the regime.[11]

In order to lay claim to rule, Aristotle insists, an individual or group must go beyond arguing about individual or collective advantage. They must argue that some quality which they possess entitles them to a share in deciding what is advantageous for the community. Where reasoned argument is not sup-pressed, it quickly becomes clear that there are a number of qualities relevant to ruling for which reasonable arguments can be made. In order to proceed in pursuing the collective advantage of the community, some decision must be made about the relative worth of these qualities, some of which will be equally distributed among the members of the community, others very unequally distributed (1283a).

Aristotle's guiding premise in Book III is that the claim to rule recognized in a political community shapes the standards of judgment and argument throughout the community. The argument about political justice provides the "decision about what is just" which is the "order of the political community" (1253a17). The proportionate worth given to equally and unequally held qualities accustoms the community to argue in terms of more or less egalitarian or inegalitarian standards.

> For all men lay hold of a certain sort of justice, but they proceed only so far, and do not argue for complete justice. It seems to them that justice is equality, as it is, but only for equals, not for everybody; or it seems to them that inequality is just, as indeed it is, but only for unequals, not for everybody. But these partisans strip away the qualifications and judge badly. The cause is that most men are bad judges when their own interests are in question. (1280a)

All political argument lays hold of a part of justice, Aristotle suggests, but only a part. For political argument involves not only our interests, but our worth; and if we are bad judges when we have an interest in the resolution of some issue, we are even worse judges when that issue is that of how to judge our worth. It is thus not surprising that:

> both parties put forward a plea that is partially just, but think that what they argue for is completely just. For one side being unequal in some things such as wealth, think themselves unequal in all things, and the other, being equal in some things such as freedom, think themselves equal in all things. (1280a)

Political justice establishes the proportions among different claims to rule. In his classification of regimes, Aristotle distinguishes between two sets of three regimes, the right (*orthos*) and the divergent or erring regimes. This distinction between two sets of regimes does not represent a distinction between just and unjust regimes, let alone the distinction between legitimate and illegitimate regimes the modern reader is tempted to see in it. Each regime, with the exception of tyranny, is partly just, for a regime is a decision about the standards of political justice. As long as it establishes *some* proportion among claims to rule, a regime is lawful and just, no matter how much that proportion usually exaggerates the worth of equally or unequally held qualities. Only an absolute tyranny, in which standards change from day-to-day according to the tyrant's whim, deserves to be called absolutely unjust; for in an absolute tyranny, there is, in reality, no regime at all (1275a).[12]

Familiarity with Aristotle's analysis of political regimes and political argument in Book III makes it easier to get at the meaning of his claim that the capacity for reasoned speech makes man a political animal. When individuals come together from different families and villages to form a self-sufficient community of need, their capacity for reasoned speech leads them to argue about advantage and harm. Some means of deciding among conflicting conceptions of advantage must be found in order for them to form even a community of need. The argument about advantage thus leads to an argument about who shall decide what collective advantage is, since there are many possible claims to decide, claims based on qualities which are not equally shared by all individuals in the community. It is this argument about who should rule which leads individuals into argument about just and unjust.

In the prepolitical communities, the household and the village, the problem of judging the proportionate worth of various claims to rule does not arise.

> The just in political matters is found among men who share a common life in order that their community bring them self-sufficiency and who are free and equal, either proportionately or arithmetically. Hence, in a community where this is not the case, there is nothing just in the political sense in the relations of the various members to one another, but only something which bears a resemblance to the just. (*EN* 1134a25ff)

All communities need to establish hierarchies, implicit or explicit, among various claims to make final decisions for the communities—age, physical prowess, talent, wealth, freedom, virtue, good birth, divine favor, and so on. But in households and other prepolitical communities, these standards usually remain implicit; in a political community they become the center of argument. In a household, we tend to accept the hierarchy of age because of the combination of natural inequalities and affection. Accustomed from infancy to such a hierarchy a fully mature individual accepts subordination to his parents he would never accept with regard to his fellow citizens. Primitive communities, Aristotle suggests, remain close to the patriarchical principle of the family and thus tend toward patriarchical monarchy, where claims to rule are not argued (*Politics* 1286b).[13]

In a community of free individuals, coming together from different clans, implicit claims to rule will tend to be challenged. Reading the opening pages of the *Politics* in light of his analysis of regimes in Book III suggests that Aristotle understands political community as the sharing of argument around a standard of distributive justice, a standard developed in answer to the question: Who should rule? Since the individuals who form a political community must be a somewhat heterogenous group—otherwise how would self-sufficiency be gained by their cooperation?—they will not equally possess all claims to rule, and they will thus tend to favor different standards of political justice. Political community is a community of *argument*; for the explicit standards of political justice develop only where claims to rule can be challenged. It exists only where political argument is possible. Man is a political animal because his capacity for reasoned speech compels him to argue about political justice when he gathers with others of his kind to form a self-sufficient community.

But one might ask, with Thomas Hobbes: What makes this naturally argumentative animal a political animal? In other words, in what way do our natural capacities for argument lead us into community rather than battle? Hobbes too understands man's uniqueness in terms of his capacity to calculate and communicate advantage and harm, just and unjust; but he sees in that capacity the source of the unique disorder of human life, rather than the source of a particular kind of community. The establishment of political society, Hobbes argues, requires the stifling of our inclination to argue about the justice or injustice of different distributions of advantage and honor.[14] While Aristotle suggests that the capacity for reasoned speech makes us political animals, Hobbes insists that "the tongue of man is the trumpet of war and sedition."[15] Without a convention limiting our natural tendency to argue about justice and injustice, a convention which limits the meaning of justice to the performance of contracts and the enforcement of law by a common authority, Hobbes believes there can be no political society. The agreement *not* to argue about political justice is for Hobbes the essential condition of political society.

Aristotle would probably argue against Hobbes that the establishment of a common authority establishes, willy-nilly, substantive standards of distributive justice within a community by honoring, as especially appropriate to ruling, the qualities which the sovereign possesses. Where individuals are free to use their reason, and see themselves as, at least, proportionately equal—as, of course, Hobbes insists they are[16]—a community of argument will grow up around these standards. In such a community individuals do share, among other things, a unique form of competing with each other: political argument. And conflict and distrust are unavoidable among individuals who share in political argument. Only the systematic suppression of our capacity for reasoned speech, Aristotle would argue, could keep such a community from forming among free and proportionately equal individuals. Hobbes is willing to endorse such a suppression of political argument in the name of civil peace. Aristotle is not. The distrust and conflict which tend to grow out of political argument are part of the price one pays, he would suggest, for a *political* community.

POLITICAL FRIENDSHIP

Aristotle's assertion that "friendship also seems to hold political communities together" (*EN* 1155a22) has long attracted those with a distaste for civic bonds grounded on rational calculation of self-interest or moral obligation to his concept of political community. On the one hand, Aristotle's view of the bond between citizens seems so much warmer and more humane. It makes the political community seem like an extended home rather than a marketplace where we advertise our needs. On the other hand, it seems to offer a more realistic view of the political bond, in that it recognizes that individuals share political commitments and inclinations prior to calculation and choice.

A recent work by Jeffrey Abramson illustrates the kind of enthusiasm Aristotle's concept of political friendship inspires in many modern critics of liberal thought and institutions. Abramson, like many others, turns to Aristotle's account of political friendship as the basis for an alternative to modern models of political association, based on individual calculation and liberation.

> Friendship becomes the highest virtue in Aristotle's discussion of the good life and the good city, arguably higher than even justice, because "when men are friends they have no need of justice, while when they are just, they need friendship as well." . . . From friendship to citizenship can be a very long way. In every city, Aristotle remarked, there seems to be a kind of friendship among citizens . . . to find a city where citizens have no fellow-feeling for one another at all is to find a collection of individuals which is a "city no longer." . . . At its best, politics aspires to awaken the Eros of the political animal, through the experience of friendship, to the good "we can know in common" that no one self could know alone. Citizenship—involving loyalty to a common way of life—regains its enriching impact on the self to be realized.[17]

Undoubtedly, Aristotle would consider a political community with "no fellow-feeling a 'city no longer.'" But what is the character of the fellow-feeling among members of political communities? Modern enthusiasts of Aristotle's concept of political friendship seem to assume that political friendship shares the character of personal intimacy. Indeed, when we think about political friendship, the concept has an inviting warmth, which it does not have for Aristotle, since we usually define friendship in terms of personal intimacy. Aristotle, on the other hand, speaks of the friendship characteristic of parties to a contract or travelers on ship, as well as the friendship among citizens and intimate acquaintances (*EN* 1159b). The Greek word *philia* has a far broader range than our word friendship.[18] The intimate personal friend, the *hetairos*, represents only one—and one of the least common—kind of friendship for Aristotle. It is this kind of friendship which he suggests is an essential part of the good life. But is this the kind of friendship which he believes exists among members of a political community? I think not.[19]

Every form of community, Aristotle suggests, has a form of justice and friendship appropriate to it (*EE* 1242a; *EN* 1160a). The political community and the community among intimates are very different communities. We should thus expect them to have different forms of friendship. What is the form of friendship which corresponds to the political community? Aristotle never answers that question directly, so we must reconstruct his answer.[20] To do so, we need to turn to his treatment of friendship in his ethical works.

All friends hold things in common, Aristotle notes (*EN* 1159b). What they hold in common determines the character of the friendship bond between them. Aristotle distinguishes three basic forms of friendship; they correspond to the sharing of interest, pleasure, and virtue (*EN* 1156a; *EE* 1236a). The friendship of interest or utility is the commonest; it represents the bond between individuals forged by contracts, business cooperation, and most marriages. The friendships of shared pleasure are rarer, Aristotle suggests; we usually find them only among the young. Both of these kinds of friendship can be found among animals. Only the friendship of shared virtue is peculiar to man, for only man has *logos*, which allows man to distinguish between the good and his own (*EE* 1236b). Only such a creature can share special regard for other creatures deemed virtuous.

Where does the friendship among members of a political community fit in this threefold classification? If the preceding interpretation of Aristotle's concept of political community is accurate, then political friendship fits in the first and third categories, the friendship of interest and the friendship of shared virtue. I suggest that, for Aristotle, political friendship is a friendship of shared interest which must also see itself as a friendship of shared virtue. Although Aristotle himself never explicitly defines political friendship in this way, such a definition seems the most appropriate to his work, given both his general analysis of friendship and his understanding of political community. Moreover, such a conception of political friendship seems to me a plausible and interesting interpretation of the phenomenon itself.

Aristotle does describe such a form of friendship which combines the friendship of interest and that of virtue in the *Eudemian Ethics* (1242b). (The parallel passage in the *Nicomachean Ethics* contains part of this discussion [*EN* 1162b].) He speaks there of a form of shared interest friendship which is especially prone to dissension and recrimination. There are, he suggests, two kinds of shared interest friendship: the *legal* and the *ethical*. The legal form, which is particularly appropriate to contracts, is less subject to recriminations than the ethical form since the terms on which the individual profits are laid out clearly and there is an accepted third party to enforce the agreement. Much of the cooperation among citizens clearly takes this form. In the ethical form of the shared interest friendship, however, individuals trust each other to advance each other's interest. The terms are not specified and the enforcement ignored, as if each individual has some special virtue which made him specially worthy of trust.

> This is the sort of friendship with the most accusations and recrim-
> inations, the cause of which is that it is contrary to nature. For the
> friendships based on utility and virtue are different, but these peo-
> ple want both at once; they come together for sake of the useful,
> but make it out to be an ethical friendship, portraying their rela-
> tionship as one of trust rather than legality. (*EE* 1242b38)[21]

Does this not describe the peculiar bond among individuals in political communities as Aristotle describes it? Men come together out of need, but live together for the sake of the good life. The political community forms out of the shared interest of individuals seeking a self-sufficient community. A group of individuals can serve each other's interest because of the variety of their skills and their proximity to each other. No special virtues qualify them to be members of that community. But those individuals can form a community of shared interest only through forming a community of argument around standards of political justice. They thus come to share standards of justice and expect their fellow citizens to live up to these standards. They trust their fellow citizens in a way they do not trust foreigners because of these shared standards; or, at least, they expect their fellow citizens to deserve their trust more than foreigners. They presume, without justification, that their fellow citizens will act like virtuous men, especially in times of stress, when sacrifice is called for. They thus treat political friendship as a friendship of virtue. But their expectations are bound to be disappointed, for the political community is only partly a community of virtue.

This contradictory bond of friendship, Aristotle suggests, will be especially subject to recriminations and violent distrust, for it leads individuals to expect more from their friends than they can possibly deliver. The same bond which promotes noble acts of self sacrifice and the successful pursuit of common interests, the bond of friendship which we admire in political communities, promotes the particularly violent distrust and conflict which is the most hateful aspect of political life. This bond of friendship compels us to expect our fellow citizens to be both virtuous men and partners in selfish interest at once. We suspect the interest seeker who does not appear virtuous because he may ignore our interest in the pursuit of his own; we suspect the virtuous man because he may ignore our interest in the pursuit of what is good. We want to trust our compatriots, but to be worthy of our trust they must appear to be both virtuous and self-interested at the same time. In short, as Aristotle says, we "want both at once" (*EE* 1242b40). And regardless whether it is our sense of interest or of virtue which alerts our suspicion, we have a special feeling toward the individual whom we suspect. He is not merely a liar or cheater, a breaker of agreements; he is a traitor, a betrayer of our trust. Mere power struggles or competitions for advantage rarely generate passions as violent as those fueled by a broken trust.

Given Aristotle's understanding of political community, distrust is an inescapable feature of political friendship. If that understanding is correct, then when rational creatures form a self-sufficient community of interest, they also form, in some sense, a community of virtue, or at least, the expectation of such a community. The citizen shares not only a distribution of goods, but an argument around standards of political justice which allow that distribution to be made. He shares in a regime, a way of life. He expects others to live up to that way of life. When they do not, he cannot help but wonder whether they will also distort their agreements to their own advantage. The pleasures of political friendship seem to be tied to its cruel and potentially violent inconveniences.

To rid political life of these inconveniences has been the aim of some of the most influential modern political philosophers, such as Hobbes and Rousseau. Aristotle would suggest that one could only rid us of these inconveniences by ridding us of *political* communities altogether. Or, to put it in another way, one can rid the world of the potentially violent inconveniences of political friendship only by suppressing the freedom to use our reason which leads to the establishment of political communities, a suggestion borne out by

Hobbes's and Rousseau's arguments. Both Hobbes and Rousseau try to pacify the political community by removing one of the contradictory elements of political friendship. If we treated each other merely as partners to a contract rather than sharers in some notion of the good life, as Hobbes would have us do, then we would have fewer and less explosive sources of mutual recrimination. On the other hand, if a spirit of fraternity or genuine camaraderie ruled in the breast of every citizen, such as Rousseau longs to create, then, "government becomes so easy, it needs none of that art of darkness whose blackness is its only mystery."[22] Judging their arguments from Aristotle's perspective, it appears that each tries to redesign the bond between individuals in a political community in the image of friendship among members of a subpolitical community: Hobbes looks to the friendship of interest between sharers in a contract; Rousseau looks to the friendship of virtue among comrades or the shared identity of brothers.

Aristotle's analysis of political community and communities makes, I believe, a persuasive case that neither contract nor camaraderie provides an appropriate model of political friendship. Free individuals with the capacity for reasoned speech cannot relate to each other as parties to a contract As Hobbes himself insists, there can be no contractual relations among individuals until there is some final authority to decide cases of disagreement; but to set up such an authority, Aristotle would argue, they must establish a community of argument. As long as they have the freedom to use their reason they will not remain indifferent to the relative worth of various claims to rule (see above). A consistent Hobbesian polity would require the systematic suppression of political argument. Hobbes, of course, accepts this constraint as a condition of political peace, but he also expects free men to choose to establish a Leviathan state, something they could not do without implicitly or explicitly recognizing the justice of various claims to rule. That is why wherever the Hobbesian theory of sovereignty has been institutionalized, it has always been adapted to specific egalitarian or inegalitarian standards of justice.

Rousseau, like many later radical political critics, found Hobbes's reconstruction of the political bond cold, demeaning, and alienating—as well as demonstrably false with regard to the political communities of ancient times. More than anything else, his impassioned protests against modern politics have inspired contemporary glorifications of the ideal of political friendship and community. One of the purposes of this essay is to disassociate Aristotle's concept of political community from this ideal, for many of its partisans have distorted his concept of community to suit their own. Aristotle would have rejected the romantic ideal of subordinating laws and institutions to the "genuine communal spirit, the living association, indissolubly united by the holy chain of friendship" as disdainfully as modern critics of that ideal, such as Hegel.[23] From Aristotle's perspective, one would have to say that Rousseau and his followers allow analogy to overtake analysis and try to model political friendship on forms of friendship which are inappropriate to the political community.

The models which usually inspire Rousseauian attempts to transform political friendship are fraternity and camaraderie. Political fraternity is obviously a metaphor. To demand fraternity among citizens is to demand a bond similar in strength and intensity to that among brothers.[24] Camaraderie among citizens, however, need not be metaphorical. All citizens could conceivably be each other's comrade, like Aristotelian *hetairoi* in a shared virtue friendship. But to create among a community of individuals thrown together by chance of birth and geography a friendship of shared virtue, one would have to find a way of turning them all into virtuous individuals. Since that seems unlikely, those who long for camaraderie among citizens usually shift the focus of virtue from the individuals to the regime. All individuals may not be especially virtuous, but they can all share in an especially virtuous regime. Rousseau recognizes this point, and redefines virtue as patriotism, devotion to the regime.[25] One can treat all of one's fellows as comrades only when one no longer has any standards but reverence for a particular regime to distinguish the virtuous from the self-interested. Thus one must suppress argument about political justice in order to establish camaraderie among the members of a political community, a suppression which Rousseau, as much as Hobbes, endorses. The reign of virtue and the reign of terror always go together when revolutionaries try to turn citizens into comrades. For camaraderie among all citizens requires the suppression of natural capacities which incline us toward political argument.

Members of a political community are indeed friends of a sort according to Aristotle. But political friendship, as he understands it, offers no alternative to distrust and competition within a regime. Political friendship grows out of the particular kind of sharing one finds in a political community. It is the nature of that community which creates the inconveniences of political friendship. For that community is more like a family business, than like either a family or a business. In a political community, as in a family business, shared identities and commitments facilitate the pursuit of shared interest; but, as in a family business, these affinities raise expectations of disinterested behavior and sympathy which tend to intensify distrust and turn disagreements about advantage into suspicion of betrayal. Political friendship sows the seeds of distrust as well as cooperation among members of a political community.

CONCLUSION

I have tried in this essay to correct a widespread misperception of Aristotle's political thought, a misperception shared even by his champions among contemporary political theorists: that his concept of political community is based on an image of organic growth and identity, and thus does not account for political conflict and distrust. This misperception is so widespread because contemporary political theorists tend to look to Aristotelian political concepts for a counterimage to liberalism's image of political society. If the contract dominates the liberal image of political society, then the family, personal friendship, and organic growth tend to dominate counterliberal images.

But Aristotle, unlike contemporary political theorists, does not view political community through the lens of liberal theory and practice. However he might have judged liberal theories and institutions, were he given the opportunity—and I am inclined to think that he would be far less critical of the latter than of the former—he does not view political community as a refuge from diffidence and distrust among individuals. On the contrary, he views the existence of community as a necessary condition of distrust among individuals; for only individuals who share something, be it only a particular interest, will be inclined to take issue with each other's behavior. His understanding of political community allows him to identify and analyze the kinds of conflict around which political life ordinarily revolves.

NOTES

1. A. MacIntyre, *After Virtue* (South Bend: University of Notre Dame Press, 1982), 153. This lack of interest in conflict represents, for MacIntyre, the only serious flaw in Aristotelian moral and political philosophy.

2. Leo Strauss's short essay on Aristotle in *The City and Man* (Chicago: University of Chicago Press, 1978) is an exception to this tendency among Aristotle's recent admirers.

3. Arendt's interpretation of Aristotle rests on her highly original and very misleading interpretation of his understanding of "political" action: "The 'good life,' as Aristotle called the life of the citizen therefore was . . . 'good' to the extent that by having mastered the necessities of sheer life, by being freed from labor and work, and by overcoming the *innate urge* of all living creatures for their own *survival*, it was no longer bound to the biological life process" (*The Human Condition* [Garden City: Anchor, 1958], 33). Arendt's use of expressions like "overcoming the urge of all creatures for their own survival" and "no longer bound to the biological life process" to describe political activity shows how far she has, despite her insistence to the contrary, strayed from Aristotle's understanding of political life. Such expressions make it clear that for Arendt man's political character is something asserted *against* nature, against the "biological life process." Only when we put our life at risk, only when we "overcome" natural urges, do we behave politically. Politics is for her the way in which we overcome our nature, while for Aristotle it is the development of our nature. Arendt's definition of the "political" sphere of action excludes almost the entire subject matter of the *Politics*. What would a "political" act be for her? Arendt is hard pressed to describe one. The action which most clearly fits her definition, the risk of life in war, is not one which the author of the most famous critique of totalitarianism is likely to glorify as the true end of human striving. Aristotle, on the other hand, has no trouble pointing to political actions in the day-to-day struggles over distribution of goods and honors within the political community, since he does not associate political action with self-overcoming.

4. Ritter's articles on Aristotle are collected in *Metaphysik und Politik* (Frankfurt: Suhrkamp, 1969). For a discussion of his interpretation see below. One of Ritter's students, Gunther Bien, has written a very serious and interesting full-length study of Aristotle's political philosophy: G. Bien, *Grundlagen der Politische Philosophie bei Aristotle* (Munich, 1973). It is not surprising, however, that Bien only devotes a small fraction of his analysis to Books III–VI, given that he builds on the foundations provided by Ritter's studies of Aristotle.

5. Werner Jaeger thought the contradictions between Book I and Books IV–VI so great that he developed a genetic theory to explain them. W. Jaeger, *Aristotle* (Oxford: Oxford University Press, 1934), 269ff. Jaeger's hypothesis about the different layers of the text of the *Politics* no longer dominates discussion of the work as much as it did in the first half of this century and is not relied on by the recent interpreters of Aristotle whom I am criticizing here. That hypothesis makes sense only if we assume that the approaches used in the two sections of the text contradict each other. My essay, I hope, will raise serious questions about that assumption.

6. I translate *koinōnia* as community in order to maintain the association with common (*koinon*). See R. Mulgan, *Aristotle's Political Theory* (Oxford: Oxford University Press, 1977), 16.

7. As he has often taken to be doing, Maurice Defourny, a perceptive interpreter of Aristotle, was already complaining in 1933 about social scientists who were using Aristotle's characterization of man as a political animal in order to lend authority to their understanding of human sociality. M. Defourny, *Études sur la Politique d'Aristote* (Paris, 1933), 383ff.

8. See, for example, Hegel's early essay in *Natural Law* (Philadelphia: University of Pennsylvania Press, 1975), 112–13. Rousseau's famous image of the citizen as the numerator and the community as denominator (*Emile* [New York: Basic Books, 1979], 40) draws on this "ancient" understanding of citizenship and political community.

9. It seems that Aristotle ran out of terms when he moved from his biological to his political writings. Rather than call human politics "more political" than animal politics, I have reserved the adjective "political" for the human communities examined in the *Politics*. I leave it to the biologists to find a new term to classify the "less political" animals like bees and ants.

10. J. Ritter, *Metaphysik und Politik*, 76–77. For an interesting variation on this interpretation of Aristotle, see S. Salkever, "Aristotle's Social Science," *Political Theory*, 9 (1981), 479–508.

11. Complaints about Aristotle's short-sightedness in classifying regimes in terms of the number of rulers thus reflect the short-sightedness of their authors, as in the case of W. L. Newman, *The Politics of Aristotle*, 4 vols. (Oxford: 1887), 1:225.

12. Similarly, Aristotle doubts that extreme democracies whose standards change daily according to the whims of demagogues are properly called regimes (*Politics* 1292a30).

13. Political communities grow only where individuals have developed their rational faculties and are free to make use of them. In Aristotle's opinion, the tribes of the north have not yet developed their rational capacities fully enough to form political communities, though they are second to none in attachment to their freedom. The subjects of the vast empires to the east, on the other hand, he considers rational, but lacking in the courage to assert their freedom (*Politics* 1327b).

14. T. Hobbes, *Leviathan* (London: Pelican, 1968), 96, 100, 189–90.

15. T. Hobbes, *Of the Citizen* in *Of Man and Citizen* (Garden City: Anchor, 1972), 168–69.

16. T. Hobbes, *Leviathan*, 183.

17. J. Abramson, *Liberation and Its Limits: The Moral and Political Thought of Freud* (New York: The Free Press, 1984), 127–29. The citation at the end of this quotation refers to M. Sandel, *Liberalism and the Limits of Justice* (Cambridge: Cambridge University Press, 1982), 183. MacIntyre's *After Virtue* is cited by Abramson in this section as well.

18. See J. C. Fraisse, *Philia: La Notion de l'Amitié dans la Philosophie de l'Antiquité* (Paris: 1974), for a general account of the concept of *philia* in ancient thought.

19. In speaking of political friendship, Aristotle seems to be speaking of the friendship among all members of a political community rather than among the members of the

political clubs based on friendship groups, the *hetaireia*, which played such a large role in Athenian politics. For discussions of the *hetaireia* see W. R. Connor, *The New Politicians of Fifth-Century Athens* (Princeton: Princeton University Press, 1971), 3–84; and H. Hutter, *Politics as Friendship* (Waterloo, Ontario: Waterloo University Press, 1978), 26ff.

20. In Book VIII of the *Nicomachean Ethics*, Aristotle defines the species of political friendship—democratic, aristocratic, and so on—but not the genus to which the species belong.

21. Note Aristotle's statement that this kind of friendship is "against nature" (*EE* 1242b39). Could political friendship be against nature? Aristotle calls this form of friendship against nature because it pursues both interest and virtue, the same combination we find in political communities.

22. J. J. Rousseau, *Discourse on Political Economy*, in *On the Social Contract with Geneva Manuscript and Political Economy*, ed. R. Masters (New York: St. Martin's Press, 1978), 218.

23. J. F. Fries, as quoted by Hegel, *Philosophy of Right* (Oxford: Oxford University Press, 1952), preface, 6.

24. See *Politics* 1261a15 where Aristotle ridicules the fraternity among citizens which Plato tries to create in the *Republic*. The bond between a real nephew and his uncle, he suggests, is far stronger than the bond between the so-called brothers of the Platonic republic.

25. See J. J. Rousseau, *Political Economy*, 217–24.

CHAPTER 14

THE "REALISM" OF CLASSICAL POLITICAL SCIENCE

An Introduction to Aristotle's Best Regime

ROBERT C. BARTLETT

The principal aim of these remarks is simply to offer a counterweight to the contemporary view, whose roots extend at least as far as Machiavelli, according to which classical political science is woefully naive. Leave these philosophers to their lofty talk of justice, virtue, and noble self-sacrifice: the brute facts of politics will teach those who have eyes to see the fate of such concerns in the real world. "Realism" of various stripes may be said to wish "to go directly to the effectual truth of the thing" rather than to "the imagination of it," refusing in particular ever to be tempted to lift its gaze from the harsh political "is" by the charms of any wished-for political "ought": "And many have imagined republics and principalities that have never been seen or known to exist in truth; for it is so far from how one lives to how one should live that he who lets go of what is done for what should be done learns his ruin rather than his preservation."[1] This essay argues that precisely the "imagined" republic or "best regime"[2] of Books VII and VIII of Aristotle's *Politics*, the classic of premodern political science, shows Aristotle to be in no sense naive and that he knows full well the ways of the world; that although Aristotle does indeed look to moral virtue as the standard by which to judge the seriousness or moral goodness of a political community, he is not only aware of the difficulties of that standard but attempts in a number of ways to cope with them;[3] and finally that reflection on Aristotle's imagined regime leads more surely than does "realism" to the very end the realists themselves seek, namely the comprehension of the world as it is, free of illusion or false hope. Insofar as that goal is of interest also to us here and now, not only as political scientists but as human beings, the antiquarian inquiry suggested by my title would be of more than merely antiquarian interest.

THE BEST REGIME AND THE MOST CHOICEWORTHY WAY OF LIFE

Aristotle devotes the whole of Books VII and VIII of the *Politics* to the construction in speech of his own best regime, an undertaking prepared in part by the critical analysis in Book II of other, would-be best regimes existing in both speech and deed. Since the best regime as such seeks to foster the best way of life for a human being, one cannot reach clarity about that regime without first determining the life that will be its target (1323a14–19). Accordingly, the first three chapters of Book VII are devoted to just this task. Very briefly, Aristotle there concludes that one and the same life is best for both individual and city and that this life is an active, political one properly understood (1324b41–1325b4; 1325b16–32). This conclusion implies first and foremost that participation in political life at its peak is capable of satisfying human nature at its peak or that one need not in principle look to anything beyond politics to attain human happiness. This best political life proves to be concerned with "theoretical reflections and thoughts" that are "ends in themselves and for their own sake," a goal so lofty that Aristotle here likens it to the activity proper to "the god" (1325b28–30; consider also 1323b23–26). This contemplative and quasi-divine activity is, to say the least, an odd conception of political life, and common sense rightly resists accepting it on the basis of Aristotle's brief argument in VII.1–3.[4] Indeed, by asserting the superiority of the political life concerned above all with what appears to be a nonpolitical activity, Aristotle seems to transcend the horizon of the ordinary citizen even as he praises it. To be more cautious, one might simply say that it is as yet uncertain whether the best way of life for a human being is necessarily the thoroughly political one.

This puzzling characterization of the best political life becomes all the more enigmatic in that Aristotle immediately drops it. That is, the detailed account in VII.4–7 of the practical "equipment" (1325b38) necessary to the coming into being of the best regime proves to contradict the contention of VII.3 that the active, political life of the best regime can be at the same time simply private or inward looking. To give just one example, the regime must engage in import and export trade to assure its material self-sufficiency (VII.6); this is inevitably to have dealings with other cities or nations and, as precisely VII.1–3 insists, most communities seek to dominate their neighbors (1324b3ff., esp. 7). As a result, the best regime is compelled to try to be "fearsome" in the eyes of its neighbors (1327b1).[5] Given the necessity of pursuing an active life very much in the ordinary sense, the end of the best regime appears in VII.4–7 to be action at its best, i.e., the performance of noble deeds, rather than the pursuit of self-contained "theoretical reflections" (consider, e.g., 1325a40–1325b3). At the outset of Aristotle's treatment of his best regime, then, moral virtue vies with some philosophic possibility as *the* goal of the best life.

THE PROBLEM OF MORAL VIRTUE AS
THE BASIS OF CITIZENSHIP

This emphasis on an active, political life in the ordinary sense continues when Aristotle turns to decide the question of who should enjoy citizenship and hence rule in the best regime (VII.8–9). The best city is above all a partnership among equals for the sake of the "actualization and a certain complete use of *virtue*," and while "some are capable of sharing in it, others are so only to a small degree or not at all" (1328a37–40; emphasis added). Only those persons, then, capable of leading the virtuous life will be qualified to be citizens in the best regime, a partnership in virtue (1328a40–1328b4; 1323b29–31). To decide which of the elements necessary to the city's existence should share in that partnership—farmers, laborers and craftsmen, the military, the commercial and trading elements, priests, and finally rulers or "judges of what is necessary and advantageous" (1328b22–23)—Aristotle again focuses very much on considerations of moral virtue: "Since we are in fact investigating the best regime, and this is the one under which the city would most of all be happy, and it was said previously that it is impossible for happiness to be present apart from virtue, it is clear from these things that, in the city that is most finely governed and that possesses men who are just unqualifiedly and not on the basis of a presupposition, the citizens should lead neither a banausic nor a commercial life" (1328b33–40). Such lives, Aristotle argues, are "ignoble and contrary to virtue" (1328b40–41). Different persons, then, must fill the ranks of the laboring and the trading or commercial elements, and none should be a citizen. The farmers too must constitute a separate element in the city that is similarly excluded from citizenship, not so much because of the harmful character of their work as because "leisure is required with a view to both the inculcation of virtue and political actions" (1329a1–2), and the farmers will simply be too busy to enjoy the requisite leisure.

Aristotle continues his enumeration of the parts necessary to the city by discussing the military and the adjudicative or deliberative bodies—elements that are "present in and manifestly parts of the city most of all" (1329a2–5). The assignment of the deliberative office is based exclusively on the capacity to act in accordance with moral virtue, i.e., with the dictates of *phronēsis*: the rulers rule on the grounds that they alone are prudent or practically wise.[6] Similar considerations based on the prerequisites of moral virtue ground Aristotle's resolution of the question of the distribution of property, and he concludes that "the possessions should belong to these persons [i.e., the hoplites and rulers], if in fact it is necessary that the farmers be slaves or foreign servants" (1329a24–26).

The question of the place of the farmers in the best regime requires further comment because it is the first and perhaps most massive difficulty casting a shadow on the goodness of Aristotle's "best regime." The arrangement of rule indicated presupposes not only that all citizen-rulers as such possess or will come to possess prudence, but also that the farmers and indeed all those excluded from citizenship do not possess it and never could. At the end of VII.10, however, Aristotle himself acknowledges that at the very least this latter is in fact not so, for he states that "it is better to hold out freedom as a prize for *all* slaves" (1330a32–33; emphasis added). According to his own definition in Book I, a natural slave is one who, though capable of perceiving reason, is without reason himself. Precisely because such a person could never be free, it is better and more just that he serve another than that he attempt to live on his own (1254b16–24; 1254a17–19). This means in turn, however, that if freedom is rightly held out as a prize for all slaves in the best regime, they cannot be slaves by nature and are not justly enslaved strictly speaking.[7] The best regime is compelled to look beyond those who are said in Book I to be slaves by nature because precisely the severe limitations of the rational capacity that make one a natural slave at the same time limit severely the possible number and utility of such persons. As Aristotle's discussion of the farming class makes clear, even the best political order will not be simply natural or simply just. A fundamental arbitrariness thus lies at the bottom of the ordering of office in Aristotle's best regime, and so far from being unaware of this fact, Aristotle himself draws attention to it. And this essential limitation in regard to justice proves to be only the first of two fundamental difficulties characterizing Aristotle's best city.

MORAL VIRTUE AND THE
PROBLEM OF HAPPINESS (VII.10–12)

In order to affirm or support the correctness of the arrangements indicated, Aristotle now shifts his focus from moral virtue to tradition and ancient political practice, an appeal that underscores the necessity or efficacy of these arrangements rather than their relation to moral virtue (1329a40ff.).[8] In fact, moral virtue is all but absent from the section at hand, and when it returns, toward the end of VII.11, it does so in such a way as to bring to light an additional difficulty no less troubling than the preceding one: "As for defensive walls, those who deny that cities laying claim to virtue should have them have excessively old–fashioned ideas: they even see the cities that have such pretensions refuted by fact [deed]" (1330b32ff.). It is therefore imperative that the best city preserve itself by means of the construction and maintenance of defensive walls. This is especially true, Aristotle says, in light of "the present–day discoveries pertaining to missiles and the refinement of machines used to besiege cities" (1331a1–2).

It is now clear that the best regime, which to this point has come to sight as the virtuous city *par excellence*, must attend to the nuts and bolts of its own defense; to rely on merely "human virtue" (1330b39) is not enough, and the temptation to do so, characteristic of those who are confident of their own moral goodness, must be resisted. Does this not mean, however, that Aristotle's emphasis on moral virtue is misguided or naive? If the city's concern to be morally virtuous, so far from securing its happiness, runs the risk of making it a sitting duck, should the city continue to be concerned with virtue first and foremost? More to the point, will it be permitted the luxury of so concerning itself? Despite their best intentions, the virtuous are compelled to meet and indeed to try to best the vicious in matters of potentially dubious decency or uprightness; the depths to which a virtuous city may be forced to sink in order to protect itself are determined by the viciousness of its enemies and hence are beyond its control. This means, in other words, that "the good city has to take its bearings by the practice of bad cities or that the bad impose their law on the good" (Strauss 1958, 298–99). The innovative spirit of Hippodamus—made more serious by looking to something other than attractive adornment (1267b22-30; 1330b21–31)—would ultimately seem to be more vital to a city's well-being than Aristotle's "conservative" politics of virtue.

It cannot rightly be said of Aristotle, however, that he is naive concerning the conduct of political communities as such: "most of the laws laid down among most [peoples] are as it were a jumbled heap, but if somewhere the laws look to some one thing, *all* aim at domination" (1324b5–7; emphasis added). Similarly, as we have just seen, Aristotle too criticizes as excessively "old–fashioned" (*archaiōs*, 1330b33) the view that virtuous action alone can preserve a city, and he is very much alive to the danger of what one may call technological innovation. More importantly, Aristotle grants that the determination to act virtuously is by itself insufficient to secure happiness because one must have, in addition to the opportunity, the wherewithal or "equipment" so to act, and this depends decisively on chance (1325b35–39; 1331b18–24; *EN* 1178a24 and context). The attempt to control such chance is one reason why empire is so attractive to cities and nations: "The majority of human beings envy the exercise of mastery over many because it brings about much equipment in the things of good fortune" (1333b16–18). But Aristotle goes farther. For even granting the requisite equipment, Aristotle elsewhere calls into question the presumed link between moral virtue and happiness that is the fundamental basis of his strictly speaking aristocratic ordering of office in the best regime: not only is the happiness of the virtuous fragile in the face of the cunning of the vicious, but brute fact seems to deny that the performance of virtuous deeds at their noble peak—i.e., in times of the greatest self-forgetting self-sacrifice— always brings with it the fulfillment of the ever-present (if at times somewhat obscured) desire for one's own happiness. As Aristotle says in the *Nicomachean Ethics*, even moral virtue seems "rather incomplete" as the end of political life because it is possible to possess virtue while suffering terribly, and no one would call such a person happy (*EN* 1095b30–1096a2). Since Aristotle both denigrates the worth of empire as a solution to the problem of virtue and here maintains the choiceworthiness of moral virtue, he is compelled to offer another, better solution to the problem of virtue. How then does Aristotle cope in practical terms with the exposedness or fragility of the happiness of the virtuous to which he himself draws attention?

The next chapter, VII.12, bears on the problem of moral virtue in its relation to happiness insofar as it continues the same theme with which the discussion of "defensive walls" is concerned, namely the city's security. According to Aristotle, "it is fitting that the dwellings assigned to divine matters and the common messes for those in the most authoritative offices occupy the same location appropriate to them" (1331a24–26). The most important rulers, then, should dine together in or near the temples, and they are in this way continually reminded of the presence of the city's gods. Aristotle acknowledges two exceptions to this rule: some temples may have to be set aside according either to a given law or to some Pythian prophecy (1331a26–30). This reference to the Pythian oracle is the first indication that the best regime will be concerned with the worship of Olympian as opposed to "cosmic" gods (cf. 1331a27–28 with 1323b23–27 and 1325b28–30). It would appear that sacrifices must be made to the gods of the best regime; they must be appeased by burnt offerings and presumably can be appealed to for solace and succor (consider 1330a9–13). These gods who issue prophetic utterances (1331a27) are very different indeed from "the god" or "whatever it is that keeps this All together" (1326a32–33) who performs no external actions beyond the ones appropriate to Him, who leads an altogether "private," contemplative life, and who requires no external goods—e.g., burnt offerings—in order to be happy (VII.3, end; 1323b23–29; see also *EN* 1178b9–24).

In the immediate sequel, Aristotle sketches the two sorts of public squares the best regime is to have, one being a "necessary marketplace" used for trade and commerce, the other a liberal or free meeting place accessible only to citizens in which no commercial activity is permitted (1331a30–36). It is fitting, Aristotle says, for certain of the rulers to spend time there with the younger citizens, just as it is fitting for "the older to be with the rulers" (1331a39–40). The young—i.e., the soldiers—will benefit from this association with the rulers because "being before the eyes of the rulers most of all instills genuine reverence and the fear belonging to the free" (1331a40–1331b1). The rulers will presumably reap a comparable benefit from their association with "the older"—i.e., the priests (see 1329a27–34). As the soldiers are reminded, through their association with the rulers, of their duty to and place in the city, ennobled and restrained by reverence and fear, so the rulers are benefited by being together with the priests. Aristotle concludes VII.12 by saying that arrangements similar to these should be made for the rulers in the countryside (the "foresters" and "field managers"), and that, in particular, "temples should be distributed throughout the territory, some for the gods, others for the heroes" (1331b17–18). More than any other chapter, VII.12 makes clear that the best regime, though not a "theocracy," will be suffused with the presence of watchful or providential gods. When the citizens of the best regime look up, they see, not indeed empty sky, but an ordered heaven ruled by superintending gods; heaven encompasses and completes earth in such a way as to form a unified whole at the center of which is the political life of the best regime.

It remains to make more precise the necessity of the care of the divine, and hence of priests, to the city's well-being. To repeat, the chapter in which the gods make their most marked appearance in Book VII is concerned with the topic "security"; it follows the statement of the problem posed to the virtuous city by the cunning of vice. It is not difficult to see that, insofar as the city is unified through the proper arrangement of common messes and through shared worship, it is thereby made more secure. Still, such security does not speak adequately to the most profound and at the same time most fragile hope for happiness of the virtuous. It would seem that only benevolent, all-powerful gods can rectify the perhaps rare but nonetheless harsh or heartbreaking discrepancies between noble service and just reward; only such gods can set aright, in life or after death, the misery that the just sometimes suffer (consider Xenophon, *Symposium*, IV. 48 and context). Belief in such gods is the capstone completing the best regime, for without it the service and sacrifice the community must of necessity demand would be carried out only with difficulty.[9]

To sum up thus far: the necessary exclusion of some human beings from office (VII. 8–9) has little to do with their natural potential to be virtuous and is therefore arbitrary according to Aristotle's own standard. The conclusion of VII.11, moreover, makes clear the exposedness of virtue to vice and raises doubts concerning the simple equation of the happy city with the morally virtuous one that is the fundamental premise on which Aristotle bases his ordering of office (1328b33–37; 1329a21–24). It therefore becomes a question both whether the distinction Aristotle makes between citizens and noncitizens really accords with his avowed standard and whether that standard is itself sound. VII.12 attempts to cope with this second and more fundamental difficulty by outlining ways to compensate for the shortcomings of moral virtue in securing one's happiness: the best regime must be militarily secure, unified, and devoted to providential gods.[10]

THE BEST REGIME AND THE GOOD LIFE (VII.13–15)

The introduction of the gods into the best regime is a kind of watershed, and after it Aristotle makes something of a new beginning: "It is necessary to speak about the regime itself, both out of whom and of what sorts [of persons] the city that is to be blessed and nobly governed should be constituted" (VII.13, beginning). That Aristotle still thinks it necessary to address this question is odd, since the whole of VII.8–12 concerns the ordering of office in the best regime, the most obvious task of a city's regime (1328b25–33), and at the end of VII.7 Aristotle clearly indicates that he has spoken sufficiently about the sorts of persons who are to make up the best regime's citizen-body (1328a17–18). One may suppose that, in returning to the question of "the regime itself" and its composition, Aristotle wishes to add to or revise his preceding remarks. In fact, the end to which his best regime is devoted is about to undergo a fundamental transformation.

The nature of this transformation becomes clearest by comparing Aristotle's restatement here of the basis of rule in the best regime with his earlier account (cf. 1332b29–42 with VII.9, esp. 1328b33–39 and 1329a2–9). In the earlier version Aristotle had stressed that, prudence being the product of maturity, it is right for the older citizens to fill the authoritative political offices, the younger and therefore more powerful the military offices. In the present account this same arrangement is choiceworthy because it alone is sufficient to restrain the hoplites from demanding their share in rule rather than awaiting their own maturity, based as it is on the obvious and therefore noncontroversial difference in age between ruler and ruled, i.e., father and son. The arrangement is praiseworthy because it is conducive to civil stability. It is safe. "No one is indignant or believes that he is superior when ruled on the basis of age, especially when he will receive his share in return upon attaining the requisite age" (1332b38–41). Although this consideration was present in the earlier account (1329a9–12), it was not the fundamental consideration, as here. It now seems that the older citizens should rule *whether or not* they possess prudence—and while a prerequisite, age is hardly a guarantee of it—just as the soldiers *must* be given rule in their turn whether or not they come to be prudent. The ordering of rule that Aristotle describes wishes to provide for a perfect natural aristocracy, but it must in practice accommodate itself both to the scarcity of those fit to rule wisely and to the claims to rule of those who, possessed of arms, cannot safely be ignored. To repeat, considerations of merit based on natural capacity to rule must give way in the political community to the demands of civil stability or peace.

If, then, moral virtue seems to have been dropped as the defining characteristic of the best regime,[11] what takes its place apart from calculations concerning civil peace? One clue is supplied by comparing the formulation of the task initially guiding this section—namely that "it is necessary to investigate how a man becomes *morally serious* [*spoudaios*]"—with the one that, in its new form, will guide the remainder: "this would have to be a matter of concern for the legislator, namely how men become *good*" (cf. 1332a35–36 with 1333a14–15; emphasis added). This distinction recalls that between the "serious" citizen and the "good" human being in III.4 and therewith the difference between a political and a transpolitical criterion of excellence.[12] The importance of some notion of human goodness thus seems to ascend in proportion as that of moral virtue descends. And while Aristotle never addressed adequately the "target" at which the education to seriousness should aim, he chooses to make

clear the corresponding target or aim related to "goodness." That target is theoretical virtue:

> Two parts of the soul have been distinguished of which one has rea-
> son in itself, the other does not in itself but is capable of harkening
> to reason. We assert that it is in accordance with the virtues of
> these parts that a man is said to be in some way good. It is not
> unclear to those who make the distinctions as we do in which of
> these two [virtues] the end is more to be found. For always what is
> worse is for the sake of what is better—this is equally clear in both
> artificial and natural things—and that which possesses reason is
> better. This also has been divided in two, in accordance with our
> usual manner: the one part is practical reason, the other theoreti-
> cal. It is clear, then, that this part [of the soul] must be divided in
> this way. (1333a16–27)

Aristotle proceeds to expand on this superiority of things rational to non-
or subrational, on the one hand, and the superiority of theoretical to practical
reason, on the other: "And we shall assert that actions must be analogous [to the
division in the parts of the soul] and that the more choiceworthy [actions]
belong to what is better by nature for those capable of attaining either all of
them or the two [lesser parts]" (1333a27–29). The two "lesser parts" here are
the simply nonrational part of the soul on the one hand and that possessing
practical reason on the other. The highest part of the soul thus is or possesses
theoretical reason, and the action or activity belonging to it is best. One can
now see the *political* consequences of this psychology:

> Life too has been divided into occupation and leisure and war and
> peace, and of matters involving action some are directed toward
> necessary and useful things, others toward noble things. Concern-
> ing these things there must of necessity be the same choice as in
> the case of the parts of the soul and their actions: war must be for
> the sake of peace, occupation for the sake of leisure, necessary and
> useful things for the sake of noble things. The statesman must leg-
> islate, therefore, looking to all these things in the case both of the
> parts of the soul and of their actions, but particularly to the things
> that are better and possess to a greater degree the ends. And he
> should legislate in the same way in connection with the ways of life
> and the divisions among activities. For one should be capable of
> being occupied and going to war, but should remain at peace and
> be at leisure, and one should act to attain necessary and useful
> things, but noble things more so. (1333a30–1333b3)

We now see that the end of the best community is the enjoyment of leisure properly understood (see also 1334a3–10). The goal of the lives of the citizens of the best regime thus changes from the concern for self-contained "theoretical reflections" in the manner of the god or "whatever it is that keeps this All together" (VII.1–3); to the performance of morally virtuous deeds supported by the belief in active, providential gods (VII.4–7, 8–12); to the enjoyment of noble leisure (VII.13ff.). This means among other things that for the best regime to exist, "the virtues contributing to leisure must be present": although leisure was said previously to be a necessary *means* "with a view to the inculcation of virtue and to political actions," leisure is now the *goal* to which the moral virtues have become means (cf. 1334a13–14, 16–17 with 1329a1–2). The moral virtues are now choiceworthy only insofar as they contribute to leisure properly understood. Aristotle may argue explicitly in VII.1–3 that the political life is superior to the philosophic, but—as precisely VII.1–3 anticipates—he comes eventually to depict a political life that is as philosophic as possible and that is judged in terms of a philosophic standard: as theoretical virtue is superior to moral virtue, so leisure is superior to occupation. To put this another way, Aristotle judges political life ultimately in terms of "goodness" rather than "seriousness," the former being determined by at least a provisional sketch of the human soul. This shift from "seriousness" to "goodness" is therefore of crucial importance for Aristotle's argument as a whole because it amounts to a shift from moral to theoretical virtue as *the* standard by which to judge both cities and human beings.

LEISURE AND THEORETICAL VIRTUE

I suggest, then, that Aristotle alters the focus of his best regime from the performance of morally virtuous deeds to the enjoyment of leisure properly understood, in accordance with what he argues is the supremacy of theoretical to practical virtue. But what is the precise relation between theoretical virtue and leisure? In the list of the various virtues necessary to securing and enjoying leisure, Aristotle mentions "philosophy," and it would therefore seem that philosophy is merely a means to leisure (1334a23 and context). On the basis of Aristotle's remarks in the *Nicomachean Ethics*, however, it would seem that leisure is with greater justification seen as a *prerequisite* to philosophy or contemplation, for contemplation alone is loved for its own sake or is an end in itself (consider, e.g., *EN* 1177b1–2). While the various virtues thus contribute to the possibility of "leisure," leisure itself seems to be ancillary to philosophy. To put this another way, leisure is the end of the lives of the citizens of the best regime but it is not the end of human life simply. The noble appreciation of beautiful things that is evidently to be the focus of the leisured conduct (*diagōgē*)[13] of one's life in the best regime is informed by the philosophic preference for rest over occupation, but it does not share the same goal as the philosophic life, namely wisdom or a discursive understanding of the whole in terms of natural necessity. As Aristotle asserts in Book VIII, it is inappropriate for the citizens of the best regime to pursue the understanding of the liberal sciences to the point of "precision" (1337b15–17). Leisure is a step in the direction of philosophy, but it is not philosophy. The cultivation of leisure is only a half-solution, then, to the problem of the life concerned with moral or political virtue, and to the extent that the citizen's soul will be concerned with something other than the true end, it will remain torn or in turmoil. The best regime is best only insofar as it most fosters this politically feasible reflection of the philosophic life that supplies to the citizen-body the most satisfying life possible within the context or confines of the political community. The fact that the best regime is otherwise deeply flawed does not constitute a criticism of Aristotle's politics; all to the contrary, that fact constitutes Aristotle's criticism of politics.

The discussion of "leisure" in Book VII is arguably the peak of the *Politics*, then, not because it outlines the genuinely satisfactory end of life but because it points to the true peak, the truly satisfying and altogether private activity of philosophic contemplation. Aristotle's discussion of the best regime as a whole is meant to show to those who are moved by the concern to make political life as good as possible that the hope hinging on politics—the hope, namely, of finding one's happiness through the participation in a just community—can in the end be satisfied only by participation in the philosophic life. This is not to deny, of course, that a political community and the goods it makes possible are necessary prerequisites to the best life, but the tendency on the part of contemporary scholars to make *theōria* essentially political is, it seems to me, mistaken, obscuring as it does the transpolitical character of the peak of Aristotle's moral and political philosophizing.

Aristotle goes on in Book VIII to prescribe the purgative or "cathartic" effect of music as a kind of palliative for the shortcomings of political life; the distance by which leisure falls short of philosophy is made up for, in a manner, by music broadly understood. As will be clear in the next section, however, this musical catharsis is a further step away from reason or philosophy, for music at its most serious proves very much to be linked with belief in the gods. I cannot do more than indicate those features of Aristotle's complex treatment of music that bear most directly on my theme.

MUSIC AND THE HEALTH OF THE CITIZEN'S SOUL (VIII)

I begin with the first of what prove to be three enumerations of the ends of a musical education.[14] It is possible that one should share in music for the sake of (1) play and rest (1339a16–21), (2) moral character (1339a24 and context), or (3) *diagōgē* and prudence (1339a25–26). Concerning the first, Aristotle argues as follows: "Now that one should not teach the young [music] for the sake of play is clear, for those who are learning it are not at play: learning is accompanied by pain" (1339a26–28). Since learning music is painful rather than pleasant, it cannot be for the sake of inherently pleasant play. Aristotle does not now comment on the relation between music and moral character, as one would expect, but rather on the third possibility enumerated, that of *diagōgē* and prudence: "Moreover, it is inappropriate to grant *diagōgē*, at any rate, to children and to those of such an age, for the end [*telos*] is improper for anything incomplete [*atelei*]" (1339a29–31). If, then, the musical education of the young cannot be for the sake of *diagōgē*, one might nevertheless hold that children should take music seriously when young in order that it may improve the character of their *diagōgē* when "complete," i.e., as adults. At this suggestion, there erupts what appears to be a tangential debate concerning the merits of having children learn to play musical instruments as opposed to acquiring what we might today call "musical appreciation." Aristotle himself seems to side with those—the Spartans in particular—who argue against the learning of musicianship, that is, against "doing" rather than understanding or judging alone (1339a2–4; cf. however VIII.6, beginning). This tangential quarrel moves so much to the fore that it all but as it were swallows up the discussion of the second of the three aims of a musical education, that of the improvement of moral character: "The same question [as to whether one should learn to play instruments oneself] holds even if [music] has the capacity to improve moral habits. For why should they themselves learn [to play] and not, by listening to others, be capable of rejoicing therein and judging correctly?" (1339a41–1339b1).

This first enumeration in VIII.5 of the possible ends of a musical education takes its bearings exclusively by the highest attainable for a human being or by the fact that humanity's true end is theoretical. The statement of the third and highest end, that of *diagōgē*—the stand-in for philosophy in the city and which in the present context is said to be *the* end of human beings—is here given its most intellectual formulation: "*diagōgē* and prudence" (1339a25–26). In this same context, "liberal *diagōgē*" is also linked with "contentedness" (*euēmeria* 1339b4–5), i.e., with that state of soul claimed, by the critic of political life in

VII.1–3, to be impeded by participation in politics (1324a38). And to repeat, Aristotle seems to agree with those who advocate the purely "theoretical" appreciation of music; he goes so far here as to adduce the example of Zeus who does not deign to play but rather is played to.

Aristotle makes something of a new beginning in the course of VIII.5 and offers the second enumeration of the goals of a musical education: "But perhaps it is necessary to make a further investigation concerning these things later. The first inquiry is whether or not one should make a place for music in education and what its capacity in regard to the three things mentioned is, namely education, play, and *diagōgē*" (1339b10–14). Aristotle now suggests that music "is reasonably arranged with a view to all of these and seems to share [in all]" (1339b14–15). Play is for the sake of rest, and rest must be pleasant; the pleasure music naturally affords is therefore reasonably a part of play. Similarly, since it is agreed that *diagōgē* should possess not only the noble but also the pleasant, and all agree that music belongs among the most pleasant things, it is clear that music should adorn *diagōgē* as well (1339b16–21). The remarkably more accommodating tone Aristotle here takes is the result of the following view: "All the pleasures that are harmless are appropriate not just with a view to the end [*telos*] but also with a view to rest. *And while it rarely happens that human beings attain the end*, they frequently are at rest and make use of play not for some further purpose but on account of the pleasure it affords. It would [thus] be useful to take rest in the pleasures that arise from this [i.e., music]" (1339b25–31; emphasis added).

Whereas in the first enumeration of VIII.5 Aristotle had calculated the proper place of music by looking only at the end or completion of human beings, in the second enumeration he takes his bearings by the fact that "human beings rarely attain the end." This means that they rarely lead theoretical lives and that they are therefore more or less devoted to a political, active life. The majority of human beings are thus cut off from that self-contained pleasure and happiness said to accompany the philosophic life. For political human beings who as such are "occupied" most of the time, there is always the sense of something lacking, a constant striving toward a never-realized goal: "the one who is occupied is so for the sake of an end which is absent, but happiness is an end which all suppose is not accompanied by pain but rather by pleasure" (1338a4–6; consider *EN* 1177b4ff.). While in the first enumeration "*diagōgē* and prudence" loomed large as "the end" and moral character was all but absent, in the second enumeration *diagōgē* in its brief appearance is equated with "social gatherings" (1339b22–23) and the topic of music in its relation to character takes up the rest of the chapter; to put this another way, "education" in this second enumeration takes the place of "moral character" in the first but seems to include nothing more than the habituation to moral virtue (cf. 1340a5ff. with 1339a21–25 and 41ff.).

How, then, will a sound musical education help to form noble characters? By making use of those rhythms and harmonies in which are found "particularly close likenesses to the genuine natures of anger and gentleness, and further of courage and moderation and all their opposites, as well as the rest of the moral virtues" (1340a18–21), we may experience through music the variety of passions most associated with virtue and learn to do so in a manner appropriate to free human beings. Properly conducted, then, a musical education refines and ennobles the passions. This explanation of the utility of a musical education does not quite account, however, for the examples with which Aristotle begins of the effects of the tunes of Olympus[15] and the imitations of those tunes,[16] the former instilling "divine inspiration" or "enthusiasm," the latter feelings "sympathetic" to that inspiration (1340a7ff.). There seems to be another function performed by music quite apart from the educative refinement suggested. Indeed, while the flute has no place in education proper because it impedes *logos* both in the sense that one cannot speak while playing it and in the sense that it is most inclined to induce in those who listen to it a frenzied, *alogon* state of soul (1341a21–22; 1341b2–8; compare 1342b1–3 with 1340b4–5), nevertheless there are "right times" or "opportune moments" to hear it played, namely when "catharsis rather than learning" is required—the first appearance in the *Politics* of this important term (1341a21–24).[17]

Those human beings who require "catharsis rather than learning" feel most deeply and urgently the exposed character of their own happiness and that of their loved ones, feelings present to all souls but in widely varying degrees (1342a4–6). To experience the extreme state of "possession" that certain "sacred" and "frenzy-inducing" tunes induce is evidently to believe that one is as close as possible to the gods, the only agents of delivery from the fears and worries of this life (1340b4–5; 1341a22; 1342a7–11). The resulting "catharsis" seems to be a calming of the greatest disquiet of the virtuous soul, a temporary release from the concerns accompanying the life of virtue and self-sacrifice. Not least among these is the fear of one's own death, the occurrence and consequences of which are known only to gods. Since music is held to be a means of access to the gods, the saying of Musaeus makes sense: "'For *mortals* to sing is most pleasant'" (1339b22; emphasis added). To a limited degree, then, the catharsis Aristotle here describes and makes a place for in the best city actually performs the function of the gods. And while it is true that children are not to learn to produce such frenzied music themselves, it appears that the city as a whole, the men and the women, the citizens and the noncitizens, may experience the musical performances in question (consider 1342a18–22). There certainly are no restrictions here comparable to those in the section of VII.16–17 treating of comedy (1336b20 and context).[18] Political life seems to require what one might call tragic frenzy to purge, if only for a time, the apprehensions and disappointments accompanying that life. Although Aristotle denies us the expected discussion of the education of the intellect by means of argument (*logos*), he does discuss an *alogon* state of "possession."[19]

According to the third and final enumeration of the ends of a musical education, one may make use of music "for the sake of education, catharsis . . . and third with a view to *diagōgē*, to the relaxation and the rest from strain" (1341b38–41). "Play" drops out of the list and is replaced by "catharsis," and this seems reasonable since the functions of each are similar: catharsis provides a necessary respite from the exertions associated with moral virtue and is needed especially by those given to pitying, fearing, and to the passions in general, as Aristotle indicates (1342a11–15). Moreover, since we have left *diagōgē* in its highest sense far behind, it is here given its least intellectual formulation; so far from being linked with prudence and the end of man, it is now indistinguishable from "relaxation and rest." The whole discussion of music in Book VIII attempts to cope with the limits, seen in Book VII, to even the political life that "accords with what one would pray for."[20]

CONCLUSION: ARISTOTLE'S "REALISM"

It is fair to say that nothing characterizes Aristotle's political science so much as its concern for moral virtue. At the same time, when the exposition of that science reaches its culmination in the description of the best regime, Aristotle makes clear his awareness of the problem of moral virtue as a simply just basis of the distribution of political office and as a means to attain happiness. He tries to cope with the latter problem in part by encouraging hardnosed calculation concerning one's military security in a world where all nations that are not simply confused may be assumed to aim at domination (1324b5–7). Aristotle's appeal to and encouragement of moral virtue cannot be called naive.

Is not Aristotle himself confused, however, insofar as he insists on appealing to moral virtue while being aware of and even stressing the so to speak "Machiavellian" character of politics? Why not either jettison moral virtue as an impediment to sound politics or, more cautiously, try to define virtue in terms of what is politically expedient? I suggest that Aristotle refuses to encourage the utilitarian pursuit of moral virtue, or to dismiss the concern for virtue as naive, because to do either would be to distort the fundamental human attachment to justice or moral excellence understood as an end in itself. Accordingly, Aristotle begins his investigation into the best regime by making explicit, and by taking his bearings from, the highest and most serious hopes attending political life (VII.1–3). For it is only by first becoming fully aware of those hopes and the attachment to justice they imply that we can come eventually to understand them and ourselves better; to begin by discounting or dismissing as naive our devotion to the common good is therefore to make self-knowledge impossible, and insofar as we cannot come to know the world as it is without first seeing ourselves as we are, as beings whose profound moral hopes inform from the outset the way we look upon the world, the adoption of such a "sophisticated" but unearned view of morality is fatal to philosophy. Aristotle's clear-eyed attachment to moral virtue is thus motivated at bottom by the desire to preserve philosophy as a possibility, the possibility lying behind even the refined goal of leisure in the best regime.

One may say, then, that the "realism" of Aristotle's account of the best regime consists above all in the naiveté of its starting point, for by taking most seriously our moral and political concerns as citizens, it is true to our prephilosophic experience, i.e., to the necessary beginning point of reflection. As I have tried to indicate, such reflection leads in the case of Aristotelian political science from the devotion to noble political action, to the priority of leisure over activity, to, finally, the recognition of contemplation as the best means to secure a worthy human happiness. It hardly needs to be said that what such contemplation is or entails requires further study; let it suffice for now to note that Aristotle's inquiry into the best regime as the sum of our hopes for political life seems to point beyond any political association, beyond any best regime, to the philosophic life as their deepest fulfillment. As for "realism," to the extent that it denies or distorts our moral attachments from the very beginning, it is unrealistic, and to the extent that it remains wedded to the hope of a purely political solution to the problem of human happiness, it remains, in the decisive respect, naive.

NOTES

1. Machiavelli, *Prince*, ch. 15 (consider also Spinoza, *Political Treatise*, I.1). According to Thomas Hobbes, the moral and civil philosophy of Aristotle—"the worst teacher that ever was"—wrongly takes its bearings by a wish rather than necessity, i.e., by a necessarily fanciful conception of the supposed *summum bonum* rather than by certain knowledge of the undeniable *summum malum*. And that theoretical error has proved practically disastrous: "Their [sc. the ancient philosophers's] Morall Philosophy is but a description of their own Passions. . . . they make the Rules of Good and Bad, by their own Liking, and Disliking: By which means, in so great diversity of taste, there is nothing generally agreed on; but every one doth (as far as he dares) whatsoever seemeth good in his owne eyes, to the subversion of Common-wealth" (Hobbes, *Leviathan*, ed. C. B. Macpherson, [Penguin] 686; 369 and 697–700; see also *De Cive*, Ep. Ded., Preface, III.13, 32; VII.2–3; X.2; XII.3; XIV.2).

2. Unless otherwise indicated, all references in the text will be to the *Politics* by book and chapter (roman and arabic numerals respectively). Where a more precise citation is required, I have made use of the standard Bekker numbers as these appear in Alois Dreizhenter, *Aristoteles' Politica* (Munich: Wilhelm Fink, 1970). Translations from the Greek are my own.

3. So far as I am aware, none of the secondary literature takes up the question whether Aristotle himself is satisfied with the goodness of his "best regime." See William T. Bluhm, "The Place of 'Polity' in Aristotle's Theory of the Ideal State," *Journal of Politics* 24 (1962): 743–53; George Huxley, "On Aristotle's Best State," in *Crux*, ed. Paul A. Cartledge and F. D. Harvey (London: Duckworth, 1985); Paul A. Vander Waerdt, "Kingship and Philosophy in Aristotle's Best Regime," *Phronesis* 30 (1985): 249–73. Otherwise helpful discussions of Aristotle's best regime in the context of his political philosophy as a whole include Ernest Barker, *The Political Thought of Plato and Aristotle* (New York: Dover, 1959); Harry V. Jaffa, "Aristotle," in *History of Political Philosophy*, ed. Leo Strauss and Joseph Cropsey. 2d ed. (Chicago: Rand McNally, 1972), 125–28; John B. Morrall, *Aristotle* (London and Boston: G. Allen & Unwin, 1977), 104–11; and Richard G. Mulgan, *Aristotle's Political Theory* (Oxford: Clarendon Press, 1977). For an overview of the "best regime" in the history of political thought, see James V. Schall, "The Best Form of Government: the Continuity of Political Theory," *Review of Politics* 40 (1978): 97–123.

4. Aristotle's argument here is limited in the decisive respect, as appears not least from the following: "But these two things now require investigation: in the first place what the more choiceworthy way of life is, the one that takes part in citizenship and shares in a city, or rather the one characteristic of a foreigner and that is separated from the political community; and secondly what regime and what condition of a city one should set down as best, *whether or not it is choiceworthy for all to share in a city or whether it is so only for most and not for some*. For this [inquiry into the best regime and city] is the task of political understanding and contemplation, *but not that which is choiceworthy for the individual*, and we have deliberately chosen this as the present inquiry, for the one [i.e., that which is best

for the individual] is beyond the task of the present investigation, the other [i.e., the question of the best political life] being its task" (1324a14–23; emphasis added). An adequate inquiry into the question of the best life simply cannot begin by presupposing the superiority of the political life. See the helpful discussions of Carnes Lord, *Education and Culture in the Political Thought of Aristotle* (Ithaca: Cornell University Press, 1982), 181 and Gerald M. Mara, "The Role of Philosophy in Aristotle's Political Science" *Polity* 19 (1987): 375–78; cf. Richard G. Mulgan, *Aristotle's Political Theory*, 208–11 and Stephen G. Salkever, *Finding the Mean* (Princeton: Princeton University Press, 1990), 148.

5. This conclusion is confirmed by Aristotle's discussion in VII.14 of the ends with a view to which courage ought to be fostered: (1) the maintenance of one's own freedom in the face of hostile enemies, (2) the exercise of leadership (*hēgemonia*) among cities, and (3) the enslavement of those fit to be slaves (1333b38–1334a2). Precisely because all cities look to their own good first and foremost, the best city will require considerable military might and will exercise an empire of a kind, what today might be called a "sphere of influence."

6. It is true that Aristotle also entertains a consideration of a quite different kind as regards the soldiers (1329a9–12), but he concludes this section with a firm statement that the arrangement indicated is "in accordance with *merit*" (1329a17), i.e., merit judged in terms of the capacity to act virtuously.

7. See Leo Strauss, *The City and Man* (Chicago: University of Chicago Press, 1964), 22–23; Nicholas D. Smith, "Aristotle's Theory of Natural Slavery," *Phoenix* 37 (1983): 111; Wayne H. Ambler, "Aristotle on Nature and Politics: The Case of Slavery," *Political Theory* 15 (1987): 404–7. In his enumeration of the elements requisite to the city, Aristotle speaks of a twofold necessity demanding the presence of arms: "for those who share [in the regime] must necessarily have arms among themselves both with a view *to those who disobey the rule* and those foreigners who undertake to act unjustly" (1328b7–10; emphasis added). The army, then, must be capable of acting against the city's inhabitants—e.g., the farmers—no less than against foreign invaders.

8. Similarly, the mention of Hippodamus in this section (1330b21–31) recalls Aristotle's contention in II. 8 that the political community is not and cannot be fully rational (cf., e.g., 1269a20–24).

9. Aristotle's view of the divine is complicated to say the least. On the one hand, piety is not among the virtues cited in the *Nicomachean Ethics* as belonging to a gentleman, and Aristotle makes it clear in the course of the *Politics* that the care of the divine is separate from and inferior to political office strictly speaking (1299a17–19; 1322b18–22; 1328b11). On the other hand, Aristotle admits providential gods into his best regime, and he maintains that the care of the divine is *essential* to the city's existence. The very statement of this necessity captures Aristotle's ambivalence: the care of the divine is "fifth and first" in importance (1328b11–13). Since the gods are the most important and perfect beings, the care of and service to them must be "first." Aristotle wishes to curb any overzealous reliance on the divine, however, and to foster in particular a moderate, sober analysis of political fact or necessity—the kind of analysis that characterizes VII as a whole. The care of the divine is therefore also "fifth" in rank. For recent discussions of the religious dimensions of Aristotle's political thought, see Thomas K. Lindsay, "The 'God-like Man' versus the 'Best Laws': Politics and Religion in Aristotle's *Politics*," *Review of Politics* 53 (1991): 488–509 and

Lionel Ponton, "Le divin comme préoccupation politique chez Aristote et Hegel," in *La question de Dieu selon Aristote et Hegel*, ed. Thomas De Konnick and Guy Planty-Bonjour (Paris: PUF, 1991).

10. Leo Strauss suggests also that "the good city in the classical sense" is impossible only if science ceases to be, as Aristotle argued it must be, essentially theoretical (*Thoughts on Machiavelli* [Chicago: University of Chicago Press, 1958]); the application of natural science to the relief of man's estate must be strictly limited by political science (consider *EN* 1094a26–1094b11). Furthermore, "the opinion that there occur periodic cataclysms in fact took care of any apprehension regarding an excessive development of technology or regarding the danger that man's inventions might become his masters and his destroyers" (ibid., 299); consider *Politics* 1268b22ff. and Plato *Laws* III, beginning.

11. Similarly, whereas Aristotle had maintained in VII.7 that the citizens should be by nature "easily led by the legislator toward virtue" (1327b38), in the present context he suggests only that they be capable of being "easily taken in hand by the legislator" (1332b9): virtue is no longer explicitly the end.

12. Compare Robert Develin, "The Good Man and the Good Citizen in Aristotle's *Politics, Phronesis* 18 (1973): 71–79.

13. The term, usually rendered "pastime," refers to the way in which one spends one's time when inactive or free of business. Since Aristotle argues that leisure is of higher importance and dignity than activity ordinarily understood, it is more, not less, serious than "business." I shall hereafter simply transliterate the Greek rather than settle for the somewhat frivolous-sounding "pastime" (see Salkever, *Finding the Mean*, 78 n.46). On the meaning of *scholē* ("leisure") see J. L. Stocks, "*Scholē*," *Classical Quarterly* (30) (1936): 177–87.

14. For a learned and detailed treatment of music in the *Politics*, see Lord, *Education and Culture*. The principal difference between my discussion and Lord's is that whereas I try to present the musical education of Book VIII as responding to a *political* problem, Lord more or less divorces the presentation of music from its political context; the argument of VII.1–3, for example, is treated only comparatively briefly as the final chapter of the book.

15. Olympus was a legendary figure of the eighth century, hailing from Phrygia, who composed tunes for the flute: see W. L. Newman, *The Politics of Aristotle*, 4 vols. (New York: Arno Press, 1973), 2:536; and Carnes Lord, *The Politics of Aristotle* (Chicago: University of Chicago Press, 1984), 269 n.11.

16. The referent of *tōn mimēsiōn* at 1340a12 is unclear. According to Carnes Lord, *Politics* (269 n. 12), "it seems most likely that poetic imitations in the broadest sense are what is meant here," but the narrower sense indicated in the text is at least as plausible.

17. On the meaning of "catharsis," see W. L. Newman, *Politics of Aristotle*, 2:563–65; Carnes Lord, *Education and Culture*, 156–64; Jonathan Lear, "Catharsis," *Phronesis* 33 (1988): 297–326; and D. J. Depew, "Politics, Music, and Contemplation in Aristotle's Ideal State" in *A Companion to Aristotle's Politics*, ed. David Keyt and Fred Miller (Cambridge: Blackwell, 1991), 362–74. The classification in VIII.7 of the kinds of tunes and rhythms and their corresponding harmonies sheds some additional light on the need for such frenzied music (1341b23ff.). According to this classification, which is philosophic in origin (1341b28), there are three kinds of tunes, those bearing on or contributing to (1) moral character, (2) action, and (3) divine inspiration. According to Aristotle's own view, "one

should make use of music not for a single benefit but for the sake of many" (1341b36–38); "It is clear that one should make use of *all* the harmonies" (1342a1; emphasis added). Since the active, political life devoted to the moral virtues and the performance of the deeds that accord with them requires and is completed by the worship of just gods, the three kind of tunes here indicated themselves form a kind of whole, and all would be necessary to that happiness possible within political life. Thus "those educated with a view to political virtue" (1340b42–1341a1) must at times make use of inspirational music and hence of the flute.

18. The importance of comedy, as well as that of the worship of the god to whom the law has assigned "scurrilous mockery" (1336b16–17), is linked with the presentation in this context of the "speeches and myths" it is necessary to tell children on the one hand and the fact that we most cling to what we are first told on the other (1336a30–31 and 1336b28–32): to laugh at something is already to gain for oneself a certain distance from it.

19. Compare VIII.6–7 with 1337a38–39 and 1338b4–6.

20. Aristotle's frequent formulation: 1260b29; 1265a17–18; 1288b23; 1295a29; 1325b36, 39; 1327a4; 1331b21.

Contributors

WAYNE AMBLER is Associate Professor of Political Science, University of Dallas. His dissertation on Aristotle's *Politics* won the American Political Science Association's Leo Strauss Award for the best dissertation in political theory, and his studies of Aristotle's political thought have appeared in the *Canadian Journal of Political Science, Political Theory*, and the *Review of Politics*.

ROBERT C. BARTLETT is Assistant Professor of Political Science at Emory University. He is the editor of Xenophon's *The Shorter Socratic Writings: Apology of Socrates to the Jury, Oeconomicus, and Symposium* (Cornell, 1996) and has published studies of Aristotle in the *American Political Science Review* and the *American Journal of Political Science*.

RONALD BEINER is Professor of Political Science, University of Toronto. He is the editor of Hannah Arendt's *Lectures in Kant's Political Philosophy* (Chicago, 1982) and the author of *Political Judgment* (Metheun, 1983) and *What's the Matter With Liberalism?* (California, 1992). He has most recently published a collection of his own essays *Philosophy in a Time of Lost Spirit: Essays on Contemporary Theory* (University of Toronto, 1997).

RICHARD BODÉÜS is Professor of Philosophy, University of Montreal. His works include *Le philosophe et la cité* (Les Belles Lettres, 1982) and *The Political Dimensions of Aristotle's Ethics* (SUNY, 1993).

DAVID BOLOTIN teaches at St. John's College (Sante Fe). He is the author of *Plato's Dialogue on Friendship* (Cornell, 1979) and *An Approach to Aristotle's Physics* (SUNY, 1997).

HAUKE BRUNKHORST is Professor at the Kulturwissenschaftliches Institut (Essen). His works include *Theodor Adorno: Dialektik der Moderne* (Piper,

1990) and *Der entzauberte Intellektuelle: uber die neue Beliebigkeit des Denkens* (Junius, 1990).

SUSAN D. COLLINS is Assistant Professor of Political Science, Southern Illinois University. She is at work on a critical study of neo-Aristotelianism and on a book-length treatment of the moral virtues in Aristotle's *Nicomachean Ethics*.

HANS-GEORG GADAMER'S many works include *Truth and Method* (2d ed., 1993), *The Idea of the Good in Platonic and Aristotelian Philosophy* (Yale, 1986) and *Plato's Dialectical Ethics* (Yale, 1991).

DAVID K. O'CONNOR is Associate Professor of Philosophy, University of Notre Dame. He is the co-editor, with Carnes Lord, of *Essays in the Foundations of Aristotle's Political Science* (California, 1991).

LORRAINE SMITH PANGLE is co-author, with Thomas L. Pangle, of *The Learning of Liberty* (Kansas, 1993). She is at work on a book-length study of Aristotle's *Nicomachean Ethics*.

JUDITH A. SWANSON is Associate Professor of Political Science, Boston University, and the author of *The Public and the Private in the Political Thought of Aristotle* (Cornell, 1992).

ARISTIDE TESSITORE is Associate Professor of Political Science, Furman University. His many studies of classical thought have appeared in the *American Political Science Review*, *Political Theory*, and the *Journal of Politics*, among other journals. He is the author of *Reading Aristotle's Ethics: Virtue, Rhetoric, and Political Philosophy* (SUNY, 1996).

FRANCO VOLPI is Professor of Philosophy, University of Padua and Witten-Herdecke. He is the author of many studies spanning ancient and contemporary thought, including *La rinascita della filosofia pratica in Germania* (Francisi, 1980), *Heidegger e Aristotele* (Daphne, 1984), and, with Enrico Berti, *Storia della filosofia* (Laterza, 1991).

BERNARD YACK is Professor of Political Science at the University of Wisconsin (Madison). He is the author of *The Longing for Total Revolution*

(Princeton, 1986), *The Problems of a Political Animal* (California, 1993), and *The Fetishism of Modernities: Epochal Self-Consciousness in Contemporary Social and Political Thought* (Notre Dame, 1997).

INDEX

Abramson, Jeffrey, 283

Action: existential specificity of, 117–18, 128n2; Kant on, 8; and knowledge, 9; moral, xi, xiv; nobility of, 183–84; Platonic idea of, 117–18; political, xi, 121, 124; priority of leisure over, 309; purposeful, 189; role in happiness, 110, 113–18, 119, 121, 124, 129nn6–7; sociability in, 198. *See also Energeia*; Tyranny

Adultery, in *Nichomachean Ethics*, 150, 164

Affection: in friendship, 177–78, 181; and sociability, 197

Ambition, 207, 271n18; in *Nichomachean Ethics*, 142; in *Politics*, 109

Ambler, Wayne, 236, 315

Anaxagoras, 125, 126, 129n14

Androgyny, biological, 231

Anger: and music, 307; in *Nichomachean Ethics*, 143

Animals, 227–28; gender of, 229–30; generation of, 229; gregarious, 276

Annas, Julia, 101n17, 112, 128n2; on friendship, 201n4

Antimodernism, 69

Apodeixis (proof), 12–13

Apology, 221n7

Aporiai (puzzles), 212, 222n13

Arendt, Hannah, 25n44; on civil disobedience, 31–32; on communities, 274; on feminism, 30; on freedom, 27–28; on political activity, 290n3; on *praxis*, 5; on religion, 27; on republicanism, xiv, 30–35; *On Revolutions*, 28; on slavery, 30; on the state, 34, 36n23; on theocracy, 33; on universalism, 34; *Vita activa*, 4–5

Aretē, 55; in *Nichomachean Ethics*, 58

Argumentation, modes of, 12–13. *See also Logos*

Aristotle: Anglo-American interpretations of, 109–10; Aquinas on, 154n5; construction of concepts, 60, 67n3; on dialectics, 24n41; doctrine of intellectual virtues, 60; dogmatism of, 225–26, 228, 242; eighteenth-century scholars on, xi; exile of, 204, 221n4; as founder of ethics, 54; as founder of practical philosophy, 56, 57; Hobbes on, 310n1; on human excellence, 220, 223n21; influence on Christianity, xii; influence on literature, 22n17; on justice, xv, 83, 102n21; on law, 32–33; logico-metaphysical works, 226, 245n11; misogyny of, 231; modes of inquiry, 220; on moral behavior, 53, 239–40; on natural right, xv, 70–72, 79–86; and necessity, 56; on poets, 108–9; on practical life, xv; realism of, 308–9; recovery of practical philosophy of, xiv, 5, 10, 69, 100n1;

319

(*Aristotle continued*)
 on slavery, 72, 102n24, 103n29; on
  socialization, 45; on the soul, 61–62;
  and Stoicism, 70; teleological
  reasoning of, 275, 276, 277, 278; view
  of freedom, 78–79; on virtue, 32–33,
  60, 120–21, 128n2, 131–53, 154n4,
  211. Works: *See* individual works
Aspasius, 155n7
Aubenque, Pierre, 24n42
Audience, Aristotle's, 128nn2–3,5, 221n2,
  225–26; moralizing account of,
  111–12; morally minimalist account
  of, 109–13, 128n6; philosophers in,
  129n12
Autonomy: Kant on, 64; public *versus*
  private, 31; in self-love, 193
Axiological neutrality (Wertfreiheit), 9

Bacon, Francis, 21n12
Bartlett, Robert C., 315
Beatitudo, 22n14
Beaufret, Jean, 38, 41
Beiner, Ronald, xiv–xv, 315
Being: modes of, 12; perfection of, 16
Benefactors, 199; love felt by, 188–91; love
  for, 192
Berman, Harold, 34
Bernstein, Richard, 47
Bien, Gunther, 290n4
Biology, Aristotelian, 244n7, 245n11;
  procreation in, 230–31, 244n8; sex
  differentiation in, 229–32, 244n6
Bloom, Alan, 222n19
Boasting, in *Nichomachean Ethics*, 145, 146,
  208
Bodéüs, Richard, xv, 315
Boethius, 21n12
Bolotin, David, 315
Book of Judges, monarchy in, 33
Brunkhorst, Hauke, xiv, 315

Brunner, O., 23n17
Brutishness, in *Nichomachean Ethics*, 161
Burnet, John, 157n16, 158nn9–11

Callicles, 121, 122, 127, 250, 269n3
Callicles' challenge, 110, 122, 123
Camaraderie, political, 287, 288
Categorization, Aristotle's scheme of, 226
Catharsis, 312n17; through music, 307–8
Causality: of freedom, 55; physical, 8
Chance, in practical philosophy, 12
Children: as common good, 259; musical
  education for, 305, 307; souls of, 238
Christianity: Aristotle's influence on, xii; in
  public sphere, 27
Cicero, 21n12; on duty, 56
Citizens, 269n7; and bourgeois, 32, 33;
  common advantage of, 270n14;
  fraternity among, 287, 288, 292n24;
  polis's service to, 236; self-organization
  of, 32–33, 34. *See also* Rulers and
  subjects
Citizenship: in the republic, 32; role of
  moral virtue in, 295–96
City. *See Polis*; Political community
Civil disobedience, 31–32
Civitas Dei, 54
Cognitivism, 50n22
Collins, Susan D., 316
Comedy, 147, 308, 313n18
Common advantage, 96, 260, 271n19; in
  democracy, 97; of goodness, 265; in
  justice, 97–98; in *Nichomachean
  Ethics*, 270n15; and partisan
  controversy, 270n14; in political
  community, 276, 280; in *Politics*,
  249–68, 270n13; in regimes, 250–51,
  261–62, 264, 266, 270n16; for rulers
  and subjects, 265, 267, 270n17; and
  self-love, 195; in slavery, 92
Communism, Socrates on, 218

Communities: Arendt on, 274; *ethos* of, 40–41, 43, 52n41; prepolitical, 281. *See also Polis*; Political community

Confidence, in *Nichomachean Ethics*, 133–34

Conflict, in Aristotle's political philosophy, 273–89, 290n1

Consent, legitimacy of, 40

Constitutions, justness of, 74–78, 81, 83

Constructivism, 4

Consumerism, 28, 29, 31

Contemplation: Aristotle on, 118–19, 123, 250; divine, 129n14; of the good, 176; in *Nichomachean Ethics*, 196; as *praxis*, 124, 126; role in happiness, 309

Conversation, in friendship, 199

Cooper, John M., 112, 201n2

Cosmic order, 100nn7–8, 246n33

Courage: Aquinas on, 155n6; and happiness, 134–35, 155n8; and magnanimity, 140; in *Nichomachean Ethics*, 133–35, 151, 205–7; nobility in, 205; Socrates on, 128n1, 205–7; types of, 205

Curtius, E. R., 23n17

Davis, Michael, 222n18

Death: in *Nichomachean Ethics*, 133–35, 205; Socrates on, 207

Decisionism, 17

Defourny, Maurice, 291n7

Deinotēs (cleverness), 14, 55

Democracy: common interest in, 97; Lincoln on, 34; in *Politics*, 34, 278; scientific foundation of, xiii

Democracy, Western: Arendt on, 28; and Christian tradition, 32

Demon worship, 156n12

Deutsche Gesellschaft für Soziologie, 5

Diagōgē (pastime), 146, 157n19, 312n13; prudence in, 305, 306, 308

Dialectics, 24n41

Difference, and otherness, 234–35, 245n19

Dilthey, Wilhelm, 8

Discourse: ethics of, 4; on norms, 46–47

Divinity: contemplation of, 129n14; in *Nichomachean Ethics*, 139; in *Politics*, 298–300, 311n9

Doxa, 15

Duty, 56; Kant on, 63–64

Economics: in practical philosophy, 6; science of, 22n15

Education: Gadamer on, 51n28; musical, 305, 307; in *Politics*, 108; practical philosophy in, 11; resistance to, 102n25; Socrates on, 217; for virtue, 169

Eidos (species), 233, 245n11

Embryology, 230, 244n6

Empedocles, 214

Encyclopedias, medieval, 6, 16, 21n12

Energeia (activity), 113–14, 115, 116; of intellect, 125; and *praxis*, 126–27, 129n7; theoretical activity as, 124, 125

Enlightenment: human perfectibility in, 64, 65; ideals of, 59; political thought of, 236; rationalism of, 46

Epistēmē: Aristotelian account of, 15; in *Nichomachean Ethics*, 61; and *phronēsis*, 63

Equality: before law, 85; natural, 90

Equity: in gender roles, 222n16; in *Nichomachean Ethics*, 72–73, 137; in *Politics*, 74–76; regulation by norms, 74

Erotic love, 175

Ethics: Aristotle as founder of, 54; classical, 38; dissociation from morality, 17; Habermas on, 39–40, 50n22; Heidegger on, 40–41; of imperatives, 55–56; Kantian understanding of, 25n44; medieval teaching of, 22n14;

(*Ethics continued*)
   philosophical achievement of, 247n33;
   in politics, 21n11; in practical
   philosophy, 6; relationship with
   metaphysics, 38–39, 49n5
Ethnicity, in statehood, 34, 36n23
Ethos (custom): of communities, 40–41, 43,
   52n41; concreteness of, 17; as
   condition of virtue, 46; and *logos*, 54;
   of modernity, 48; normative function
   of, 43; priority over theory, xiv; and
   rationalization, 45; role of *phronēsis* in,
   62
Eudaimonia, 22n14; Kant on, 65
Eudemian Ethics, audience of, 128n6;
   community in, 275; friendship in,
   284, 285; happiness in, 108; reason in,
   89; relationship with *Nichomachean
   Ethics*, 155n5; soul in, 90–91
Eurymedon, 221n4
Evil, in *Nichomachean Ethics*, 159–69
Existence, Kierkegaard on, 60

Family: common advantage in, 262, 264,
   265, 270n11; gender roles in, 237–38,
   246n27; governance of, 215, 222n10,
   237–39, 257–65; as model
   association, 259; natural role of,
   236–37, 260; in *Politics*, 214–16,
   262–65; role in the *polis*, 215, 236
Farmers, in best regimes, 296, 311n7
Fear, in *Nichomachean Ethics*, 133
Femaleness: metaphysics of, 233–35; norms
   of, 237; politics of, 235–39; principle
   of, 229–32; in procreation, 230–31,
   244n8; psychology of, 232–33. *See also*
   Gender roles; Women
Feminism, Arendt on, 30
Ferry, Luc, 100n7
Form, 227; in semen, 230, 231
Formalism, Kantian, 42–43, 50n20, 53
Fortenbaugh, W. W., 246n28

Founding events, 31–32
Fraternity, political, 287, 288, 292n24
Freedom: Arendt on, 27–28; Aristotle's view
   of, 78–79; biblical idea of, 33;
   causality of, 55; of choice, 62, 179,
   201n5; classical idea of, 32; in
   friendship, 201n5; under natural right,
   86; negative, 32, 34; Pauline doctrine
   of, 28; from politics, 32; positive, 28;
   and private interests, 28–29, 33; in
   public sphere, 29, 31; from regrets,
   187; republican idea of, 29, 32; for
   slaves, 296; universal, 49n9
Friendship: among philosophers, 200;
   conversation in, 199; ethical, 180–85,
   285; in *Eudemian Ethics*, 284, 285; as
   external good, 201n7; freedom of
   choice in, 179, 201n5; goodness of,
   196–200; Hobbes on, 287; kinds of,
   173–77, 284; legal, 181–82, 285; and
   magnanimity, 172; Montaigne on,
   173, 178–80; against nature, 285,
   292n21; in *Nichomachean Ethics*, 116,
   144, 172–200; nobility of, 172; of
   pleasure, 173–77, 181, 197–98, 284;
   political, 285–88, 291n19, 292n20;
   rank of, 177–80; role in happiness,
   141, 172–73, 176, 198; role in self-
   sufficiency, 201n7, 202n13; sacrifice
   in, 188, 286; self-identity in, 188; self-
   love and, 185–88; unequal, 185; of
   utility, 173–76, 179, 180–81, 201n2,
   284–85; as virtue, 144, 157n20, 174,
   177, 179–83, 283
Functionalism, 242, 243

Gadamer, Hans-Georg, xiv–xv, 316;
   antifoundationalism of, 51n39;
   Beyond Objectivism and Relativism,
   47–48, 51n27; on education, 51n28;
   on intellectuals, 43–44, 51n35; on
   justice, 101n18; on metaphysics, 39;
   on modernity, 45–46; on moral life,
   37; on *Nichomachean Ethics*, 24n40;

"On the Possibility of a Philosophical Ethics," 42; on *phronēsis*, 18, 48; on Plato, 49n11; on practical knowledge, 37; on primacy of *ethos*, 37–48; on universal freedom, 49n9; universalism of, 40, 45–46; *Wahrheit und Methode*, 5, 40, 41

Galston, William, 158n25

Gamikē (maternal rule), 237

Garver, Eugene, 102n27

Gauthier, R. A., 157n23

Geisteswissenschaften (sciences of the mind), 11, 55, 57

Gender roles, 225, 229–32; equity in, 222n16; in family, 237–38, 259; metaphysics of, 233–35; norms of, 237; in the *polis*, 239–42; political implications of, 226, 235–42; psychology of, 232–33; virtue in, 215

Generation and Corruption, 82

Generation of Animals, 82, 229

Genos (genus), 231–32, 234, 245n11

Gentleness: and music, 307; in *Nichomachean Ethics*, 143–44, 157n15, 207

German Convention of Philosophy, ninth, 4

Gods: Aquinas on, 156n12; Aristotle on, 298–300, 311n9, 313n17; belief in, 304; immortality of, 139; sacrifice to, 299

Good, The: Aristotle on, 57, 76, 119, 173; friendship and, 173, 175, 198; norm of, 99; Plato on, 57, 119; in political community, 149; in practical philosophy, 58; role of moral virtue in, 131–32, 152–53; and self-interest, 186; Socrates on, 53–54

Good deeds, motivation for, 190

Goodness: common advantage of, 265; of friendship, 196–200; of honor, 178; and moral virtue, 301–2; in political life, 303; and self-love, 191

Goods, external: Aquinas on, 154n5; communism of, 218; friendship as, 196–97, 201n7; in the *polis*, 217, 296; rejection of, 140

Goodwill: in friendship, 173, 174–75, 176, 195, 201n2; role of sociability in, 197

Gorgias, 122, 269n6

Grant, Sir Alexander, 154nn5, 8; 157n15

Greed, 167–68; as injustice, 161; of rulers, 263; as vice, 138

Grosseteste, Robert, 22n14

Habermas, Jürgen: on communal ethos, 44, 49n7; on ethics, 39–40, 50n22; in Frankfurt school of philosophy, 4; on *hexis*, 50n24; on modernity, 45; on moral theory, 44–45; on neo-Aristotelianism, xiv, 37–39, 49n2; on prudence, 47; on rationality, 43; on reason, 51n35; universalism of, 51n32

Habit. *See Hexis*

Happiness, 22n14, 101n17, 202n12; activist ideal of, 110, 113–18, 119, 121, 124, 129nn6–7; and courage, 134–35, 155n8; in *Eudemian Ethics*, 108; in good deeds, 190; hyperactivist ideal of, 118–22, 123, 124; Kant on, 65; under law, 152; magnanimity and, 141, 171; in *Nichomachean Ethics*, 113–18, 125–26, 129n9, 168, 169; political action as, 121, 124; of political community, 149, 304; in *Politics*, 108, 297; and pursuit of justice, 171–72; role of contemplation in, 309; role of friendship in, 141, 172–73, 176, 198; role of moral virtue in, 115–16, 132, 134–35, 141, 171, 297–300; role of pleasure in, 115, 306; sacrifice of, 195–96; self-love in, 191, 194–95

Hardie, W. F. R., 155n5

Hare, Richard M., 4

Hedonism, 114–15; as life goal, 58

Hegel, Georg Wilhelm Friedrich, 288; on
community, 276, 291n8; on Socrates,
43; speculative idealism of, 60
Heidegger, Martin, 24n40, 48; on dianoetic
virtues, 61; on ethics, 40–41; *Letter on
Humanism*, 38, 41; on metaphysics,
39
Heine, Henrich, 29–30
Hermeneutics, 49n12, 61; German, 4
Hetaireia (friendship groups), 292n19
Hexis (habit), 15, 208; in friendship, 176;
Habermas on, 50n24; in
Nichomachean Ethics, 111–12, 116;
virtuous, 132
Hiero (tyrant), 120
Hippodamus, 297, 311n8
History: of ideas, xii; progressive view of,
10–11
History of Animals, 227–28, 232, 276
Hobbes, Thomas: on Aristotle, 310n1; on
disinterested rule, 258, 270n10; on
political community, 286, 287, 288;
on reasoned speech, 282–83
Honor: as external good, 196; goodness of,
178; love of, 142
Honors: for courage, 134, 177; distribution
of, 163, 196; for magnanimity, 140,
171, 172, 201n3; for war dead, 205
Horowitz, Maryanne Cline, 244n7, 246n28
Household. *See* Family
Hume, David, 75
Humor, in *Nichomachean Ethics*, 146–47
Husserl, Edmund, 58, 59–60

Idealism, German, 58
Immortality, through good deeds, 190
Imperatives: ethic of, 55–56; of natural
justice, 71
Incontinence, in *Nichomachean Ethics*,
212–14, 222n12n14
Indignation, in *Nichomachean Ethics*,
162–63, 168, 169

Injustice, 159–60; involuntary, 167
Innovation, 242–43
Institutions: anthropo-biological grounding
of, 4; basis for, 45; ethical, 43
Intellectualism: ethical, 17; Gadamer on,
51n35; Plato's, 49n5
Intelligence, in self-love, 192–93, 194
Irony, in *Nichomachean Ethics*, 145–46,
147, 207–9
Isonomy, 31, 33

Jacobinism, 29
Jaeger, Werner, 290n5
Jaffa, Harry V., 154n5
Jason of Thessaly, 120, 121, 127, 129n11
Joachim, H. H., 154n5
Jolif, J. Y., 157n23
Judeo-Christian tradition: in modern state,
27; republicanism in, xiv; rights under,
34
Judgement, reflective, 25n44
Jurisprudence: Aristotle on, 73–74, 81;
noninterpretive, 75; norms in, 70,
74–75, 77, 83
Justice: absolute, 34; Aristotle on, xv, 83,
102n21; common interest in, 97–98;
commutative, 150, 163, 164, 165;
distributive, 150, 163, 165, 166, 267,
282; in laws, 79–80, 151, 160; as a
mean, 157n22; as moral virtue, 160,
171; motivation for, 190; in
Nichomachean Ethics, 85, 102n23,
142, 143, 149–53, 163–68;
nonpartisan, 267; partial, 150–51;
Platonic, 71, 100n9; and political
authority, 268; in political argument,
280; and *praxis*, 118; in *Republic*, 151,
160, 241, 251, 269nn3, 8; in *Rhetoric*,
120; role in happiness, 171–72;
strength as, 255, 263; variability of,
101n18; as virtue, 150–53. *See also*
Natural justice; Political justice

Kant, Immanuel: categorical imperative of, 42–43, 53, 59, 65; *Critique of Practical Reason*, 64; on duty, 63–64; on eudaimonism, 65; formalism of, 42–43, 50n20, 53; *Foundations of the Metaphysics of Morals*, 42, 59, 64; on human freedom, xii, 55; moral philosophy of, 40, 58, 66, 239–40; on practical knowledge, 8; on the republic, 35; universalism of, 40

Keuls, Eva C., 244n8

Kierkegaard, Søren, 60

Knowledge: and action, xiv, 9; Aristotelian model of, 5–7, 226–27; authoritative, 214; classification of, 16, 226, 228; disregard of, 212, 213–14; Hellenistic view of, 21n12; moral action and, xiv; and moral virtue, 211; of natural justice, 241; sociology of, 5; systems of, 6, 7–9; unity of, 10, 24n41. *See also* Practical knowledge

Knowledge, scientific: of human action, 8–9; Plato on, 23n28

Koinōnia (community), 274, 291n6. *See also* Political community

Krüger, Gerhard, 64

Kullmann, Wolfgang, 102n27

Law: Aristotle on, 32–33; in correct regimes, 74–78; defective, 74–75; equality before, 85; happiness under, 152; morality in, 76–77; in *Nichomachean Ethics*, 73; practical philosophy in, 10–11; relationship to justice, 151, 160; Roman, 34; of slavery, 87, 94; universal, 101n13; violence of, 94. *See also* Positive law

Lawgivers, 169

Laws: Aristotle on, 217, 218; politics in, 214, 216

Lebensbedeutsamkeit (life-significance), 9

Legitimacy, political, 33–34, 46

Leisure: in best regimes, 296; moral virtues and, 303; in the *polis*, 296; in *Politics*, 304; priority over activity, 309; role of music in, 305–6; and theoretical virtue, 303–4

Lennox, James G., 245n19

Liberalism, in Christian tradition, 32

Liberality: and magnanimity, 156n10; in *Nichomachean Ethics*, 136–38, 151, 207; noble deeds in, 142; as virtue, 136–38, 250

Life-projects, 57–58

Lifeworld, 59–60

Lincoln, Abraham, 190; *Gettysburg Address*, 32, 34

Lloyd, G. E. R., 103n32

Logic, deontic, 57

Logos: Aristotle's doctrine of, 14, 62; in political community, 276–83, 287; role in political justice, 282. *See also* Reason

Lord, Carnes, 312nn14, 16

Lorenz, Konrad, 4

Lorenzen, Paul, 4

Love: erotic, 175; in ethical friendship, 183; felt by benefactors, 188–91; in friendship, 180; of honor, 142; maternal, 178; nobility of, 199. *See also* Self-love

Luhmann, Niklas, 4

Machiavelli, Niccolò, 293, 308

MacIntyre, Alasdair, 38–39, 50n22, 155n5; *After Virtue*, 43; on conflict, 273, 290n1; on Socrates, 221n6

Madison, James, 267

Magnanimity, 156n13; and courage, 140; and friendship, 172; and happiness, 141, 171; honors for, 140, 171, 172, 201n3; liberality and, 156n10; in *Nichomachean Ethics*, 116–17, 139–41, 151, 207, 209; and nobility, 148; as virtue, 136, 139–41, 250

Magnificence, as virtue, 136, 138–39

Maleness: metaphysics of, 233–35; norms of, 237; politics of, 235–39; principle of, 229–32; in procreation, 230–31, 244n8; psychology of, 232–33. *See also* Gender roles

Masters: authority of, 90; natural, 88

Master-slave relations, 92, 96, 103n32; self-interest in, 258, 265

Mathematics, Greek view of, 57, 61

Matter: Aristotle on, 227, 245n19; in menstrual blood, 230, 231; soul's dominance over, 230–31

Maus, Ingeborg, 33

Menger, Carl, 5

Meno, 210–11, 222nn8–9

Metaphysics, 228, 234

Metaphysics, relationship with ethics, 38–39, 49n5

Military. *See* Soldiers

Mill, John Stuart, 55

Minimalism, moral, 109–13, 128n6

Moderation: in *Nichomachean Ethics*, 135–36, 137; as virtue, 135–36, 250

Modernity: concept of science in, 6, 65; *ethos* of, 48; Gadamer on, 45–46; Habermas on, 45; neo-Aristotelianism's opposition to, 10–11; role of *prudentia* in, 54–55; self-representation of, 17; view of practical knowledge, 16

Monarchy, 85; decision-making in, 281; justice under, 98; self-interest in, 258; self-sufficiency of, 266. *See also* Regimes

Money. *See* Wealth

Montaigne, Michel de, 173, 178–80; on Aristotle's dogmatism, 225, 242

Morality: biological basis of, 4, 239; dissociation from ethics, 17; laws of, 55; role of *phronēsis* in, 53; role of practical philosophy in, 59

Moral sciences, 8, 9

Moral theory: Habermas on, 44–45; in *Nichomachean Ethics*, 37, 169; purpose of, 37

Moral virtue: ambition as, 142; as basis of citizenship, 295–96; in best regimes, 301, 303; and goodness, 301–2; habituation to, 307; justice as, 160, 171; and knowledge, 211; in *Nichomachean Ethics*, 131–53, 171, 298; nobility in, 132, 137, 141, 155n7; in political communities, 293; in political science, 308; role in leisure, 303; role of happiness in, 132, 134–35, 141, 171, 297–300; utilitarian, 309. *See also* Virtue

Mother love, 178

Musaeus, 307

Music, 312n14; catharsis through, 307–8, 312n17; and nobility of character, 307; role in political community, 304, 305–8

Natural justice, 101n13, 165–66; changeability of, 240; knowledge of, 241

Natural law: as part of morality, 100n3, 240; and positive law, 84–85; universality of, 84. *See also* Law

Natural right: Aristotle on, xv, 70–72, 79–86; common interest in, 82; freedom under, 86; in *Nichomachean Ethics*, 71, 79–81, 269n2; in positive right, 101nn11, 14; renewed interest in, 100n4; in slavery, 92, 95–98, 101n15; Wolff on, 38. *See also* Positive right; Rights

Nature: in Aristotelian corpus, 226–29; changeability of, 226, 246n32; duality of, 228; effect on man, 23n18; gender roles in, 225; metaphysics of, 8; moral standards in, 240; in *Nichomachean Ethics*, 196, 197, 198; plurality of,

226–28; in political thought, xii; in *Politics*, 103n32; teleology of, 227

Neo-Aristotelianism, 154n1; and conservatism, 20n5; German, xiv, 10, 15, 163; Habermas on, xiv, 37–39, 49n2; opposition to modernity, 10–11; programmatic theses of, 11–16; roots of, 4–7

Neo-Kantianism, 60

Nichols, Mary, 222n19

Nichomachean Ethics, xi; activity in, 115, 117, 119; *alēthē* in, 24n34; ambition in, 109, 142; anger in, 143; *aretē* in, 58, 63; audience of, 109–13, 119, 128nn2–3; boasting in, 145, 146, 208; brutishness in, 161; common advantage in, 270n15; community in, 275; contemplative life in, 118–19, 126; courage in, 133–35, 151, 205–7; death in, 133–35, 205; divinity in, 139; *epistēmē* in, 61; equity in, 72–73, 137; *ethos* in, 41; evil in, 159–69; friendship in, 116, 144, 172–200; function argument of, 113–14; gentleness in, 143–44, 157n15, 207; habits in, 111–12, 116; happiness in, 113–18, 125–26, 129n9, 168, 169; humor in, 146–47; incontinence in, 212–14, 222nn12, 14; indignation in, 162–63, 168, 169; irony in, 145–46, 147, 207–9; justice in, 85, 102n23, 142, 143, 149–53, 159, 163–68, 241; knowledge in, 13–14, 63; law in, 76; leisure in, 303; liberality in, 136–38, 151, 207; *logon echein* in, 61, 62; magnanimity in, 116–17, 136, 139–41, 151, 207; magnificence in, 136, 138–39, 156nn10–11, 207; moderation in, 135–36, 137; moral theory in, 37, 169; moral virtues in, 131–53, 171, 298; natural right in, 71, 79–81, 269n2; nature in, 228–29; nobility in, 134, 136, 152; passions in, 162; *phronēsis* in, 14–15, 63; pleasure in, 96, 114–15, 135–36, 146–47, 172; *praxis* in, 123–27; *proairēsis* in, 17, 61, 62; prudence in, 209–12; psychological plan of, 157n15; regimes in, 262, 266; relationship with *Eudemian Ethics*, 155n5; self-sufficiency in, 97; shame in, 148, 207; slavery in, 96; Socrates in, 203, 205–14, 219, 220, 221n6; soul in, 227; straightforwardness in, 208–9; *technē* in, 14; truthfullness in, 144–45, 207, 208, 209; vice in, 132, 138; viciousness in, 161; virtue in, 111, 154n3, 160; wittiness in, 207

Nietzsche, Friedrich, xii; on Socrates, 43

Nobility, 250; of action, 183–84; of benefactors, 189–90; in courage, 133, 205; of friendship, 172; of love, 199; and magnanimity, 148; and moral virtue, 132, 137, 141, 155n7; of motive, 184–85; in *Nichomachean Ethics*, 134, 136, 152; role of moderation in, 136; self-love and, 191, 192–94; in wisdom, 196

Norms: discourse on, 46–47; ethical, 41–43; of family, 237–39; of gender roles, 237; internal, 212; in jurisprudence, 70, 74–75, 77, 83; of liberty, 85; regulation of equity by, 74; of right, 70–71, 95, 101n21; theoretical knowledge of, 47

Nous, 218, 245n9

Nussbaum, Martha, 158n25, 222n19

O'Connor, David K., 316

Office holding: in best regimes, 296, 298, 300, 301; in political community, 163–64

Oikos, action in, 21n11

Oligarchy, 78, 279

Olympus (musician), 307, 312n15

Organon, 6

Ostracism, 83, 87, 94

Ostwald, Martin, 156n13

Parts of Animals, 231–32

Passions: of anger, 143, 307; control over, 186–87; expression through music, 307; internal, 157n22; in *Nichomachean Ethics*, 162; in *Politics*, 233

Patrikē (paternal rule), 237

Paul, Saint, 28

Pellegrin, Pierre, 231, 232, 234, 245n11

Pericles, 221n10

Phaleas of Chalcedon, 121, 122

Phenomenology, 59–60

Philia, 284, 291n18

Philosophers: as Aristotle's audience, 129n; friendship among, 200; German, 3–4; Hellenistic, xii; medieval, xi–xii; modern, xiv; natural, 213; as paradigm of *praxis*, 124; presocratic, 15; rule by, 217, 218, 269n5

Philosophia mechanica, 6, 7

Philosophia practica. See Practical philosophy

Philosophia theoretica, 6, 7

Philosophy: as action, 198; consequences for civic life, 204; Frankfurt school of, 3–4; hermeneutic, 49n12; importance to *polis*, 204, 220; pleasure in, 200; and political authority, 267; political responsibility of, 256; and political science, 5; as *praxis*, 123–27; superiority to politics, 119, 122, 124, 303. *See also* Political philosophy; Practical philosophy

Phronēsis, 16, 296; Aristotle's view of, 14–15, 48, 62–63; definition of, 5; and *epistēmē*, 63; in moral law, 53; normative function of, 43; and other knowledge, 61; practical character of, 24n40; and practical science, 15; rediscovery of, 18; role in *ethos*, 62;

role in happiness, 115; and *sophia*, 41, 61, 63; specificity of, 44; and *technē*, 13–15, 24n34; types of, 21n11; and virtue, 53

Piety, 139

Plato: on community, 275; intellectualism of, 49n5; *praxis* in, 13; on scientific knowledge, 23n28; Socratic dialogues of, 60, 109, 128n1, 203, 204. Works: *See* individual works

Play, in *Nichomachean Ethics*, 146–47, 148. *See also* Leisure

Pleasure: in friendship, 173–77, 181, 197–98, 284; in gain, 161; in good actions, 197; moderation in, 135–36; in music, 306; in *Nichomachean Ethics*, 114–15, 135–36, 172; overwhelming of reason, 213; in philosophy, 200; in play, 146–47; role in happiness, 115, 306

Pleines, Jürgen-Eckhart, 11

Poetics, 107

Poets: Aristotle on, 108–9; Plato on, 107

Poiēsis, distinction from *praxis*, 11, 13, 23n28

Polis: action in, 21n11; authority of, 249, 254–55; commercial elements of, 295–96; common advantage in, 96, 260; in constitutional revolutions, 27; decline of, 56; dominant groups of, 255, 256; gender roles in, 239–42; importance of philosophy to, 204, 220; leisure in, 296; moral decline in, 43; natural existence of, 235–36, 251; property in, 217, 296; religion in, 298–300; role of family in, 215, 236; role of military in, 296; of Roman empire, 54; rulers of, 265–66; security of, 298, 300, 311nn5, 7; Socrates on, 206; unity of, 216–17; women's role in, 225. *See also* Political community; Regimes; Rulers

Politeia (political regime), 278, 279. *See also* Regimes

Political action: as happiness, 121, 124; and rationalism, xi

Political animal, human, 236, 250, 291n7; Hobbes on, 282; in political community, 274–83

Political authority: attacks on, 249–50; and justice, 268; and philosophy, 267; and reason, 282

Political clubs, 292n19

Political community: in Aristotle's philosophy, 273–89; common advantage in, 276, 280; exchange in, 164–65; friendship in, 285–88; good life in, 277; goodness of, 294; happiness of, 149, 304; identity in, 275, 288, 289; justice in, 162, 165, 168, 264; *logos* in, 276–83, 287; moral virtue in, 293; office holding in, 163–64; political animal in, 274–83; priority over individual, 274; rationality in, 291n13, 311n8; role of music in, 304, 305–8; sacrifice in, 276, 286; self-sufficiency of, 278, 282, 285; speech in, 276–78; standards of judgment in, 280. *See also* Polis; Regimes

Political justice, 101n20, 142, 168, 264; distribution of goods under, 286; and gender roles, 239–42; natural basis for, 240; role of *logos* in, 282

Political philosophy, 5, 243; community in, 273–89

Political science: classical, 293–309; conceptual foundations of, 5; moral virtues in, 308; in nineteenth century, 55

Politics, xi; catharsis in, 307–8; common good in, 249–68, 270n13; democracy in, 97, 278; despotism in, 76; divine in, 298–300, 311n9; education in, 108; equity in, 74–76; ethos in, 48; family in, 214–16; foresight in, 91; Gadamer on, 48; gender in, 235–42; good in, 76; happiness in, 108, 297;

jurisprudence in, 73–74, 81; leisure in, 304; master-slave relations in, 96; natural right in, 71, 72; nature in, 103n32; office holding in, 163–64; ostracism in, 83; passions in, 233; *phronēsis* in, 48; Plato's *Republic* in, 213–19; political community in, 273–74; political rule in, 261–68; recreation in, 147; rediscovery of, 6; regimes in, 166, 217, 251, 262–63, 269n2, 277, 279, 293–303; slavery in, 86–87, 91–93, 237; Socrates in, 203, 214–19, 220; soul in, 89, 90, 233, 302; tyranny in, 159, 280; virtue in, 120–21, 214–16, 297, 303

Politics: change in, 243–44; debate in, 36n20; ethics in, 21n11; freedom from, 32; Kantian understanding of, 25n44; Machiavellian, 308; in *Nichomachean Ethics*, 109; nineteenth-century concept of, 54; philosophy's superiority over, 119, 122, 124, 303; Plato on, 23n28, 128n3; in practical philosophy, 6, 204; and rationalism, xii–xiii

Politis, Vasilis, 202nn9, 11

Positive law, 71–72, 73, 79–80, 166–67; natural right in, 84–85; of slavery, 94–95, 98

Positive right, 71–72, 74, 77–78, 80–81; in common law, 85; natural right in, 101n11; slavery under, 87–88

Positivism, logical, 69

Postmodernists, French, 50n27

Power, social relations of, 32

Practical knowledge: Aristotelian account of, 10; concreteness of, 37; and deontic logic, 57; Kantian paradigm of, 25n44; modernity's view of, 16; Plato on, 13, 23n28; specificity of, 13–15. *See also* Practical philosophy

Practical philosophy, 6; Aristotle as founder of, 56, 57; in education, 11; German debate on, 3–4; good in, 58; John

(*Practical philosophy continued*)
Stuart Mill on, 55; Kant on, 59;
modern alternatives to, 7–9; as
philosophia minor, 12; in political
science, 10; recovery of, xiv, 5, 10, 16,
17–18, 69; scholastic tradition of, 6–7,
22n15; scientific basis of, 58; topo-
dialectical quality of, 24n41; tripartite,
6, 7, 21nn11–12

Practical reason, 64, 240; and theoretical
reason, 302; theory of, 37

Praotēs, 157n16

Praxis: Aristotelian account of, 5, 11;
autonomy from theory, 11–13, 16;
contemplation as, 110, 124, 126;
distinction from *poiēsis*, 11, 13, 28n28;
and *energeia*, 126–27, 129n7;
epistemological examination of, 15; in
happiness, 110; and justice, 118;
perfection of, 13; philosophy as,
123–27; priority over theory, xiv, 124;
rediscovery of, 16

Precision, in practical philosophy, 12

Prejudice, pre-Enlightenment sense of, 51n31

Price, A. W., 201n4, 202n11

Private sphere, in civil society, 30–31

Procreation, 230–31, 244n8

Production, 5

Progress, 10–11, 242

Proairesis, 17, 61, 62

Property. *See* Goods, external

Protagoras, 221n14

Prudence, 5; in best regimes, 301; Christian
understanding of, 54; Habermas on,
47; and moral virtue, 209–10, 212,
222n8; in *Nichomachean Ethics*,
209–12; in pastimes, 305–6, 308;
practical character of, 24n42. *See also*
Phronēsis

Pseudo-Aristotle, *Oikonomikos*, 21n11

Public sphere: Christianity in, 27; in civil
society, 30–31; freedom in, 29;
republicanism of, 30

Punishment: in *Nichomachean Ethics*, 167;
in *Rhetoric*, 162

Pythian oracle, 298–99

Rationalism: critical, 4; of Enlightenment,
47; and moral action, xi; origins of,
xiii; and politics, xii–xiii

Rationality: control over science, 66;
Habermas on, 43, 47; overwhelming
by passions, 213–14; in political
communities, 291n13, 311n8; in self-
love, 194; of virtue, 152, 210

Realism: in best regimes, 308–9; of classical
political science, 293–309

Reason: acquisition of, 89–90; Aristotle's
conception of, 100n8; collapse of, xiii,
xiv; and decision, 17; effective, 64;
Habermas on, 51n35; in Kantian
philosophy, 8; love of, 196; in the
political community, 279; in
procreation, 230; and self-love, 192;
universal principles of, 70; and virtue,
210. *See also* Logos; Practical reason

Regimes: best, 293; basis of rule in, 301;
choiceworthy life in, 294–95, 303,
310n4; commerce in, 299; common
advantage in, 261, 264; common good
in, 250–51, 260n16, 261–62, 266;
correct, 166, 261, 280; deviant, 74,
76–78, 83, 251, 263, 280; farmers'
role in, 296, 311n7; good life in,
300–303; goodness of, 310n3; justice
under, 262; law in, 74–78; legitimacy
of, 280–81; leisure in, 296; moral
virtue in, 301, 303; number of rulers
in, 279, 291n11; ordering of offices in,
296, 298, 300, 301; philosophic, 217,
218; in Plato, 217; realism in, 308–9;
right in, 80–82, 85–86, 87, 102n22;
rulers and subjects in, 299; sacrifice in,
298; self-sufficiency of, 295; slaves in,
296; types of, 81, 256, 261, 267, 280;
vice in, 300. *See also* Political community; Rule

Relativism, 51n27; cultural, xiv, 18; in ethics, 47; Habermas on, 49n12

Renaut, Alain, 100n7

Republic, 128n3; Aristotle on, 213–19, 222n11, 223n20, 243, 269n8; ethics in, 117; justice in, 151, 160, 241, 251; poets in, 107, 109; politics in, 214, 216; regimes in, 217; soul in, 62; "third wave" of reform in, 217, 222n18; Thrasymachus in, 250, 251–56, 257, 261, 269n3

Republicanism: Arendt on, xiv, 30–32; classical, 29–30, 32, 33–34

Republics: as communicative power, 34; modern, 27–28, 32–35

Revolutions: classical roots of, 28; eighteenth-century, 27, 34

Rhetoric, 84; indignation in, 162; injustice in, 159, 161; justice in, 120; punishment in, 162

Right: absolute, 97; Aristotle's principles of, 72–79; conventional, 81; in correct regimes, 80–82, 85–86, 87; distinction from morality, 100n6; and natural slaves, 86–95; nature of, 98; norms of, 70–71, 95, 101n21; philosophy of, 70. *See also* Natural right

Rights: individual, xii, xiii; under Judeo-Christian tradition, 34

Ritter, Joachim, 11, 278–79, 290n4

Rorty, Richard, 51nn27,32

Rousseau, Jean-Jacques: on communal *ethos*, 52n41; *Contrat Social*, 32; on modernity, xii, 65; on political community, 286, 287, 288, 291n8

Rule: accidental consequences of, 257–61; challenges to, 282; despotic, 256–57, 261, 263; familial, 257–64; natural, 263–64, 265; in *Politics*, 261–68; self-interest in, 253–54, 263; selfless, 252–53, 264; Socrates on, 265–66; types of, 256; unselfish, 256–61. *See also* Political community; Regimes; Tyranny

Rulers: greed of, 263; number of, 279, 291n11; self-interest of, 253–56; Socrates on, 265–66

Rulers and subjects: in best regimes, 299; common advantage for, 265, 267, 270n17; in the family, 262; Hobbes on, 270n10; in the *polis*, 266, 269n7; self-interest among, 253–61, 264

Sacrifice: in best regimes, 298; in friendship, 188, 286; to the gods, 299; of happiness, 195–96; nobility of, 202n11, 205; in political community, 276, 286; self-love in, 191–96; Socrates', 195

Salkever, Stephen, 128n2

Saxonhouse, Arlene W., 246n27

Schelsky, Helmut, 11

Schmoller, Gustav, 5

Schnädelbach, Herbert, 20n5

Schofield, Malcolm, 102n24, 103n35

Science: application to human welfare, 312n10; Aristotelian classification of, 21n12; Aristotle's influence on, xii; destructive power of, 66; practical, and *phronēsis*, 15, 24n41; value systems in, xiii

Self-interest: in rulers, 253–56; in virtue, 286

Selflessness, 252–53, 254, 264

Self-love, 202n9; autonomy in, 193; and common good, 195; and love of others, 194; in nobility, 191, 192–94; reasonableness of, 202n10; and sacrifice, 191–96; as standard of friendship, 185–88

Self-sufficiency: in *Nichomachean Ethics*, 97; in political community, 278, 282, 285; in politics, 227; role of friendship in, 201n7, 202n13

Self-understanding, 202n11

Servility. *See* Souls, servile

Sex differentiation, 229–32, 244n6. *See also*
    Gender roles
Sextus Empiricus, 21n12
Shakespeare, William, 190
Shame, in *Nichomachean Ethics*, 148, 207
Simonides' challenge, 110, 120–22
Slavery: Arendt on, 30; Aristotle on, 72,
    102n24, 103n29; common interest in,
    92; law of, 87; natural right in,
    101n15; in *Nichomachean Ethics*, 96;
    in *Politics*, 86–87, 91–93, 237; positive
    law of, 94–95, 98
Slaves: deliberative capacity of, 91; freedom
    for, 296; natural, 86–95, 258, 265;
    natural right of, 92, 95–98; rule over,
    258; souls of, 238
Smith Pangle, Lorraine, 316
Snow, C. P., 66
Sociability, need for, 187, 197–99
Social theory, modern, 275, 276, 279
Society: legitimacy of, 47; private interests
    in, 29. *See also* Communities; Political
    community
Socrates, 43; on courage, 128n1; debate with
    Thrasymachus, 250, 251–56, 257,
    261, 269n3; defense of justice, 269n4;
    on education, 217; as exemplar of
    irony, 146, 147, 207–9, 219; historical,
    203–4, 221n3, 222n17; on injustice,
    161; intellectualism of, 49n5; mode of
    inquiry, 221n14; in *Nichomachean
    Ethics*, 203, 205–14, 219; on
    philosophical engagement, 107; on
    poets, 107, 109; political teaching of,
    216–19; in *Politics*, 203, 214–19; on
    rulers, 265–66; sacrifice of, 195; trial
    of, 203–4; on virtue, 210–11; on wage-
    earning, 253–56, 270n9
Socratic dialogues, 60, 109, 128n1, 203,
    204; moral virtues in, 211
Soldiers: in best regimes, 296, 311n6;
    courage of, 206–7
Solitude, need for, 187

Solon, 125, 126–27
Sophia, 16; and *phronēsis*, 41, 61, 63; Plato
    on, 24n42; role in happiness, 115
Sophocles: *Ajax*, 215–16; ethos of, 41
Soul: catharsis for, 307; domination over
    matter, 230–31; in *Eudemian Ethics*,
    90–91; in *Nichomachean Ethics*, 227;
    in *Politics*, 89, 90, 233, 302; proper
    function of, 118; rational and
    nonrational, 302
Souls: Aristotle on, 61–62; gender
    differences in, 231, 238; servile,
    89–92, 95–98, 102n25, 238. *See also*
    Slaves, natural
Sparta: musical education in, 305; virtue in,
    269n2
State: Arendt on, 34, 36n23; Judeo-
    Christian tradition in, 27; legitimacy
    of, 47; modern idea of, 22n15. *See also*
    Polis; Political community; Regimes
Stern-Gillet, Suzanne, 201nn5, 7, 13
Stoicism, 55–56, 155n6; cosmic order in,
    100n7
Strauss, Leo, 5, 49n3, 222n19, 290n2,
    312n10
Student unrest, 28
Subjectivism, 56
Sunesis (understanding), 63
Swanson, Judith A., 316
Syllogisms, 57
Symposium, 175

Tact, in *Nichomachean Ethics*, 148
Taylor, Charles, 50n22
Technē: perfection of, 14; and *phronēsis*,
    13–15, 24n34
Tertullian, 27
Tessitore, Aristide, 128n3, 316
Thales, 129n14
Theōria: distinction from *praxis*, 11–13, 16;
    goals of, 11; and *scientia*, 16. *See also*
    Moral theory

Theoricism, 17

Thomas Aquinas: on Aristotle's virtues, 154n5; on courage, 155n6; on the gods, 156n12; on justice, 157n22

Thrasymachus (*Republic*), debate with Socrates, 250, 251–56, 257, 261, 269n3

Thucydides, 160

Totalitarianism, 28, 29

Truth: general *versus* specific, 44; as goal of theory, 11; love of, 209; natural, 241

Truthfulness, in *Nichomachean Ethics*, 144–45, 207, 208, 209

Tyranny: as active ideal, 117–18, 120–22, 128n3, 129n11; in *Politics*, 159, 280–81

Universalism, 34; Gadamer's, 40, 45–46; Habermas's, 51n35; Kantian, 40

Utility: of benefactors, 189–90; in friendship, 173–76, 179, 180–81, 201n2, 284–85

Utopianism, 46

Value judgements, 5

Verein für Sozialpolitik, 5

Vice: in best regimes, 300; continuum with virtue, 228; greed as, 138; injustice as, 160; in *Nichomachean Ethics*, 132; of prodigality, 137; and self-hatred, 186

Viciousness, in *Nichomachean Ethics*, 161

Violence, legitimacy of, 94

Virtue: active ideal of, 118; Aristotle on, 32–33, 60, 120–21, 128n2, 131–53, 154n4, 211; in common relations, 144, 148; continuum with vice, 228; definition of, 131; education for, 169; in ethical theory, 154n1; friendship as, 144, 157n20, 174, 177, 179–83, 283; gender differences in, 215–16; in human disposition, 144; instrumental view of, 158n25; justice as, 150–53; as

a mean, 145; moderation as, 135–36; moral *versus* dianoetic, 62; in *Nichomachean Ethics*, 22n14, 111, 154n3; in *Politics*, 120–21, 214–16, 297, 303; and prudence, 209–10, 212, 222n8; rationality of, 152, 210; rewards for, 171, 184–85; role in happiness, 115–16, 141, 187; self-interest in, 192, 286; Socrates on, 128n1, 210–11; Spartan, 269n2; of *technē*, 14–15; theoretical, 302, 303–4, 305; of women, 215–16. *See also* Moral virtue

Virtue-science, Socratic doctrine of, 24n42

Vlastos, Gregory, 221n3, 222n17

Voegelin, Eric, 5, 246nn32–33

Volpi, Franco, xiv, 316

Voluntarism, 17

Wage-earning art (*misthōtikē*), 253, 260, 270n9

Wealth, 164; in households, 237; liberality with, 137–38

Wellmer, Albrecht, 46

Wieland, G., 22n14

Will, individual, xiii

Willensbildung, 36n20

Williams, Bernard, 111–12, 113, 117

Wolff, Christian, 22nn16–17, 38; *Philosophia practical universalis*, 7

Women: deliberative capacity of, 238–39, 246n28; emotionalism of, 238, 246n28; in Plato's *Republic*, 218; role in *polis*, 225; under Spartan law, 74; as species, 245n19; subordination of, 33; virtue of, 215–16

Xenocrates, 21n12

Xenophon: *Hiero*, 120, 129n11; on Socrates, 203, 204; *Symposium*, 300

Yack, Bernard, 101n21, 222n19, 316